Business Telecommunications

Concepts, Technologies, &
Cases in Telematics

The Irwin Series in Information and Decision Sciences

Consulting Editors   **Robert B. Fetter**   **Claude McMillan**
                          Yale University   *University of Colorado*

Business Telecommunications

Concepts, Technologies, & Cases in Telematics

Jay Misra
ROLM, an IBM Company
Visiting Lecturer,
Harvard University and
Stanford University

Byron Belitsos
Golden Gate University
University of San Francisco

Homewood, Illinois 60430

ISBN 0-256-05617-X

Library of Congress Catalog Card No. 86–81956

Printed in the United States of America

1 2 3 4 5 6 7 8 9 0 MP 4 3 2 1 0 9 8 7

*This book is dedicated by
BB to his parents, for their long and
loving support.*

*and
by JM to Bapa, Maa, Munu and Sanju*

PREFACE

Business Telecommunications explains the basic technical concepts, surveys the key telecommunication technologies and applications, and provides cases required for an introductory course in Telecommunications and/or Data Communications.

OBJECTIVES

The fundamental objective of this text is to present an organized, up-to-date, and relevant survey of the technologies resulting from the convergence of telecommunications and computer technology, framed in terms of their strategic impact in the business environment. Of the many student-oriented objectives, the primary one is to provide an easy-to-read primer on the state-of-the-art in the telecommunications industry today.

AUDIENCE

Business Telecommunications can be used effectively for an introductory course at both the undergraduate and graduate levels. Courses stressing telecommunications management, whether in business schools, management information systems programs, engineering administration programs, or in telecommunications programs have found draft versions of this text helpful.

Students in communication programs can use this text for a survey of technologies and applications. Continuing education programs can benefit from the currency of topics in this text.

FEATURES

The most salient features of this book are its content, writing style, and pedagogical support material. The content stresses the newer communication technologies and applications, plus case studies and real-world examples. For example, Part III on office communication networks emphasizes Local Area Networks, and Private Branch Exchanges, and the current PBX versus LAN controversy. Part IV on interoffice networks emphasizes the newer Bypass networks and Integrated Services Digital Networks (ISDN). All through the text, the emphasis is on integrating management issues and telecommunications industry dynamics with an understanding of technology.

The second facet in content is the discussion of applications. Chapters on micro-to-mainframe links, teleconferencing, business videotex and electronic mail are an example. Each of these applications are supplemented by examples showing practical uses.

The content of the book also stresses cases. The range of companies includes a small public relations firm and the giant Hewlett-Packard. These cases have been developed from first-hand interviews with the key managers and users. Smaller case examples are interspersed throughout the text.

In writing style, we have stressed readability, organization, and liberal illustrations over depth of technical detail.

These features were developed as a result of draft versions being used in a variety of settings, including MBA programs, M.S. in telecommunications programs, B.S. in business programs, and B.S. in Information Resource Management programs, and in company training programs.

PEDAGOGICAL FEATURES

The intent is to have each chapter serve as an independent building block towards understanding the most complex communication networks in use today. Specifically, we have divided the book into seven parts to make for easier comprehension. Each part has an overview. Each chapter has a detailed outline, learning objectives, liberal illustrations in the text, review questions, discussion questions, and selected references for further study. At the end of the text, there is an extensive glossary.

For the instructor, we have an Instructor's manual containing suggested course outlines, class outlines, transparencies, answers to review questions and discussion questions, and sample examinations.

ORGANIZATION OF TEXT

The text is divided into seven parts. Each part is designed to accomplish a specific purpose and provide a foundation for the next part.

- Part I—The Telematics Revolution presents a clear definition of telematics, the convergence of telecommunications and computer technology. Then, it shows the fundamental driving forces behind the growth and future importance of telematics.
- Part II—Fundamentals of Telematics presents the fundamental technical ingredients of data communications and, voice communications. Historical vignettes are interspersed between the technical descriptions to allow easier comprehension.
- Part III—Office Communication Networks discusses the two primary schemes for information transport within an office, LANs and PBXs. A model to demystify the LAN market, along with the role of PBX in data switching is discussed. Then, the PBX versus LAN controversy is described, followed by a discussion on integration of Mainframe computers, PBXs and LANs to form a true office communications network.
- Part IV—Corporate and Public Networks builds on the previous part by discussing communications between disparate sites. Classical telephone company offerings and their limitations are described. Then the public data networks' needs and limitations are described. A detailed look at the Bypass technologies follows, accompanied by a framework to understand the plethora of offerings. Finally, ISDN is described, both technically and its role in the telecommunications industry.
- Part V—Applications in Telematic networks presents the technologies, uses, and benefits behind micro-to-mainframe links, videotex, electronic mail, and teleconferencing. The first two chapters focus on communication with databases; the second two on communications between people.
- Part VI—Case Studies covers the spectrum of telematic technologies used in business today. The first looks at the emergence of an office communications network in a firm, Regis McKenna, Inc. Hercules Incorporated has built an

integrated digital network which strategically emphasizes its network as a competitive weapon. Finally, an extensive study of Hewlett-Packard is presented.
- Part VII—concludes the text with a discussion of strategic and organizational impact of telematic technologies.

ACKNOWLEDGMENTS

The inputs of hundreds of students, several universities, and scores of companies were needed to make this text a reality. We would like to specifically thank the faculty of Harvard Business School, Yale University, Stanford University, Columbia University, Naval Postgraduate Academy, University of Southern California, Golden Gate University, University of San Francisco, and finally San Jose State University. We are also grateful for permission to use selected portions of "Handbook of Telecommunications," by Harry Green (Dow-Jones Irwin) and IBM's "Vocabulary for Data Processing, Telecommunications, and Office Systems" in our glossary.

Jay Misra
Byron Belitsos

CONTENTS

a PBX: *Corporate Politics. PBX Reliability. Today's Applications. Looking to the Future.* References.

Management. New Roles for Telecommunications Office Automation, and Data Processing Managers. Notes for Chapter Nineteen.

PART ONE

The Telematics Revolution

HIGH
- PERFORMANCE
    PRODUCTIVITY

— D, V, T, I

CHAPTER ONE

Introduction: Telecommunications and Computers Converge

OUTLINE

DEFINING TELEMATICS
   The Evolution of Telematics
   Telematics in the Workplace
TELEMATICS AND INFORMATION TECHNOLOGY
TELEMATICS AND BUSINESS COMMUNICATION
   Transparency
   Selectivity

OBJECTIVES

- **Define the term telematics.**
- **Discuss the three stages in the evolution of telematics.**
- **Describe information technology and the role of telematics.**

— INFO. AS A STRATEGIC RESOURCES

— HIGH PERFORMANCE

GLTOP SURVIVAL VAS COMPETIVENESS
SABRE AM HOSP. SUPPLY

Telematics—a hybrid technology based on the convergence of computers and telecommunications— is now emerging after 150 years of sustained evolution in electronics and electronic communication technology. Telematics is *modern* telecommunications; it is electronic communication as it has evolved to meet the demands of the information age.

For business, building corporate networks based on telematic technology is becoming essential to competitive survival in an information economy. Developments in telecommunications over the past century have always accompanied business expansion; but telematics is proving to be even more essential to businesses operating in the 1980s. As the communications core of information technology, telematics is a key element in the future success of many manufacturing and most service businesses in the late 20th century.

A brief look at the history of telecommunications and computers over the past century and a half reveals how electronic communications has become increasingly central to business.

This history begins with the invention of telegraphy—the first flowering of electronic communications. Western Union Telegraph Company's telegraph wires greatly facilitated the expansion of business and trade early in the industrial age. Later in the 19th century, American Telephone & Telegraph Company (AT&T) was primarily responsible for building the world's first nationwide telephone network. This system fulfilled Alexander Graham Bell's dream of universal end-to-end service and made the telephone a way of life for business.

Business telematics was born when the first mainframe computers and minicomputers entered the business environment in the 1960s, just as the information age was dawning; soon after, the first networks that allowed these computers to exchange data began to evolve. As the percentage of white-collar and office workers in corporations grew, the influx of word processors, microcomputers, and other microprocessor-driven devices into offices and factories helped companies manage the increasing complexity of business operations.

Then came networks for linking these desktop computers to each other, to large data bases, and even to telephones. Computer intelligence was added to telephone network equipment, and new, high-capacity transmission media were developed. Teleconferencing—the technology of group communication—grew steadily in its variety of forms. And now telematic networks, based on the eventual convergence of all these technologies as one integrated digital communication system, are being established by companies attempting to cope with the burgeoning information economy of the late 20th century.

Generally speaking, telematics is the union of computers and telecommunications: This means that the transmission of voice, data, and visual information is increasingly handled by telecommunications media and equipment undergoing digitalization (or computerization).

Corporate networks based on this new hybrid technology provide a company with a better "nervous system" for processing and filtering information. Telematic networks can act like sensitive nerve pathways that channel needed information to the right person at the right time, allowing white-collar workers or knowledge workers—who represent the "brains" of a company—to convert that information into business intelligence. Like an intelligent person who is well adjusted to his or her own inner and outer experiences of the world, business organizations can use telematics and other information technologies to adjust more intelligently to their own internal and external information environments.

Because of its potential to improve the productivity of communications, telematics can provide a significant competitive edge in an increasingly information-based society. Establishing networks for the effective and timely communication of voice, data, and visual information—within the office, between company sites, and with the outside world—has become a strategic imperative for business in the 1980s.

DEFINING TELEMATICS

The new term *telematics* is derived from the French word *télématique*[1] and has become a common European term for the merging through a common network of the communication capabilities of telephones, computers, video technology, and other information technologies; this new network is evolving (over the next two decades) from the traditional analog telephone system toward a worldwide voice, data, and video network capable of integrated digital transmission. For the typical business, this digital network will consist of high-speed office communication systems at any local site, which in turn will be linked to other company office systems located in disparate sites, via the public networks (or, in large companies, through company-owned private networks); or, to the offices of other businesses or organizations external to the company's network, via the public networks.

The technical advantage of the emerging corporate telematic networks is clear: Telematics will allow voice, data, and visual information to be digitized for integrated transmission over the same telecommunications medium, under computer control. This capability for digital transmission—the sending of discrete coded pulses produced and controlled by computers through a variety of transmission media—offers important improvements in speed, capacity, efficiency, and reliability over the older wavelike analog transmission technique used by the telephone system.

The definition of telematics can be expanded further by considering the stages of its technical evolution and the variety of communication capabilities it is bringing to the workplace.

The Evolution of Telematics

The evolution of fully digital telematic networks is occurring in three stages.

The *first stage* is the use of ordinary telephone lines as the transmission medium for both voice and low-speed computer communications. In this case, the computer link is made possible via modems placed on either end of the analog telephone line. This stage of telematics will have run its course by the mid-1990s.

The *second stage* involves the first phase of the digitalization of the two elements of the communication link—both the transmission media and communicating devices.

- Transmission media—a variety of innovations based on the computer chip are allowing a quick transition to fully digital, high-capacity office networks for voice and data transmission based on fiber, coaxial cable, and twisted-pair telephone wires. Meanwhile, related technical progress is allowing the eventual digitalization of the entire public telephone network. This includes the computerization of network equipment such as switches, plus the installation of digital transmission lines based on fiber, coaxial cable, microwave, or satellites. But integrated digital office communication systems will evolve long before the public networks are fully digitalized.
- Communication devices—the addition of computer circuitry to these devices allows them to send information digitally over the new digital transmission media. In addition to computers, this includes telephones, facsimile machines, telex machines, video teleconferencing equipment, and other devices.

Second-stage telematics means, therefore, the first appearance of end-to-end digital transmission over a variety of high-capacity media, which link computerized communication devices capable of digitizing voice, data, and, in some cases, video input. The first manifestations of this stage of telematics are the intraoffice digital networks examined in Part Three of this book, which include local area networks, and especially the newer digital private branch exchanges for integrated transmission of voice and data in a single company site. Some corporations, such as Hercules Incorporated (see Chapter Sixteen), have had the foresight to simultaneously install intra- and inter-office digital networks, resulting in a fully digital companywide voice, data, and video network. But most corporations, such as Regis McKenna, Inc. (see Chapter Fifteen), will have to await the arrival of the third stage of telematics (the full digitalization of the public networks) before all of their electronic communication can benefit from transmisssion over digital networks.

The *third stage* of telematics involves the connection of high-speed office networks to one another over private companywide networks (in the case of large corporations) or via fully digitalized public voice and data networks, plus the eentual integration of video into digital transmission systems. Part Four of this book covers these new "metropolitan area" and "wide area" transmission networks now emerging.

By the end of this century, if the plans of AT&T and the local telephone companies are realized, the public network itself will be able to regularly transmit digital video as well as digital voice and data. All forms of information will enter the network through a single standard interface to voice, data, or video terminals of any kind and will run over a single digital network consisting largely of satellite, microwave, and fiber optic links. This plan for providing integrated communication services via a network capable of end-to-end digital connectivity is known as ISDN (Integrated Services Digital Network).

An increasing number of large corporations also will have built their own private integrated digital networks for voice, data, and video, based on a similar standard. Hewlett-Packard Company (examined in Chapter Seventeen) is well on its way to building a corporate network based on third-stage telematics.

Telematics in the Workplace

Telematics, as the term is employed in this book, means much more than digital transmission technology. Our definition of business telematics also includes the interface of communication device users to the new digital networks. We will examine how telematic technology brings new and more effective forms of electronic communication to managers and office workers.

Part Five of this book explores how telematics enhances business communication in two general directions:

- Between people engaged in one-to-one or group communications (through electronic text and voice messaging, electronic file transfer, improved telephony, and audio-, video-, and computer teleconferencing).

- Between people and data bases (through terminal or microcomputer-to-mainframe links, business videotex, and other on-line data base communication systems for business).

Our definition of business telematics includes the fact that the communication devices being used by information workers are located closer to where their work actually occurs—the teleconferencing room just down the hall, the mobile phone in the executive's car, and, most importantly, the personal computer and telephone on the worker's desktop. Whether these terminal devices are linked by cable to others within a small office or via a satellite link across a continent, telematic technology collapses the traditional barriers of time and distance. As a result, managers and their support people have far more timely electronic access to people and to electronically stored information.

Telematic technology, of course, has a sociological impact far beyond its mere application for business communications. Telematics will also have far-reaching effects on government, education, entertainment, and many other sectors of modern life—even on the home. Indeed, many of the same technologies, applications, and management problems covered here will apply to public sector organizations. But the focus of this book is limited to the communication issues facing modern corporations, a formidable topic in itself.

Management and policy issues raised by the use of telematics in the workplace are suggested throughout the book and are taken up systematically in the final chapters in Part Seven.

TELEMATICS AND INFORMATION TECHNOLOGY

As we examine the technologies resulting from the union of computers and telecommunications, it must be remembered that the telematic convergence is one aspect of an even broader convergence of the technologies used by information workers in today's corporations. Three once-separate islands of technology—the data processing center, the automated office, and the telecommunications facility—now are converging through computer technology. The result is a broad new category of business tools known as information technology, of which *telematics technology is the communications core*. It is important to approach telematics via this larger framework of technological convergence, realizing that telematics itself is one manifestation of this convergence.

Seen from this perspective, telematics is that form of information technology that interconnects voice, data, and video devices in the so-called automated office, links the whole company with its centralized data processing facilities, and connects these varied company networks across numerous corporate sites.

Even though the data processing center, the automated office, and the telecommunications department have traditionally been managed independently, this grand convergence has now made possible the *coordinated management* of entire corporate information systems for the attainment of specific corporate goals. These goals can be built around a corporate information policy.[2]

Telematics is one of the major technical issues needing attention in a corporate information policy; in many progressive companies, a corporate telecommunications policy will evolve as an essential part of the company's overall information policy.

A telecommunications policy can be used by senior management to harness the productivity potential of telematics. Cases of the implementation of a corporate telecommunication policy will be presented in Part Six of this book. Part Seven then examines how corporate management should set goals and policies that will blend the interests of three parties in the corporation: the efforts of technical personnel in telecommunications and data processing departments to build functional telematics

*THREE PRINCIPAL
(PARTICIPANTS)
— MAIL
— CUSTOMER
— PROVIDERS*

CUSTOMERS

networks, the needs of end-users of communication technology in the office for a better communications environment, and the strategic and productivity goals of departmental, divisional, and corporate managers.

TELEMATICS AND BUSINESS COMMUNICATION

Information technology—with telematics as its communications core—is causing a revolution in business communication.

Consider the following stories about telematic technologies in use in large and small companies. These stories suggest the range of valuable applications of telematics in typical business environments.

We begin with the story of a work group in the Wells Fargo Bank whose communications have been enhanced by the installation of an electronic messaging system.

*VALUE OF
PC'S,*

- One component of Wells Fargo Bank, called the Real Estate Industries Group (REIG), manages the financing of 300 to 400 large construction projects at a time. Its work often requires the organization of bid proposals by several Wells Fargo offices around the state of California.

  Before the computer network was installed, changes in the bid proposals were put together by telephone calls and a flurry of memos.

  "Our managers are scattered among eight offices," says the vice president of business and systems planning for REIG. "In going through the decision-making process, we would spend all day chasing each other by telephone."

  *TELEPHONE
  TAG*

  In 1983, employees of REIG were given personal computers linked to the bank's seven mainframe computers (three in Los Angeles, four in San Francisco) as a pilot project for the bank.

  *SEND / RECEIVE
  RECORD NOT
  IMMEDIATELY*

  Instead of playing "telephone tag," they are now able to exchange information by electronic messaging. Inefficient procedures typical of paper-based communication, such as writing memos on paper, as well as copying, mailing, and waiting for mailed information, have dropped off dramatically.

  As a result, Wells Fargo estimated that the $500,000 spent on the equipment and connections to the mainframes was returned in 15 months through increases in the productivity of REIG employees.[3] *WHAT ABOUT THE NEXT 15 MOS.*

Next is the story of a typical application of Hewlett-Packard's nationwide video teleconferencing network.

- The marketing communications manager for Hewlett-Packard's Components Group uses the company's video-conferencing network to broadcast new product demonstrations and technical training to the group sales force. The live multisite hookup allows salespeople to ask on-the-spot questions through an audio link.

  Speakers have ranged from product marketing engineers to vice presidents. "We usually choose the person closest to the product to announce it," explains the manager. "In that way we maintain maximum credibility and assure that everyone receives consistent information. In the near future, we will broadcast live to our independent distributors and someday directly to our customers around the country for major new product introductions."[4]

Zapata Corporation, an oil and gas exploration company, uses facsimile to cut communication costs between multiple sites.

- In 1984, an internal study at Zapata determined that employees were spending too much on expensive telex messaging and air courier services for routine communications between remote sites. So the firm decided to install digital facsimile machines at 10 key company sites in the U.S. and three foreign countries. The facsimile system was found to be even more cost-effective than had been sus-pected: Communication costs between these sites dipped nearly 90 percent. Now company headquarters receives some 85 faxed messages daily and typically sends out 60 pages over the network.[5]

These examples show how telematics is reshaping business communications, making access to needed information significantly easier and less expensive. Because of these changes, we believe that basic terms describing communication in the corporate environment now need to be reexamined.

Data is the traditional term used to designate the raw material for corporate information systems. But the recent merger of computers and telecommunications requires us to view this term in a new way. Gone are the old data processing days of the 1960s and 1970s when information systems involved narrow accounting-oriented applications run on large mainframe computers by specialists with minimal understanding of the information needs of managers. The stories of useless thousand-page computer printouts are well known. Instead, in the 1980s,

[handwritten margin notes: SLIDE / INFORMATION PROCESSING, with a circular diagram labeled DATA, VOICE, TEXT, OJT, IMAGE, EO, BUS, KNOW]

micro-to-mainframe links (as in the case of Wells Fargo above), corporate videotex, local area networks, and other on-line data base communication systems have changed the nature of data processing and information systems.

Telematics allows "value-added" data processing; it improves the value of electronically stored data by making the data more easily and inexpensively available. This same principle holds true for data in the possession of a living person, which needs to be communicated efficiently in order to be useful; mobile telephony, electronic text and voice mail, and teleconferencing allow people far easier access to others for retrieving or sending needed information.

Thus the new business communications environment growing up around telematics allows us to take a different perspective on the problem of data processing. Properly managed telematic systems can convert data through several levels of increasing usefulness for managers: Basic data, stored electronically or possessed by a person, are converted into *information* which then, because of the unique capabilities of telematics, can be turned into *business intelligence.*[6] For our purposes, these terms—data, information, and intelligence—will have the following definitions:

1. *Basic data:* a record of a primary event, state, or relationship. Basic data are the fundamental building blocks of information.

2. *Information:* When data is analyzed and aggregated (i.e., processed), stored in some repository, and available through an electronic network, it becomes information. The repository of information is usually a person or some form of electronic storage. Thus, for our purposes, information is defined as processed data available over an electronic communication medium and ready for access by another party via electronic communication devices.

3. *Business intelligence:* In the information age, managers usually do *not* need easier access to more information; most are overwhelmed with information from a myriad of electronic, print, and interpersonal sources. Instead, they need access to intelligence—the right information made available in time to be useful for problem solving and decision making. As a vice presi-

dent at Aetna Life & Casualty Company puts it, the problem is to "get the right information to the right guy to make the right decision to beat the other guy out in the marketplace."[7]

Because of telematics, electronic communication can play a critical role in the manager's quest for business or organizational intelligence.

The computer intelligence that has been added to telecommunication media and equipment allows more intelligent managerial communications; this technical convergence provides the basis for us to speak of electronic communication systems that convert data and information into business intelligence. In this usage, the term *intelligence* signifies that a receiver (end-user of a communication device) can *easily* extract or select the right amount of needed information in a timely way, either from data bases or other people; conversely, a person or organization that is a source of information can become a purveyor of intelligence, (again, via data bases or electronic communication with people). All of the new techniques of electronic communication surveyed in this book—microcomputer-to-mainframe links, corporate videotex, electronic voice and text messaging, and teleconferencing—can help managers and office workers filter intelligence from the oceans of information available to them from these sources.

The concept of intelligence can be simplified by highlighting two key attributes: First, telematic network technology potentially allows the connection to an information source to be virtually *transparent,* that is, simple and largely invisible to the user. Second, the new technology gives the user the power of *selectivity*—the ability to easily retrieve the right amount of needed information from that source (or conversely, to make the needed information available for selective access by others). Transparency refers mainly to the benefits arising from the technical capabilities of digital transmission networks as covered in Parts Three and Four of this book; selectivity refers to the benefits arising from the specific uses of the communication applications of telematics in the workplace, especially as discussed in Part Five. Let's examine these two key perspectives.

Transparency. If telematics is to live up to its promise to cut communication costs and improve the productivity of information workers in the corporate environment, then transparency should be a design goal of telematic networks.

A manager with transparent access to business intelligence resides, in effect, at the *center* of a vast network of accessible information resources. The manager can tap into the network with voice, data, and visual communication devices that are simple to use and close at hand. Use of these communication tools makes the manager immediately aware of other person(s) or of specific files of information on a data base; moreover, once the user has entered the network, the existence and operation of intervening network technology or any devices on the network has faded from view. By this definition, for example, the U.S. telephone system had attained virtual transparency by the late 1930s (for its intended purpose of "real-time" person-to-person communications).

Of course, transparency in the realm of telematics is a much greater technical challenge. In addition to the telephone system, the design goal of telematics is development of transparent data and video networks. (Telematics will also make the telephone a better information system.)

In the current telecommunications environment, transparency can be created more easily when business communication is limited to intraoffice or intersite connections within a private corporate network. (This is illustrated in examples and case studies cited later in the book, where telecommunications managers have nearly complete control over the operation of the network); eventually, however, the full standardization and digitalization of public networks will also bring increasing transparency to data and video communication *between* businesses within the next decade.

Finally, it is important to remember that a key by-product of network transparency is the speed and timeliness of electronic communication via telematics. This benefit especially stands out when compared to the postal mail system.

Telematics decreases the "information float"—the time a message spends traversing the geographic distance between sender and receiver—from days to minutes. A transaction occurring through the mail can consume up to a week for physical ground and air transport to and from the two parties; by contrast, two parties communicating over an electronic mail system could complete the same transaction in hours or even minutes.

The concept of timeliness implies both this speedy flow of information, plus delivery of the latest and best information *in time to be useful*. Telematic applications such as electronic mail and voice mail allow messages in transit to be inexpensively stored in computer memory; the recipient can then forward the stored information when it is timely and convenient. Similarly, videotex systems and micro-to-mainframe links store information on large data bases from which users can extract intelligence on demand. Teleconferences—electronic meetings in which a number of communicating parties are simultaneously available—allow reductions in travel time and numerous other benefits.

Selectivity. The concept of intelligence also implies that managers (or support people who work for the manager) have enhanced powers of accessing accurate, timely, and reliable information via the transparent communication system. The manager can easily extract from among available data the intelligence needed to quickly make decisions and solve problems; the telematic network becomes, in effect, the manager's primary information-filtering system.

Selectivity is especially the design goal of all systems in which people interact with data bases, in applications such as microcomputer-to-mainframe links and corporate videotex. In addition, systems for people-to-people communications, because these are mediated by computers, also provide numerous filtering mechanisms for the senders and recipients of information.

Through a corporate information or telecommunication policy, corporate management can systematically pursue the benefits offered by transparency and selectivity to improve the productivity of managers and office workers and to improve the company's responsiveness to external market conditions. In this sense, we can say that the most progressive companies of the 1980s will use telematics to convert data into business intelligence as part of a competitive strategy for survival in the information age.

Having defined telematics and its potential impact on business, the next chapter explores the powerful forces motivating the growth of the telematics industry. These technological, economic, and regulatory forces are establishing telematics as a leading factor in the development of business.

QUESTIONS FOR REVIEW:

1. Define the term telematics.
2. Recount the history of telecommunications and the computer, briefly.
3. Describe the three stages in the evolution of telematics.
4. Describe transparency and selectivity.

FOR DISCUSSION:

1. Discuss how telematics enhances business communications? What are some of the implications for you as a professional in a business?
2. What would some of the components of a corporate telecommunications policy be? Corporate Information Policy?
3. How is telematics reshaping the concept of business intelligence?
4. Describe how John Diebold in, *Managing Information* (New York: AMACOM, 1985), views the role of communications technology in business.

ASSIGNMENT —

NOTES FOR CHAPTER ONE

1. The term was first used in report to the President of the French Republic by Simon Nora and Alain Minc, entitled, "L'Informatisation de la Société, La Documentation Française," January 1978.

2. John Diebold, *Managing Information* (New York: AMACOM, 1985), Chapter 4.

3. Jane Ferrel, "Computer Networks Boost Productivity," *The San Francisco Examiner,* April 7, 1985, p. 37.

4. Marika Ruumet and David Green, "Pull It Together with Videoconferencing," *Communications Age,* March 1985, p. 24.

5. International Data Corporation, "Business Communication in the '80s," *Industry Week,* September 16, 1985, p. 43.

6. The concept of managerial and organizational "intelligence" is developed at length in Goldhaber et al., *Information Strategies* (Norwood, New Jersey: Ablex, 1984), Chapters 1 and 2.

7. Quoted in "Information Power," *Business Week,* October 14, 1985, p. 111.

Forces Shaping the Evolution of Telematics

OBJECTIVES

- Describe three major forces shaping the evolution of telematics and their roles.
- Describe the major players and their strategies in post-divestiture communications.
- Provide framework for the rest of the text.

*DRIVING
FORCE
IN DIGITAL
PROCESSING*

*INFORMATION
EXPLOSION*

*INDUSTRY
CHANGE*

Dazzling improvements in the cost-effectiveness of semiconductors over the past decade are the main technological force motivating the rapid growth of information technology and are a primary cause of emergence of telematics. But two other motivating factors must also be considered in the case of telematics: the radical change in market forces resulting from the breakup of AT&T in 1984 and the rising demand by corporations for *integrated* communication and information systems to help them cope with the emerging information economy. Of the many powerful technological, economic, and regulatory forces shaping telematics, these three are the most important.

THE SEMICONDUCTOR REVOLUTION

The semiconductor—also known as the chip or very large scale integrated (VLSI) circuit—is the core technology of the computer. Over the past 20 years, the cost of semiconductors has dropped 99.9 percent—a cost reduction equivalent to a $10,000 automobile being reduced in price to just $10. As the price of semiconductors has fallen, manufacturers have also radically improved their efficiency, speed, and reliability.

Telematics is the result, quite simply, of the fact that telecommunications providers now find it economically feasible to add semiconductor technology to every kind of communication tool and function. Once-exotic telecommunication technologies have now become cost-effective tools available to almost any size business.

Consider the change that has occurred, for example, in modern switching devices. (Switches automatically connect telephone users anywhere on the telephone network to each other.) The first automatic switches were once bulky electromechanical machines with many moving parts; they filled large rooms at the local telephone company's central office and required frequent maintenance. Now, because of semiconductor technology, these devices have become elegant cabinets filled with trays of circuit boards quietly controlled by software. They use digital circuitry to automatically switch incoming and outgoing calls to their destination. This radical improvement in cost-effectiveness allows a corporation and even departments within an organization to own and operate their own digital switch (known as the digital private branch exchange, or PBX). In addition, many other value-added features are now possible with the new digital switches: voice messaging (a digital voice storage and forwarding service); cost-cutting capabilities such as least-cost call routing (automatic connections to the cheapest available lines) and call detail recording (providing daily telephone usage information). Finally, because the new computerized switches are made to handle digital signals, they can simultaneously be used to switch data between desktop computers that are linked in computer networks, while offering numerous value-added services to the users on these networks.

New transmission equipment and media introduced over the past three decades—satellites, fiber optics, coaxial cable, and microwave relay equipment—are also undergoing steady improvements through the application of digital technology. The main result of the digitalization of telecommunications media and equipment is the evolution of higher speed, more reliable, more cost-effective transmission systems for voice, data, and video.

For example, for most forms of computer communication, transmission reliability is essential; the loss of a few bits in transmission can render the communication useless. The analog transmission of data over telephone wires, however, is prone to transmission errors. Analog signals traveling down a telephone line must be boosted periodically by amplifiers, which can't distinguish between the actual signal and any noise on the line; thus, as the signal is amplified, transmission errors become inevitable. But if new wires and telecommunications equipment capable of digital communication are installed, transmission reliability improves significantly. (AT&T began installing such lines as far back as the early 1960s.) The digital signals are simply and cleanly regenerated by computerized devices known as repeaters as they pass through the network. (A vivid example of the impact of computer technology on the existing *analog* transmission systems is packet switching technology, covered in detail in Chapter Eight, which allows relatively high-speed data transmission with low error rates over ordinary telephone wires.)

As noted before, the current evolution of second-stage telematics also means that the voice, data, and video communication devices attached to networks are undergoing digitalization. Some examples: The human voice can be digitized inexpensively by adding a specialized chip called a codec to the telephone handset; semiconductors have turned the latest facsimile machines into desktop, digital devices capable of far higher transmission speeds than before, with much improved document resolution; miniaturization of various components permitted by VLSI circuitry has allowed the development of desktop workstations capable of combined digital voice and data communication. Even television technology is being computerized: Industrial-grade cameras, recorders, and video switchers (and soon most television sets) are made with digital circuitry. All these devices join the personal computer as communication tools capable of digital transmission.

Anticipated breakthroughs in the application of computerized technology will soon usher in the most advanced stages of telematics: the integration of voice, data, and video terminals, network control equipment, transmission media, and network services into what may be called an intelligent digital network. Such networks will not only move digital voice, data, and video signals from point to point, but will also provide the capability to process, store, and manipulate the information it moves or collects. Thus, because of the power of semiconductor technol-

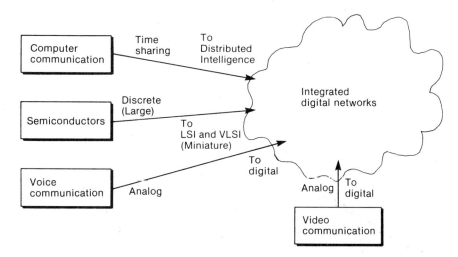

FIGURE 2–1: Factors in the evolution of integrated digital networks.

AT&T VISION

ogy, public telecommunication systems and private corporate networks will behave like vast, integrated, software-controlled, distributed data processing systems—much more flexible and efficient than any previous system—and capable of transmitting information in a variety of forms.

Figure 2–1 shows how the co-evolution of computer communications, semiconductor technology, and digitalization of voice and video transmission is resulting in the establishment of integrated digital networks.

THE DIVESTITURE

A major factor that many believe may have impeded the development of telematics—AT&T's regulated monopoly of the telecommunications system—was struck down by the recent government-ordered divestiture of AT&T. This momentous event can be seen as government's way of recognizing the potential impact of the merger of computers and telecommunications on economic growth; deregulation was regarded as the best technique for spurring technological innovation and improvement in services through the development of a competitive marketplace.

The official breakup of the Bell System on January 1, 1984, was the largest corporate reorganization ever undertaken. The Bell monopoly—formerly with more than $100 billion in assets—was divided into eight major entities. (See Figure 2–2.) According to the federal consent decree issued in 1982 by the Justice Department, the new remnant of AT&T would be allowed to handle long-distance service only, plus pursue the development and manufacture of technologies merging computers and telecommunications. The other seven entities that once comprised the Bell System were designated as regional holding companies (also known as the RBOCs—the regional bell operating companies); they were given responsibility for providing regional telephone service under state regulation. Each RBOC was subdivided into numerous "local access and transport areas" (LATAs), and the local telephone companies generally were restricted to intra-LATA transmission. The Justice Department's "equal access" ruling required that long-distance calls (i.e., inter-LATA) no longer would be passed automatically to AT&T's network. Instead they would be passed to whatever long-distance carrier the customer chose.

LATA's ARE IMPORTANT AREAS FOR COST

Before the divestiture of the Bell operating companies by AT&T on January 1, 1984, the telecommunications industry was fairly simple. Customers leased their phones from Ma Bell and received one phone bill for equipment and services. Customers never thought about who provided their phone service or who they should call if they had a problem.

Divestiture separated the suppliers for long-distance and local telephone service. Each of the 22 Bell operating companies (BOCs) was incorporated into one of seven regional holding companies. Under divestiture, AT&T supplies almost all long-distance services. AT&T Communications, the unit responsible for long-distance transmission, continues to be regulated by the Federal Communications Commission and local agencies. AT&T Technologies is a new umbrella organization for manufacturing, marketing, and servicing computer and communications equipment.

AT&T: **BEFORE AND AFTER**

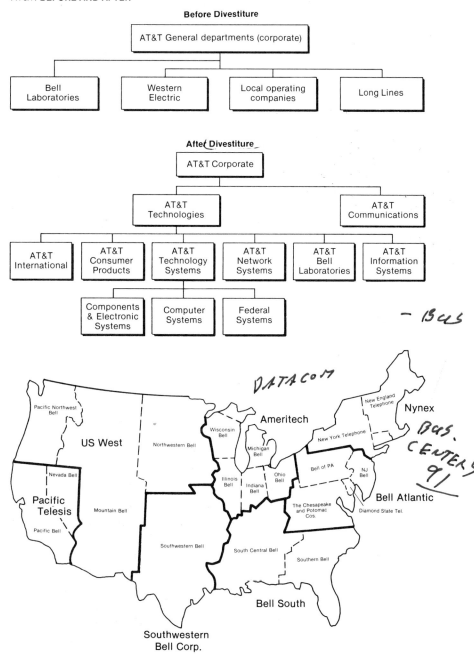

FIGURE 2–2: AT&T: before and after.

Divestiture altered AT&T's operations in other ways too. AT&T's virtual monopoly of telecommunications had included more than just local and long-distance carrier lines; it also embraced the manufacture of transmission network and switching equipment, network services such as WATS lines and leased lines, and even "customer-premise" equipment up to and including the very telephone on the desktop. Deregulatory decisions in the past two decades had begun to reduce AT&T's stranglehold in a few of these areas. But now, for the first time since the creation of the Bell System monopoly in the early 20th century, the divestiture also subjects each of these technologies to free market competition. The RBOCs are now permitted to manufacture and sell telecommunications equipment to businesses in competition with their old mother company, and a large variety of small, technologically advanced companies, which were waiting in the wings for a chance to compete, are now entering the market.

[handwritten margin note: SHOULD RBOC BE IN ANY OTHER BUS. THEN UTILITY]

AT&T before Divestiture

The divestiture was the culmination of a series of government actions against the monolithic Bell System, stretching back to the 1940s.

The first formal antitrust suit was filed against the Bell System in 1949. The suit was resolved in 1956, with the out-of-court Consent Decree: AT&T would be allowed to remain intact, on the condition that it not enter the business of selling solid-state components or computers (and thus become, in potential, a telematics provider). It could continue offering ordinary local and long-distance service under Federal Communications Commission (FCC) regulation.

Barriers to competition in telecommunications were not eased until a 1968 court decision finally allowed customers to connect non-AT&T equipment to the Bell network. This was followed in the mid-1970s by a series of rulings that permitted other companies, such as MCI (Microwave Communications, Inc.), to effectively compete in the long-distance marketplace. At this juncture, the Justice Department and the FCC realized that by loosening the reins somewhat, the government had created an awkward regulatory environment: The

[handwritten margin note: DECISIONS INFLUENCE TELEMATICS PROGRESS]

industry had become part competitive and part monopoly. By 1974 the Justice Department had moved to break up the remaining monopolistic sector with another antitrust suit against AT&T.

When the suit moved to trial in 1982, AT&T negotiated a settlement with the government that allowed it to retain its profitable business of long-distance service and equipment manufacturing, while spinning off the RBOCs. In exchange, AT&T was released from the 1956 Consent Decree, which prohibited it from entering the computer business.

This bargain now appears to have been a wise technical move for the telecommunications giant. As we have seen, the emerging synergy between computing and telecommunications has created the new future for the communications industry: the telematic technologies. It was clear to the management of AT&T—once divestiture was a foregone conclusion—that competitors with computer expertise would mount the biggest challenge to AT&T in the newly restructured market. By moving toward computers, AT&T was preparing itself for the onslaught of competition in the new telematics marketplace.[1]

Telecommunications after Divestiture

AT&T had been nearly every company's one-stop telecommunications provider—but the divestiture has changed all that forever. The government's goal of bringing competition into what had once been a single-vendor marketplace has succeeded almost too well: Corporate telecommunications managers are being bombarded with a confusing array of products and services offered by a multitude of new vendors. The fierce competition is leading to severe shakeouts in a number of product areas. At the same time, a number of new computer products and office communication systems—each in need of links to larger public and private networks—are entering the marketplace, adding a new element of complexity. Many observers consider this post-divestiture computer and communications marketplace to be chaotic, and some wonder whether the divestiture has been worth all the disruption and difficulty it is causing business (as well as ordinary consumers). After all, the post-divestiture telecommunications environment differs sharply from the former ar-

 # FEATURES
↓ ↑

rangement, which provided everyone with reliable end-to-end telephone service from a regulated public utility.

On balance, however, companies adjusting to the information economy are better served by the newly competitive, flexible market in communications equipment and services that has resulted from the breakup of AT&T. The new competition is stimulating rapid growth of new technologies. Many vendors are able to offer better service than the old Bell operating companies, which were known to be bureaucratic, unresponsive entities; in addition, advanced services and improved equipment are being brought to market faster and at lower prices than was possible under the regulated AT&T monopoly. In fact, the success of the deregulatory movement in the United States has led the way for a worldwide trend toward the privatization of telecommunications; for example, government-run telecommunication systems in Japan and the United Kingdom have recently been turned over to the private sector, and other industrialized countries are considering similar actions.

THE DEMAND FOR TELEMATICS: COPING WITH THE INFORMATION AGE

WORKER PERFORMANCE

The increasing supply of new telecommunication and information technologies has been eagerly adopted by American businesses, and for good reason: The United States and all other industrialized nations are moving toward an information economy, where data and information have become the strategic "raw material" for a wide array of occupations.

The trend to an information economy first became apparent in the 1950s, when the percentage of white-collar workers began to exceed that of blue-collar workers. By the mid-1970s, according to a major study by the Department of Commerce titled "The Information Economy," more than half the labor force was working in an information-related job. By 1985, the percentage of professional workers alone—scientists, engineers, lawyers, architects, accountants, doctors, and so on—exceeded the percentage of workers in manufacturing. And now, with the advent of robots and microcomputers in manufacturing, even blue-collar jobs are becoming information-intensive.

The rise of the information worker reflects the overall trend in advanced industrialized societies toward a postindustrial information economy in which knowledge and information technology are the dominant forces of production. Industrial-age work, by contrast, was based on energy-intensive machine technology and the hierarchical division of labor for manufacturing efficiency.

The demand side of the telematics industry is driven by management's new concern for the productivity of information work. Business is seeking new formulas for increasing the information productivity of information workers; the general goal is to match the successes achieved in the manufacturing productivity of blue-collar workers over the past century. Telematics—as the communications core of information technology—is increasingly seen as essential to any strategy for coping with productivity problems in the information age.

After surveying telematic technologies and applications in Parts Two through Six of this book, Part Six will consider various cases in which telematics has been used to solve information productivity problems. Part Seven will recommend an approach to the problem of managing telematic corporate networks in the information age. (In this section we will introduce the problem in terms of the rising demand for communications solutions in America's corporations.)

The Information Explosion

As the information age progresses, telematic corporate networks will become information workers' scouting system for uncovering the intelligence they need to perform competitively. It's their best tool in the battle against the main enemy of people engaged in information work: inaccurate, irrelevant, and untimely information.

Unfortunately, many white-collar and office workers are overwhelmed with useless information in their daily work. Take for example the manager who when asked what is the greatest communication problem he faces responded:

> Communication problem? I'll tell you my biggest communication problem. Just look at this desk! Reports, computer printouts,

telephone messages, letters, journals, telegrams. My biggest communications problem? I'm overloaded. I'm getting so damn much information from so damn many people that I can't see the top of my desk! I'm drowning in paper: drowning in information.

His answer to a follow-up question regarding his second-biggest communication problem reveals a lot about the quality of the information he is bringing to his desk. His response was, "I never know what the hell is going on around here!"[2]

Such is the communication paradox of most managers: too much data, not enough useful information—i.e., not enough of the essential business intelligence they need to make decisions in an increasingly ambiguous and complex environment. Instead, they either receive too little information about major decisions, irrelevant information that doesn't answer questions, or information in the wrong form or with too much detail or frequency.

Unlike most clerical and support workers, who rely heavily on structured, internally generated data, managers deal with data from both internal and external sources—usually in an unstructured, ad hoc environment defined by the needs of the decision to be made or the problem to be solved. Such workers typically spend more than 50 percent of their time communicating with people in meetings, on the telephone, and through electronic communication devices. Their own use of communication technology—or its use by subordinates to gather and filter relevant information—is becoming the basis for their decision-making power, their *information power*. Managers and others who communicate in unstructured work environments will increasingly demand telematic technologies as a solution to their burden of useless information.

Telematics is therefore in transition from a technology-driven to a demand-driven industry. The benefit of telematics for bringing intelligence to the desktop of harried managers and office workers is becoming increasingly clear. As these technologies mature and as prices continue to fall, the technological and regulatory forces that are currently the dominant forces shaping the industry will be replaced by a booming business demand. This force will be as strong as was the demand for cost-cutting manufacturing technology during the industrial age.

THE POST-DIVESTITURE COMMUNICATIONS BATTLEGROUND: AT&T AND ITS OPPONENTS

What kind of marketplace will companies building telematics corporate networks encounter in the late 1980s?

The first point to understand is that the 1984 divestiture unleashed powerful competitive forces that were already present. As early as the 1960s, when partial deregulation began to soften AT&T's monopoly, innovative products began chipping away at AT&T's dominion. For example, by the early 1970s, entrepreneurial companies such as MCI started offering inexpensive microwave transmission and access to communications satellites that began to threaten AT&T's lead in long-distance services.

Now that the players in the telecommunications market have been put on a (theoretically) equal competitive basis, the new AT&T must compete shoulder to shoulder with powerful competitors, like MCI and many new players in the long-distance telecommunications market, and with computer giants such as International Business Machines Corp. (IBM), Digital Equipment Corporation (DEC), and Hewlett-Packard in the computer and communications market.

However, as we will see, IBM is clearly shaping up as AT&T's largest competitor in the emerging telematics industry.

AT&T Versus IBM

Many observers date the real beginning of the new era of competition in telematics from January 1982. In this one month, the Justice Department dropped its antitrust suit against IBM and negotiated the settlement with AT&T that culminated in the 1984 breakup. The current consensus is that this date marks the genesis of a competitive market environment dominated by AT&T and IBM, and their respective allies.

The future of IBM and AT&T is in many ways the future of the telematics industry. The market strategies of these behemoth corporations do appear to guide the development of the cutting edge technological developments. In fact, they are taking their cues from the inevitable direction of technical evolution in an information economy.

Those companies making their bid for a piece of the post-divestiture communications marketplace must respond to the logic of the convergence of computers and telecommunications. As we have seen, convergence is being pushed by the cost-efficiencies offered by digitalization and pulled by the demand of business for communication tools that increase information productivity.

It is interesting to note how the recent histories of AT&T and IBM actually follow the line of convergence of computer and telecommunication technologies. IBM, of course, has long been the leader in computers; AT&T still dominates in telecommunications. But it is now in each company's interest to expand its product line to cover the traditional marketplace of the other. In fact, ever since divestiture, IBM and AT&T have discovered that they have little choice but to compete with one another in the newly emerging telematics marketplace. Each has lost market share in its traditional markets in recent years and needs to expand into new markets in search of profits. It happens that their most lucrative opportunities lie in each other's markets, with IBM moving into telecommunications, and AT&T migrating toward computers. The eagerness of the two giants to combine computer and telecommunication technology confirms that the era of telematics has truly arrived.

IBM's Strategy

Consider IBM's aggressive communications strategy since divestiture. Late in 1984, IBM bought ROLM Corporation, a leading manufacturer of digital PBXs. Then, in early 1985, IBM proposed to buy 18 percent of MCI, with an option to expand its holding to 30 percent. With IBM's resources and data processing expertise behind it, MCI, which is AT&T's primary long-distance competitor, will have the potential to challenge AT&T in voice telecommunications (where AT&T holds about an 80 percent market share) and possibly in data communications.

Part of IBM's purchase agreement with MCI includes the acquisition by MCI of IBM's satellite network, Satellite Business Systems (SBS). This makes MCI/SBS one of the largest computerized transmission networks in the country for voice, data, and video communication. This arrangement, plus access to ROLM's advanced switching equipment, combined with IBM's installed base of computers, will give IBM the foundation for establishing business telematic networks; IBM could become an integrated supplier of both computers and voice and data communications services. Indeed, many analysts predict that IBM will fully acquire MCI within a few years, making such a capability fully under its control.

AT&T's Reaction

Like IBM, the key to AT&T's strategy is the integration of computers and telecommunications. However, its approach to integration differs significantly. AT&T, the now-independent RBOCs, and many other telecommunications vendors are now rallying around a common vision of the future, which will help bring some coherence to the unsettled telecommunications market. Central to this vision is a digital network that relies heavily on sophisticated digital switching equipment and on the prodigious transmission capacities of fiber optic links. A day is foreseen—perhaps in the late 1990s—when virtually all voice, data, and video signals will travel over a unified digital network, operated according to international standards. The network, known as the integrated-services digital network (ISDN), will evolve from today's telephone system, which was originally designed to handle voice transmission only; end-users of data and video communication devices will find it as easy to interface with as the current telephone system. Most telecommunication specialists throughout the world, and the resources of such diverse organizations as AT&T, Japan's Nippon Electric Company (NEC), and Germany's Siemens are focused on making the network a reality. (See Chapter Ten for more details on ISDN.)

The short-run result of the breakup of AT&T has been fierce competition, but in the long run the U.S. market may revert to an oligopoly. U.S. companies are looking for vendors who can usher them quickly into the age of telematics: who can help them build a system that integrates the company's automated office systems and data processing center with a worldwide digital network for transmission of voice, data, and video. This demand, and the advanced nature of telematics technology, will favor the larger competitors such as IBM and AT&T.

In this interim period, the communications marketplace, though chaotic in many ways, should prove highly responsive to the needs of business. Companies wishing to tap the productivity and cost-cutting potentials of telematic technology have numerous options. The payback period for investments in telematic technologies and services—even for building private corporate networks—is relatively short.

THE PLAN OF THE BOOK

Companies wishing to turn this opportunity into a competitive advantage will need an intimate understanding of the post-divestiture communications environment. This book provides a guide through the broad spectrum of new technologies and applications now available.

Part One has provided a definition of telematics and a brief review of the forces motivating the growth of the telematics industry.

Part Two extends the definition of telematics in two dimensions: the technical and the historical. Telematics has given rise to a new lexicon of technical terms that must first be mastered if the coming presentation of telematic technologies and applications is to be understood. In addition, the historical vignettes on the progress of electronic communications should help bring some human perspective on the field and perhaps add a bit of comic relief from the abstruse technical discussion.

Once the fundamentals are presented, the current state of telematics can be understood on at least three levels, which account for the next three sections of the book (Parts Three through Five). Figure 2–3 depicts these as three circular layers. Communication devices located in the office or workplace are the point of departure. The inner two layers (representing Parts Three and Four of the book) are the transmission pathways for information being sent or retrieved by these devices, both intraoffice and between sites. The last layer (representing Part Five) indicates the major communication applications that run over these information pathways.

Part Six presents telematic corporate networks actually in

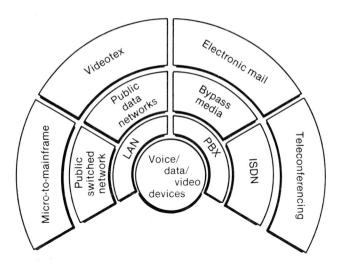

FIGURE 2–3: A model of the spectrum of telematic devices, networks, and applications covered in this book.

operation. These cases show how three very different companies have made varying choices among technologies and applications to suit unique problems. The case of Regis McKenna, Inc., shows the predicament of a small information-intensive company on the verge of making crucial choices for office integration. Hercules Incorporated is a medium-size chemical company that has advanced very quickly toward the establishment of a satellite-based integrated digital network for voice, data, and video communication among multiple sites. The case study of Hewlett-Packard Company, the most comprehensive of the three, shows what advanced telematics—guided by a comprehensive corporate telecommunications and information policy—will look like in progressive Fortune 500 companies in the coming decade.

Part Seven concludes the book with a look at a number of issues pertinent to the socio-technical management of telematics. The real purpose of corporate telematic networks is to help solve the communication productivity problems posed by the information age: A new era of information management will be the likely response to the awesome productivity potential of telematics and the other information technologies.

QUESTIONS FOR REVIEW:

1. What are the three major forces shaping the evolution of telematics?
2. What factor makes telecommunications technologies cost-effective?
3. What are some advantages of digital transmission over analog transmission?
4. Briefly describe divestiture.
5. What is "equal access"?
6. Recount the history of AT&T before divestiture.
7. Describe the role for AT&T after divestiture.
8. What is the "information economy"?
9. What drives demand for telematics?
10. Who are the major players and what are their strategies in the post-divestiture communications era?
11. Discuss the content in Figure 2.3.

FOR DISCUSSION:

1. What are some forces (other than in text) that are shaping the evolution of telematics?
2. Why was divestiture important to households?
3. What are AT&T and IBM battling over?
4. Who do you think will win the IBM versus AT&T contest?

NOTES FOR CHAPTER TWO

1. As we enter the post-divestiture era, it is interesting to note that today's computer and communication industries were spawned at AT&T Laboratories in the 1940s. In 1947, both the transistor and information theory emerged from this laboratory center. Innovations based on these two developments ultimately led to the development of telematics. See "The Future of Telecommunications," *IEEE Spectrum,* December 1985, p. 49.

2. Source: Goldhaber, et al., *Information Strategies* (Norwood, New Jersey: Ablex, 1984), p. 19.

Fundamentals of Telematics

Part Two presents an overview of the basic technical concepts and terms of telematics. This is supplemented by short portraits of key stages in the history of electronic communication. Together, the technical overview and the historical vignettes provide a foundation for understanding the three major levels of telematics to come in Parts Three through Five.

Part Two assumes that the reader has no more than a layperson's knowledge of communications. Readers with strong backgrounds in these basic concepts can skip these chapters and go on to Part Three. Because each key concept or historical event is encapsulated in short modules, those readers possessing a moderate familiarity with electronic communications are able to pick and choose the topics they need to review.

The technical content of Part Two is presented in two chapters. Chapter Three defines electronic communications and surveys the basic means by which information in its various forms can be transmitted. First, digital and analog signaling—as modes of information and transmission—are introduced. Then, in the second half of the chapter, we present the fundamental technical concepts of voice and data transmission.

Chapter Four builds on the basic grounding of the preceding chapter. Transmission media—including each type of wired or wireless scheme—are surveyed, according to their places on the electromagnetic spectrum. The variety of types of terminal attachments are introduced. With this background, we revisit the issue of analog versus digital transmission. This discussion includes the transmission of digital information digitally and in analog form and the transmission of analog information in both analog and digital form. We conclude with an introduction to the telecommunications regulation and standardization efforts that are moving telecommunications toward a future of integrated digital transmission of voice, data, and video information.

CHAPTER THREE

Basic Concepts

OBJECTIVES

- Provide the fundamental concepts in communications.
- Understand the differences between analog and digital information and analog and digital signaling.
- Understand the fundamentals of data transmission, voice transmission and video transmission.

HISTORICAL OVERVIEW

Business has always sought improved methods of communication. Historically speaking, any technique that delivered needed information in a timely fashion has been regarded an asset. For example, the foundation of the Rothschild fortune was a message delivered by carrier pigeon indicating the defeat of Napoleon at Waterloo. This advance information gave the Rothschilds an advantage in making market decisions that anticipated the crisis.

Since the evolution of language, major advances in business or organizational communications have derived increasingly from new communication technologies.

Perhaps the earliest innovation in communications was the invention of writing instruments. Also among the early innovations were simple signaling techniques for relaying coded messages over distances. For example, coded smoke signals or beacon fires at night were used by many ancient civilizations for long-distance signaling. One vivid example of the importance of speedy, long-distance communication to ancient peoples was recorded by the Greek poet Aeschylus in 1084 B.C. Beacon fires set up on nine hills over a distance of 500 miles brought the message of the fall of Troy to the queen Clytemnestra and her lover—and the news of her husband's imminent return.

The invention of printing in the 15th century was the next major step in communication technology. This included the invention of movable type, the construction of presses, the manufacture of paper in large quantities, and the distribution of books. After the printing revolution, nearly four centuries passed before the next important step, the sudden arrival of electrical methods of communication: telegraph, wireless telegraphy, radio, and telephone.

Today we are witnessing an unprecedented explosion of innovation in communication technology, mainly spurred by the convergence of communications and computers. Telematics—the technology for business communication in the late 20th and 21st centuries—is providing technological innovations worthy of an evolving planetary system of industry and commerce.

Module 1   A Model of the Communication Process

Communication does not occur when one person sends a message. The message must be received by another person, and its meaning understood, to be considered part of a communication process. (This process can also be defined to include the *effect* the message has had on the behavior of the recipient.)

Claude E. Shannon of Bell Laboratories, the originator of mathematical communication theory, proposed an elegant model of the communication process built on these basic concepts.[1] The model is applicable to most forms of communication, from human speech to the most advanced computer communications. The communication process includes five major elements.

1. The *source* of a message, the person intending to send a message to another, say a person picking up a telephone to make a call. *KEYBOARD, POS*

2. The *transmitter,* which normally transforms the source's message into the form required for transmission. In the telephone system the transmitter is a vibrating mechanism in the telephone handset. *INPUT DEVICES CODES THE INFOR. FO*

3. The *communications channel,* which is the physical means for sending the message from one point to another, such as telephone wires. *MICROWAVE, FM, STATELLITES*

4. The *receiver,* which captures the message from the chan-

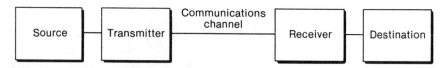

FIGURE 3–1: A model of the communications process.

nel and converts it into a form that can be understood. This would be the receiving telephone, for example.

5. The *destination*, which is the addressee or target of the message. This is typified by the person who picks up the phone at the other end. *OUTPUT TO PEOPLE*

OERSTED AND ELECTROMAGNETIC WAVES

THE BIRTH OF ENERGY FOR INFOR. FLOW BY SIGNALING

1819

Hans Christian Oersted, an unknown physics professor, was giving his routine lecture in which he demonstrated the elementary properties of electric current by connecting a wire to a strong battery. But this day in 1819, the Danish physicist thought he would close his lecture with a new experiment. Though historians are not certain what point he was trying to make, it is known that Oersted placed a current-carrying wire parallel to the north-south alignment of a compass needle. Suddenly, the needle turned violently, reorienting itself on an east-west alignment.

Both Oersted and his students were surprised. Oersted decided to test the compass's reaction if he inverted the flow of current by connecting the wire to the electrodes in reverse manner. Now the compass needle turned violently in the opposite direction.

Soon after Oersted announced his discovery, physicists all over Europe began to experiment further, until it quickly was established that electricity could be used to transmit information. Oersted's discovery led to an explosion of inventions. Not the least of these, as we will see, was based on the principle revealed by Oersted's twitching compass needle: the concept that

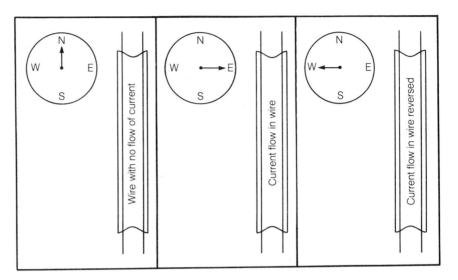

FIGURE 3-2: Current flow in an adjacent wire changes compass needle direction. Reversing the current flow turns the needle in the opposite direction.

the flow of electric current could provide the basis of a new form of signaling. (See Figure 3-2.)

Module 2 Fundamentals of Electrical Communications

Oersted's discovery paved the way for others to show that electrical current flows not only could be harnessed for communicating information but also could be used to transmit information over great distances.

An electrical current flow is generated by introducing an electric charge at one end of a transmission medium. In essence, electrical current flow, or *signaling,* is the movement of these charges down a transmission medium such as a wire. There are two methods of signaling: analog and digital.

Analog signals consist of continuous oscillating waves, which can have an infinite number of values, like our voices. These waves have three characteristics that can be varied, individually or in any combination, to carry information: amplitude, frequency, and phase.

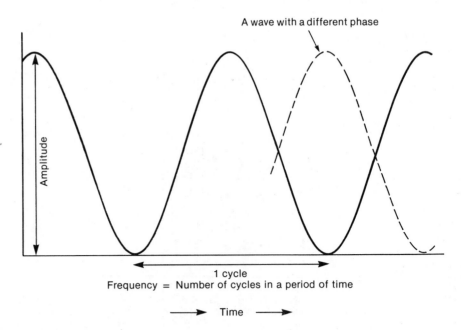

A wave with a different phase

Amplitude

1 cycle

Frequency = Number of cycles in a period of time

Time

FIGURE 3–3: Characteristics of analog signaling. Amplitude is the peak value of the wave; frequency is the number of complete cycles in a period of time; and phase is the point in time at which the wave peaks. A second wave with a different phase is shown with the dotted lines.

Amplitude is varied by the amount of electrical charge inserted into the transmission medium. *Frequency* is the number of complete oscillations or cycles per unit of time (usually expressed in number of *Hertz* or cycles / second).*

The *phase* of an analog signal describes the point to which the signal has advanced in its cycle. (See Figure 3–3.) To visualize these three properties more readily, one can think of the human voice, with amplitude as volume, frequency as pitch, and phase as rhythm.

Digital signals can be visualized as discrete pulses of electrical energy. These discrete pulses typically take one of two values, called 0 and 1. (See Figure 3–4.)

---

*The metric scale uses the prefixes kilo-, mega-, and giga- to represent 1,000, 1 million, and 1 billion. So,

Kilo-Hertz or kHz   = 1,000 Hertz or 1,000 Hz
Mega-Hertz or mHz = 1,000,000 Hz
Giga-Hertz or gHz = 1,000,000,000 Hz

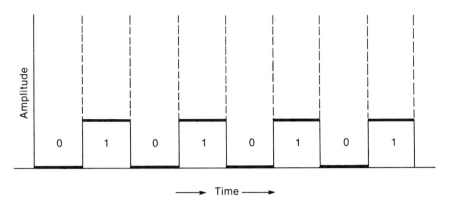

FIGURE 3–4: Digital signaling uses a discrete set of values, typically called 0 and 1.

In electrical communications, information can be sent from the transmitter to the receiver through either analog or digital signals. Voice communications through a telephone represent analog transmission of analog information. The newer telephone systems within large companies transmit voice digitally.

Computers are the prime example of devices that work with digital information. Computer communications initially involved transmission of digital information through analog telephone lines, with use of attachments. When computers are connected directly and communicate with each other, digital information is transmitted digitally. A summary of this description of choices is presented in Figure 3–5.

It is important to understand the choices highlighted in Figure 3–5, since it encompasses the fundamental definition of telematics. Before the invention of devices that process digital information (computers), telematics was virtually nonexistent. Once the computer arrived, and communicated with other computers using analog transmission through the telephone network, first-stage telematics was born.

Now, telematics has taken on added significance with the continuing digitalization of the telephone system. The new digital telephone systems allow not only the analog waves of the human voices to be transmitted digitally, but also the digital transmission of digital information among computers. This we have termed second-stage telematics.

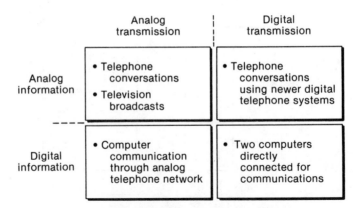

FIGURE 3–5: Examples of analog and digital information transmitted through analog and digital means.

THE GROWTH OF TELEGRAPHY

Oersted's observation that electric current can deflect a magnetized needle led others to predict the communications applicability of the idea. As early as 1832, a Russian inventor had built a primitive telegraph that linked the czar's winter and summer palaces in St. Petersburg.

Cooke and Wheatstone of England patented the first commercial telegraph device in 1837. The six-wire, five-needle apparatus could be read visually. The needles moved clockwise or counterclockwise pointing to letters of the alphabet, as current was fed through the respective wires.

Instead of sending current over six wires to change the position of magnetized needles, the American Samuel Morse developed a telegraph device that sent coded electrical signals over a single wire. The code was based on a binary system of dots and dashes that represented letters, numerals, and punctuation.

Morse patented his telegraph machine and the dot-and-dash-based Morse Code in 1840. Amazingly, three years passed before his world-transforming device attracted financial support. In 1843 he persuaded Congress to appropriate $30,000 to build a test line between Washington, D.C., and Baltimore. On May

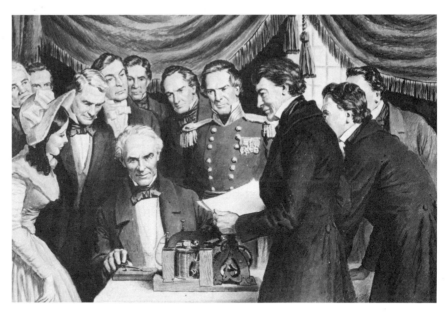

Courtesy of AT&T Bell Laboratories

FIGURE 3–6: An early version of Morse's telegraph instrument. The key, being pressed and released, regulated the flow of current to the telegraph instrument at the destination.

24, 1844, Morse sat at a sending device in the Supreme Court chamber in Washington and tapped out the rather pompous biblical phrase, "What hath God wrought!" In Baltimore, his assistant received the message and sent it back to Washington. After the dramatic success of this demonstration, telegraphy expanded rapidly in the United States.

Module 3 Codes in Computer Communications

Morse's binary dot-dash code was one of the first clearly defined electrical transmission codes. With increasing applications of computer communications, an alarming proliferation of codes has developed. However, the basic structuring of computer (data) codes is still derived from the binary system.

The term binary indicates a condition capable of existing in only two different states, such as the on or off states of a light switch. The binary system uses 1 and 0 to represent the on and off pulses. Strings of 1s and 0s or binary digits (*bits*) are used to encode digital information. Eight bits are called a *byte*.

A binary *code* is characterized by the number of bits it contains. The bit is the smallest unit of information in a digital communications system. The rate at which bits are transmitted are usually calculated as the number of bits per second (bps).

A one-bit code can represent two characters, say "1" representing the letter A and "0" representing B. A two-bit code handles four characters based upon one of four possible combinations: 00, 01, 10, and 11. A five-bit code handles 32 characters; a seven-bit code handles 128 characters.

COMBINATION TO REPRESENT INFOR.

Just as alphabets are standardized, codes have been standardized for addressing specific applications. The examples below describe some of the more popular codes in use today. ASCII, Baudot, and EBCDIC are typically used for conveying digital information through an analog transmission system. Digital codes are used for digital transmission of digital information only.

Baudot Code. The five-bit *Baudot* code has been used in the modern-day equivalent of the telegraph, the international telex network, since its introduction in the 1950s. An example of this representation is 10100 followed by 00110 to possibly encode the greeting "hi." This code is meant for the simplest of transmissions, since the use of five bits places a 32-character limit on the entire code.

ASCII Code. *ASCII* (American Standard Code for Information Interchange) is an eight-bit code. Seven of the bits are used to represent data, and the eighth bit, called the *parity* bit, results from algorithms used for error-checking transmissions. The seven bits can encode 128 characters. This gives ASCII the capability to handle upper and lower case letters, digits 0 through 9, and additional special characters used in data transmission. ASCII is by far the most popular of all the codes used in data communications today, especially for desktop devices such as terminals and personal computers. Several dialects of ASCII are in use today.

EBCDIC Code. *EBCDIC* (Extended Binary Coded Decimal Interchange Code) is an eight-bit code used by larger computers *(handwritten margin note)* YOU NEED COMPLEX SYSTEM TO MAKE AN INTELLIGENT MACHINE TO PROCESS INFO.

a) ASCII code

Bits	b4	b3	b2	b1	column / row	0	1	2	3	4	5	6	7
b7 →						0	0	0	0	1	1	1	1
b6 →						0	0	1	1	0	0	1	1
b5 →						0	1	0	1	0	1	0	1
	0	0	0	0	0	NUL	DLE	SP	0	@	P		p
	0	0	0	1	1	SOH	DC1	!	1	A	Q	a	q
	0	0	1	0	2	STX	DC2	"	2	B	R	b	r
	0	0	1	1	3	EXT	DC3	#	3	C	S	c	s
	0	1	0	0	4	EOT	DC4	$	4	D	T	d	t
	0	1	0	1	5	ENQ	NAK	%	5	E	U	e	u
	0	1	1	0	6	ACK	SYN	&	6	F	V	f	v
	0	1	1	1	7	BEL	ETB	/	7	G	W	g	w
	1	0	0	0	8	BS	CAN	(	8	H	X	h	x
	1	0	0	1	9	HT	EM	)	9	I	Y	i	y
	1	0	1	0	10	LF	SUB	*	:	J	Z	j	z
	1	0	1	1	11	VT	ESC	+	;	K	[	k	{
	1	1	0	0	12	FF	FX	,	<	L	/	l	|
	1	1	0	1	13	CR	GS	-	=	M	]	m	}
	1	1	1	0	14	SO	RS	.	>	N	>	n	~
	1	1	1	1	15	SI	US	/	?	O	—	°	DEL

b) EBCDIC code

Bits 4567		00				01				10				11				← Bits 0,1
		00	01	10	11	00	01	10	11	00	01	10	11	00	01	10	11	← 2,3
0000	0	NUL	DLE			SP	&	-									0	
0001	1	SOH	SBA				/			a	j			A	J		1	
0010	2	STX	EUA	SYN						b	k	s		B	K	S	2	
0011	3	ETX	IC							c	l	t		C	L	T	3	
0100	4									d	m	u		D	M	U	4	
0101	5	PT	NL							e	n	v		E	N	V	5	
0110	6			ETB						f	o	w		F	O	W	6	
0111	7			ESC	EOT					g	p	x		G	P	X	7	
1000	8									h	q	y		H	Q	Y	8	
1001	9		EM							i	r	z		I	R	Z	9	
1010	A					¢	!	|	:									
1011	B					,	$	.	#									
1100	C		DUP		RA	<	.	%	@									
1101	D		SF	ENQ	NAK	(	)	_	.									
1110	E		FM			+	;	>	=									
1111	F		ITB		SUB	|	—	?	"									

FIGURE 3–7 Examples of codes: (a) A seven-bit dialect of the ASCII code used in data transmission. (b) EBCDIC code as used for data transmission primarily by large computers.

for intracomputer and intercomputer communications. The eight bits have sufficient encoding capacity to include nonprinting (control) characters used in controlling data communications. EBCDIC has a different representation for characters than ASCII and other encoding schemes as seen in Figure 3–7.

Digital Codes. The above codes are primarily used by computers for transmission through the analog telephone. The newer digital telephone systems have codes, like Manchester, Non Return to Zero (NRZ), and others in common use today.

DEVELOPMENTS IN TELEGRAPHY

JOHN

A BIT OF HISTROY

MARKET FACTORS & DYNAMIC EVOLUTION

AND ELECTRONIC TECHNOLOGY

FORMES TEXT COMMUNICATIONS

1851

By 1851, more than 50 telegraph companies were operating in the United States. Newspapers began running columns of "telegraph news." Later, the Associated Press agency was formed to help share the cost of telegraphed news among many newspapers. In 1856, 12 telegraph companies were combined into the Western Union Telegraph Company. This marked the beginning of a unified telecommunication system for the United States.

Western Union extended its telegraph line to the California coast in 1861 and laid the first transatlantic telegraph cable in 1866. The transcontinental telegraph ended the Pony Express, which had operated only about 19 months. When the first telephone patents were issued in 1876, 100,000 miles of telegraph wire had been built. This was the first time an entire continent had been bridged by electrical communications.

The next step was development of systems for sending many messages over one wire. In 1874, Thomas A. Edison developed the quadruplex system for sending four messages simultaneously. This was increased to eight in 1915.

Devices that sent and received messages in printed form, rather than in code, were developed in the early 1900s. Starting in 1927, teleprinters were adopted. The first commercial facsimile system went into operation in 1934. (For a discussion of the current state of facsimile, see Chapter Thirteen.)

Today the telegraph industry has millions of miles of land wire, ocean cable, and microwave-radio circuits throughout the world. In the United States, Western Union, which held a monopoly over telegraphy until 1979, has built a nationwide network including multiple satellites, a transcontinental microwave system, electronic switching centers, and local transmission lines. Western Union was a pioneer in the commercial application of data communications.

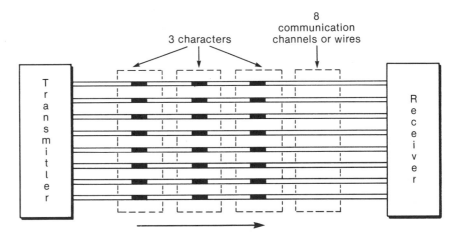

FIGURE 3–8: Parallel transmission using eight communication channels or wires to transmit eight bits at a time. Eight-bit parallel transmission is in popular use today for linking microcomputers to printers.

Module 4 Concepts of Data Transmission

In order to transmit data, the bits of the coded characters, such as the letters a, b, or z, must be sent through transmission media to their destination. The characters can be transmitted serially or in parallel, and asynchronously or synchronously. Transmission can be through simplex, half-duplex, or full-duplex communication channels. These concepts are explained below.

Parallel versus Serial Transmission. In *parallel* transmission, all the bits within an encoded character are transmitted at the same time, and the numerous characters within a message are transmitted one after the other. The *communications channel* is the portion of a transmission medium (like a wire) in which a message is carried. In fact, an eight-bit code in parallel transmission would require eight associated transmission channels. Typically, each of these channels is located within individual transmission media, so that eight wires, for example, would be needed. (See Figure 3–8.)

Over long distances, the cost of providing multiple channels, one for each bit in a code, can be prohibitive. However, the use of these separate channels can increase the speed of data trans-

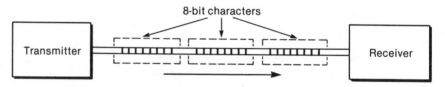

FIGURE 3–9: Serial transmission. Bits within each encoded character are transmitted one after the other.

mission. An analogy is that a one-lane highway for handling traffic may be less congested if increased to five lanes, but more expensive to build and maintain.

Parallel transmission is typically used for intracomputer communications, because distances are short when the transmitter and receiver are within a manufactured unit. The most commonly used method of transmission between computers over long distances involves sending bits of each coded character *serially* (one after the other) through one channel. Our previous example showing parallel transmission now becomes as shown in Figure 3–9.

Like the one-lane highway, serial transmission slows the potential speed of transmission, because it reduces the number of channels needed for data transmission to one. The following section discusses serial transmission in more detail.

Asynchronous and Synchronous Transmission. Most low-speed computer devices use *asynchronous* (async), sometimes called, start-stop transmission. Async transmission envelops individual encoded characters with a start bit and stop bits. These start and stop bits help a receiving device recognize the beginning and end of a character. (See Figure 3–10.)

Because of the individual start and stop bits, characters can be sent at random times because each transmission contains all the information necessary for the receiver to decode the character.

The advantage of async transmission is derived from its simplicity, while the drawback is the inefficiency caused by the nonmessage bits in the start and stop bits. In Figure 3–10, 2 out of the 10 bits are *overhead* used by the receiver to decode the other important bits.

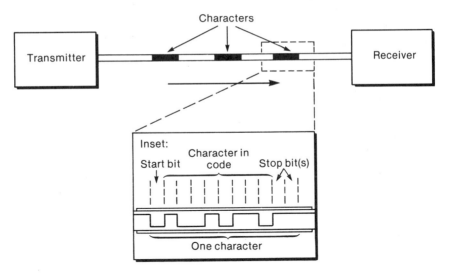

FIGURE 3–10: Asynchronous transmission. Each character is preceded by a start bit and followed by one or more stop bits. Asynchronous transmission is designed for sending characters at random.

In *synchronous* (sync) transmission, encoded characters follow one after the other with the entire block enveloped by a header and optional trailer bits. (See Figure 3–11.)

Synchronous transmission is faster than async data transmission due to reduced nonmessage overhead, but it requires expensive circuitry at both sender and receiver. Another way to contrast asynchronous and synchronous transmission is to look at the coordination required between the transmitter and receiver. In synchronous transmission, both the transmitter and receiver are coordinated through a common clock and know when to decode the many transmitted characters sent at one time.

In asynchronous transmission, the transmitter must send a special signal (the start bit in the message) that tells the receiver to expect an upcoming character. Typical transmission rates for asynchronous transmission of data through telephone lines are 1,200 bits per second, while synchronous transmission is about 9,600 bits per second.

Both asynchronous and synchronous transmission have choices in the type of communications channel used.

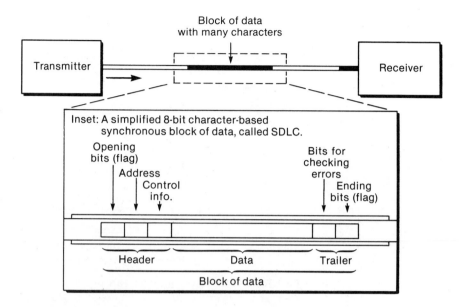

FIGURE 3–11: Synchronous transmission. Each block of data carries one to several characters. The block is preceded by several bits, called header bits and is trailed by several bits known as trailer bits. The inset shows more details on a commonly used synchronous block of data, called synchronous data link control, or SDLC.

Simplex, Half-Duplex, and Full-Duplex. The simplest type of communication channel allows one-way transmission or *simplex*. Examples are radio and television where a transmitter broadcasts the signal outward to a passive audience.

Half-duplex (HDX) channels allow transmission in either direction but only in one direction at a time. An analogy is a single railroad track (two rails) where trains can move only in one direction at a time.

Full two-way conversation is know as *full-duplex* (FDX) transmission. The railroad analogy can be extended to include a pair (four rails) of railroad tracks allowing simultaneous two-way travel. Full-duplex systems are sometimes called four-wire systems. Figure 3–12 shows these three options.

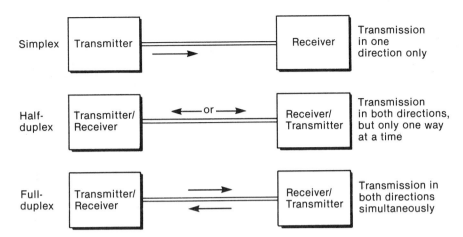

FIGURE 3–12: A communications channel can be either simplex, half-duplex, or full-duplex.

INVENTION OF THE TELEPHONE

Western Union developed technology that for the first time permitted duplex transmission over a single telegraph wire in 1872. Because this doubled the capacity of the network, the commercial value of any mechanism that permitted more channels to be carried over a telephone wire became immediately apparent to entrepreneurs and inventors. Two inventors attempting to develop an improved telegraph system instead independently developed devices capable of transmitting and sending human speech. They were Elisha Gray and Alexander Graham Bell.

Alexander Graham Bell filed a patent for his telephone device on the morning of February 14, 1876. That afternoon, the professional inventor Elisha Gray filed a description of a similar device, not as a patent but as a "notice of invention." Convinced that the telephone offered little commercial value, Gray made no attempt to block Bell's patent, which was issued March 7, 1876.

The 1876 Centennial Exhibition opened in Philadelphia just two months later. Bell's invention went on exhibit in the company of the first electric light and Western Union's new printing telegraph. The first telephone sat at an inconspicuous table, unknown and unrecognized for more than six weeks.

Courtesy of AT&T Bell Laboratories

FIGURE 3–13: Alexander Graham Bell at the New York end of a call to Chicago during an exposition in 1892. Bell conversed with William H. Hubbard at Chicago, the same man who helped Bell introduce the first telephone at the Philadelphia Centennial in 1876.

Finally, after some difficulty, Bell and his friend William H. Hubbard managed to persuade the judges to visit Bell's out-of-the-way exhibit. One member of the prestigious panel of scientists, Sir William Thomson, later known as Lord Kelvin, wrote of his encounter with Bell and the first telephone, "I heard it speak distinctly several sentences. . . . I was astonished and delighted. . . . It is the greatest marvel hitherto achieved by the electric telegraph."[2]

Module 5   The Telephone and Voice Transmission

An important rule was usually posted near the first public telephones, "Don't talk with your ear or listen with your mouth." Figure 3–14 shows one of these early phones.

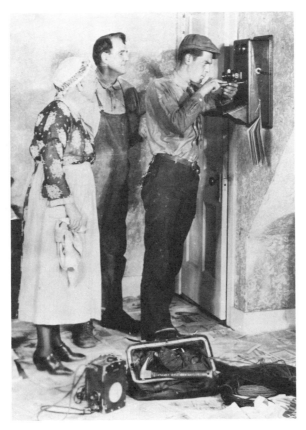

Courtesy of AT&T Bell Laboratories

FIGURE 3–14: One of the earlier telephones in commercial use.

The components of a telephone include the handset, which houses the speaker and listening device; the hookswitch, which is a cradle or button on which the handset rests when not in use; a bell or buzzer for ringing; and a rotary dial for calling other lines. (See Figure 3–15.)

A pair of wires, colloquially called tip and ring, provide the electrical connection between the telephone instrument and the local telephone company's office, called the *central office*. Lifting the handset off the hookswitch (*off-hook*) sends a signal to the central office indicating that the user is ready to dial a telephone number. The central office responds with *dial-tone*. Then, rotary

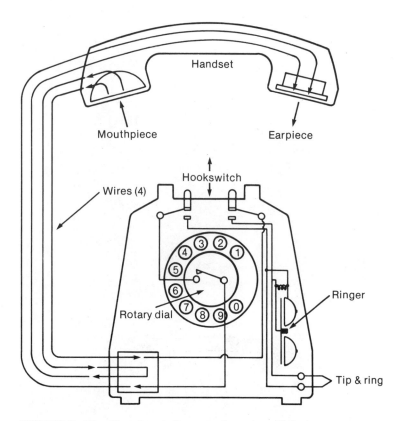

FIGURE 3–15: Functional diagram of a rotary-dial phone.

dialing of digits sends a series of electrical impulses to the telephone office. For example, dialing seven represents seven impulses to the telephone office.

Modern telephones use push-button dialing, with *dual-tone multifrequency signaling* (*DTMF*). When any button is pushed, two tones are sent simultaneously. These series of tones are recognized by modern equipment in central offices. (See Figure 3–16.)

When the destination phone is located, the central office sends a ring signal that activates the bell or electronic buzzer in the phone being called, along with a ring-back signal to the calling telephone. Lifting the handset off-hook at the destination establishes a communication channel for conversation.

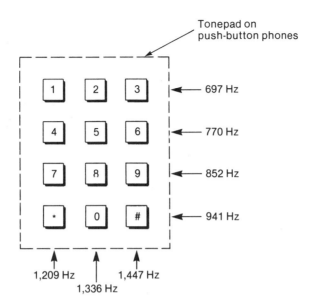

FIGURE 3–16: Tonepad for push-button phones. Dual-tone multifrequency signaling is used. For example, pressing 0 generates two frequencies, 1,336 Hz and 941 Hz. In addition, the tonepad may also be used as a push-button input device in a voice store and forward system.

BELL'S VISION OF THE TELEPHONE NETWORK

After the principle of electrical transmission of voice became accepted, it was not at first obvious how it would be used. For example, Bell himself briefly considered using the telephone for broadcasting messages from a central location, much like modern radio. But Bell quickly came to the clear perception of the telephone as a conversational device. By March 1878 he was able to make a very prescient forecast of where his new Electric Telephone Company should take the new technology. In a letter to his investors, he outlined a system that permitted universal, switched, long-distance service.

At the present time we have a perfect network of gas pipes and water pipes throughout our large cities. We have main pipes laid under the streets communicating by side pipes with the various

STRATEGIC THINKING VISION

dwellings, enabling them to draw their supply of gas and water from a common source.

In a similar manner it is conceivable that cables of telephone wires could be laid under ground, or suspended overhead, communicating by branch wires with private dwellings, shops, manufactories, etc., *uniting them through the main cable with a central office where the wire could be connected as desired, establishing direct communication between any two places in the city.* Such a plan as this, though impracticable at the present moment, will, I firmly believe, be the outcome of the introduction of the telephone to the public. Not only so, but I believe *in the future wires will unite the head offices of telephone companies in different cities,* and a man in one part of the country may communicate by word of mouth with another in a distant place. [emphasis added][3]

Module 6   Network Configurations and Switching

A *network* is an interconnected set of two or more sending and receiving devices and the communication channels that link them. Networks in use today are made of complex and numerous transmitters, receivers, and channels. Of course, the telephone system (public switched network) is the most extensive network in use today. Computer networks and other telematic networks in place today supplement the public switched network.

Network connections can be either point-to-point or multipoint. (See Figure 3–17.) In a *point-to-point* connection, two devices are connected only to each other.

Multipoint links are typically used when a specific set of devices needs to be interconnected through a shared transmission medium. A common example is a large computer and its links to peripheral devices, such as printers, disk drives, and terminals.

Multipoint networks are particularly suitable for applications in which each device transmits infrequently, thus allowing more efficient use of the lines in the network. Multipoint networks are also known as multidrop networks.

An expansion of the point-to-point and multipoint layout is extended point-to-point, also known as a *star* network. Such a network consists of a central station that connects each element in

a) Point-to-point

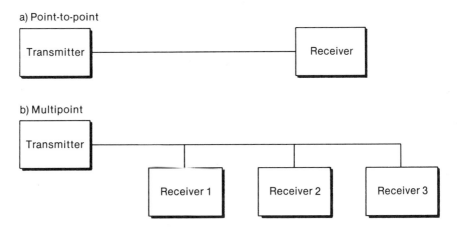

b) Multipoint

FIGURE 3-17: Two primary types of network connections: (a) point-to-point and (b) multipoint.

the network to itself through a set of point-to-point links. (See Figure 3-18.)

Star networks are necessary for networks connecting numerous terminals or phones, in which point-to-point links between all devices would be highly impractical. For example, suppose 5,000 phones had to be connected to each other through point-to-point links. This would require more than 12 million connections.

The cost-effective solution to this mathematical dilemma is to configure a star network, thus reducing the number of individual connections to 5,000. However, accomplishing this feat requires a sophisticated central station to *switch* any sending device's transmission to any receiving device. Switching allows information to travel across a star network, by establishing a transmission path between the sender and the receiver. The two major switching techniques used today are known as circuit switching and packet switching.

The public switched network uses *circuit switching* to connect any two telephones. In circuit switching, a dedicated physical communications link is established and used. After the connection is made, the use of the circuit is exclusive and continuous for the duration of the conversation.

A different approach, called *packet switching,* is used in public data networks. Public data networks are the chief method by which

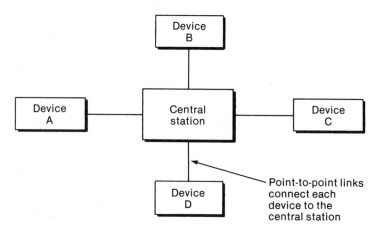

FIGURE 3–18: An extended point-to-point, or star network. The central station, or switching device, sets up the connection between any two communicating devices.

digital information is exchanged by computers over long distances. In this case, it is not necessary to have a dedicated physical communications link, since data transmission tends to require brief bursty usage of the communications channel. Figure 3–19 illustrates circuit switching and packet switching. (For more details on public data networks, see Chapter Eight.)

THE EVOLUTION OF SWITCHING AND CENTRAL OFFICES

Just two years after the introduction of the telephone at the Centennial Exhibition, the number of new telephone subscribers was growing quickly. With the evolution of central telephone company exchanges and manual switchboards, Bell's concept of universal point-to-point service began to materialize much as he envisioned. See Figure 3–20 for a typical scene in one of the early telephone exchanges.

However, young boys handled the switchboards in the very first exchanges. There was no number system for dialing the intended party; everyone was called by name. New York's system had 1,500 subscribers by 1880, but the switching boys still

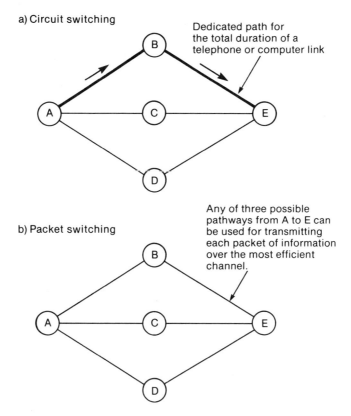

a) Circuit switching

Dedicated path for
the total duration of a
telephone or computer link

Any of three possible
pathways from A to E can
be used for transmitting
each packet of information
over the most efficient
channel.

b) Packet switching

FIGURE 3–19: A simplified illustration of circuit switching
and packet switching.

had to match each name with the proper circuit on a huge central board. Two to six boys were needed to handle each call.

A well-known technology journalist of the time, writing in 1910, describes the improved efficiency that accompanied the transition to female operators.

A telephone call under the boy regime meant bedlam and five minutes; afterwards, under the girl regime, it meant silence and twenty seconds. . . . Here at its best was shown the influence of the feminine touch. The quiet voice, pitched high, the deft fingers, the patient courtesy and attentiveness—these qualities were precisely what the gentle telephone required in its attendants.

Courtesy of AT&T Bell Laboratories

FIGURE 3–20: A large central office in the late 1880s.

Commenting on the state of the exchanges in his own time, he writes:

> These telephone girls are a part of a great communication machine. How many possible combinations there are with the five million telephones of the Bell system, no one has ever dared to guess. But whosoever has seen the long line of white arms waving back and forth in front of the switchboard lights must feel that he has looked upon the very pulse of the city's life.[4]

The linkage complexity of the networks proved to be the system's greatest weakness. Bell had recognized the limits of manual switching of the networks. He argued that as the num-

Courtesy of AT&T Bell Laboratories

FIGURE 3–21: A manual switchboard, circa 1930.

ber of subscribers increased, the burden on the switchboard operators was expanded exponentially.

Here was the biggest dilemma facing the Bell system. The company's cost of serving each subscriber was greater with each addition of a new subscriber. One early telephone manager complained that "so far as he could see, all he had to do was get enough subscribers and the company would go broke."[5] The only solution would be the automation of switching.

A. B. Strowger's automatic switch, invented in 1891, was the first of a long series of automatic switching devices to come. Along with many other innovations, automatic switching was the key to the realization of universal service that Bell had predicted.

FIGURE 3–22: Circuit packs being examined are part of a new electronic switching system. This room is filled with rows of electromechanical step-by-step switches. When the electronic switching system fully replaces it, only one-fourth of the space will be used.

Module 7 Switches and Central Offices

Strowger's invention was the first step in the evolution of automatic switching devices used in today's central offices. In the telephone network today, older electromechanical switches and newer electronic switches coexist. The older electromechanical switches have remnants of manual switchboards. The old manual systems relied upon an operator who used a series of patch cords and plugs to connect two telephones. (See Figure 3–21.)

Strowger and cross-bar switches are the prevalent types of electromechanical switches. In both switches, a rotary dial telephone's pulses during dialing causes a step-by-step advancement mechanically to a contact position representing the dialed digit.

FIGURE 3–23: AT&T's first no. 5 electronic switching system (ESS) being installed.

The sequence of dialed digits resulted in an individual circuit being selected.

Electromechanical switches are prone to heavy maintenance requirements. This problem provided the main motivation for the creation of electronic switching systems.

The first electronic switching systems were installed in the mid-1960s. Since these switches were controlled by stored computer programs, the mechanical step-by-step advances from a dialed digit required in older electromechanical switches were not needed. Instead, the program helped decode the dialed digits and set up a connection path electronically. These electronic switching systems are rapidly replacing the electromechanical versions. (See Figures 3–22 and 3–23.)

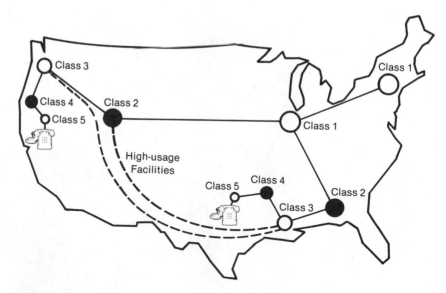

FIGURE 3–24: Central offices—the hierarchy. The solid line represents the path of last resort. Dotted lines show high-usage facilities typically used to shortcut the last resort path.

The total public switched telephone network built by the predominant vendor, AT&T, and the local telephone companies is divided into 10 regional centers in the United States and 2 in Canada. They are each served by a class 1 regional center office.

The next largest center is called a class 2 sectional center, followed by class 3 primary centers, class 4 toll offices, and class 5 *end offices.* Class 5 end offices are also called *local central offices,* where the actual connection to telephone users is made through lines called *local loops.* If the telephone user is a large business with its own switching facility, then these media are labeled *trunks.*

A typical call between telephones, known as a dial-up connection, could be routed through the hierarchy as follows: from the telephone to end office, end office to toll office, toll office to a primary center, primary center to a sectional center, and then to a regional center. Then the regional center assigned to the called party's phone would be linked and the route would be connected downward to the end office through the intermediate offices.

Most calls use this extensive transmission path only as a last resort. A call typically does not need to go to the top of the hierarchy, but links to one of the called party's intermediate offices from one of the sender's intermediate offices through high-usage transmission facilities. See Figure 3–24 for an example. Furthermore, some calls can be made over permanent connections, called *leased lines.* Leased lines are point-to-point connections, typically used for linking a branch site of a company with its headquarters complex.

QUESTIONS FOR REVIEW:

1. Sketch the main components in communications.
2. What is signaling? What is analog signaling? Digital signaling?
3. What is analog information? Digital information?
4. Describe the contents of Figure 3.5.
5. Why are codes needed in data transmission?
6. Provide some details characterizing ASCII code, EBCDIC code.
7. Contrast Digital Codes, in general, with Baudot, ASCII and EBCDIC.
8. Contrast parallel and serial transmission.
9. What is a communications channel? Describe the three types.
10. Contrast asynchronous and synchronous transmission.
11. What is DTMF?
12. What is a network? Specifically, sketch a star network and a multipoint network.
13. Contrast circuit switching and packet switching.
14. How is a typical long-distance call routed?
15. Contrast dial-up and leased lines.

FOR DISCUSSION:

1. Speculate on how analog information can be transmitted digitally.
2. Speculate on how digital information can be transmitted in analog form.

NOTES FOR CHAPTER THREE

1. C. Shannon and W. Weaver, *Mathematical Theory of Communication* (University of Illinois, 1959).

2. Herbert Casson, *The History of the Telephone* (Chicago: A.C. McClurg & Co., 1910), p. 41.

3. Ithiel de Sola Pool, editor, *The Social Impact of the Telephone* (Cambridge, Mass.: The MIT Press, 1977), p. 156.

4. Casson, *The History of the Telephone*, pp. 154–57.

5. Pool, *The Social Impact of the Telephone*, p. 130.

REFERENCES

ASIMOV, ISAAC. *Understanding Physics, Light, Magnetism, and Electricity.* New York: New American Library, 1966.

BAKER, W. J. *A History of the Marconi Company.* New York: St. Martin's Press, 1971.

BELL, DANIEL. "Communications Technology—For Better or Worse." *Harvard Business Review,* May–June 1979.

CASSON, HERBERT N. *The History of the Telephone.* Chicago: A.C. McClurg & Co., 1910.

LANDES, DAVID. *The Unbound Prometheus.* Cambridge University Press, 1969.

MABON, PRESCOTT. *Mission Communications: The Story of Bell Laboratories.* Bell Laboratories, 1975.

MARTIN, JAMES. *Future Developments in Telecommunications.* 2nd ed. Englewood Cliffs, N.J.: Prentice-Hall, 1977.

MARTIN, JAMES. *Telecommunications and the Computer.* 2nd ed. Englewood Cliffs, N.J.: Prentice-Hall, 1976.

MEADOW, CHARLES T. and Tedesco, A.S. *Telecommunications for Management.* New York: McGraw-Hill, 1985.

POOL, ITHIEL DE SOLA. *The Social Impact of the Telephone.* Cambridge, Mass.: The MIT Press, 1977.

Transmission—Devices and Methods

REGULATION OF TELECOMMUNICATIONS AND DATA COMMUNICATIONS
Module 14   Regulatory and Standards-Setting Bodies
Regulatory Agencies
Standards Bodies

OBJECTIVES

- Understand the role and limitations of transmission media within the electromagnetic spectrum.
- Describe the role of terminals and list several types.
- Understand the various modulation and multiplexing schemes.
- Name and describe the roles of the major regulatory and standards-making bodies.

THE INVENTION OF WIRELESS TRANSMISSION

Guglielmo Marconi was the first to find success among the many who struggled to build a commercially viable device for transmitting and receiving radio waves.

Marconi initially showed his wireless transmitter to the Italian government. It was a bitter blow for the 21-year-old inventor to learn that his own government was not in the least interested.

After a family conference, it was decided that Marconi's best chance of commercial success lay in Britain—then the hub of a great empire. Marconi's entry into England a few months later was hardly auspicious. An overzealous customs officer investigated his mysterious device with such thoroughness that it arrived in London broken and useless. But the young genius soon recovered and on June 2, 1886, applied for and received the first patent for wireless telegraphy.

Later that year Marconi appeared with William Preece, chief engineer of the British Post Office, for the first public lecture on wireless transmission. The London press was in attendance. Marconi was to assist Preece's lecture by giving practical demonstrations. Marconi astutely added a helpful bit of showmanship by carrying the receiver into the audience, so when Preece depressed the transmitting key 100 feet away, a bell rang in Marconi's hands, to the amazement of the onlookers. The next day Marconi awoke to find himself headline news.

Module 9   Electromagnetic Spectrum and Transmission Media

Electromagnetic Spectrum. Marconi's demonstration of wireless transmission was a huge leap forward in an ongoing search for alternate means of sending information across air and wires. This search has been partially motivated by the need for more transmission capacity. Greater transmission capacity is always needed to handle growing demand for instantaneous communications to geographically dispersed locations.

In general, increases in transmission capacity are achieved by increasing the range of frequencies (*bandwidth*) by which signals are transmitted and by finding adequate transmission media to harness the increased ranges. The bandwidth of a channel is defined as the difference between the lowest and highest frequencies transmitted. In telephone conversations, about four kHz (kilohertz) of bandwidth is used, with the actual frequency used ranging between 300 hertz and 3,400 hertz.

The complete range of known frequencies is called the *electromagnetic spectrum.* The lower range of frequencies in this spectrum is used in telephone and other wire transmissions, AM radio, FM radio, and television. Higher range frequencies are employed for shortwave radio, microwaves, and satellite transmission. The highest useful frequencies are those found in the visible portion of the electromagnetic spectrum, and involve the encoded transmission of light through fiber optic media.

The very highest frequencies are transmission frontiers and hold vast potential. To illustrate, commercially used frequencies today are less than a billionth of a billionth of the total electromagnetic spectrum. Before these frequencies can be used for telecommunications, transmission media and devices must be invented that can cost-effectively handle them.

See Figure 4–1 for an illustration depicting the electromagnetic spectrum and the frequencies used by different applications.

Transmission Media.   New *transmission media,* with ever-increasing capacities, continue to be developed for using wider bands of the electromagnetic spectrum. Each of these media, wire or wireless, is tailored to carry specific frequency ranges. The newest media are oriented toward the higher frequency ranges in

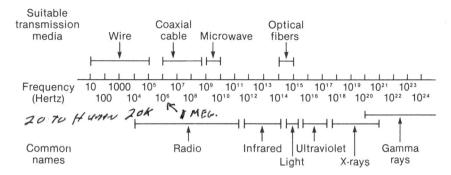

FIGURE 4–1: The electromagnetic spectrum. Suitable transmission media for different frequency ranges are shown and common names for these frequency ranges are also shown.

the electromagnetic spectrum, with bandwidths in excess of billions of hertz.

The following description of the major media starts with twisted-pair wires, proceeds to the media for higher frequency ranges, and concludes with an overview of the new high-capacity optical transmission techniques.

Twisted-Pair Wires. *Twisted-pair wires,* like those in home wiring today, are enhancements of the *open-wire pairs* used in the early days of the telephone. Open-wires typically were made of steel coated with copper in strands an eighth-inch in diameter. They usually were strung atop wooden poles. In heavily populated areas, they formed a crisscrossing spider's web, as seen in Figure 4–2.

Today, the lines connecting telephones to central offices consist of twisted-pairs one-twentieth of an inch in diameter. These wires are insulated, braided together, and grouped with other twisted-pairs within a protective sheath. These sheaths are typically laid under city streets. Individual twisted-pair wires appear as shown in Figure 4–3.

Because of the proximity of twisted-pairs in the sheaths and the small sizes of the wires, transmitted signals have to be strengthened every two to three miles in order to retain the original signal strength. These devices, called *repeaters,* are often located underneath the manholes found in city streets.

Courtesy of AT&T Bell Laboratories

FIGURE 4–2: A street in New York City around 1890. Open wires atop wooden poles cluttered the space above city streets.

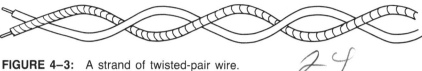

FIGURE 4–3: A strand of twisted-pair wire.

Twisted-pair wires can carry several 4 kHz voice channels, typically 24, through a technique called multiplexing, which is discussed in module 12. Frequencies in excess of 1.544 megahertz (mHz), have been transmitted on these wires over a distance of 6,000 feet. Higher frequencies have been transmitted also, although over less distance, by compensating for "skin effect."

When transmission frequencies are increased in any wire medium, the current flow moves to the outer rim of the wire. The transmitted signal also weakens quickly. This phenomenon is called *skin effect.* Relying on this very small area for transmission increases the resistance of the wire to transmission, making more frequent use of repeaters necessary.

The expense of repeaters makes twisted-pair wire uneconomical for transmission of electromagnetic frequency ranges higher than 1 mHz. Sometimes bad weather causes the transmitted signal to radiate outward from the wire, further restricting the frequency ranges.

Coaxial Cable. *Coaxial cable* (coax) was designed to allow higher bandwidth transmission by reducing skin effect. A coax cable's innermost section is typically a single copper wire. It's surrounded by an insulator, usually plastic, and then encased in a hollow copper cylinder. A protective plastic sheath surrounds the cylinder. (See Figure 4–4.) Current flow at high frequencies is constrained within the copper cylinder and the outer edge of the copper wire.

In the telephone network, a tube consisting of four to six coax cables can carry upwards of 10,000 voice transmissions at 70 mHz bandwidths. Another improvement over twisted-pairs is the transmission speed of coax cable, which jumps from one tenth of the speed of light with twisted-pairs to nearly half of the speed of light with coax cable.

Coax has been used for volume transmission between cities in the telephone network. It is also laid on the ocean floor for

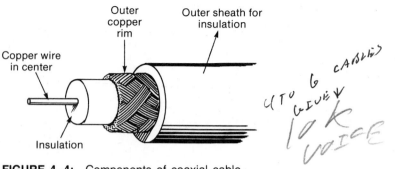

FIGURE 4–4: Components of coaxial cable.

transatlantic transmission. In addition, coax dominates in the community antenna television networks (cable TV or CATV).

Radio Waves. The commercial use of *radio waves* varies from 3 kHz to more than 40 gigahertz (gHz, or billion hertz) of the electromagnetic spectrum. Specific frequency ranges within this total are allocated by domestic and international agencies for FM radio, TV (both UHF channels and VHF channels), mobile radio, and several hundred other uses.

Here we will consider the major uses of the range between 3 mHz (shortwave radio) and the upper limit in UHF of 3 gHz frequencies. Microwave transmission overlaps these frequencies at the upper end and is important enough to cover separately.

Lying below the 3 mHz frequencies are the AM radio channels. Occupying the 3 to 30 mHz range is *high-frequency radio,* used primarily for amateur radio transmission and ship-to-shore transmission. Above this band is the *very high frequency* (VHF) band (30 to 300 mHz) used for television, FM radio, and mobile communications. *Ultra-high frequency* (UHF) forms the high end of this section with frequencies ranging from 300 to 3,000 mHz. This spectrum is used by several of the newer independent TV broadcasters. Frequencies up to 1,000 mHz are shared by mobile telephones, police radios, taxi dispatch systems, personal paging systems, and others.

All of the above frequencies are extremely congested because of the several hundred services utilizing them. This congestion impedes development of newer services, such as mobile radio.

Progress has been made through localized frequency range allocations, such as cellular radio networks in cities, which will be discussed in Chapter Nine.

Microwave Transmission. *Microwave radio transmission* has been used extensively for long-distance telephone transmission, television, telegraph, and data communications. The transmission route is a series of point-to-point links between land-based (*terrestrial*) microwave antenna "dishes," each about 10 feet in diameter. One can see these dishes atop tall buildings in suburban areas. On a transmission route, microwave antennas (*relays*) typically are located less than 30 miles apart, in line-of-sight distance. Line-of-sight requires the sending and receiving antennas to be visible to each other. Each of the relays receives a focused microwave radio frequency beam, regenerates the now-weakened signal, and retransmits it to the next relay on a slightly different frequency, thus forming a chain of point-to-point links. (See Figure 4–5.)

Satellites. A problem with long-distance transmission using microwave frequencies is the use, expense, and management of the relays. *Satellites* have come into being as an alternate relay housed in space. Satellites orbit around the earth 22,300 miles above the equator. They orbit at the same speed as the earth's rotation, making the satellite appear as a stationary point overhead (a *geostationary* orbit).

Powerful microwave antennas, called satellite *earth stations,* direct and receive microwave beams to and from the satellites. These earth stations are situated outside congested microwave frequency areas, like cities, to avoid frequency interference. (See Figure 4–6.)

Satellites use microwave frequencies primarily in two bands. The C band operates from 3.9 to 6.2 gHz, sharing land-based microwave frequencies. The Ku band operates from 12 to 13 gHz. Other bands, such as the Ka band, are used for specific applications.

Typically, the C or Ku band signals are sent to a satellite from an earth station, amplified by one of two dozen *transponders* in the satellite, and sent back to the ground at a different frequency. Because the satellite is 22,300 miles above the earth, its line-of-

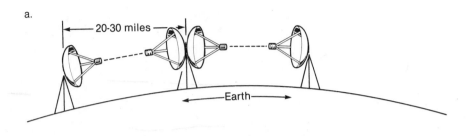

a.

20-30 miles

Earth

b.

Courtesy of MA/COM

FIGURE 4–5: (a) Microwave relays are linked through "line of sight" transmission of a focused microwave beam.
(b) Microwave relay attached outside the top floor
of a building.

a.

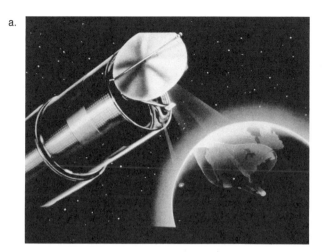

Courtesy of AT&T Bell Laboratories

b.

Courtesy of Vitalink Corp.

FIGURE 4–6: (a) A satellite in orbit.
(b) An earth station used for communications with
satellites.

sight extends more than a third of the earth's surface. By retransmitting received signals back to another satellite, the entire earth could be traversed in seconds. These retransmissions are called *hops.* Typically, 6–10 satellites are used to traverse the earth.

Optical Transmission. The frequency ranges associated with light are nearly 10 million times greater than the frequencies used in coax transmission. Harnessing this bandwidth cost-effectively can increase transmission capacities significantly.

Two modes for transmission using encoded light (*optical transmission*) are used today. One is based on *infrared* signals transmitted through the air as pencil-thin beams of light. Because of the vagaries of weather, birds, and other objects, use of infrared has been limited to well-defined, short-distance transmission.

The second mode uses *optical fibers,* which are hair-thin strands of high-purity glass, protected by a thin strand of dissimilar glass and sheathing. Encoded and concentrated light of specific frequencies is transmitted by devices called *light-emitting diodes* (LEDs) and *lasers* through this media. (See Figure 4–7 for details.)

Using light as a transmission signal offers many benefits: Light is less susceptible to interference from neighboring transmissions at similar frequencies; skin effect is minimized; and fantastic bandwidths are possible, in excess of several gigabits per second. Intensive research and development efforts continue, so expectations for better use of fiber optics to accommodate the 10^{14} hertz to 10^{15} hertz total bandwith of visible light are in the horizon.

GROWTH OF THE TELEPHONE INDUSTRY

The Communications Act of 1934 sought to encourage growth of a nationwide and worldwide communications service and to consolidate the federal government's control of the system in one regulatory agency, the FCC. It required AT&T to interconnect with each of nearly 8,000 independent telephone companies serving primarily rural areas to assure full, "universal" service.

Congress based the Communications Act on the premise that telephone service is a naturally monopolistic market. Allowing

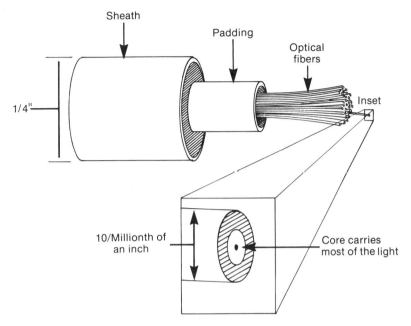

FIGURE 4–7: Components of a fiber optic cable.

several telephone companies to duplicate facilities in the same geographical area was seen to be wasteful. Thus, each independent telephone company was guaranteed an area of operation without competition; in exchange, charges for telephone service were subject to government approval through "tariffs" filed with the FCC or state regulatory bodies.

Over the next two decades, government policy served to reinforce AT&T's monopoly position in the industry. Local operating companies were forced to design their networks to comply with AT&T standards; an FCC ruling forced long-distance competitors to adopt AT&T standards for connecting to local operating companies. In addition, when microwave radio transmission emerged during the 1940s, the FCC restricted the allocation of frequency bands to established common carriers. This and other government-imposed barriers to entry into the telecommunications market served to limit AT&T's competitors.

Thus the government's anticompetitive policies allowed AT&T to enjoy a stable period as a regulated monopoly between the

1930s and the 1950s, with easy dominance over local telephone exchange service, long-distance service, and the telephone equipment market. But technological change and new economic pressures disrupted this market structure by the 1950s.

The computer's emergence as a commercial tool in the late 1940s raised new challenges concerning the nation's telecommunications system. AT&T was barred from entering the new data processing market as a result of the 1956 Consent Decree with the Justice Department. This removed the initial threat that the telecommunications giant might move to also dominate the emerging telematic marketplace.

Concurrent with this settlement, a number of court and regulatory decisions began to erode Bell's monopoly in the equipment and transmission markets as well.

The first breakthrough in the equipment market came in 1957. Until this time, AT&T enjoyed tariff provisions that prohibited the connection of any device to the network that was not telephone company-provided. The restriction was originally designed to protect the telephone system from technical damage, but it was used for years to protect AT&T's monopoly control over the network. However, the 1957 Hush-A-Phone Decision ordered AT&T to drop its restriction on foreign attachments that did not clearly damage the public telephone system.

But the truly landmark ruling involving the terminal equipment industry came in 1968 with the Carterfone Decision. The ruling prohibited AT&T from refusing to allow the Carterfone terminal device, a mobile car radio system, to interconnect with the national telephone system. This decision helped to establish a new *interconnect* industry with rights to attach communications terminal equipment to common carrier lines. The interconnect vendors continued to be boosted by even more deregulatory stances, as depicted in Figure 4–8.

Module 10 Transmission Impairments

Hearing another's conversation or your own voice as an echo on a telephone line; faintly hearing a caller's voice; garbled characters received by a computer terminal; and loud static heard during a radio broadcast are evidence of *transmission impairments*.

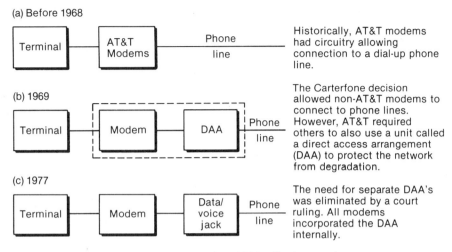

(a) Before 1968

Terminal — AT&T Modems — Phone line

Historically, AT&T modems had circuitry allowing connection to a dial-up phone line.

(b) 1969

Terminal — Modem — DAA — Phone line

The Carterfone decision allowed non-AT&T modems to connect to phone lines. However, AT&T required others to also use a unit called a direct access arrangement (DAA) to protect the network from degradation.

(c) 1977

Terminal — Modem — Data/voice jack — Phone line

The need for separate DAA's was eliminated by a court ruling. All modems incorporated the DAA internally.

FIGURE 4–8: Regulatory changes after 1968 affecting modem interconnections to the telephone network.

Most transmission impairments to telephone conversations can be overcome. We can ask the speaker to talk louder, wait for a burst of noise to pass, or guess the meaning of a lost word from the context of the conversation.

But when machines communicate with machines, as in data transmission, the human adaptability to noise is missing. A lost character or a burst of noise may require retransmitting an entire message.

Various methods of overcoming impairments exist today, tailored to alleviate each of the types of transmission impediments in the telephone network. Below is a discussion of the major classes of impairments: natural noise and network noise.

Natural Noise. The first type of transmission impairment, known as *natural noise,* occurs as a random event. Natural noise occurs in two forms: *white noise* and *impulse noise.* A common example of white noise is the hissing sound heard in the background during a telephone conversation. It cannot be removed completely, but a partial solution involves sending the signal at a higher amplitude, so the receiver does not mistakenly look for information at the white noise's amplitudes.

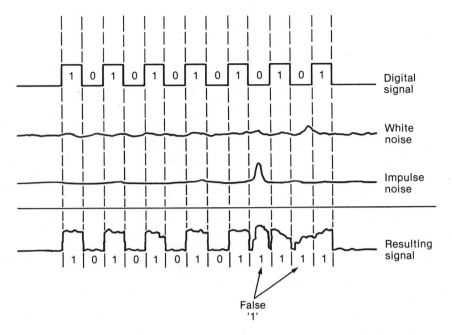

FIGURE 4–9: White noise and impulse noise can alter the original signal drastically.

Impulse noise is of great concern because it is the main reason for data transmission errors. Manifested as crackles and other audible clicks, impulse noise is caused by equipment in older central offices, atmospheric disturbances, and power lines adjacent to the transmission media. In data transmission, impulse noise lasts long enough to change several bits, causing errors. (See Figure 4–9.) Overcoming this impairment is accomplished by installing new central office equipment and re-engineering parts of the telephone network. In the short term, leased lines certified by the telephone company to be less susceptible to impulse noise are available.

Network Noise. Impairments known as network noise are of lesser concern. One of them, *cross talk*, occurs when one communications channel picks up an adjacent channel's conversation or data. Irritating or amusing in telephone conversations, cross talk rarely affects data transmission. *Echoes* also have little impact on data, but can cause a speaker to become disjointed when his voice is heard soon after he has spoken.

Conditioning. Most of the impairments discussed above can be controlled by the telephone company through leased lines that offer _conditioning._

Conditioning comes in two varieties: C- and D-conditioning. C-conditioning equipment provides compensation for most types of distortion. Different grades of C-conditioning are available, depending upon transmission speeds and requirements.

D-conditioning involves the use of leased lines that are laid out to avoid older central offices and to avoid proximity to external disturbances.

THE BEGINNINGS OF TIME SHARING

The classical mode of computer operation is known as *batch processing*. It began with programmers keypunching programs and data onto cards. The cards were submitted to special operators who placed them in a job queue at the central site. Eventually, the cards were read into the computer in batches, the job run, and the results printed for delivery to the programmer. The turnaround time was usually overnight. Often, however, the first run led to the uncovering of program bugs, requiring that the program be resubmitted through the job queue once or twice more after corrections.

Early in the history of the computer it became obvious that programmers were better off running their own programs. The programmer could supervise the operation by interacting with the program from a computer control console. Small errors could be corrected quickly and the results viewed immediately on the terminal instead of on stacks of printouts. Terminal devices and improved software were developed to simplify the task of interactive computing.

This procedure soon proved to be an expensive luxury. While the programmer sat deliberating at the console, an extremely expensive machine was sitting completely idle. And even when the programmer interacted with the machine, the program for the most part used only a fraction of the machine's resources. It was natural, therefore, to look for a means by which several programmers could use the same machine at the same time. This led to the development of the first *time-sharing systems*. New software and hardware were developed that allowed the processing time of the computer to be distributed in small intervals among several users, with the intervals being frequent enough to give the programmer the impression that he or she was the sole user. With the arrival of IBM's 370 series computers, time-sharing became the standard mode of computer use for program development.

Module 11 Terminals

Time-sharing systems helped make an important category of devices, terminals, a major element in computer communications. Terminals provide the man-to-machine interface to computers through transmission media. To unwary users, terminals represent the computer itself.

These devices are seen everywhere today; in banks, grocery stores, homes, manufacturing establishments, cars, offices, and other places. Even the ubiquitous telephone is now classified as a terminal.

We can define *terminals* to be devices through which information can enter or leave a communications network. Terminals typically consist of an input mechanism, like a typewriter-style keyboard; an output mechanism, like a visual display or a printing unit; and a communications interface to communication networks.

Several million terminals are in use today, representing several hundred types of devices. We will describe five major categories of terminals: dumb, transaction-based, programmable, multiuser, and integrated voice/data terminals.

Dumb Terminals. Before the miniaturization of electronic circuits, terminals were built with little or no storage capacity. Some were used for transmitting manually entered data only. Others were no more than slow-speed printers. Some of these *dumb terminals* had a small amount of storage that enabled an entire line to be typed and sent. Today these devices still exist, primarily for use by office workers in making data inputs or viewing a screen of data.

Courtesy of Televideo Inc.

FIGURE 4–10: A typical dumb terminal.

Classical names for them are: keyboard send/receive (KSR) teleprinters, automatic send/receive (ASR) teleprinters, and remote job entry (RJE) terminals. (See Figure 4–10.) Information typically is viewed through an attachment like a small TV, called a cathode ray tube (CRT) display.

Transaction-Based Terminals. *Transaction-based terminals* are devoted to a particular application. Major types include: point-of-sale terminals, videotex terminals, credit card authorization terminals, automatic teller machines, portable data collection devices, and facsimile terminals. More sophisticated transaction-based terminals are used for graphics applications, computer-aided-engineering applications, and computer-aided design (CAD) and computer-aided-manufacturing (CAM) applications.

Intelligent Terminals. Adding a microprocessor's capabilities to a dumb terminal elevates it to an *intelligent terminal.* This type of terminal always has both an input and output device. The microprocessor adds functions for editing text and noting mis-

Courtesy of ROLM, an IBM company

FIGURE 4–11: An integrated voice/data terminal. The keyboard slides into a slot underneath the keypad of the telephone.

spelled words, working rudimentary arithmetical calculations, and manipulating text in and out of a local storage device. Intelligent terminals can be programmed to emulate other terminals in communications networks.

Multiuser Terminals. Intelligent terminals are sometimes joined together with a group of dumb terminals to form a *multiuser terminal system.* The intelligent terminal in this system is identified as the master, or supervisor, terminal. The master terminal allows dumb terminals to be linked to it to use its resources.

OFFICE **Integrated Voice/Data Terminals.** *Integrated voice/data terminals* (IVDTs) incorporate a telephone and intelligent terminal into one physical unit. (See Figure 4–11.) IVDTs were originally designed for use in corporations having digital telephone systems.

The primary reason for IVDTs is to save space on the desktop—the alternative being a separate intelligent terminal and a telephone. Now the reason has expanded to saving space in office/desktops that have personal computers and a telephone. In the near future, IVDTs will evolve into integrated voice/data/image terminals with the added capability for slow-speed video transmission.

EVOLUTION OF ON-LINE SYSTEMS

The development of on-line data communication systems marks the true beginning of first-stage telematics: the use of the telephone network for computer communications.

On-line systems and the traditional time-sharing systems that preceded them had many points in common. The most obvious is that these were both shared-access systems allowing many simultaneous users of a single computer.

But the growth of on-line access reflected a new specialization in the use of computers. Two classes of users had appeared by the early 1960s.[1] One was the class of experts and programmers, who would share the machine for program development. Their terminals were often directly attached (*hard-wired*) to the mainframe from short distances. The other was the rapidly growing class of nonspecialists who would share the use of application programs and common data. These were information workers in offices often located at sites remote from the computer who needed access to already-established files. Their tasks, typically routine interactions known in advance, included entering data or "conversations" with the computer concerning inventory, accounts, billing, or sales statistics.

The technology of on-line systems was pioneered by the U.S. Air Force during the early 1950s. Cold War perceptions of a Soviet threat were at high pitch. The nation's current air defense then consisted of only a few radar stations with control centers on the east and west coasts. This system was inadequate for tracking Soviet bombers mounting a massive attack or flying outside or around the range of radar surveillance. The result was the appropriation of almost unlimited funds for the construction of a drastically improved air defense system.

More than a decade in development, the new system, known as SAGE (Semi-Automatic Ground Environment), was the first on-line computerized defense network. The network could coordinate in *real-time* all surveillance data acquired from a web of new radar stations spanning North America.

SAGE taught American industry how to design and build an extensive, real-time network for the transmission of digital data over voice-grade lines. The system included about a million miles of communication lines and several thousand terminals located in 26 centers around North America. The terminals were connected to central computers built by IBM based on a design by the Massachusetts Institute of Technology.[2]

IBM used its involvement with SAGE to gain an advantage in the newly emerging data communications market. It soon introduced the first commercially produced computer allowing on-line access. The new IBM 305 could be accessed by four terminals at distances of up to 1,000 yards.

But the best known of the early commercial on-line systems was SABRE (Semi-Automatic Business-Related Environment), developed jointly by IBM and American Airlines Inc. between 1956 and 1964 to handle airline seat reservations. For the first time, the control of air travel could be done in real-time instead of by the cumbersome system of keeping manual daily flight records. When completed, SABRE consisted of 1,200 teletype terminals located in travel agencies and connected to a central computer over 12,000 miles of telephone lines. A much smaller version of SAGE, SABRE became one of the first commercial examples of the association of a large data base with a communication system, which has become characteristic of modern telematic systems.

Module 12 Modulation and Multiplexing

There are two ways in which signals can be represented in transmission. They can be transmitted at their original frequency, called *baseband* signals. Or the signals can be shifted without alteration to a new position further up the frequency scale.

For example, a telephone conversation may begin by transmitting a voice signal at its original frequency of 300 to 3,400 Hz. The technique of shifting this signal to a frequency of, say, 100,000 to 104,000 Hz is a form of *modulation.* Modulation opens up the possibility of sending signals in any of a large number of frequency ranges without overlapping. A *carrier wave,* resembling a continuous signal at a specific frequency, is used to shift the original baseband signal. In our example, the carrier wave would be at 100,000 Hz.

Generally, three methods of modulation are used: frequency modulation, amplitude modulation, and pulse code modulation.

In frequency modulation, the frequency of the carrier signal is modulated to conform to the original analog signal, while the am-

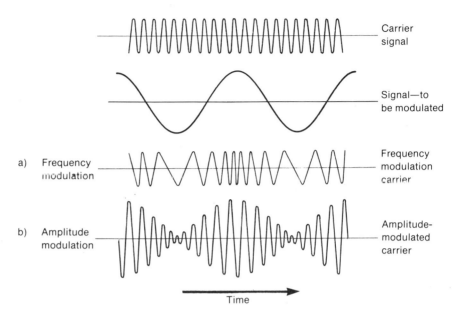

FIGURE 4–12: Frequency modulated and amplitude modulated signals. A digital signal modulated by a carrier signal follows the same scheme, except that changes from 0's to 1's or vice versa are more noticeable.

plitude is kept constant. Frequency modulation is used for FM radio broadcasts and for the sound in television.

In amplitude modulation, the amplitude of the carrier signal is altered with time. AM radio broadcasts use amplitude modulation.

Pulse code modulation will be discussed in the next module.

Figure 4–12 illustrates the first two modulation schemes.

Modulation and the reverse process, demodulation, apply equally well to transmitting data over the telephone network and most other analog transmission networks, like cable TV. Terminals transmitting data over analog telephone lines use a *modem* (modulator-demodulator) at one end to convert digital signals into voice-frequency analog signals, and another modem converts the analog signal back to digital at the end of the transmission line. (See Figure 4–13.) Typically, a specific carrier frequency within the 300 to 3,400 Hz range of a telephone channel is employed.

Multiplexing. *Multiplexing* is a scheme by which transmission media are divided into many communication channels in order to transmit several signals. By multiplexing many signals onto

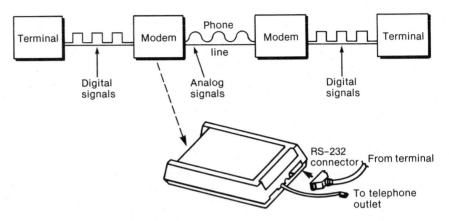

FIGURE 4–13: A modem converts digital signals into analog signals for transmission over the public telephone network. At the receiving end, another modem converts the analog signals back to digital.

one transmission medium, a much higher percentage of the medium's capacity is utilized, allowing more users to be served.

The two most common techniques of multiplexing are frequency division multiplexing and time division multiplexing.

Frequency Division Multiplexing (FDM) divides a single transmission medium into a number of smaller frequency channels. Each of these subchannels can then be used as a separate channel for transmission.

For instance, telephone conversations require a total of 4,000 Hz bandwidth in the public switched network. This includes 3,100 Hz for the voice signal and additional frequencies to serve as a buffer, or *guard band.*

The 4,000 Hz bandwidth utilizes only a fraction of the available capacity of the twisted-pair wire attached to the telephone. Hypothetically, a twisted-pair wire designed for 20,000 Hz bandwidth would have four-fifths unused capacity. Five telephone conversations could be frequency division multiplexed over the same wire.

This is done after modulating five individual telephone conversations to different frequencies, as illustrated in Figure 4–14. At the receiving end, the reverse process separates the five signals into their original baseband frequencies. Frequency division multiplexing is one of the inventions that has made long-distance calls cheap enough for common use.

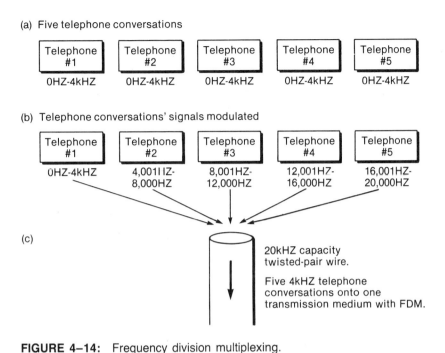

(a) Five telephone conversations

Telephone #1	Telephone #2	Telephone #3	Telephone #4	Telephone #5
0HZ-4kHZ	0HZ-4kHZ	0HZ-4kHZ	0HZ-4kHZ	0HZ-4kHZ

(b) Telephone conversations' signals modulated

Telephone #1	Telephone #2	Telephone #3	Telephone #4	Telephone #5
0HZ-4kHZ	4,001IZ-8,000HZ	8,001HZ-12,000HZ	12,001HZ-16,000HZ	16,001HZ-20,000HZ

(c)

20kHZ capacity twisted-pair wire.

Five 4kHZ telephone conversations onto one transmission medium with FDM.

FIGURE 4–14: Frequency division multiplexing.

Time division multiplexing (TDM), unlike FDM in which multiple signals are sent simultaneously, allows each signal to be sent at a different time, each completely occupying the transmission medium for an instant. TDM is typically used in digital transmission and is more economical for shorter distances. At the receiving end, the interleaved signals are sorted into baseband signals. (See Figure 4–15.) Variants of time division multiplexing use *statistical* techniques to allocate more time elements to the more actively transmitting devices. Devices called *multiplexers* are tailored for doing each of the techniques of multiplexing.

THE EVOLUTION OF VLSI AND COMPUTING

In 1947, scientists at Bell Laboratories made the electronics revolution possible by inventing the transistor.

The transistor is a semiconductor—a type of material that allows regulated amounts of electrical current flow. Transis-

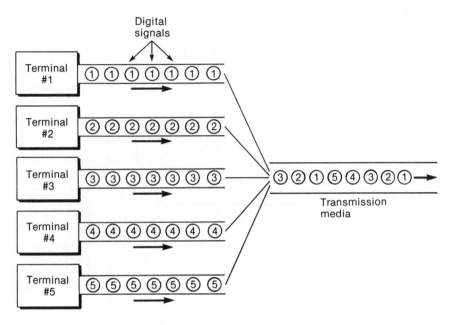

FIGURE 4–15: Time division multiplexing.

tors first reached public attention in the early 1950s as components in radios and hearing aids.

In 1956, scientists at MIT saw the potential for using the transistor as a replacement for some of the massive vacuum-tubes in the SAGE machines. As a result computers like the SAGE started becoming smaller and more reliable.

However, another technology, even more revolutionary, was suggested by the transistor. At that time, electrical circuits consisted of discrete components, individually packaged and built. An English engineer, W. Dummer, started publicizing the idea of a component, called a chip, that incorporated many transistors and other discrete parts. This spurred scientists all over the world to attempt to develop what is now called an integrated circuit (IC). Robert Noyce, a physicist in Silicon Valley in California, was one of the first designers of one of these elegant devices.

Courtesy of AT&T Bell Laboratories

FIGURE 4–16: Smaller than a dime, AT&T's new memory chip can store more than 1 million digital bits of information.

The first IC computers appeared in the mid-1960s. Throughout the next decade engineers began to cram more and more discrete components into an IC. By the early 1970s, engineers were able to place a computer's entire central processing unit onto a chip.

The result of these efforts was the microprocessor—and the evolution toward very large scale integrated circuits (VLSI). Soon after, VLSI was used to create the first microcomputers as well as components which allow inexpensive and reliable computer communications. Figure 4–16 shows a state-of-the-art VLSI component.

Module 13 Digital Voice Transmission

More than $200 billion are tied up in the nation's analog telephone system. However, if the telephone industry were born today, a completely *digital network* would be built. Our voices would be converted into a digital bit stream, with the transmission resembling computer communications. Let's consider some of the technical advantages of a digital network.

First of all, a digital network would eliminate the need for modems and other auxiliary devices required for data transmission via an analog network, reducing equipment costs. Also, costs for digital switching and transmission of voice and particularly data are lower than for analog circuitry. Digital transmission methods are more tolerant of transmission impairments, with regenerators, commonly known as *repeaters,* reconstructing the voice or data bit stream periodically, while excluding most noise in the media. Analog transmission also uses analog repeaters to amplify weakened transmitted signals; unfortunately, these analog repeaters also amplify the noise in a medium, degrading transmission quality. Finally, VLSI allows the reduction of costs for digital transmission circuitry.

Notwithstanding the advantages, the large capital investment in the analog network precludes starting over. Therefore, incremental changes toward a digital network are being made. Crowded cities and suburbs are being converted first. Eventually, we can expect all voice, video, and data to be transmitted over one common pipeline in an integrated digital network.

The previous module described the process for converting digital information from computers to a form suitable for transmission in the analog telephone network. With the conversion of the analog telephone network to digital transmission capability, the complementary problem of converting analog inputs into digital signals is important to understand.

Obviously, digital information from computers is easily transmitted through a digital network. However, converting analog signals, like our voices, into a digital stream is somewhat complex. The following model illustrates the steps needed in an analog-to-digital conversion. Imagine that a visible analog signal is coming from a source to your left. Between you and the analog signal is a bell that rings every few seconds. Although the analog signal

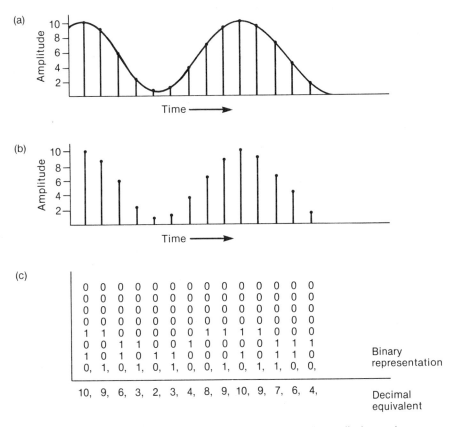

FIGURE 4–17: Analog to digital conversion. (a) A device called a codec samples the amplitude of an analog signal periodically (b) resulting in this plot of amplitudes (c) which are now shown in binary representation.

is being transmitted continuously, you can observe the signal only when the bell rings. You, as the observer, note the amplitude of the signal during each of these rings, or *sampling* instants.

Each of these amplitudes then is encoded into eight-bit binary numbers. Then, these streams of bits are transmitted digitally. At the receiving end, the digital stream is brought back into analog form, through the reverse process. (See Figure 4–17.)

A popular modulation scheme, *pulse code modulation* (PCM), refines this analog-to-digital conversion process. A device, called a coder-decoder, or *codec*, helps sample the analog waves and record the amplitudes. Then, the amplitudes of successive sam-

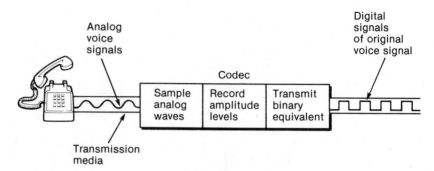

FIGURE 4–18: A codec converts analog voice signals into digital signals.

ples are represented approximately by binary numbers. These binary numbers are transmitted. At the receiving end, the codec helps perform the reverse process to reproduce the original analog inputs. (See Figure 4–18.)

In PCM, sampling of voice is done 8,000 times a second, with 7 bits used for quantization. The total bit rate transmitted is 8,000 samples per second times 8 bits per sample, which equals 64 kilobits per second.

Transmission media have bandwidths well in excess of 64 kilobits per second. Therefore, time division multiplexing is used to transmit several of these digital signals over the same channel. The prevalent digital transmission system in the telephone network using time division multiplexing with PCM is the *T1 carrier*. It is used for transmission over long distances, with regenerators every 6,000 feet. This carrier uses twisted-pair wires to carry 24 channels at a sum of 1.544 million bits per second.

The T1 carrier uses eight bits per sample in total, seven for the encoded sample and the eighth for signaling information, like establishing or terminating a call. A hierarchy based on the T1 carriers can carry more channels. T2 combines four T1 carriers. T3 and T4 multiply the channel capacity even more.

The T1 carrier is a building block for many of the newer digital networks. This technology is attractive as it takes advantage of the vast quantities of twisted-wire circuits that exist in the current telephone system. The telephone companies have an enormous investment in these installed wires. Converting these wires to carry 24-voice conversations compared to only one allows tremendous economies of scale.

REGULATION OF TELECOMMUNICATIONS AND DATA COMMUNICATIONS

After the spectacular commercial success of the American Bell Company in the 1880s, Bell's patent eventually was challenged by a number of claimants—including the early telephone experimenter Elisha Gray, who originally thought the telephone had little commercial value.

However, Bell's company emerged as the monopoly supplier of telephone service. At first, American Bell licensed local operating companies to use its patents in return for a 35 percent interest in their revenues. AT&T was formed in 1885 to assure that local companies complied with technical standards needed to carry out local interconnection with American Bell's long-distance lines. By the early 1890s, AT&T began to acquire many of these local operating companies.

When the original American Bell patents expired in 1893, a stampede of new companies entered the market. In some places this created a chaotic multiplicity of companies offering local exchange service. Many of these independents did not possess the capital resources required for survival. AT&T stepped up its acquisitions of independent local competitors again in the early 1900s. Its purchase of a controlling interest in Western Union, the largest telegraph supplier, attracted the attention of the Justice Department.

Favoring reasonable government controls over the threat of outright government takeover, AT&T agreed in 1913 to divest its Western Union holdings, halt the acquisition of independent telephone companies, and interconnect lines freely with any non-Bell companies requesting access to the network. The telephone industry has been regulated in one form or another since Congress transferred this regulatory authority to the FCC with the 1934 Communications Act.

Module 14   Regulatory and Standards-Setting Bodies

The regulation of telecommunications and data communication services within the United States derives from agencies created through the Communications Act of 1934 and the statutes of individual states.

Voluntary national and international standards bodies, not regulated by the government, set standards which ensure that degrees of compatability exist among similar telematic services. Major standards issues include transmission codes and methods for connecting devices. These organizations have helped develop a strong communications infrastructure and will continue to affect development of the telematics industry. Cooperation between nations to provide worldwide-compatible telematic services is another goal of the voluntary standards bodies and regulatory bodies.

This module describes the role of the important regulatory agencies in the United States and proceeds to a discussion about standards-making bodies.

Regulatory Agencies. *FCC:* The Federal Communications Commission, an independent federal agency, regulates interstate and foreign telephone, telegraph, radio, and television communications.

The FCC was created by the Communications Act of 1934 and is authorized to regulate companies that provide communication services to the public. These companies are called *common carriers,* with the largest being AT&T. To institute a telematic service, a common carrier like AT&T must file the details of the service, rates, and other items. These filings are called *tariffs,* which become contracts between the common carrier and the public, upon FCC approval. A rate change for an existing service is the most frequently filed type of tariff.

PUC: Each state has a public utility commission (PUC) that is responsible for regulation of intrastate communications. Different states may have different tariffs for similar telematic services.

Standards Bodies. *CCITT:* CCITT is an international standards body within an agency of the United Nations, The International Telecommunications Union. It develops standards for telephone and data communication systems among member nations. U.S. membership is through the State Department, common carriers, and other organizations. Several CCITT-study groups have been formed by the United States to focus efforts on different telematic services and have arrived at several accepted standards, especially in data transmission. The CCITT is also at the center

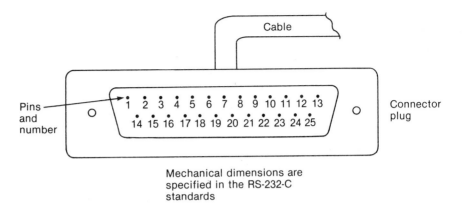

Mechanical dimensions are
specified in the RS-232-C
standards

FIGURE 4–19: An RS-232-C interface is used to connect terminals to modems for data transmission over the public telephone network. The mechanical configuration is shown. Electrical specifications help define ranges of voltage for interpreting 1's versus 0's.

of efforts to establish and deploy the ISDN (integrated services digital networks) standard throughout the world.

ISO: The International Standards Organization (ISO) consists of several national standards committees from different countries. ISO coordinates most of its activities with the CCITT and has arrived at several well-known standards. ISO has several subcommittees; the most famous has created the open systems interconnection (OSI) model to help standardization efforts focused on the exchange of information between distributed systems.

ANSI: The American National Standards Institute (ANSI) is an agency within the U.S. government for developing standards and accepting proposals from other bodies in this country. ANSI has focused on programming language standards, such as COBOL and FORTRAN. ANSI has several communication standards efforts under way.

Others: The Institute of Electrical and Electronic Engineers (IEEE), the Electronic Industries Association (EIA), the National Bureau of Standards (NBS), and the Department of Defense (DOD) are some of the other major standardization bodies. The IEEE has focused most of its efforts on creating standards for local area networks. The EIA has encompassed several standardization efforts, the most well-known are in physical and mechanical interface standards. A depiction of RS-232, one of the primary standards, is in Figure 4–19.

QUESTIONS FOR REVIEW:

1. Define bandwidth. How does bandwidth relate to the electromagnetic spectrum?
2. Name and describe three transmission media.
3. What is skin effect? Why is it important?
4. Describe optical transmission with fiber optics.
5. Classify transmission impairments and briefly describe each of the three types.
6. What are terminals? Describe two types.
7. What is modulation? Describe the three methods.
8. What is a modem?
9. What is multiplexing? Name two popular techniques.
10. Describe VLSI.
11. What is a codec? Describe the process of a analog-to-digital conversion.
12. What is the T1 carrier?
13. What are the roles of the FCC, CCITT, and ANSI?

FOR DISCUSSION:

1. Are modems and codecs functionally opposite devices?
2. Contrast analog-to-digital conversion and digital-to-analog conversion.
3. Describe a scenario in which standards-making bodies are (a) beneficial and (b) harmful. Do the same for regulatory bodies.

NOTES FOR CHAPTER FOUR

1. René Moreau, *The Computer Comes of Age,* (Cambridge: MIT Press, 1984), pp. 119–31.

2. Stan Augarten, *Bit By Bit: The History of Computers.* (New York: Ticknor & Fields, 1984), pp. 204–208.

REFERENCES

Casson, Herbert N. *The History of the Telephone.* New York: Bantam Books, 1983.

LOOMIS, MARY E. S. *Data Communications*. Englewood Cliffs: Prentice-Hall, 1983.

MARTIN, JAMES. *Telecommunications and the Computer*. 2nd ed. Prentice-Hall, 1976.

SOBEL, ROBERT. *IBM: Colossus in Transition*. New York: Bantam Books, 1983.

Office Communication Networks

About 80 percent of the information used in most workplaces is generated within the local work environment. Part Three presents the emerging role of two major telematic technologies—local area networks (LANs) and the newer digital private branch exchanges (PBXs)—for handling this intraoffice voice and data communication requirement. LANs and PBXs link communication devices in the local environment, and they provide an electronic bridge to networks outside a company's local office or local site (topics covered in Part Four).

LANs should be considered the next logical step in the progress of the microcomputer revolution. The stand-alone personal computer (and its peripheral devices) allows significant productivity gains for *individual* users, of course. But linking these devices in a local area network will bring about a transition to *improved productivity for organizations* through sharing of peripherals, file sharing, and electronic messaging. Chapter Five explains how LANs can affect organizational productivity and presents a detailed technical overview of these high-speed data transmission systems.

Paralleling the evolution of LANs as an intraoffice computer networking system has been the growth of PBXs as the on-premise controller of a company's telephone system. PBXs were once an electromechanical technology used only for switching analog telephone signals at the company site, but now they have migrated into telematics. The newest PBXs are large computers that handle the switching of both voice and data transmission via telephone wiring already installed in the office site. Applications such as voice messaging and numerous management control features enhance the usefulness of PBXs for office communications. These and many other technical and socio-technical issues concerning the PBX, also known as the office communications controller, are covered in Chapter Six.

Now that both LANs and PBXs can handle local data transmission, a complex debate is under way concerning which alternative is best for handling the increasing requirement for computer communications in the office. Part Three concludes with a look at the LAN versus PBX debate.

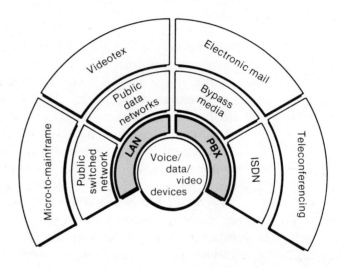

Local Area Networks

OBJECTIVES

- Describe the benefits of LANs.
- Understand the role of technology in a LAN.
- Understand the OSI model.
- Conceptualize a LAN taxonomy tree.
- Conceptualize a model to clear up the LAN market.
- Describe major product offerings.

GENERAL INTRODUCTION

In the early days of data communications, computer networks consisted of links between widely dispersed mainframes and terminals via telephone lines.[1] These premier computer networks were often referred to as wide area networks (WANs). Now that inexpensive microcomputers and other intelligent devices are crowding the workplace, a computer network is needed to connect computing devices within the "local area": an office, a building, a complex of buildings, a factory floor, or a university campus. Local area networks (LANs) have thus evolved for linking micro-, mini-, and mainframe computers, storage devices, printers, and other devices within such local work environments, using on-premise telephone wiring or customized wiring schemes based on coaxial cable or optical fiber.

The first important step in the evolution of LANs was the joint announcement in 1980 by Digital Equipment Corporation, Intel, and Xerox Corporation of a local area network product called Ethernet. Four years later, the LAN marketplace reached relative maturity with the announcement of LAN offerings by IBM and AT&T. With scores of other vendor hardware offerings in place and with networking software quickly evolving, the late 1980s will witness an explosive growth in business use of local networks.

Local area networks present a challenge and an opportunity for business on two levels: the *technical issue* of choosing appropriate LAN technology and integrating it into the larger corporate network and the *socio-technical issue* of using LANs to improve intraoffice communications.

1. *LAN technology:* The world of LANs presents a rich variety of technologies from a multitude of vendors. Offerings vary widely in physical configuration, number of workstations, and applications. Standards for LAN design are slowly emerging under the guidance of several international organizations. Meanwhile, LAN hardware and software are continually changing and increasing in sophistication, as users and manufacturers gain new experience with this versatile technology. Some observers believe LANs will be the backbone of the automated offices and factories of the future. Thus, much is at stake with the choice of LAN; understanding an organization's local networking needs and choosing the appropriate LAN hardware and software are not easy tasks.

2. *LANs and intraoffice communication:* Stand-alone personal computers can improve the productivity of individuals, but do not allow efficient coordination of jobs requiring participation of multiple personal computer users; file sharing is limited or impossible; and keeping track of information scattered across a number of segregated storage systems is awkward at best. LANs represent a major transition from this regime of personal productivity to a new era of office telematics: the networking of stand-alone computers to enhance the computing productivity of work groups or of whole organizations.

In addition to offering significant savings through shared peripherals, LANs allow more timely access to information through data base sharing and electronic messaging. LANs improve the performance of both information technology and information workers; they enhance both the productivity of individual workers and the collective performance of work groups. The potential impact of LANs on office communication is shown in the following example of a marketing work group.

- The direct marketing business unit of a California bank uses a LAN to support communication and file sharing among its employees. The group's charter is to help bank branches obtain more loan customers through telemarketing and sales support.

The department acquired a local area network that allows simultaneous access to the same customer files by employees who enter customer information and check the status of customer loan applications. Employees can also switch easily between files containing information on the bank's specific loan products and offerings. A special capability of the network is "record-locking," which allows a number of people to view the same file while the computer, acting as a "traffic cop," lets only one person at a time change information in the file.

TESTIMONIAL

The business unit's vice president says the network has saved employees hundreds of hours, thousands of pounds of paper, and file space.

This chapter begins with a definition of LANs and brief overview of the impact of LANs on the office environment; this is followed by a lengthy discussion of LAN technology, which is necessary because of the complexity of today's LAN marketplace.

Defining Local Area Networks

& COOPERATIVE FOR COMMON SHARING OF INFO & TECHNOLOGY

Despite the variety of LAN systems, a formal definition is possible: *A local area network is a high-speed information transfer system that links intelligent devices over a common transmission medium within a confined geographical area.*

An easy way to approach LANs is to think of an organization's large computers, micros, terminals, word processors, printers, storage facilities, and other devices as if they were components waiting to be assembled as a complete computer system. Once tied together, these components can form one powerful, productive system. The small distances covered in local networks, combined with their efficient transmission techniques, allows them to provide high-capacity, reliable communication at up to millions of bits per second through this system.

Most work environments have a unique mix of computing devices from a number of different vendors. LANs by definition must also be able to provide compatible communication interfaces between them, (unless all devices on a LAN and the LAN itself are offered by the same vendor). LAN software should render all machine interfaces on the network transparent to the individual user.

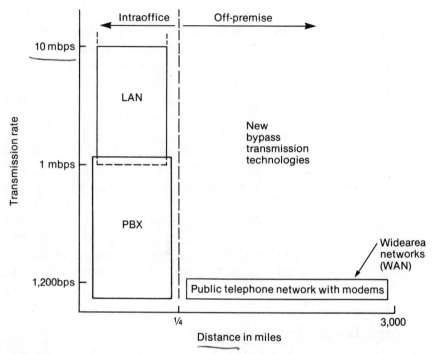

FIGURE 5–1: Differences between LANs, WANs (public telephone network transmission using modems), PBXs, and the new bypass transmission technologies.

NOT REGULATED

LANs also are generally privately owned and managed networks, whereas wide area networks usually require the leasing or buying of lines from the telephone system; thus LANs allow an organization to bypass local loops and all the regulatory and technical problems inherent in the telephone company's end-office connection. (In Part Four we will see how some organizations are now able to build completely private WANs as well.)

Perhaps the most distinguishing feature of LANs is their speed and geographic scope. For example, because they bridge short distances, LANs can run hundreds of times faster than wide area networks using phone lines. A private branch exchange can connect large numbers of data and voice users over short distances, but at lower speed than LANs. Figure 5–1 illustrates the relationships between bit rate and distance in LANs, WANs, PBXs, and the new bypass technologies.

LAN Environments

Three main environments for local area networks have evolved, with different vendors offering solutions for each environment.

1. **Peer-to-peer communications** among personal computer users in departments or small offices, with links to a mainframe.
2. **General purpose networks** for connecting a variety of terminals and peripherals in a building or set of buildings.
3. **Industrial networks** for intelligent devices on factory floors or other industrial settings.

[handwritten note: USING GATEWAYS TO CONNECT THESE NETWORK CONFIGURATIONS]

Many companies may require interconnection of all three in one intraorganizational system. A typical configuration of such a system might look as shown in Figure 5–2.

Capabilities of Local Area Networks

[handwritten note: PERIPHERAL SHARING " FILE MESSAGES GATEWAYS]

Local area networks have three essential functions in today's automated office:

[handwritten note: MAJOR BENEFITS — TEST]

1. They allow sharing of expensive peripheral devices, just as if these devices were connected to every computing machine in the network.
2. They permit users to share files and programs because data entered in any computer can be centrally stored and transmitted to all users on the network.
3. Most provide some method of electronic messaging among users of the network.

Some LANs also facilitate communication from outside the network. Shared modems on a LAN can allow access by remote users over telephone lines. In addition, LAN gateway services permit interconnection to neighboring or remotely located LANs or to large computers.

The following section examines these capabilities in greater detail.

Peripheral Sharing. The overall cost of computer hardware has dropped in the past decade, but the cost of essential

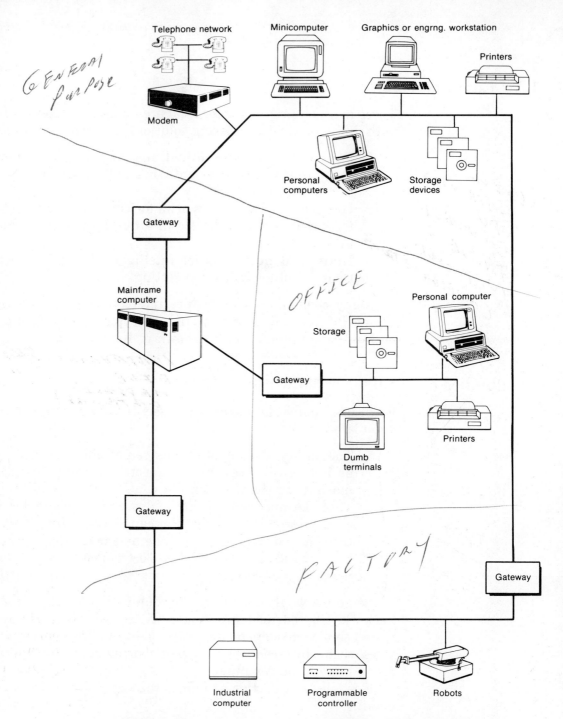

FIGURE 5–2: An example of interconnected LANs. The top portion of the figure represents devices linked by a general purpose LAN. The middle portion shows devices found in a departmental/small office LAN. At the bottom is an industrial LAN. All the LANs are connected through gateways to each other and to a mainframe.

electromechanical peripherals—high-quality printers, hard disks, or plotters—remains relatively high. Before distributed data processing, these devices were shared in data processing centers by being hard-wired directly to mainframe computers. In the era of distributed processing, LAN technology provides a way to share these expensive devices in offices and departments, allowing significant cost savings. With the more advanced network software now available, users should not have to remember a special command that tells their microcomputer how to access shared devices. *THIS IS CALLED? TRANSPARENCY*

File Sharing.   File sharing is a key productivity benefit of local area networks. According to Paul Strassman, former vice president of the Information Products Group at Xerox Corporation, "I doubt most of the claims about benefits obtained from the proliferation of personal computers without network connections and without access to shared resources."[2]

LANs that connect personal computers to mainframes even allow corporate wide data bases to become a shared resource. For example, in large companies, records of thousands of employees are usually stored on a centralized mainframe computer. A "general purpose" LAN might allow a manager easy access to data on employee salary or length of employment. (See also Chapter Eleven on microcomputer-to-mainframe links and Chapter Twelve on corporate videotex for more detail on linking desktops to centralized data bases.)

More specialized files would be shared by a group of users in a departmental "peer-to-peer" LAN environment or in the office of a small business.

Inventory management records are an example of specialized files that might be held on a departmental minicomputer. A departmental LAN would allow a manager in a sales department, for example, to have immediate access to shared files on the minicomputer to get up-to-the-minute inventory information based on changes entered by shipping and receiving employees.

A small Chicago law firm uses its LAN to facilitate editing, printing, and routing of legal files and documents within its office. Previously the firm disseminated information by carrying floppy disks from one person to another. Now all records are accessible from a shared hard disk.

There are innumerable cases where members of a project or team need to share work and information. The most efficient way by far to do so is through a LAN that links their word processors or personal computers.

Electronic Messaging. Electronic mail improves the efficiency of creating and distributing messages, memos, and reports. Electronic mail is covered in depth in Chapter Thirteen.

Gateways. Gateways do for LANs what LANs do for microcomputers. Gateway technology allows LANs to bridge to other LANs of the same or differing types and to mainframes or minicomputers, via local links (if in the local work environment) or through public data networks if the LANs are isolated from one another over long distances. Gateways are typically not included as a standard part of the LAN, but are usually an enhancement added by specialized vendors. *TEST*

The Workplace Impact of Local Area Networks

LANs allow vital information to be quickly accessible from network data bases. In addition, each device on a LAN may instantly communicate with any other device or any group of devices at virtually any time.

From the socio-technical point of view, these capabilities allow LANs to strengthen both the *individual* and *collective* business intelligence of LAN users.

Individual Impact

You can sit at the center & not be able to access files (print) to the last person who sat in the center

LANs vividly illustrate the general networking principle that each individual on an electronic network *sits at the center* of a vast pool of accessible information resources. LANs potentially make the information resources of all network users, of the company as a whole, and of public data bases transparently available to each individual user.

For example, imagine that a product manager needs to generate a forecast of next month's manufacturing volume. He presses a few keys on his desktop computer to retrieve an inventory list from the warehouse manager located at the other side of the building. Next he enters the sales forecast data base for the most recent forecast of next month's sales. Then, by accessing the inventory control group's data, he discovers the desirable inventory level for the next month. Now he merges this data on his screen to calculate his forecast. Finally, he sends the finished report electronically to a standardized distribution list. Through this use of the LAN, the product manager has been made the center of a paperless electronic information-delivery system.

Collective Impact

LANs also strengthen the collective mind of work groups. Each member of the group can work individually on different parts of a project, then store the work on a shared storage device. Access to current information on the project data base helps team members avoid repetition of data gathering and data entry.

The electronic messaging capability allows users to send memos or transfer files to a colleague with the same facility as they can access the shared data base. Or the group manager (or anyone else) can send the same message simultaneously to the entire group via the LAN's automatic distribution function; for example, the manager can type in a meeting time and automatically dispatch an electronic "broadcast" of that message to everyone on the network distribution list. (An example of the use of a departmental LAN among a group of writers at Regis McKenna, Inc., is given in Chapter Fifteen.)

Thus, a new group synergy is permitted when each project member sits at the center of an electronic network.

On the other hand, local networks have potential pitfalls if not planned and managed correctly. Chief among these is the inability to control information available through the network. Because data is accessible to multiple users, questions of data security and privacy need to be addressed through encryption software and special data management procedures.

LOCAL AREA NETWORKS:
THE TECHNOLOGY

Potential LAN users are frequently bewildered by a vast number of hardware and software choices. More than 150 offerings

Courtesy of 3-COM

FIGURE 5–3: Equipment offered in a local area network by 3-COM, a subsidiary of Convergent Inc. Storage devices, called servers, are in the foreground.

already are available and many additional ones are on the way. One such offering is shown in Figure 5–3.

To provide structure for understanding these wide-ranging options, we propose a taxonomy (classification scheme) of LANs. The taxonomy isolates the fundamental technical ingredients of LANs. These include topology, transmission techniques, transmission media, and access control techniques. Manufacturers of LANs mix and match among these design options to arrive at specific products to meet the varying needs of offices and factories.

Topology: The Overall Shape of the LAN

Topology refers to the overall geometric arrangement of the transmission media and devices comprising a LAN. Topology influences a LAN's performance, reliability, and control strategy.

Four basic topologies are in popular use: bus, tree, star, and ring. These shapes can be individually used for constructing LANs or as building blocks for more complex LANs.

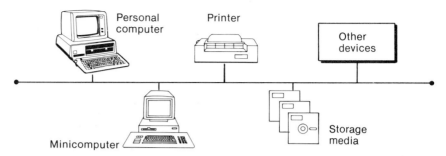

FIGURE 5–4: LAN based on a bus topology.

Bus Topology. In a *bus* topology, all attached computers and peripherals (stations) share a common transmission medium. The bus system does not require a central controller and can operate even if one or more of the attached stations malfunction. Bus systems allow the easy addition of computers and peripherals to the LAN and internetwork connections. (See Figure 5–4.)

EXPANDED BUS

Tree Topology. The *tree* topology builds on the bus by joining several of them together. The tree provides the wiring flexibility needed to carry LAN services to several floors of a building or to several buildings in a campus setting. (See Figure 5–5.)

Star Topology. In the *star* topology, each station is connected by a point-to-point link to a central switching station. Thus, communication between any two stations is via the switching station.

The centralized communication control strategy of star LANs requires an exceptionally reliable switching station. (See Figure 5–6.) Specific LANs based on the star topology are the newer voice/data private branch exchanges and the more popular data switches. *Specifics on the star topology LAN will be covered in Chapter Six.*

Ring Topology. A ring-shaped LAN consists of a set of repeaters joined by point-to-point links, usually in the shape of a circle. Stations are attached to the LAN at a repeater. The repeater is capable of receiving data on one link and retrans-

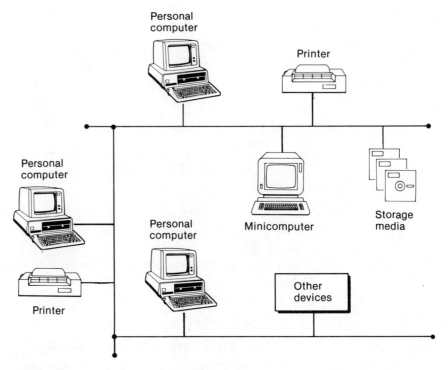

FIGURE 5–5: LAN based on a tree topology.

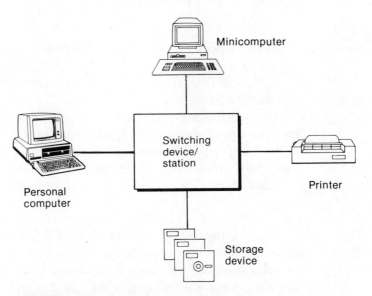

FIGURE 5–6: LAN based on a star topology.

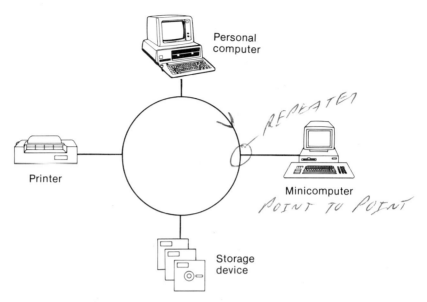

FIGURE 5–7: LAN based on a ring topology.

mitting it to the other link. Data circulates around the ring in one direction. (See Figure 5–7.)

Star-Shaped Ring Topology.   The *star-shaped ring* combines the features of the star and ring topologies. The gross topology is the star, with each branch consisting of two links, one for reception of data, the other for transmission. Each station communicates, through repeaters, with the next station via a "wire center." These wire centers contain bypass circuitry to allow LANs to operate, even with a station failure. (See Figure 5–8.)

Bridges and Gateways

Organizations considering a LAN purchase often look for a single topological layout that solves all existing LAN needs. In most such purchases a compromise approach is taken.

An organization may opt for unique LANs that satisfy each department's functional area's need. Others may seek to interconnect these disparate LANs to amass a corporatewide net-

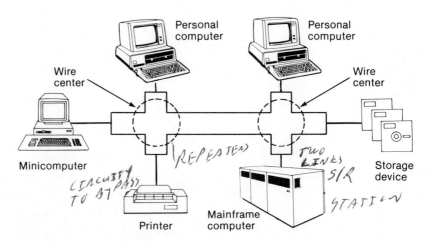

FIGURE 5–8: Star-shaped ring topology. Wire centers are physically located at the junction of several devices.

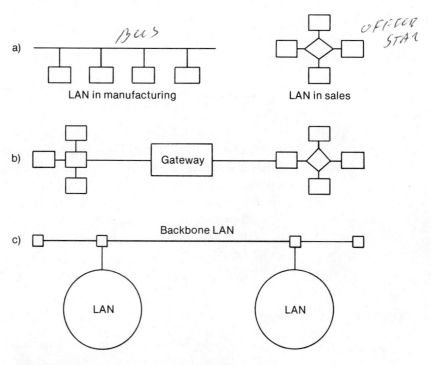

FIGURE 5–9: Choices for interconnecting LANs.
a) Unique LANs within an organization.
b) LANs connected through a gateway.
c) LANs connecting through a backbone LAN.

KA7

work; such interconnections can be done through bridges and gateways, which interconnect two LANs. Or a large backbone LAN could be purchased, enabling individual LANs to have access to each other through the backbone LAN. For an illustration of these three approaches, see Figure 5–9.

Open Architecture for Communications

During the early 1980s, versatile and inexpensive desktop microcomputers became firmly established. Unfortunately, many vendors contributed to the proliferation of dissimilar computing devices within organizations. Users of these devices were soon demanding a common software architecture to allow computer-to-computer communications among these incompatible devices.

One of these architectures used today was developed by the International Standards Organization (ISO), and is named the *Open Systems Interconnection* (OSI) model. OSI uses a concept of "layers" to aid in the design of software. OSI's layering partitions computer communications into seven hierarchical elements. Seven was chosen to make each layer a small enough element for a manageable software development task.

Each layer performs a subset of the total computer communications requirement. Its work relies on a summary of the next lower layers' performance of its functions, called services. OSI defines what each layer's functional responsibilities are. OSI has attempted to define each layer so changes in the implementation of a layer require no changes in any of the other six layers. This layer independence in implementations permits a modular approach in software development. Each layer and its services to the next higher layer can be written independently and then all the layers are consolidated to form a communications program.

Thus, ISO's OSI model specifies an open architecture for computer communications. The figure following shows the seven layers and summarizes their responsibilities.

OSI MODEL

Device #1 in LAN	Device #2 in LAN	Explanations on layers
Layer 7 "Application"	7 Application	Applications to be run on the LAN
Layer 6 "Presentation"	6 Presentation	Code and syntax translation
Layer 5 "Session"	5 Session	Controls dialogue
Layer 4 "Transport"	4 Transport	Reliable exchange
Layer 3 "Network"	3 Network	Intersystem (LAN) communication
Layer 2 "Data link"	2 Data link	Frame of data to be sent
Layer 1 "Physical"	1 Physical	Mechanical & electrical specs. for physical interfaces

Physical connection

OSI Model: Open Systems Interconnection model.

OSI Model—Details

The purpose of OSI is to solve the diversity of intercomputer communications problems. Two devices must implement identical communication functions, organized so that peer layers (i.e., layer 4 in device A and layer 4 in device B) provide the same communications functions.

Therefore, standards for defining protocols for each layer are needed. OSI provides the basis for formulating these standards. Physically, OSI transmits data by the process of *encapsulation*. The application layer (layer 7) takes the data,

TEST

performs its functions, and appends a header to the data. Then, layer 6 takes layer 7's message consisting of the header and data, processes it, adds its own header, and passes it down to layer 5. This process continues until layer 2's work is done, when the resulting frame is transmitted by layer 1 to the receiving device. The receiving device performs the reverse process, called *decapsulation*. The received frame is stripped of the header, beginning in layer 2, and continuing until only the data remains after layer 7 decapsulates the last of the header information.

We will discuss bridges, gateways, and related devices in this section. Interconnections through a backbone LAN will be covered when specific LAN products are described later in this chapter.

A *bridge* acts upon the data (frames) sent over the LAN, storing and forwarding them to their proper destination within the LAN. In terms of the OSI model, layers 1 and 2 connections are made. Bridges require the interconnected LANs to have identical layers 3 and 7 in the OSI model; in other words, similar software must be resident on stations attached to both LANs. Typically, bridges connect LANs of identical topologies and access methods, although these connected LANs may run at different transmission rates. (See Figure 5–10.)

By contrast, gateways can potentially connect any two LANs. In practice, gateways are designed to allow any two specific LANs to be interconnected. (See Figure 5–11.) Another function for a gateway is to connect a LAN to non-LAN resources, such as the telephone network or mainframe computers.

[handwritten margin note: BRIDGES & OSI →]

Controversies in Topology

LAN vendors opt for differing topologies according to varying strategies for controlling the network. The two main strategies are centralized control and distributed control.

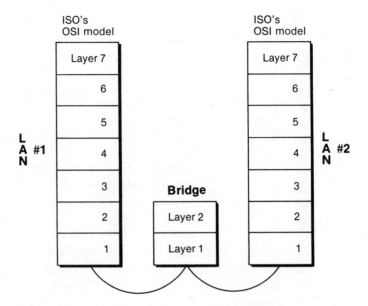

FIGURE 5–10: Bridges connect LANs through compatibility with layers 1 and 2 of the OSI model.

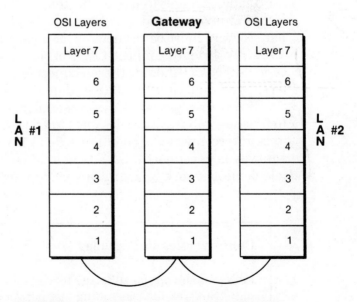

FIGURE 5–11: Gateways connect LANs through compatibility of all seven layers of the OSI model.

Centralized control topologies tend to centralize the management and maintenance of the LAN in one group, while distributed control requires individual departments to manage and maintain their own LAN.

Another controversy depends on the increased reliance placed on the switching station in a centrally controlled LAN. The switching station routes all data from one device in the LAN to another; however, if the switching station were to fail, the entire LAN becomes inoperative.

Some LAN vendors who offer LANs with distributed control have pointed to switching station reliance in attempts to discredit centrally controlled LANs. In reality, all product offerings are a mixture of the two control strategies; in which case, critical components such as the switching station are constructed with highly reliable components. In general, the chances of prolonged disability in any LAN is minimal. Therefore, the discrediting of centrally controlled LANs in the trade press should be overlooked. The important difference is in the network control strategies offered by the centralized and decentralized LAN, and the impact control strategies have on the management and maintenance of the LAN. That is where the choices should be made.

Transmission Techniques in LANs

Two general transmission techniques are used in LANs: baseband and broadband. These techniques partially determine the type of transmission possible in a LAN.

Baseband. Generally, baseband refers to the transmission of an analog or digital signal in its original, unmodulated form.

In the LAN world, *baseband* is defined as a transmission technique using digital signaling.

Broadband. Like baseband, broadband has a more restrictive meaning in LANs than in general communications parlance.

In LANs, *broadband* refers to the use of analog transmission, with one of many frequency division multiplexing techniques. Because devices connected to a broadband LAN transmit digitally, the use of special modems known as *radio frequency (RF) modems,* is required.

The Baseband-Broadband Controversy

The controversy over which LAN transmission technique is optimal continues to be a popular topic in conferences and the trade press. Baseband partisans argue that lower cost, simplicity in implementation, higher transmission speeds, and lower maintenance requirements make it the clear winner. Broadband advocates point to its support of more users in a LAN over longer distances, plus its capability to support audio, video, and data transmission.

In fact, the two transmission techniques are suited for different applications. Baseband satisfies the need to interconnect devices within an office or department. Users can most benefit from the higher transmission speeds offered by baseband LANs; their lack of video or audio capability is not important because of the close proximity of the users.

Broadband is better adapted for communication between larger complexes of offices and buildings. A broadband LAN can accommodate more users, though there is a trade-off of slower data transmission rates. The broadband LAN also can carry video and audio signals between disparate locations for teleconferencing, perform security monitoring, and other similar applications.

Transmission Media Used in LANs

The transmission medium provides the physical connection between equipment in a LAN. The choice of medium influences the transmission capacity, reliability, ease of installation, and maintenance of the LAN. Although several types of media exist, LANs typically use either coaxial cable or twisted-pairs and, to a lesser extent, fiber optics.

Coaxial Cable. Coaxial cable has been the most popular medium for LANs. Coax provides very high bandwidth and has good resistance to noise. However, it is expensive and difficult to install because of its stiffness. Not requiring any surrounding conduit, it is best suited for installation in false flooring or ceilings. Because of its historically popular use in the cable television industry, coax is readily available and technologically proven.

Two types of coax are generally used:

- 50-ohm cable, about three-eighths inch in diameter.
- 75-ohm cable, about one-half inch in diameter.

Baseband LANs use 50-ohm cable with data rates typically below 10 to 15 megabits per second. Broadband LANs normally employ 75-ohm cable, which is also used in cable television systems. The 75-ohm cable provides hundreds of low-speed data channels, and several voice, video, and high-speed data channels within the 300 to 400 mHz current capacity of the medium.

Twisted-Pairs. Although ubiquitous in telephone communications, twisted-pairs are only now becoming important in LANs. Twisted-pair wire is easy to install and move around. The potential for environmental noise interference usually requires the use of a conduit to protect the wire, making the sum of installation costs and material costs approach that of coax.

Twisted-pairs have severe distance limitations as transmitted signals attenuate quickly. Their theoretical data rate potential is roughly below 10^9 meter-bits per second, so a 1 kilometer length LAN transmits at 1 megabit per second, or a one-fourth kilometer length LAN transmits at 4 megabits per second. But these transmission speeds are seldom achieved in real-world environments.

Fiber Optics. As in other communications, fiber optic media are making an entry into LANs. They are immune to noise interference, have significantly higher potential bandwidth, and are secure from intruders tapping into LANs. However, the technology is still evolving and the cost of fiber-based LANs remains high at the time of writing.

Today's early users of fiber optics in LANs typically turn to it because of noisy environments, security-consciousness, and very high-speed data requirements between two devices, such as mainframes.

10 MB
VBS
1 MB
WHEN CONNECTED
& MULTIPLE USERS
REDUCES THE
DIFFERENCE TO
2 TO 3

The Battle over Data Rates

Twisted-pair wires, coaxial cables, and fiber optics have unique strengths and weaknesses for transmission within LANs. We have described some of their varying qualities. Unfortunately, the LAN community unnecessarily emphasizes only one of these qualities, transmission speed capabilities, in evaluating various media for LANs. For example, Ethernet is listed as a 10 megabits per second LAN with the use of coax. Another popular variety, Starlan, features a transmission speed of 1 megabit per second over twisted-pair wire. Does this mean that Ethernet runs 10 times faster than the 1 megabit per second Starlan? Not at all. Transmission speeds are the maximum throughput rate of a LAN. The *effective* throughput rate is controlled by several factors, such as the software resident in the equipment and hardware attachments.

LAN software packages differ considerably in program execution speeds. In addition, most hardware attached to LANs is unable to handle the maximum data rate. The mechanical characteristics of most printers and storage devices limits effective throughput; personal computers also have internal speed restrictions that prevent them from taking full advantage of the LAN's transmission speeds (See Figure 5–12).

The basic premise for offering LANs at megabit rates is to make the time required for any station to send a message as short as possible. This allows many stations to share the channel. However, empirical studies have shown yet another limitation to LAN data rates: the speed of a LAN usually degrades after a certain number of users are on it. For example, the 10-fold difference we discussed is normally reduced to 2- or 3-fold in practice.

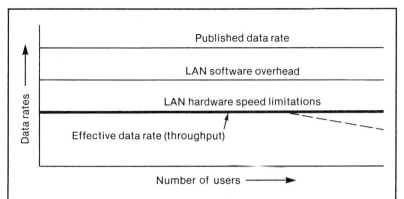

FIGURE 5–12: Effective data rate of LANs versus published data rates.

Only benchmark tests of applications programs running on LANs under varying numbers of users can provide a realistic measure of effective throughput. Relying solely on the published data rate of a LAN is misleading.

Controlling Access to the LAN

LANs connect intelligent devices, allowing them to share the network's transmission capacity. Because each attached device operates independently, each will need access to the network at unpredictable times. Therefore, some means of controlling access to the medium by multiple devices is needed.

The most commonly used access control techniques are the following:

- CSMA/CD—Carrier-Sense Multiple Access/Collision Detection.
- Token passing ring.
- Token passing bus.

CSMA/CD. According to this technique, any station (call it A) on the bus wishing to transmit must "listen" to the transmission medium to see if any other station is transmitting. If another station is, A must "defer," or wait, until the sending station is done before transmitting its message. If no other station is transmitting, A can immediately send its message.

If two or more stations need access to the LAN and are separated by significant distances on the bus, one can foresee that simultaneous transmission may occur. The reason for this is that the carrier sense feature of CSMA/CD does not detect another station transmitting until the other's signal is received, and this signal does take time to reach the other devices if it has a distance to travel. During that small time segment, multiple devices could be transmitting signals. When this happens, a "collision" occurs. CSMA/CD contains algorithms for detecting and handling the results of such collisions. It is able to direct each station to cease transmission and wait a random length of time before attempting retransmission.

This collision-handling technique was developed to regulate the kind of bursty traffic typically produced in computer-aided-engineering workstations, computer-aided-design workstations, or personal computers requiring bursty communications.

CSMA/CD's main advantage lies in the simplicity of its access control technique. Its main disadvantage is the increased probability of collisions under heavy communication environments. This access-control method is best suited for bus and tree topologies.

Token Passing Ring. Although different methods exist for controlling access to the LAN in a ring topology, the token passing ring is the predominant method. This technique involves the use of a token (a special bit pattern) that circulates around the ring. A device wishing to transmit must wait until it detects a token passing by. The device appends its data to the token and lets the other stations know that the token contains data by changing one of the bits in the special bit pattern characteristic of the token.

The token passing ring method allows a station exclusive use of the network during the time of transmission. This monopoly of the network is given up once the appended message circulates all around the ring and returns to its sender. As the token circulates the ring, each station on the ring receives the message and decides whether the message is intended for it. Figure 5–13 illustrates the token passing ring concept.

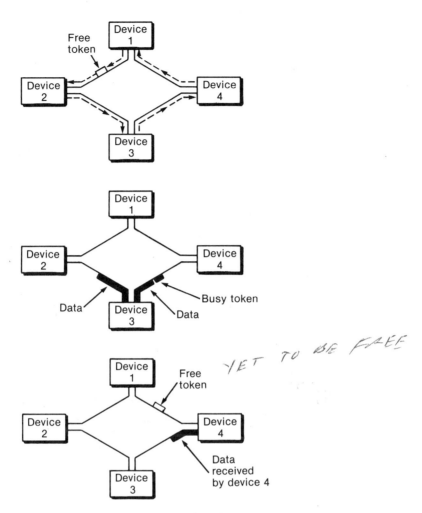

FIGURE 5–13: The token passing ring concept.

a. Device 2 awaits a free token.
b. Once a token is found, device 2 appends data; the data is destined for device 4.
c. After device 4 receives the data, the token returns to device 2, which changes it back to a free token.

Token Passing Bus. In a token bus network, devices on a bus or tree topology LAN are each assigned numbers in an ordered sequence. Each device knows the "identity" of the ones preceding and following it. The last device in the ordered sequence is assigned to precede the first one, forming a logical ring. The physical ordering of the stations on the bus is independent of the logically ordered sequence.

As in the above method, a token regulates the right of access to the bus. Whichever station receives the token controls the medium for a specified time. This station may transmit one or more strings of data or request other stations to send information, such as an acknowledgment of a received message or status. When time expires or the station is done, the token passes to the next device in the sequence.

The token bus control scheme is common in factory settings for interconnecting programmable controllers, industrial microcomputers and minicomputers, and robots.

The Deterministic-Probabilistic Controversy

Each of the access control schemes discussed above is in use today. The advantages and disadvantages of each have led to what is called the "deterministic-probabilistic" controversy.

Token passing rings and token passing buses offer "deterministic" access to a LAN, since every station is able to monopolize the medium during its transmission period. In contrast, CSMA/CD allows only "probabilistic" access since any transmission can potentially produce a collision.

This weakness of probabilistic access gives token passing rings and token passing buses (both deterministic access schemes) a marked advantage for real-time process control applications, such as in an automated factory. However, theoretical papers and other documents continue to show the likelihood and unlikelihood of the probabilistic behavior in CSMA/CD, especially when a significant number of users share the LAN. These papers also show the real-world possibility of transmission errors in a deterministic LAN because of a lost token, making these control schemes probabilistic.

Today, the deterministic-probabilistic choice for a LAN should be regarded as inconsequential; both deterministic and probabilistic LANs have found secure market niches. Factory networks are primarily based on deterministic implementations, whereas office networks are primarily based on probabilistic schemes. Backbone networks normally employ deterministic schemes.

New vendors may seek to revive the controversy if they have probabilistic-based products for deterministic environments.

The Taxonomy Tree

To recap the previous discussion, the fundamental technical ingredients of LANs are: topology, transmission techniques, transmission media, and access control techniques. Manufacturers mix and match these ingredients to arrive at LAN offerings. To further structure these choices, we offer a taxonomy tree, as shown in Figure 5–14. This taxonomy depicts four categories from which a LAN designer can choose a number of options to construct a LAN. Because of technical limitations, prohibitively high costs, and dependencies between the different sections of this taxonomy tree, actual implementations can be simplified as shown in Figure 5–15. The taxonomy shows the spectrum of choices within the LAN industry. Let's now examine these choices critically and consider how standardization efforts and other factors will help potential LAN buyers narrow their options.

DEMYSTIFYING THE MARKET

The LAN market is highly competitive and more than a bit confusing. Many vendors are making spirited claims about their LAN capabilities. Some promise compatibility with prevalent standards, while still others offer connection costs of less than $100. At the same time, traditional LAN offerings like Arcnet

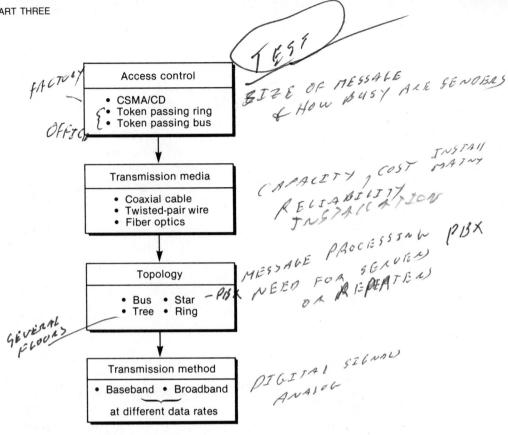

Handwritten annotations:

FACTORY

OFFICE

TEST

SIZE OF MESSAGE & HOW BUSY ARE SENDERS

CAPACITY, COST INSTALL MANY RELIABILITY INSTALLATION

MESSAGE PROCESSING PBX NEED FOR SERVER OR REPEATERS

SEVERAL FLOORS

DIGITAL SIGNAL ANALOG

FIGURE 5–14: General LAN taxonomy.

and Omninet are slowly diminishing in the marketplace. All of this makes for a confusing maze of information to wander through.

Our taxonomy tree should help simplify the jargon and the myriad technical claims in the market. We now offer a guide to understanding the utility and survivability of LAN products. This guide has four aspects:

- Standards
- Major company backing
- Cost considerations
- Applications software

These four factors should be evaluated before users seriously consider buying a LAN offering. First, compliance with

ANALYSES *TEST*

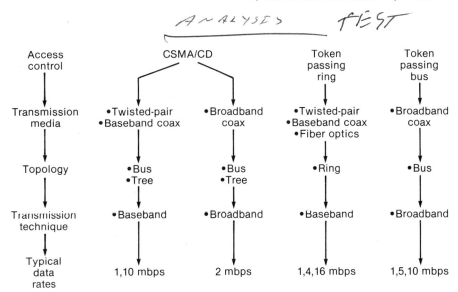

Access control	CSMA/CD		Token passing ring	Token passing bus
Transmission media	•Twisted-pair •Baseband coax	•Broadband coax	•Twisted-pair •Baseband coax •Fiber optics	•Broadband coax
Topology	•Bus •Tree	•Bus •Tree	•Ring	•Bus
Transmission technique	•Baseband	•Broadband	•Baseband	•Broadband
Typical data rates	1,10 mbps	2 mbps	1,4,16 mbps	1,5,10 mbps

*mbps = Million bits per second

FIGURE 5–15: Detailed LAN taxonomy tree.

important standardization efforts must exist. Second, major computer companies and other companies must back the LAN. Third, a cost decrease path for the future must be evident. And finally, applications software enabling the practical use of a LAN must exist.

This chapter concludes with an examination of LANs, *all* of which have a promising future based on these criteria.

GUIDE 1

Explaining Standards

CONCEPT

The very notion of LANs is their ability to interconnect computing devices and share peripheral devices within local work environments. Historically, these devices and peripherals have been supplied by a multitude of vendors, without specific products to allow easy interconnection. With the perceived need for LANs, dozens of manufacturers rushed to the market with proprietary and incompatible local area networks. Standardization *ONE REASON* efforts began in order to assure that potential purchasers would not be locked into a single LAN vendor and only their proprietary software offerings.

As stated earlier, initial standardization efforts were made

SECOND
–PREDICT DESIGN
& ENSURE COMPLIANCE

by the Digital Equipment Corporation-Intel-Xerox triumvirate with the rallying call for Ethernet, a 10 megabits per second, baseband, CSMA/CD, bus topology LAN. But skepticism arose when Ethernet's installation base did not meet expectations. Further skepticism arose when the International Standards Organization (ISO) issued the Open Systems Interconnection (OSI) scheme at the end of 1980.

Because of Ethernet's failure to immediately become a formal standard, a committee of the Institute of Electrical and Electronic Engineers (IEEE), called Project 802, was formed to devise interconnection standards for the bottom two layers of the ISO hierarchy, the physical and link control layers. With support from the European Computer Manufacturers' Association (ECMA) and several computer vendors, Project 802, with a subcommittee called 802.3, announced an Ethernet-like set of specifications as a standard.

Despite these efforts, Project 802 was bombarded with alternative standard proposals from vendors promoting their own implementations and by users finding Ethernet to be unsuitable in certain environments. Some newer standardization bodies also began soliciting proposals for some of the higher layers in the OSI model. In theory, layers 3 through 7 of the ISO model, once implemented with a LAN product, can be placed upon any of the lower two layer implementations. This would guarantee true portability of software being placed in LANs.

What has followed is a deluge of proposals, primarily to Project 802, for standards comprising different access control methods, transmission media, topology, transmission techniques, and speeds.

IEEE 802 LAN Standard Proposals. The emerging IEEE 802 standards are in fact a family of standards. These standards have four primary elements and two overseeing elements (See Figure 5–16).

The standards as illustrated form a tree-like expansion of options from top to bottom. The four primary elements are shown beside the medium access control layer. The overseeing elements are established by Project 802.1, which describes the relationships between the family of standards in Project 802 and the ISO model. Project 802.2 is the second overseeing element

ETHERNET

FACTORY

IBM

OSI Layer	IEEE 802 Sublayer	Elements					
2 (Data link)	Logical link control	*ALL* IEEE 802.2					
	Medium access control	802.3 CSMA/CD			802.4 Token bus	802.5 Token ring	802.6 Metro-politan
1 (Physical)	Physical signaling	1,10 mbps Tree	2,10 mbps Tree	10 mbps Tree	1,5,10 mbps Bus	1,5,10 mbps Tree	1,4 mbps Ring · 4,16,40 mbps Ring	?
—	Transmission medium	Baseband coax	Broadband coax	Fiber optics	Broadband coax (1 channel used)	Broadband coax	Baseband Twisted-pair · Baseband coax & fiber optics	?

FIGURE 5–16: IEEE 802 LAN standards work.

DIFFUSE & SIMPLIFY + CREATE COMPLEXITY

DEPARTMENTAL

(shown in the logical link control section above), which describes the exchange of data between access points in the LAN.

Revisiting the chart on Projects 802.3 to 802.6 with a specific example, we see 802.3 CSMA/CD as a medium access control standard. It has three different signaling options and transmission media specified. One of the 802.3 standards would be a LAN based on CSMA/CD access using baseband coax in a tree topology having either a 1 or 10 megabits per second transmission rate.

The Standards Confusion. Why have so many LAN standards been proposed with yet more on the way? The answer often given is that no one standard fits all the applications of local area networks and no single transmission medium is the most suitable one for all applications. For example, standard 802.3 is suitable for a departmental LAN in an office environment, where the probabilistic nature of CSMA/CD has less impact, while 802.4 is reportedly the most appropriate for factory

TEST

process control and factory automation. Standard 802.5 is proposed as the best single highway for interconnecting the variety of computers made by IBM, and 802.6 has been proposed specifically for citywide networks.

Readers may still ask, "When will there be a universal LAN standard?" In the sense of a single, generally accepted standard, the answer is never. Instead, as in other markets, a small number of LAN leaders will emerge. These will, by the sheer size of their installed base, become tomorrow's true de facto standards. Further, these winners will comply with a subset of the various standards we have discussed. Major computer vendors and user backing will be one of the other ingredients needed to create these winners.

Major Company Backing

The IEEE 802 project has maintained an open-door policy regarding proposals for standards. LAN vendors have seized this chance to make proposals to the 802 committee hoping that standards certification would help in increasing the popularity of their LAN. Even with the intense scrutiny placed on 802 by the computer industry, the standard makers have buckled under to the demand for more and more standards as evidenced by the large number of current efforts.

Of course, not all the current proposals will be winners in the market, even with IEEE standards acceptance as a backing. To be legitimate in the marketplace, LAN vendors will also need major companies' support. This backing will make the offering more attractive to new users and will also encourage semiconductor manufacturers to produce more LAN chips (VLSI) thereby driving down the cost of interconnection. LAN software vendors will also be encouraged to support the product.

Ethernet is the prime example of the impact of major company backing in the success of a LAN. More than 50 major computer vendors and users have publicly stated their support for Ethernet. It thus comes as no small surprise that IEEE 802.3's standard at 10 megabits per second, using baseband coax, is similar to Ethernet. The 1 megabits per second version of Ethernet is backed by AT&T, Intel, and several other vendors. The 2 megabits per second broadband coax version is backed by

Sytek, General Instruments, Intel, IBM, and others. The 5 megabits per second version of IEEE 802.4 using broadband coax is supported by General Motors, Motorola, Japan's Fanuc, and other major factory automation vendors. Finally, IEEE 802.5's 4 megabits per second token ring based on twisted-pair wire is strongly supported by IBM.

GUIDE # 3

Cost Considerations

The popularity of LANs has been restrained by long-standing complaints about costs. Many prospective buyers have found the high cost of cable, connectors, installation, and interface boards hard to justify. LAN vendors recognize that costs cannot be reduced drastically in the short term. However, a cost decrease path can be analytically derived and presented by vendors to prospective buyers so that the costs of future expansion can be determined.

As a rule, VLSI follows a steep price decrease with increases in production volume. When it can be shown that VLSI vendors for a LAN are increasing volume, this should assure LAN vendors and users a proven cost decrease path.

CHIP PRODUCTION

LAN vendors have also been working with connector manufacturers and media suppliers to arrive at a more cost-effective product. Installation cost reductions are also a consideration. For example, AT&T's IEEE 802.3 implementation at 1 megabit per second (Starlan) utilizes existing twisted-pair wiring, installed as spares in a company's telephone system, reducing installation costs dramatically.

What is important is not the specific approach taken by the LAN vendor to reduce interconnection costs, but that a specific cost decrease path exists. An important subset of LANs has a planned cost decrease path.

GUIDE # 4

Applications Software

The OSI model calls for the eventual standardization of a seven-layer communications structure. IEEE's Project 802 addresses the first two layers only. For the most effective use of LANs, however, all seven layers must be specified and products implemented.

For the time being, only proprietary software is available for the non-IEEE 802 layers. Standards bodies, such as the National Bureau of Standards, and government agencies, such as the Department of Defense, have proposed solutions for the transport layer. Software vendors, however, face a formidable task in developing software according to the OSI model. Therefore, each of them has sought major hardware vendors to adopt their proprietary seven-layer solution, hoping it bypasses ISO efforts and becomes a de facto standard.

Major hardware vendors have welcomed their software allies. Applications commonplace now, such as spreadsheet, file access, and data base management programs, have been modified for LANs to allow multiple access. Standardization efforts for the OSI's session and presentation layers continue in parallel. Even an electronic mail application is nearing an application layer standard.

All indications are that soon, ISO's efforts, although meritorious, will lag behind proprietary implementations for all seven layers by software vendors that are backed by their hardware counterparts. This is because of the critical need for software solutions that make LANs useful in everyday business. An example of a defacto standardization effort for software is NET-BIOS (or network basic input/output system), which has been an architectural foundation for constructing complementary seven-layer solutions by IBM and others.

A Model to Clear up LAN Confusion

As we have said, standards, major company backing, cost decrease path, and applications software are necessary ingredients for evaluating the current and future viability of a LAN. The model in Figure 5–17 depicts these four factors necessary for a successful LAN.

Some of the more promising LANs are listed and described below. They will continue to be successful as long as all four ingredients are present. Other LANs that arrive at these four ingredients will add to this list. Those currently meeting our four criteria conform to the following specifications:

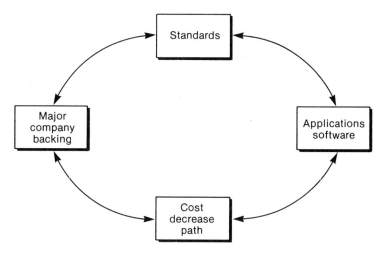

FIGURE 5–17: Four interdependent factors needed for a successful LAN.

- IEEE 802.3 Ethernet.
- IEEE 802.3 2 Mbps broadband.
- IEEE 802.3 1 Mbps baseband.
- IEEE 802.4 5 Mbps broadband (10 Mbps possible also).
- IEEE 802.5 4 Mbps baseband.

The next section will describe sample products based on some of these specifications.

PRODUCT OFFERINGS

IBM's PC Network

This LAN links personal computers in a small office environment. It transmits data at 2 megabits per second, and uses the CSMA/CD access control technique over standard 75-ohm CATV cable with broadband transmission techniques.

All the necessary ingredients—standards (802.3), major company backing, cost decrease path, and applications software—are in place. PC Network is optimized for users needing data transmission now, with capabilities for voice and video transmission in the future.

The IBM offering is a hardware/software package that connects up to 72 personal computers (primarily IBMs) in a bus topology via broadband coax within a 1,000-foot radius. Expansion units allow up to 1,000 PCs to be interconnected.

At the network's hub is a translator unit that converts the signals sent from PCs on the receive frequency and resends it on the transmit frequency. The unit comes with a connector assembly for attaching as many as eight PCs within 200 feet, sometimes more. It also has an expansion port for attaching a network base expander. The expander along with the network cabling components allows as many as 72 PCs to be linked.

Within each PC, a network adapter add-on card contains the circuitry and radio frequency modem for allowing interconnection to the LAN. The physical connection is made through 75-ohm cables.

The network adapter also contains NETBIOS support. To fulfill the remaining layers of the OSI model, additional diskettes are required that contain a multiuser operating system and network application programs. These application programs enable electronic mail and file or printer sharing.

Hardware and software is now being developed for video and voice transmission on the PC network. With the 75-ohm cable's capacity of 50 television-like channels, the two channels used by the PC network leave substantial flexibility for the future.

Ethernet

The term *Ethernet* has become almost synonymous with local area networks. Among the first commercial LAN offerings, Ethernet remains one of the more preferred designs in use. Designed for high-capacity, "bursty" traffic networks, it links computer-aided-engineering, computer-aided-design, and other engineering and graphics workstations and minicomputers. Some personal computer LANs continue to use Ethernet, but their migration to lower-cost, lower-performance networks is under way.

Ethernet's specifications are identical to the 10 megabits per second IEEE 802.3 standard. A separate standardization effort within IEEE 802.3 for 10 megabits "Cheapernet" using cheaper coaxial cable and less expensive interfaces has been proposed. These less expensive interfaces and cabling will satisfy more cost-sensitive users that would like to retain Ethernet's features, with a reduced number of users linked to the LAN. Software support for Ethernet is extensive, with several vendors offering full application-layer support.

AT&T's Starlan

AT&T has proposed a 1 megabit per second CSMA/CD baseband LAN, called Starlan, to the 802.3 committee as a standard for personal computer interconnection within a building. Some office buildings have telephones wired with cables containing 25 pairs of twisted-pair wires. Only a few of these are used for voice communications. Starlan uses two pairs of these preinstalled wires as the initial transmission media for the LAN. The building's telephone-wire closets, where all the wires come together, house the LAN wire and bus.

Factory LANs

Using local area networks within a factory environment is a recent phenomenon. The predominant LAN proposal for factories is the manufacturing automation protocol (MAP) hardware and software specification. MAP employs broadband CATV cable and uses the token passing bus topology compliant with the IEEE 802.4 standard. Applications of MAP are now in place for networking factory information sources. Process control systems, quality assurance systems, and material handling applications are some of the uses now.

MAP's lowest two layers, the physical and data link layers, are compatible with IEEE 802.4 broadband standards at 5 megabits. Because of current debates, 1 megabit and 10 megabit rates are also in the running. This implementation is being spearheaded by General Motors and supported by more than 20 major manufacturing and computer companies.

IBM's Token Passing Ring

The IBM token ring conforms to IEEE 802.5 standards for a token passing ring network using baseband transmission. The devices transmit within the LAN at 4 megabits per second. The

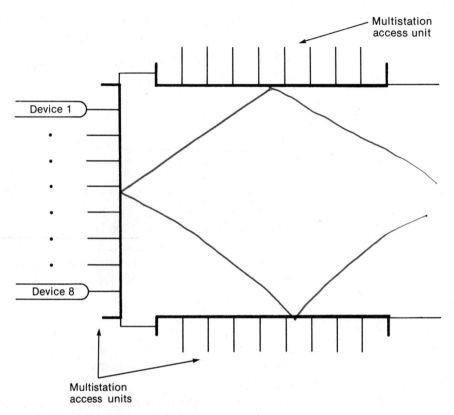

Multistation
access unit

Device 1

Device 8

Multistation
access units

FIGURE 5–18: Multistation access units connect to eight devices. These access units can be connected to form a star-shaped ring.

transmission media can be either twisted-pair wire or shielded twisted-pair wire (a higher quality variant). The number of devices interconnected can be up to 75 with twisted-pair or 260 with shielded twisted-pair wire.

Devices supported are the IBM PC family and other computers in the IBM product line. A token ring adapter card located in the device connects to the transmission medium. At the most, eight of these connected devices are then attached to a multistation access unit. Then the multistation access units are interconnected in the shape of a star-wired ring. See Figure 5–18 for an illustration.

Software needed to run the LAN can be based on the same NETBIOS core as IBM's PC LAN.

CHOOSING A LOCAL AREA NETWORK

Unwary purchasers can easily end up with a LAN that does not fulfill their needs and expectations. The previous section describing popular product offerings limits the set of choices to relatively riskless categories. The section on LAN classification highlights the important terminology and concepts that a potential LAN user must understand.

Even with this preparation, specifications of a company's real requirements from a LAN are necessary to choose an appropriate one. These requirements must be determined by surveying end users, department managers, and members of senior management. The following list of questions may be helpful in this effort.

Common LAN Requirements

FORMULATE REQ.

Bus. function

1. What kinds of applications (i.e., electronic mail, file sharing, and so on) will be needed?

topology   *CAPACITY*

2. What types of transmission and what level of effective throughput are required now and in the future?

GATES   *CUSTOMERS*
BRIDGES

3. How many sites must the LAN support? Over what distances must devices be interconnected in the LAN?

MEDIA

TYPE OR COM.

4. Are there any special data requirements, such as bursty traffic or the need for deterministic transmission times?

ACCESS
CSI

TECHNOLOGY

5. What are the number and types of computing devices, printers, storage devices, modems, and interconnection schemes (gateways) existing or needed now? In the future?

DESIGN

6. What types of network administration, control, and security do the users and managers need?

1)

7. What is the cost per connection, or total cost, that the LAN can be?

The successful outcome of the LAN choice depends most on managerial competence. It is not an application of a standard formula. But the above framework may help structure management's understanding of its LAN needs. As a final note, the following vendor qualities are needed to evaluate the vendors' capabilities for fulfilling the LAN's expectations:

- Quality of user training and documentation.

- Quality of software, hardware, and maintenance support.
- Verification of performance claim/track record.

QUESTIONS FOR REVIEW:

1. Define Local Area Networks.
2. Define the four main benefits for LANs.
3. Describe the workplace impact of a LAN.
4. Contrast bus, tree, star, and ring topologies.
5. What are the pros and cons of the star-shaped ring topology?
6. What are the roles of bridges and gateways?
7. What is the controversy in topology?
8. Contrast baseband and broadband transmission.
9. Describe the CSMA/CD, token passing ring, and token passing bus algorithms.
10. What is the deterministic-probabilistic controversy?
11. Sketch and describe the taxonomy tree.
12. Why must the LAN market be demystified?
13. Explain the IEEE standard proposals.
14. Why is there a standards confusion?
15. Describe the model that clears up the LAN market confusion.
16. Describe the components of two of the many product offerings.
17. How would *you* choose a LAN?

FOR DISCUSSION:

1. What are the negative impacts of a LAN?
2. How would you resolve the battle in data rates?
3. Come up with your own model to show what the *unsuccessful* LANs must have.
4. What are some of the problems in managing a LAN?
5. How would you introduce the concept and benefits of a LAN to senior managers?

NOTES FOR CHAPTER FIVE

1. The quest to improve computer productivity has driven the evolution of communication networks over the past 30 years. Geographically dispersed large computers were first networked in the 1950s. In 1964, the first commercial computer network was established for handling airline passenger information and reservations. Another milestone was the construction in 1968 of a nationwide network for air-route traffic control. Arpanet was developed in the early 1970s to connect computers in universities and research institutions. Telenet and Tymnet introduced the concept of time-shared systems in the mid-1970s. With the advent of personal computers, LANs became a need and reality for the same reasons.

2. Paul Strassmann, *Information Payoff* (Free Press: New York, 1985), p. 43.

REFERENCES

CABELL, DALE, and CABELL, DOUG. "Bridges and Gateways" *Micro Communications,* July–August, 1985.

CHORAFAS, DIMITRIS N. *Designing and Implementing Local Area Networks.* New York: McGraw-Hill, 1984.

FLINT, DAVID C. *The Data Ring Main: An Introduction to Local Area Networks.* New York: John Wiley & Sons, 1983.

GUTTMAN, MICHAEL K. "Strategies For Sharing Resources." *PC Magazine,* February, 1985.

HALL, MARK. "Factory Networks." *Micro Communications,* February, 1985.

McNAMARA, JOHN E. *Local Area Networks: An Introduction to the Technology.* Maynard, Mass: Digital Press, 1985.

RUSSEL, WAYNE. "A High-Level Approach to Local-Area Nets." *Computer World,* February 6, 1985.

STALLINGS, WILLIAM. *Local Networks: An Introduction.* New York: MacMillan, 1984.

Private Branch Exchanges

OBJECTIVES _____

● Describe the need for PBXs.
● Describe some basic PBX features, network features, management control features, and applications.
● Differentiate Centrex and PBX.
● Describe the technology and benefits of integrating voice and data in a PBX.
● Differentiate the roles of LANs and PBXs.

INTELLIGENT ADVANCEMENT BASE [TWISTED WIRE
USING THE INSTETATIAL EXISTSAL SWITCH
WITH EXPANDED FEATURES
FOR MNG., CONTROL, TRANSPARANCY
INTELLIGENT SWITCH
UNIVERSAL INTERFACE

In the competitive battle to add features that improve telephone communication, today's PBX vendors have turned away from analog, electromechanical devices toward digital technology, making PBXs a key element in emerging telematic networks. A side benefit of that shift from analog to digital is the PBX's ability to deliver data as well as voice over the telephone wiring already installed on a corporation's premises. This ability to distribute data instantly to information workers' desktops will become more important as the efficient handling of ever-increasing amounts of data becomes more and more crucial to an organization's success.

ADVANCES IN VOICE PROCESSING

PBXs offer numerous features that can improve the efficiency of an organization's voice communications. For the end user, the company's PBX simplifies placing or receiving a telephone call through such features as four-digit dialing of a co-worker's extension, speed dialing of frequently used numbers, and call forwarding. For management, the PBX offers greater control over a company's telephone costs via reporting capabilities that can reveal communication trends and identify possible abuses of telephone privileges. To further control costs, a PBX can automatically route calls to the least expensive long-distance carrier.

In addition, the PBXs reduce the waste of telephone tag. An optional voice store and forward system added to a PBX, for example, can eliminate the two out of three business calls that fail to reach the intended recipient on the first try.

For data communications, a PBX-based network can serve

as an intraorganization network and a gateway to the outside world. In general, a PBX can be thought of as a large-scale, complex modem linking a corporation's data network to the analog telephone network. With tomorrow's completely digital telephone network—or with some of the bypass technologies described in Part Four—the PBX becomes a gateway for high-speed digital links between any two points.

Finally, the digital PBX can deliver something new: the synergy of voice communication closely coupled with data. Some observers foresee large productivity gains resulting from the integrated voice and data workstations just beginning to appear on corporate desktops.

THE PBX: AN EVOLVING TECHNOLOGY

The PBX is essentially a switch, much like the switches at a telephone company's central office. Instead of providing connections among a telephone company's subscribers, a PBX can link telephones and data devices on a company's premises to each other and to the public telephone network.

The PBX increases efficiency by reducing the number of local telephone company lines (trunks) needed by a company. Before the advent of the PBX, separate wires connected each telephone installed on a business's premises to the central office. Most of the time the trunks were idle: Only one-sixth of a typical business's telephones are in use during the busiest hour of the day, and most of these phones are in use for intraoffice calls. By installing a switch on a company's premises that shares lines to the central office at a ratio of about 1:6, the corporation is able to eliminate five of the six lines it had formerly paid for. (See Figure 6–1.)

The PBX also eliminates the requirement for several operators dedicated to answering a company's main number and routing calls to desired extensions. With special trunks, called direct inward dialing trunks (DID), any telephone user can access a specific person hooked to a PBX without operator intervention.

Thus, the businesses that install a PBX benefit by paying for fewer trunks and by gaining greater control over their communications system.

The first PBXs were electromechanical devices. There were

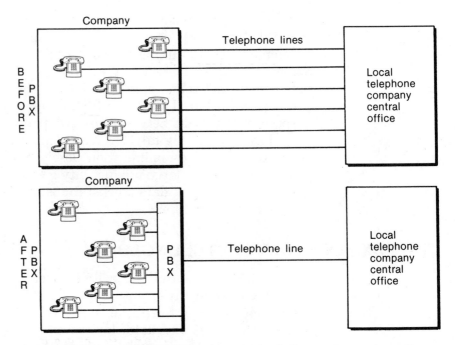

FIGURE 6–1: Installing a PBX on an organization's premises reduces the number of lines needed from the telephone company.

several reasons for the evolution to purely electronic switching. For one, although electromechanical switches are reliable, they are bulky and require expensive maintenance. In addition, electronic switches based on VLSI technology are small and require less maintenance—parts (or boards full of parts) are simply replaced as they fail. Perhaps most important, computer control and management of an electronic network proved far more flexible and cost-effective than control by the analog components used in an electromechanical system.

Competition Engenders Innovation

It was only after the 1968 Carterfone decision, which allowed other companies to sell equipment that attached to the public telephone network, that innovation began to make the PBX a more ubiquitous, cost-cutting device. The PBX offerings from pre-divestiture AT&T were primarily analog, electromechanical switches run by outdated methods. The PBXs competitors developed in hopes of winning customers away from AT&T were devices that transmitted the analog voice wave digitally within a company's premises.

One benefit of this fundamental change was that stored computer programs (software) controlled the PBX instead of hard-wired logic. Thus when people moved from one office to another, their extension number could be moved with them simply by changing a line in a computer program. The older PBXs had to be rewired, a much more difficult undertaking. Employees are relocated within most companies so regularly that this increased ease of handling moves and changes provided substantial savings to buyers of the new PBXs.

Being software based also meant that PBXs could be upgraded. Features such as least-cost routing (finding the cheapest long-distance telephone call route) can be offered simply by adding new modules to the software.

THE PBX TODAY: VOICE CAPABILITIES

Today's typical PBX is made up of one to several refrigerator-sized cabinets. It is usually located on a company's premises. Opening its doors reveals a computer card cage filled with printed circuit boards, as seen in Figure 6–2. Connected to those circuit boards are twisted pairs of wires that run to outlets located throughout a building. A range of devices can plug into these outlets, including telephones, dumb terminals, personal computers, and integrated voice/data terminals. Despite all the talk about carrying data, graphics, and video to the desktop, however, one cannot forget the reality of business: A large part of the daily activity of a typical information worker involves the phone. Therefore, we will save consideration of nonvoice devices for later and concentrate first on the various voice communication aspects of a PBX, which can be broken into: basic features, network features, management control features, and advanced features (application processors).

Basic PBX Features

Ordinary push-button phones attached to the PBX can provide a multitude of valuable features. These capabilities are activated by pressing a several-button sequence such as "#11." More

Courtesy of ROLM, an IBM company

FIGURE 6–2: An inside look at the PBX.

advanced *single-line telephones* offer dedicated buttons for one-touch access to features. Some of the most common features are listed below:

- *Call back* can be activitated when a busy signal indicates that the extension of the co-worker being called is in use. When the co-worker's phone is no longer busy, the caller's phone will ring and reconnect the caller without the need to redial the extension.
- *Conference* allows the caller to engage several parties in one telephone conversation.
- *Hold* allows the user to place a caller temporarily on hold.
- *Speed calling* allows a user to load frequently called numbers into memory for access by a short dialing code.
- *Call forwarding* allows a person to direct incoming calls to another extension.
- *Paging* allows a user to page from his extension after keying in a special company paging code.
- *Call waiting* uses a distinctive tone to alert a person using the phone that another call is coming in.
- *Do not disturb* allows blocking of incoming calls when one does not want to be interrupted, although certain callers can be given executive privileges to override.

ANY COMMENTS ON THEIR OWN EXPERIENCE WITH THEIR CO.'S PBX?

Courtesy of ROLM, an IBM company

FIGURE 6–3: An advanced electronic telephone for the PBX.

Advanced electronic telephones (Figure 6–3) may add an alphanumeric display and therefore accommodate such features as:

- *Message reminder* allows a station user to leave a "call me" message on another employee's visual display, with an extension number shown on the display.
- *Save and repeat* allows a user to save and repeat an external number with the touch of a single button.
- *Speaker and microphone* allow hands-free conversation.
- *Programmable keys* can activate a variety of functions. This technique allows a hierarchy of several levels of choices (or menus) to be presented to the user. This flexibility proves especially useful with some of the special PBX applications discussed later in the chapter (such as voice store and forward).

Attendant's consoles provide all the features just described plus

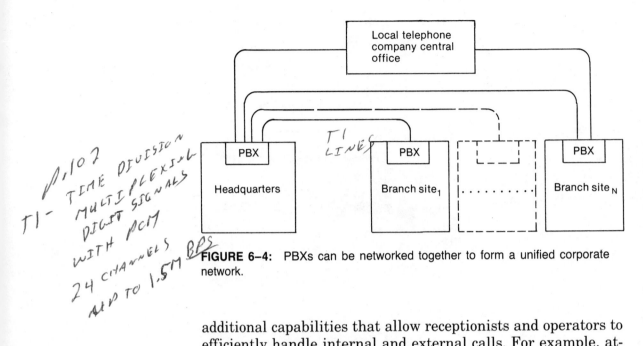

(handwritten margin notes)
P,102
T1 - TIME DIVISION MULTIPLEXING DIGIT SSGNALS WITH PCM
24 CHANNELS
UP TO 1.5M BPS

T1 LINES

FIGURE 6–4: PBXs can be networked together to form a unified corporate network.

additional capabilities that allow receptionists and operators to efficiently handle internal and external calls. For example, attendant's consoles usually include a screen display of an organization's directory with a search feature to quickly match a name with the appropriate extension number. Both telephone handset and headset operations are available with most types of consoles.

Network Features

(handwritten margin notes)
— UTILITY
— LANS

One PBX feature that has broad appeal is the ability to tie together several geographically separated company premises with a unified telephone system. Leased (tie) lines or higher capacity T1 lines provided by the telephone company for linking several PBXs allow users to simply dial a four-digit number to reach any extension on the unified corporate network. (See Figure 6–4.) Benefits accruing from network features can include:

- Simplified station-to-station calling.
- Consolidation of trunks. Long-distance trunks are used more efficiently because all outgoing traffic is pooled through one central group of trunks. The total number of trunks may even be reduced.

- Consolidation of attendants. Attendants can be centrally located, reducing the number of attendants needed.

Management Control Features

There are four basic ways a PBX helps telecommunications managers save on overall telephone costs: least-cost routing, call restrictions, station message detail recording, and system performance monitoring.

Least-Cost Routing. The equal-access scheme that went into effect in the mid-1980s allows a choice of one long-distance carrier (AT&T, MCI, and so on), permitting a company to use the one that is least expensive for its needs. A PBX can provide transparent access to the most economical carrier on a call-by-call basis. The user need not think about nor dial the extra digits necessary to route a call through other than the primary carrier.

When a user dials a long-distance number, the PBX might also consider the cost of the following kinds of telephone lines when computing the cheapest call routing:

ROUTE
SELECTION

- Tie lines—leased line connections to another location.
- FX—a special line to a distant central office that provides local calling access to and from that exchange.
- WATS (Wide Area Telephone Service)—reduced calling rates to specified geographic areas.

The PBX selects the route that will cost least by scanning internally stored tables of information on telephone rates (including variations for time of day, day of the week, and so on). If the least expensive route is "busy" (for example, if all the WATS lines are in use), the PBX system can either queue the caller for the next available WATS line or place the call through to the next least expensive route automatically, depending on how the system administrator has configured the system.

A feature known as local cost control extends least-cost routing to calls within the local calling area. Route optimization software can select use of tie lines or bypass technologies when they are more economical than the use of the local telephone company network.

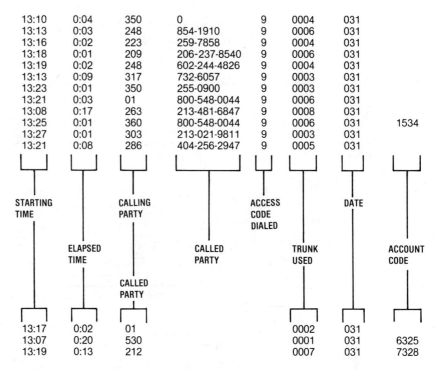

FIGURE 6–5: A typical report generated by a PBX to list calls made. This information can be presented in many types of readable formats.

Station Message Detail Recording. PBXs also allow management to look for communication patterns that may need correcting. Station message detail recording (SMDR) captures more information than found on a phone bill. That information, stored on tape or floppy disks, can be massaged into management reports.

Data recorded on outward calls include the starting time of the call, its duration, the caller's extension number, the called number, the trunk number used, the access code dialed, if any, and any other account codes. (See Figure 6–5.)

The recorded details of inward calls include the starting time, the duration, the extension that answered the call, the incoming trunk used, the date, and other accounting information.

Some of the reports provided by a typical PBX's SMDR include:

- Summary of total calls by company, division, department.
- Distribution of calls by geographic destination.
- Exception reports that summarize calls exceeding specified duration and cost parameters.
- Account code reports for chargeback.

Variations of SMDR reporting capabilities allow PBXs to satisfy the special needs of particular businesses, most often those that can resell calls. Systems designed for hotels and hospitals, for example, provide immediate call costing, include a markup above the actual cost of a call, and record call charges by room number. SMDR systems are available from PBX vendors, with such names as CDR, for call detail recording, as well as from third parties.

Finally, it is expected that display of the cost of a call will soon find its way into PBXs installed in ordinary business. The idea is to reduce overall phone costs by making users aware of how much they are spending on each toll call.

Call Restrictions. The PBX can limit which kinds of calls can be placed from specific extensions. Before switching a call, the PBX checks internal tables to make sure the class of service and trunk access needed to complete the call is available from the originating extension. For example:

- Phones in lobbies and reception areas will usually have long-distance access only with operator intervention.
- The extensions of some employees can be programmed for access to a few area codes (or even a limited number of telephone exchanges) only.
- Most extensions, of course, will have full access to all functions.

Forced authorization codes provide complete accountability and control of toll calls. PBXs can require users to enter a 4- to 10-digit personal authorization code before placing any outside call. Some extensions can be configured to require no such code, but, in general, codes are assigned to all individuals, projects, or clients for control and billback of toll charges. The users' calling privileges follow them to any extension on the PBX.

System Performance Monitoring. A PBX's system performance monitor collects data on trunk usage, attendant console usage, and so on. If trunk lines are underutilized, for example, it may be possible to reduce the number of trunks leased to save local phone company charges. On the other hand, if callers are finding themselves unable to get a dial tone (a condition known as blocking) on a regular basis, it may be that not enough trunk lines are installed or that the capacity of the current PBX configuration has been exceeded. Technical reports make the cause of the problem clear. They can be formatted to show:

- Measure of productivity in terms of:
  —Number of calls handled.
  —Average talking time.
  —Speed of answer to external calls.
  —Speed of answer to internal calls.
- Actual trunk facility usage versus capacity.

Communication networks, like the organizations they serve, should be dynamic. System monitor reports allow a PBX to be reconfigured as needed in order to handle changing communication demands.

Advanced PBX Features

PBXs can be enhanced by adding sophisticated software or stand-alone computer systems that attach to the PBX and provide advanced functions to PBX users. The most common of these applications are for automatic call distribution and voice store and forward.

Automatic Call Distribution. Automatic call distribution (ACD) is available from both PBX vendors and third parties. This PBX subsystem technology is used by airline reservation systems, ticket agencies, catalog sales departments, police departments, and a long list of other sales and service organizations. All depend on ACD to allow callers to get through even when the number of incoming calls exceeds the number of available agents. (See Figure 6–6.)

During such times, "overflow" calls are queued to a message playback device that informs callers they have been queued

TELEMARKETING

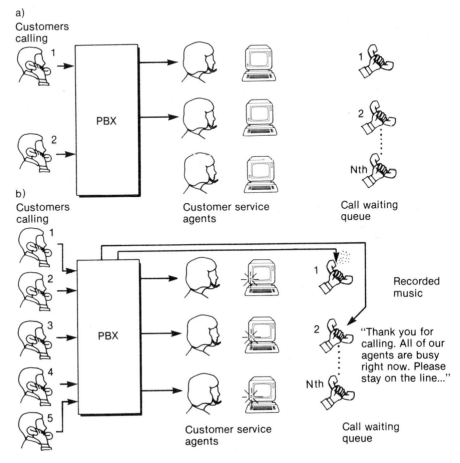

FIGURE 6–6 General Principles of Automatic Call Distribution:
a) Initially, there are enough agents to handle both incoming calls. b) Now, with five incoming calls, callers four and five first hear a recorded announcement. They wait in the queue until a busy customer service agent becomes free.

"in the order received." The caller at the head of the queue is connected to the first agent to become free while all other callers move toward the front of the line. After a specified amount of time, a waiting caller may be connected to a second recording in the hopes that some variation of the following message will reduce the number of callers who hang up: "All agents are still busy, but please remain on the line . . . ."

The increased availability and lower cost of toll-free 800 numbers (inward WATS lines) have made ACD more common. Moreover, companies are seeking to reduce overhead by selling goods and services over the phone. It is estimated that by 1990 one-fourth of all retail sales will take place over the phone, making the technology still more important.

The Atlanta Gas Light Company provides an example of how much an ACD system can improve the distribution of incoming calls over simple rotary distribution of incoming calls.

TESTIMONIAL

> Before installation of its stand-alone ACD at the Atlanta Gas Light Company's center for the handling of service requests, billing, and general information, the first few agent positions were hot seats. (If the first line was busy, the call went to the second, if the first two lines were busy it went to the third, and so on.) Agents in the end positions rarely handled calls. Management was forced to rotate staff throughout the day. Now the ACD provides even distribution of calls to agents without that administrative headache.
>
> With calls spread evenly among all agents at all times, and with the ACD system's comprehensive reporting system allowing accurate forecasting of the need for staff, the company decreased its hang-up rate from 30 percent to 3 percent. Further, using a report that listed average number of calls by time of day, managers determined the peak calling times and arranged agent breaks and lunches to accommodate them. Reporting on the productivity of individuals also allows the star performers among agents to be rewarded.

Voice Messaging: An End to Phone Tag. The most necessary piece of office equipment, ironically, is also a major roadblock to increased productivity. While phones are eminently useful, their use is marred by inefficiency. Studies of business communication indicate that three of four business calls do not reach the intended party on the first try. Moreover, nearly half of these uncompleted calls could be handled as a one-way message given a reliable medium for leaving the message.

The PBX provides a solution through the attachment of a voice store and forward (VSF) system, as seen in Figure 6–7. A VSF (also known as voice mail or a voice messaging system) is a computer that records digitized voice messages on a high-capacity disk storage unit.

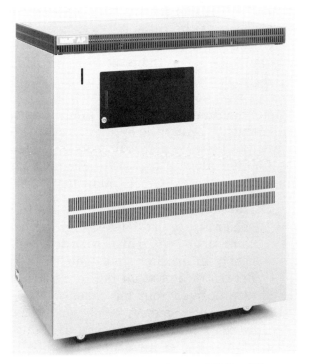

Courtesy of ROLM, an IBM company

FIGURE 6–7: A voice store and forward system. This unit would typically be attached to a PBX.

Voice store and forward is activated if a call has not been answered by a specified number of rings. Most VSF systems allow each user to record a personalized greeting that instructs the caller to leave a message after the tone, much like home answering machines.

Voice store and forward combines the best features of telephone conversations and postal mail: the spontaneity of picking up the phone and the time independence of a letter. The message reaches the intended party even if the receiver of the message is occupied when it is sent. Thus, information workers can carry on a task without interruption by a ringing phone; VSF eliminates the inefficiency of constantly shifting and refocusing attention between a task and a caller's demands. They can review and respond to spoken messages at their convenience rather than at the caller's.

Of course, there are alternatives to voice mail that are considerably cheaper—the pink message pad, for example. Unfortunately, it has been estimated that as many as 3 of 10 handwritten telephone messages fail to reach the intended party in a timely manner. Besides, the information recorded on message slips tends to be cryptic and inaccurate; a message pad usually is unsuitable for a detailed message.

Another alternative to the VSF system, the answering machine, cannot provide the following benefits:

- The ability to forward messages to an individual, an ad hoc group, or established mailing lists (perhaps at a time when phone rates are lower or when appropriate to reach people in another time zone).
- Return receipts that indicate someone else on the system has received your message.
- Private messages (when a particular extension calls, VSF systems can play a special announcement message).
- Skipping over messages to handle more urgent ones.

Finally, (when compared to postal mail, an interoffice memo, or electronic mail), voice mail offers an advantage of communicating information that is difficult to put into a written message: There are subtleties of meaning that can be conveyed only by the human voice; getting these nuances across can be essential in managerial communications.

PBX ALTERNATIVE: CENTREX

Before PBXs offered a vehicle for networking phones across several premises, the only way a company spread over several sites could easily share a unified phone system was to use the PBX alternative provided by local phone companies, a central-office-based service called Centrex.

Centrex provides PBX-like service by dedicating part of the central office's switching capability to a particular organization. Instead of twisted-pairs going from each desktop to an organization's on-site PBX, lines must be run from each desk to the central office. In effect, a company that opts for Centrex is getting an off-site PBX. The phone company is paid to worry about wiring, the environmental needs of the switch (air-conditioning, power supply, floor space), maintenance, and so on. Until direct inward dialing was added to PBX offerings in the early 1980s, Centrex also had the advantage of being able to provide DID while calls to an organization with an on-site PBX had to be forwarded by an attendant.

DIRECT INWARD DIALING

Centrex has disadvantages as well. In most cases, Centrex is based on analog equipment and offers fewer of the features and control functions (call forwarding, least-cost routing, call detail recording) we have been discussing.

Indeed, AT&T, realizing that the decreasing costs of computing meant the future lay with the more capable, less costly on-site PBX, began to raise Centrex rates in the late 1960s. This encouraged companies to switch from Centrex to the PBX, and such sales helped make up for the lost Centrex revenue. The tactic was so successful that the days of Centrex looked numbered.

SWITCH TO PBX

The divestiture of AT&T, however, left the local phone companies with large investments of Centrex equipment and minimal sales of PBXs to offset lost revenue when customers switched. To leverage the capital tied up in switching capacity, the local phone companies began to make Centrex more attractive by adjusting rates and adding PBX-like features to it.

While such moves brought the voice capabilities of Centrex nearly in line with what was available from PBXs, there was no way to overcome Centrex's limited capability for data transmission. Trunk lines to the local phone company's central office are almost exclusively analog, which limits data transmission to the speeds and reliability possible with modems.

This data capability is an essential difference between PBXs and Centrex today. As we shall see in the next section, the data capabilities of the PBX are substantial; transmission speeds far above those possible over analog trunks are supported.

Local telephone companies are quick to tell their Centrex customers that many companies offer premise-based systems that add data capabilities to Centrex. Moreover, when the long-awaited integrated services digital network (ISDN) becomes a reality (see discussion in Chapter Ten), Centrex itself will be able to offer full data services because ISDN involved the digitalization of the local loop. Local telephone companies are telling Centrex customers that ISDN will become available near the end of the decade.

DATA AND THE PBX

Thus far, we have limited our discussion to the voice capabilities of the PBX. But the modern PBX is actually a digital switch under computer control. Because it switches voice as if it were data, the actual handling of data is a natural extension of its capabilities.

Leveraging this data is important to PBX vendors because data transmission is growing at a rate of 30 to 35 percent a year, while voice transmissions are growing at a much slower 6 to 8 percent pace.

Approximately 75 percent of corporate communication is comprised of voice transmission. Another 10 percent to 15 percent of corporate communication involves the kind of low-speed data transmission (less than 9,600 bits per second) that PBXs are most adept at handling. Meanwhile, PBX vendors are enhancing their offerings to handle the remaining 5 percent to 10 percent of data transmission that requires higher data rates. Close links are being forged between LANs and PBXs for those applications that demand high-speed LAN solutions. And, perhaps most important, applications are emerging that leverage the integration of voice and data.

There are several advantages to using a digital PBX to switch data as well as voice. Twisted-pair wiring is estimated to be in place in more than 95 percent of the offices in North America. Carrying data on this in-place wiring is an attractive option for most businesses in the face of the rising cost of installing cable. (See Figure 6–8.)

One-Stop Shopping

The giants of the information processing industry are forming alliances to make sure they will have a PBX-based ability to direct not only voice and data but also graphics, facsimile, video, and all other forms of information to workers' desktops through this in-place wiring. By the mid-1980s, the largest computer manufacturer and one of the three largest makers of digital

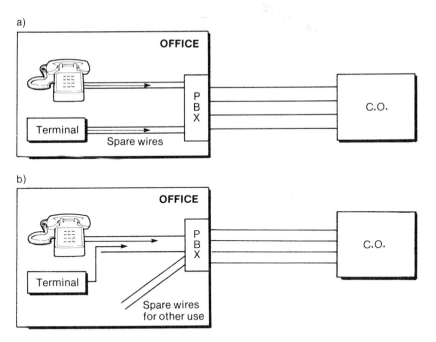

FIGURE 6–8 Using Telephone Wiring for Voice and Data: a) Spare wires not used by the telephone can be used to carry data to a PBX. b) Sharing the same wire used by the telephone through multiplexing techniques.

PBXs—IBM and Rolm, respectively—had merged, and it appeared the PBX was going to have a key role to play in IBM's architecture for communication among all of its computers, Systems Network Architecture (SNA). Office automation leader Wang Laboratories, Inc., had bought 15 percent of a leading edge PBX vendor, InteCom. European PBX vendor Ericsson had joined forces with Honeywell, while Northern Telecom worked out a computer-to-PBX interface with DEC, agreed to cooperate on servicing with major computer vendors including Data General and Honeywell, and added a full local area network capability to its Meridian PBXs. Then there was AT&T, inventor of the PBX and still a major PBX supplier, divesting itself of its local operating companies in order to enter the computer business. There is no doubt: These companies were positioning themselves to provide a PBX that worked hand in hand with computers. Any organization that was still thinking of the PBX solely as a telephone switch was not seeing the whole picture.

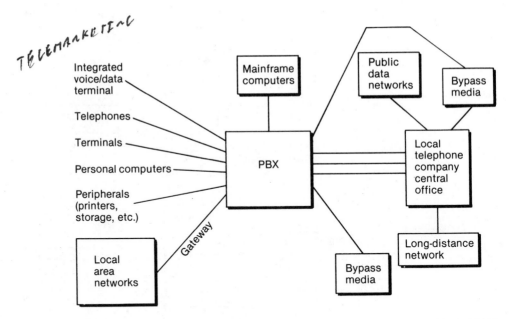

TELEMARKETING (handwritten)

Gateway (diagram label)

FIGURE 6–9: A typical installation of equipment linked to a voice/data PBX.

A Typical Installation of a Voice/Data PBX

A voice/data PBX can interconnect data terminals, integrated voice/data terminals, computers, and computer peripherals. It also can provide computers with access to public data networks or LANs. (See Figure 6–9.)

Part of the advantage of using a PBX to switch data is that the features that enhance voice communications enhance data communications as well. Station message detail recording of data calls can be used to bill computer charges to various departments, for example, or a user's access can be limited to only certain resources hooked up to the PBX network. The ideal, of course, is to make establishing a link to another computing device on the PBX network as easy as it is to establish links between voice communication devices (i.e., no more difficult than making a phone call).

CONNECTING AS EASY AS A PHONE CALL (handwritten)

Indeed, making a data call with a voice/data PBX is not much more difficult than making a phone call. With most voice/data PBXs, an asynchronous terminal or personal computer attaches via a modular connector to a small data terminal equipment (DTE) interface box that fits under (or inside) the telephone. To initiate a data call, the request for service switch on the DTE must be pressed.

The PBX responds by sending a message to the terminal of the PC screen that prompts the user to enter the "extension" of the desired computing resource. After the number is typed in, the PBX connects the call if the corresponding resource is free. If it is busy, the user can select the automatic callback feature and go on with his or her business. When that computing resource becomes free, the PBX calls back and reinstitutes the data call.

Dealing with Diversity

Although telephones have reached a state of standardization (at least as far as the public phone network is concerned) that makes them universally understood by users and compatible with other telephones, there is no equivalent in the world of data terminals. Different types of computers—even those from the same manufacturer—are designed to work with different types of terminals operating under different protocols.

Therefore, if a PBX is going to link the user to a variety of computing resources, it must serve not only as a multipurpose switch but as a multipurpose interface as well. Once data has been transmitted from the desktop to the PBX, it must be translated into the correct format and converted to the speed expected by the computer.

PBX to Computer Interfaces. The primary method of linking a PBX to a local computer in the middle 1980s was via banks of data modules. While more efficient than dedicated links from each terminal to each port, racks of data adapters and a fair amount of additional wiring in the computer room were still required for large installations. (See Figure 6–10.)

Further complicating matters, each PBX maker used its own unique and proprietary interface to link to computers. Maker A's PBX would not work with Maker B's data models.

Morever, as applications grew in sophistication, users were spending more time on their terminals. More connections were required between the PBX and the computer, increasing the physical congestion between the computer and PBX and raising costs to unacceptable levels.

Two standards have been proposed to solve these problems,

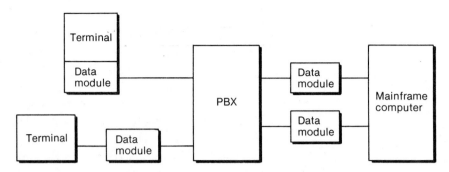

FIGURE 6–10: Primary method of linking PBXs to mainframe computers before the new PBX-mainframe interfaces. The new interfaces reduce the need for data modules between PBXs and mainframe computers.

the computer to PBX interface (CPI) and the digital multiplexed interface (DMI); both allow as many as 24 terminal links between a PBX and host on two sets of twisted-pair wiring. With the solidification of the primary ISDN specification (see Chapter Ten), these two proposals will most likely be brought into line; ISDN will provide a common "pipe" for data across most available physical media.

Synchronous Links. Linking devices such as personal computers and inexpensive terminals to synchronous devices (IBM mainframes, for example) requires a more complex link than required for asynchronous devices like minicomputers. One common practice in the world of micro-mainframe links is to make a microcomputer emulate an IBM 3270 family terminal. (See Chapter Eleven for details.) It takes a sophisticated add-on board to convert the micro's asynchronous transmission into a synchronous data stream with emulation of the screen-handling and network address of a 3270 terminal. It is more economical to eliminate this duplication of function by switching traffic from the micros to a central protocol converter linked to the PBX. Moreover, coaxial cable must then be run only from the PBX to the host's cluster controller. (See Figure 6–11.)

For connecting to remote host computers, a pool of modems can be used similarly to serve a large number of users on a contention basis. (See Figure 6–12.)

Speed of the Data Link. Of course, the transparent connections provided by a PBX to a number of different computing

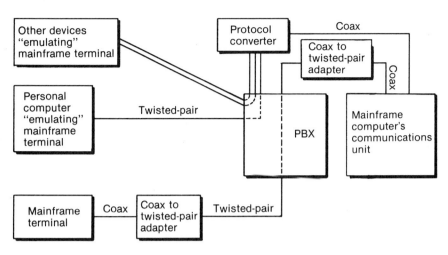

FIGURE 6–11: Common techniques for linking mainframe computers through the PBX.

resources could not boost an organization's communication efficiency if the data transfer rate between the desk and the PBX were insufficient. While much has been made in the trade press of the speed limitations of today's typical voice/data PBX compared with speeds possible on a LAN, in most applications the digital PBX is more than adequate. The most popular transmission rate in use in the mid-1980s in business was 9.6 kilobits per second, or about one-seventh the 64 kilobits per second bandwidth that some PBXs provide to the desktop without interfering with voice transmission over the same line.

Such speeds easily meet the needs of transaction-based applications (that is, applications in which people enter data by hand at a terminal or workstation).

The PBX is also well suited to handling the telecommunication needs of a microcomputer user. Microcomputer users typically desire access to a variety of services—electronic mail, the public data base, a letter-quality printer down the hall, a synchronous link to a remote mainframe—and often the speed required is no more than 1,200 bits per second. Again, the PBX serves this need by allowing the microcomputers to contend for the expensive hardware links necessary to access other data devices. Examples include modem pools, protocol converters, and PBX-to-computer links. Other options include packet switching

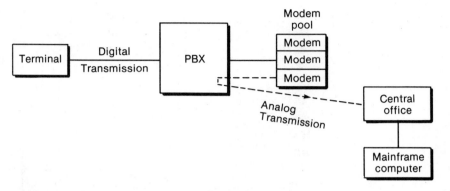

FIGURE 6–12: A modem pool configuration.

interfaces (based on the X.25 protocol) for direct connection to private packet-switched networks and public data networks. (See Chapter Eight.) Also important are T1 interfaces for high-speed, long-distance digital transmission.

PBX VERSUS LANs

Nearly any discussion of data transmission using a PBX prompts a mention of the LAN as a better alternative. While PBXs and LANs do compete with each other for office automation dollars, many experts expect the two technologies will coexist quite peacefully. As we have just discussed, a link through a PBX may be best for casual access to a number of different computing resources. On the other hand, the higher data rates supported by a LAN may be called for to serve the subset of an organization's users who require it for file transfers and for special-purpose workstations that support high-resolution graphics. In such cases, the rest of the population can also benefit from the LAN if access is provided via a gateway from the PBX network.

Sometimes the LAN Wins. In some cases, however, a LAN may be a better choice than a PBX network. The head of information services for Dataquest, Inc., for example, considered using an already installed voice/data PBX to link the many personal computers that had come into use at the market research firm's main office. But because the analysts' work is data

C A $ual

intensive—they retrieve rather large subsets of data off a mainframe, use data base tools on the PC to manipulate that data, and then share the resulting data base with others in the company—there was a call for faster data transfer than that supported by the PBX.

Indeed, the primary advantage of a LAN over a PBX network for PC users is its capability—made possible by a LAN's higher bandwidth—to appear to provide multiple simultaneous access to a storage device or, through the technique known as spooling, to a high-speed printer.

TEST

INTEGRATED VOICE/DATA TERMINALS

Thus far we have considered how the digital PBX can facilitate the use of the telephone for voice communications and the desktop terminal or microcomputer for data communications. But the voice/data PBX also makes possible a new kind of desktop workstation, the integrated voice/data terminal (VDT). (See Figure 6–13.) The VDT may have a significant impact on office productivity. VDTs integrate a terminal and phone, or personal computer and phone, into one housing. Designed for communication-intensive information workers, they provide effective, easy-to-use desktop access to both the voice and data features of the PBX.

Cited as the desktop device that will merge telephony and data worlds in offices, these VDTs offer several advantages:

- Complete integration with the PBX for simpler access to PBX features.
- Simultaneous use of the telephone handset and computer terminal.
- Use of existing telephone twisted-pair wiring.

Part of the potential of these new terminals is in integrating all of the office's desktop tools into one compact device. Synergism makes the computerized combination of these functions far more powerful than the use of stand-alone items such as the telephone, calculator, dictation machine, calendar, message pad, address book, and Rolodex.

OFFICE FUNCTIONS ACTIVITES

With such a combination, for example, a user can stop work on a spreadsheet, electronically search for the phone number of

FIGURE 6–13: An integrated voice/data terminal.

a colleague who has a needed figure, dial the number with a single keystroke, and return instantly to the spreadsheet to type the number in as the colleague delivers it over the speaker of the VDT. If the user wanted to set up a meeting later, he or she could search the calendars of several people for the first time all are free, write a quick electronic memo asking them all to confirm the time, and distribute it with a single keystroke.

A New Synergy: Voice Annotation of Text. But it is the ability of the digital PBX to integrate voice and data that may be its greatest advantage. One application that depends on this integration is the voice annotation of text.

Voice annotation provides the ability to append and annotate electronic text with voice messages. For example, the recipient of an electronic document can add verbal suggestions and editing instructions and return this mixed voice/data message to the sender. In a sense, voice annotation serves the same purpose for an electronic document that penciled comments in the margin serve for paper documents. It also allows the hunt-and-peck typist to respond more easily to electronic mail.

Before integration of voice and data can have a significant impact, however, users will have to make cultural adjustments. Indeed, if the software that links voice to text is not as easy to use as the PBX functions on an advanced electronic phone, many people simply won't use it.

DATA PBXs: ANOTHER ALTERNATIVE   *Two PBX's*

All corporations are not integrating voice and data, despite the promise of the synergy of voice and data. Other alternatives may be less expensive than installing a voice/data PBX, including adding a data-only PBX to an existing voice-only PBX.

Data PBXs are optimized for data traffic. They provide similar speed (19.2 kilobits per second), resource sharing, and switching for terminals and data devices at a fraction of the cost of a voice/data PBX ($150 to $300 per line versus $800 to $1,200 per line).

Even though two PBXs are involved, it is possible to use a single set of twisted-pair wires to transmit voice and data. A terminal's data traffic can be multiplexed over a phone's voice traffic with the use of data over voice (DOV) products. DOV equipment then separates the signals immediately before the PBX location and directs them to the voice or data PBX as appropriate.

Although some consultants advise clients to consider data-only PBXs as a fine short-term solution for connecting a number of asynchronous terminals to a number of minicomputers, all but a few data processing (DP) diehards feel the data-only PBX will disappear as its price advantage narrows and fully integrated PBXs with very high bandwidths become the norm.

A TECHNICAL LOOK AT THE PBX

Fully understanding the potential of a voice and data PBX to improve the productivity of an organization requires a technical understanding of how a PBX works. Although this is true to a degree for any piece of telematics technology, a technical understanding of the PBX is even more crucial because much of the potential for the all-in-one digital network of tomorrow lies buried in the bandwidth at the heart of the switch.

Converting Voice to Digital

To send voice over a digital network, the analog voice signal must be encoded in digital form, as described in Chapter Four. A voice signal that has been converted through pulse code modulation (PCM) is well suited for computerized switching using time division multiplexing (TDM). Instead of creating a unique physical path for each call switched, a digital PBX interleaves the strings of numbers representing each call on a single pathway called a bus.

Time Division Multiplexing

In the simplest case of time division multiplexing, two strings of numbers representing two voice signals are interleaved. The source and destination of the first voice are told, respectively, to send and receive numbers on the odd ticks (or time slots) of the PBX's internal clock, while the source and destination of the second voice are told to send and receive numbers on the even ticks of the clock.

It should be clear that digital switching can move bits from a terminal to a computer as easily as it can move the bits of a PCM voice signal from one phone extension to another. Moreover, carrying data digitally offers considerable efficiency over the use of a modem to carry data over a voice channel. Instead of the 64,000 bits per second of bandwidth required for one direction of voice carrying only the 300 to 9,600 bits per second possible from cost-effective modems, the time slot used for a PCM voice channel ideally can be divided (or submultiplexed) in some products to carry a number of data channels.

Just as it is possible to send voice and data down the same PBX pathway, it is possible to send them to the PBX on the same pair of wires. The digitized voice signal and the data signal from a terminal or PC can be multiplexed and transmitted to the section in the PBX that provides access to the bus. The voice stream can go to another telephone or a trunk line while the data stream goes to a computer.

Wiring

SMA

Most buildings are wired for voice service and essentially all PBX installations utilize a star wiring topology. Each station is supported by dedicated twisted-pair wires that run from the user's desk to the PBX. The number of pairs of wire required for each user depends upon the services provided to each desk and the type of transmission used. PBX vendors typically require one to four pairs of wire between the PBX and the end-user locations.

Just as the more powerful of today's PBXs have more traffic capacity than called for by today's applications, PBX wiring plans may also provide capacity for growth.

There are limits to the data-carrying capability of twisted-pair wiring, for example. Most common PBX requires 24 gauge unshielded twisted-pairs of insulated solid-copper wire. Wire of this type, sometimes referred to as voice-grade media (VGM) or telephone twisted-pair (TTP), has demonstrated an ability to carry data at rates above 4 megabits per second, but experts agree that such rates approach the physical limits of reliable transmission even if short distances separate stations and a PBX (often no more than 200 to 300 feet).

MANual Switch Note

Several computer manufacturers have recommended a structured wiring scheme that involves routing several pairs of voice-grade twisted-pair wires with a few shielded twisted-pairs (to support higher data rates) between each workplace and a wiring closet. Doing so at the time of building construction provides several benefits. Several universal connectors provided at each workplace mean moving a device requires nothing more than unplugging it from one outlet and plugging it into another: No additional wiring is needed to attach a device to the network. Management is easier because it is simpler to monitor uniform cabling; fault detection and repair are easier.

Installation of a structured wiring scheme with extra bandwidth makes sense for the same reason PBX manufacturers are building extra bandwidth into their voice/data switches: It is

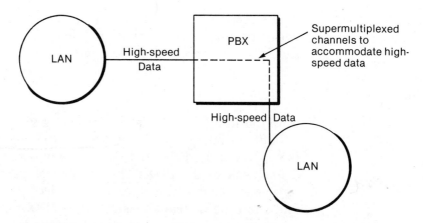

FIGURE 6–14: Using the PBX as a gateway or bridge between LANs through supermultiplexing.

only a matter of time before corporations will need it to remain competitive.

Future Uses of the PBX

The throughput of the buses built into today's most robust PBXs is far greater than could be used practically by voice and today's typical point-to-point data connections.

Today, the typical bandwidth derived from assigning a connection a single time slot is 64 kilobits per second. To obtain higher bandwidth for special purposes requires assigning a group of time slots to a single connection. This technique available in some products, called supermultiplexing, can even be used to establish high-speed data-switching services, such as transmission paths for LAN gateways and bridges. (See Figure 6–14.)

PBX: TRANSMITTING HIGH SPEED DATA

Initially, a PBX will have hundreds, even thousands, of users satisfied by the data bandwidth possible on twisted-pair wiring, while it is left to LANs to support the class of users who need higher bandwidth. When these LAN users want access to other facilities or resources that are available on the PBX network, a gateway between the PBX and LAN networks will provide it.

LAN Support

PBXs will also serve as high-speed links between physically separated LANs. Already, PBXs use high-speed digital links to connect PBX modules within an organization. Similar techniques could be used to link two networks of the same type over a T1 (1.544 megabits per second) or even higher speed link. This, in effect, would provide the benefits of a local area network over a wide area network. Users pulling documents off a file server would not notice the difference between local storage and storage that was thousands of miles away. Eventually, this bridging ability could be extended to link two dissimilar networks, allowing the PBX to serve as a gateway, say, between a token passing ring LAN and an Ethernet or PC network LAN on opposite coasts.

[handwritten margin note: TIME DIVISION MULTIPLEXING WITH PCM IS T1 CARRIER]

[handwritten margin note: INTERFACE]

Major PBX vendors also foresee continuing bandwidth increases in order to accommodate new applications. What speeds PBXs will support to the desktop in the future is uncertain. VGM twisted-pair has already been pushed to 4 megabits and higher by the IBM token passing ring. Conversion to fiber optic cable to the desk, on the other hand, would provide all the bandwidth needed for interactive video, transmission of facsimile images, or any other application we can conceive of today.

As far as links to host computers and its role in computer-oriented networking schemes such as IBM's Systems Network Architecture (SNA), PBXs for the short term will communicate to IBM and non-IBM hosts through one of the proposed standards for PBX to host communications or via the existing proprietary data modules that link terminals to a host through the PBX on a line-by-line, contention basis.

The PBX and SNA

By the end of the 1980s, PBXs will have native SNA support. Depending on how things evolve, the PBX may serve first as a terminal supporting device, much like the cluster controllers that control the mainframe's terminals in current SNA environments. (See Chapter Eleven for background.) Eventually, the PBX could become the local collection point for data from a large group of cluster controllers. Once that data was multiplexed, it could be sent by any of a number of different high-speed digital links to the mainframe.

SELECTION OF A PBX

Despite the many benefits of the PBX, not every business is large enough to make the purchase of a PBX cost-effective. For businesses with fewer than 40 telephones, the best choice may be a key system. Although the only features available on the original 1A2 key system produced by Western Electric were lights that indicated when a line was in use, the competition engendered by the Carterfone decision has pushed key system technology far. Today, key systems offer several of the voice communication features of the PBX, including last-number redial, music on hold, two-line conferencing, and hands-free station-to-station intercoms.

APPARTMENT COMPLEX

A new trend from the competitive world of real estate provides an alternative to key systems for small businesses. Space for lease in many new buildings is wired to an advanced PBX that is centrally located and designed to be shared among all a building's tenants. Thus, small businesses have the option of leasing advanced PBX service along with office space. The potential benefits of the basic PBX voice features as well as the advanced applications and data capabilities discussed in this chapter—all without capital expenditures or a need to go through an arduous selection process—make premise-based PBX service a promising option for small businesses.

Corporate Politics

COMING UP TO SPEED ON TRAINING & AREAS OF RESPONSIBILITY

In many companies there is disagreement on whether the PBX will be the center of the all-in-one digital network of the office of tomorrow. Some DP managers may argue against a voice/data PBX and in favor of a data-only PBX separate from the company's phone system, and the telecommunications manager may go along. Such a DP manager probably has no interest in a company's telephone network and is unwilling to relinquish the data communications function to a telecommunications manager. Similarly, that telecommunications manager is leery of the data aspect of an integrated PBX.

If the full benefits of switching voice and data are to be realized, the PBX cannot fall between the traditional realms of the telecommunications manager and the data processing department. But that is exactly where it falls in many companies. Often the manager of telecommunications has responsibility for the PBX, while the data processing manager has control over host computers and terminals, and individual managers have control over personal computers. Given this situation, it is difficult to design and implement an office communication system that effectively leverages the stand-alone power of the individual technologies, much less their synergistic possibilities. Let's now turn to a discussion of some of the important technical issues in selecting a PBX.

PBX Reliability

HIGH

2 MTN OUTAGE FOR YEARS 40 YEARS SERVICE

One of the main requirements is that a PBX be reliable. It can't be said too many times: The phone system cannot fail, even for short periods. This is an argument that can be put to the reluctant DP manager in favor of a voice/data PBX. While most users of data networks expect them to go down as a matter of routine, it is simply not permissible for a phone system to go down. Data users on a voice/data PBX therefore are treated to a level of reliability they have never experienced.

Although a certain amount can be told about a system's reliability by examining its architecture, more important is the vendor's reputation and ability to provide support. What is the professional competence of the vendor? How does the quality of the product, the user training, and the maintenance compare?

Today's Applications

Another factor to consider is the applications that will be implemented immediately. The telephone convenience features available from the vendor must satisfy the needs of users. Is voice store and forward or automatic call distribution available from the vendor, or would it be necessary to secure stand-alone systems from another company? Are the data capabilities of the switch sufficient to meet current and future needs?

On the other hand, all the features in the world do little good if users cannot get a dial tone when they need one. It is important to determine current usage requirements and prospects for growth. Telephone switches are expensive, and installing them is complex and costly. Having insufficient capacity due to lack of preplanning may cause the PBX to not generate dial tone. A PBX should be designed to accommodate the number of lines and trunks a company will need over the life of the system.

Then there is the matter of cost/benefit analysis. This is elusive, because it is not easy to put a dollar value on the benefits of good communication. There may also be difficulty in comparing the total cost of competing systems because of the need to evaluate both the purchase price and ongoing costs of a system. Which system will save more on transmission costs? Do both system prices include training and documentation? How does the cost of system expansion compare? What about service?

A subset of the above question is the matter of management information and control. The ability of a PBX to more closely monitor system usage and to automatically warn of patterns that might indicate abuse of the phone system can save significant sums over the life of a PBX. The system administrator can also use such reports to reconfigure the PBX network to better distribute the communications load, which maximizes resource sharing and avoids unnecessary or premature additions of equipment.

Then there is the question of choosing a PBX vendor. The two main outlets are the direct sales forces of some manufacturers or the various interconnect companies. An interconnect company has the advantage of offering several manufacturers' products, perhaps increasing the likelihood that the PBX it suggests is chosen will be the best possible fit to the company's needs. The manufacturer of a PBX, on the other hand, has the advantage of the intimate familiarity that comes from designing equipment. Similarly, the manufacturer may provide better service simply because it has to know how to configure and maintain only one line of equipment.

Looking to the Future

The need to anticipate the future makes such choices even trickier. A PBX is a large capital investment, amortized only over half a dozen or more years. Will a given manufacturer still exist in five years? How does one account for the new applications that may become common midway through the life of a system?

Probably, the key question to ask concerning future applications is whether the architecture of a PBX holds the right combination of processor power and bus bandwidth in reserve to handle whatever opportunities for increased productivity may come along. The day is not far distant when organizations will need to distribute graphics, video teleconferencing, and programs to a variety of desktops in order to remain competitive.

For widely dispersed organizations, it may be that the ability to switch information from a mainframe on one coast to desktop workstations on the other will prove key. Will a particular PBX be easily able to do that? Will a particular PBX be able to be the hub of the office of tomorrow? These are not easy questions, given the incredible increase in the amount of information organizations have had to cope with over the past few years and the equally astounding advances in information handling technology. Whatever the future holds, the telematic capabilities of the PBX will continue to be extremely important.

As data becomes more important and the data capabilities of the PBX increase, and as voice/data PBXs are integrated into the large networks of computers specified by such schemes as IBM's SNA and Digital Equipment Corporation's DECNET, it will become more and more difficult to make a case for a multiple switch solution. Pure voice PBXs in combination with a data PBX, LAN and/or high speed micro-to-mainframe links will not be attractive compared to single-switch solutions. The added expense of separate wiring and separate management of the various switches, plus the difficulty of implementing applications that closely couple voice and data, will probably make the single-switch solution the future's only viable option.

QUESTIONS FOR REVIEW:

1. Describe the evolution of PBXs.
2. Why are PBXs needed?
3. Name three basic PBX features.

4. Name two network features.
5. Describe how ACD is used.
6. Describe how VSF is used.
7. Summarize the basics behind integrating voice and data in a PBX.
8. What are the main differentiating points between PBXs and LANs for data transmission?
9. What is PCM? What is TDM?
10. Describe the role of imbedded wiring in an organization.
11. What are some possible future uses of a PBX?
12. How would you select a PBX?

FOR DISCUSSION:

1. What type of organization prefers Centrex over a PBX? Why?
2. What are the disadvantages of integrating voice and data in a PBX?
3. In what scenario can LANs replace PBXs?
4. In what scenarios can data PBXs replace voice/data PBXs?
5. What are the benefits of integrating a PBX within a computer communications network, like SNA?

REFERENCES

ANGUS, IAN. "Networking Micros on the Digital PBX." *Computerworld*, October 3, 1984.

ANONYMOUS. "Atlanta Gas Light Company Improves Customer Service with Call Distributor." *Communications News*, July 1985.

AZZARA, MICHAEL. "IVDTs: The Information Age Tool." *Communications Week*, January 28, 1985.

BARLIN, DAVID. "Switch Hitter: A Data Man's Guide to the World of Voice." *Data Communications*, October 1984.

BARTEE, THOMAS C. *Data Communications, Networks, and Systems.* Howard W. Sams & Co., Inc., 1985.

BERGMAN, MARK. *Hambrecht & Quist's Investment Strategies in Telecommunications: PBX Market.* March 1984.

CABELL, DOUG and CABELL, DALE. "LAN or PBX: A Strategic and Critical Look." *Micro Communications,* April 1985.

Datapro Research Corp. "An Overview of Key Telephone Systems." January 1985.

JANCA, PETER. "Comparing the Two PBX-to-Computer Specifications." *Data Communications,* May 1984.

OCCHIOGROSSO, BENEDICT. "Voice Mail Technology Comes of Age, Part One." *Telephony,* September 10, 1984.

PATRICK, MICHAEL. "The Heat Is on for Phone Switches that Do a Lot of Fast Shuffling." *Data Communications,* March 1985.

PART FOUR

Corporate and Public Networks

[handwritten note: Public switched — voice network in place — digital being developed or replacing the analog]

The ever-growing need to transmit data as we move deeper into the information age is a need the public switched network—which was designed to carry voice transmissions—is ill-suited to meet. Thus, although it is clear that the regional Bell operating companies (RBOCs) will carry most of a corporation's local telephone traffic while the interexchange carriers compete on an equal footing for its long-distance business, a company's data communication business is largely up for grabs. The RBOCs, the interexchange carriers, new competitors encouraged by divestiture, and the larger corporations themselves are rising to meet these needs by deploying a number of new technologies. Collectively, these are the *bypass technologies,* so-called because they bypass the public switched network.

Bypass is an important topic for a number of reasons. Bypass technology presents an opportunity to cut communication costs and give telecommunication managers more control over the corporate network: Its use may be necessary to remain competitive. In many cases, bypass can be used to turn a company's network into a strategic weapon. Bypass, with its emphasis on digital technology, is necessary today for any company hoping to take a true telematic approach to communication in the 1980s.

Indeed, bypass technologies pose such a competitive threat to the local telephone companies that the companies are fighting back with a plan to convert the entire public switched network to a completely digital system that will be able to handle data as well as it currently handles voice. The prospects for the success of this scheme, called the integrated services digital network (ISDN), are not completely clear. Nevertheless, it is an important consideration for today's corporate telecommunication planner. If it succeeds, ISDN will provide the standard, unified digital pathway needed to implement true, telematic networks.

To understand either ISDN or bypass technology requires an understanding of what is being bypassed; thus, we begin Part Four with a chapter on the public switched network. Then, the public data networks are described. The bypass option is then detailed. Part Four ends with a discussion on ISDN.

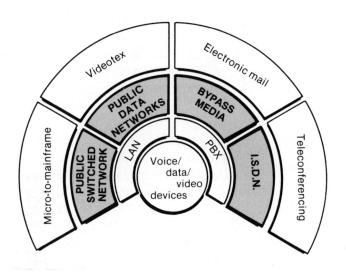

The Public Switched Networks

OBJECTIVES

- Understand the structure and limitations of the public telephone network before divestiture.
- Understand the structure and limitations of the public telephone network after divestiture.

While the private branch exchanges and local area networks provide the pathway for information movement in the office, the primary pathway for moving information between physically separated offices is the public switched network, better known simply as the telephone network.

Use of the telephone network has been complicated by divestiture. Instead of a monolithic entity controlled by AT&T, businesses now deal with a network that has been broken into pieces controlled by different vendors.

This breakup of the Bell System comes at a time when the importance of data communications transmitted by large corporations is approaching the importance of voice communications. This chapter will look at the current public switched network as a prerequisite to understanding more cost-effective alternatives for data communications.

BEFORE DIVESTITURE

Voice Communications

Before the breakup of the Bell System, AT&T's regional Bell operating companies, along with independent local companies such as GTE, were the local exchange carriers (LECs). The LECs provided the dial tone, local calling service and links to AT&T's long-distance service for each telephone in the geographic area assigned to them by the FCC.

Then, as now, single line telephones were connected to a

local exchange office switch by a twisted pair of wires known as the "local loop." Although the length of local loops averages several miles, this wiring and the local exchange office to which it connects is known in telephony jargon as "the last mile."

The primary services provided by the local phone company were direct-dial local calling and, through a link to one of the long-distance carrier's switching networks, long-distance service. Although several alternatives to AT&T existed before divestiture, including MCI and Sprint, they were available only to subscribers who had Touch-Tone phone service (approximately half of all phones installed at the time of divestiture). Users of the alternative long-distance carriers also had to dial special access codes.

LoCAL
To
NETworks
To
volume
TRAFFIC

Special services that provided more economical alternatives to long-distance service also were available before divestiture:

- Wide Area Telephone Service (*WATS*) provide a bulk discount on long-distance calls placed to specific geographic areas a company might call frequently.
- A service once known as inbound WATS (now called *800 service*) allows companies to pick up the charges for calls to a special telephone number making them free for the calling party.

Local Versus Long Distance

An understanding of how calls were handled before divestiture makes the fragmented post-divestiture scheme seem more logical. Before divestiture, the local exchange office was at the bottom of AT&T's switching hierarchy; its traffic was handled by the lowest level of switch, dubbed class 5. Calls between phones connected to the same local exchange involved only the local class 5 switches (see Chapter Three) and were considered local. A call between phones connected to two different local exchanges was still considered local if it passed through only a single trunking system that directly linked the class 5 switches in those two local offices.

A call became "long distance" only when it had to be passed from the local central office class 5 switch, known in the AT&T

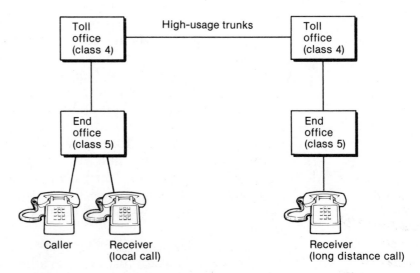

FIGURE 7–1: Before divestiture, a call became long distance if it passed through class 4 switches.

switching hierarchy as an end office switch, to a class 4 switch, known as a toll office switch. This is illustrated in Figure 7–1.

AFTER DIVESTITURE

Local Versus Long Distance

CHANGE IN SWITCHING TO BEYOND LOCAL NETWORK

Divestiture changed several aspects of how long-distance phone calls are routed. The "equal access" ruling meant that direct-dial long-distance calls would not be automatically passed to the AT&T network at the toll office; instead, the FCC ruled that all long-distance carriers would have "equal access" to subscribers. Customers could choose long-distance services from among all carriers (the largest of which at the time of divestiture were AT&T Communications, MCI, GTE Sprint Communications, and Allnet Communications).

TEST

To implement equal access, the class 4 switches were designated interexchange points of presence (IXC POP). Long-distance providers, renamed as "interexchange carriers," were permitted to directly attach their networks to these IXC POPs.

In connection with this scheme, the divestiture established

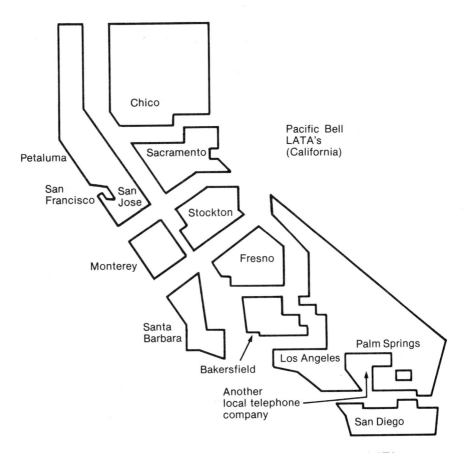

FIGURE 7-2: LATA boundaries in California. After divestiture, LATA boundaries define a long-distance call. Calls between LATAs must be carried by interexchange carriers, even if the calls do not leave the local telephone company's territory.

regions called local access transport areas (LATAs). <u>LATA boundaries define where local telephone companies have to pass a call to an IXC POP</u> and thus to one of the long-distance, interexchange carriers. A local telephone company's service area will be made up of several LATAs; thus, the local company must pass a call that crosses LATA boundaries to an interexchange carrier even though the call never leaves the local company's service area.

LATAs correspond only roughly to the area code calling regions—several area codes may be combined in some LATAs—and it is LATAs, not area codes, that affect billing.

The impact of this scheme on billing can be a bit confusing. A call that is made within California from San Francisco (area code 415) to Petaluma (area code 707) crosses LATA boundaries. Therefore, one of the POP interexchange carriers (AT&T or MCI, for example) is involved and will bill the caller for a long-distance call even though Petaluma and San Francisco are served by the same local telephone company, Pacific Bell. On the other hand, because San Francisco (area code 415) and San Jose (area code 408) are part of the same LATA, a call between these two California cities involves only Pacific Bell and is not considered "long distance" even though it crosses area code boundaries. (See Figure 7–2.)

DATA SERVICES AND DIVESTITURE

The local loop combines a twisted-pair for each phone line into larger cables. Transmission impairments caused by the close proximity of all these wires (interference known as "cross talk," for example—see Chapter Four) was not a severe problem for voice communication. However, as businesses began to use local loops for data communications via the use of modems, these inherent transmission impairments limited the speed of data communication.

The needs of data users were not ignored by the telephone company before divestiture. The services available to individual subscribers were determined by the facilities at the local central office. Besides ordinary switched services—which could be used to carry low-speed data—nonswitched private circuits called leased lines were available. Leased lines are useful when a high volume of voice or data traffic between two points makes use of the switched network uneconomical. Because they can be "conditioned" to achieve higher transmission speeds and lower error rates, leased lines are especially advantageous when significant amounts of data are to be sent. Several other types of special services also originated from most central offices, including dataphone digital services (DDS), which carries data digitally on telephone system twisted-pair lines. DDS provides speeds of up to 56,000 bits per second. T1 links provide digital

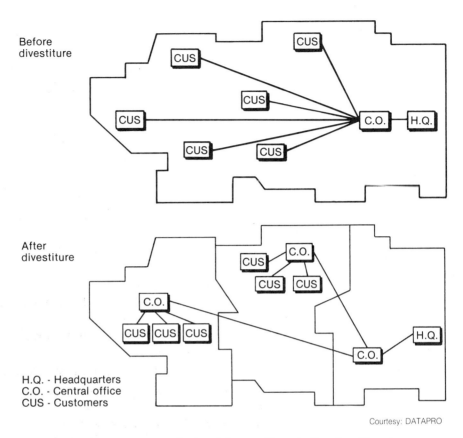

Before divestiture

After divestiture

H.Q. - Headquarters
C.O. - Central office
CUS - Customers

Courtesy: DATAPRO

FIGURE 7–3: Leased lines had to be reconfigured after divestiture because crossing LATA boundaries involved the interexchange carriers. Before divestiture, "tail circuits" were usually cost-effective.

transmission at a rate of 1.544 megabits per second, which can be used for 24 data conversations.

The introduction of the LATAs has affected use of these special data services. For example, before divestiture a company might have leased point-to-point lines from the local telephone company to tie its field offices to a host computer at corporate headquarters. After divestiture, that configuration was not possible: The interexchange carriers, not the local phone company, would have to carry that data once each line crossed LATA boundaries. But interexchange carrier rates decrease with increased volume on a single line. The more cost-effective configuration for the same service would therefore be a "tail circuit," as illustrated in Figure 7–3. A tail circuit connects each field office within the LATA to the LATA's IXC POP. At the POP the circuits from each field office within the LATA are multiplexed onto a single line to the host computer at corporate headquarters, thus taking advantage of volume transmission discounts.

QUESTIONS FOR REVIEW:

1. What is the primary pathway for voice communications between offices?
2. Describe the role of local exchange carriers before divestiture.
3. What is the "local loop?"
4. What are some special long-distance services available before divestiture?
5. How were local calls handled before divestiture? Long-distance calls?
6. Answer question 5 for after divestiture.
7. What is "equal access?"
8. What are IXC POPs? LATAs?
9. Describe some data services before divestiture.
10. How have LATAs affected data service?

FOR DISCUSSION:

1. Who do you think competes against the PSN?
2. Speculate on some reactions from the public switched network vendors if customers want large amounts of data transmission capacity.

REFERENCES

Link Resources Corporation. *Data Communications in the Local Loop, 1984.*

MEADOW, CHARLES and TEDESCO, ALBERT. *Telecommunications for Management.* New York: McGraw-Hill, 1985.

REYNOLDS, GEORGE W. *Introduction to Business Telecommunications.* Columbus, Ohio: Charles E. Merrill Publishing Company, 1984.

The Public Data Networks

OBJECTIVES

- Understand packet switching and public data networks.
- Understand the X.25 standard.
- Understand how public data networks are used.

[handwritten margin note: How to obtain the most responsive circuit that will not be fully utilized unless they accumulate & send packets of data]

Public data networks, also called value added networks (VANs), arose before divestiture from the need for better data transport than was provided by the use of modems on the public switched network. Analog transmission of data over long distances is vulnerable to noise and errors that limit transmission speeds. In addition, the "bursty" or intermittent nature of most data transmissions causes most of the bandwidth dedicated to a data call by the public switched network to be unused.

In most interactive applications, an operator at a terminal is thinking or typing information most of the time, and no information is being transmitted. Only when the input data or the application program's response is sent—a "screenload" or "page" at a time—is the circuit being used. The result is that most of the time no data is flowing, making a dedicated circuit highly inefficient and costly. In order to allow data terminals to communicate with remote host computers more easily and efficiently, some way to use the wasted bandwidth and to better control errors is needed.

PACKET SWITCHING TECHNOLOGY

The technology commercialized by the first data networks, called packet switching, uses bandwidth only when a terminal or host computer is sending data. Packet switching breaks that data

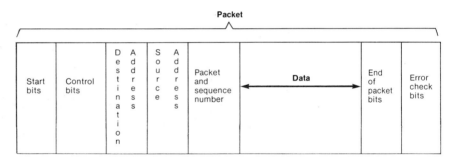

FIGURE 8–1: A simplified format for a data packet.

flow into individual blocks, called packets, as illustrated in Figure 8–1. Each packet of information travels to its destination over a series of connections that last only long enough to transmit that particular packet one "step" toward its destination.

Little bandwidth is wasted because the packets of data from a number of sources are interleaved, or multiplexed, onto a network's trunks. These trunks interconnect a series of network nodes controlled by minicomputers. One of these network control centers is pictured in Figure 8–2. Addressing information contained in each packet's "data envelope" is read by the minicomputer at each node on the network. The minicomputer dynamically establishes a temporary physical link through the network to another node closer to the receiving station listed in the address and transmits the packet there. When the packet arrives at that node, the contents of the packet are checked against the error correction code also contained in the data envelope to see if an error has been introduced. If so, a retransmission is requested. If not, the connection is broken. Each packet is thus routed from node to node, over a series of temporary connections, until it arrives at its destination. It has traveled over what is called a "virtual circuit," as seen in Figure 8–3.

Packet routes are chosen to minimize transmission delay and maximize use of the network's trunking resources. The result is that the packets making up a data transmission may each travel a different route to the receiving station. Some packets also are delayed by retransmissions. Thus, packets may arrive out of order at their ultimate destination and must be reassembled into their original order.

FIGURE 8–2

Early Packet Networks

Several small public packet switching networks arose in the 1960s and early 1970s. The first, built by Datran Corporation and subsequently taken over by Southern Pacific Communications and dedicated to private use, was unusual because it used microwave transmission techniques to carry data. The public data networks that followed used conditioned lines leased from the public telephone network carriers.

These early public data networks were not very successful, however. Most computer manufacturers were reluctant to provide the software necessary for interfacing to the various networks because each one defined its own network access and error correction protocols.

An industry standard was needed, and the most sophisticated model was the protocol used by the ARPANET network, which linked computer users at educational institutions involved in defense research across the United States. In 1976, the international standards body, CCITT, considerably modified that protocol and adopted it as recommendation X.25. With the implementation of the X.25 protocol by Telenet that year, the age of economical data communication over public networks began.

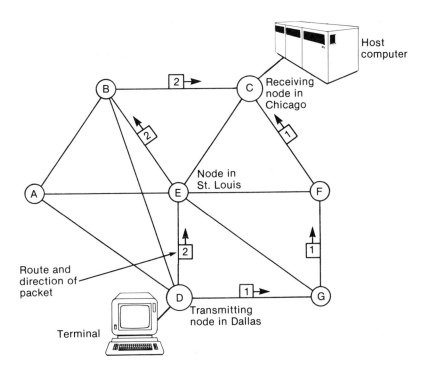

FIGURE 8–3: Individual packets of a message may travel over different routes to the destination as minicomputers at network nodes balance the load in the packet network's trunks. Thus, no circuit is dedicated to a transmission, since the circuit may change with each new packet. Instead of a dedicated circuit, a virtual circuit is established.

The X.25 Standard

LATER 1

LATER 2

HAND OUT OF X25

X.25 defines how devices connect to a packet switching network. It further specifies the physical form of transmission in terms of voltage levels, timing, and so on as well as the logical format of each packet, including the length of the data portion of the packet and the syntax of the address and control information. It defines how calls are set up and disconnected and how network errors are detected and corrected.

Access to the public data networks does not require hardware and software based on the X.25 standard. It is possible to make a telephone connection to one of the network nodes using a modem. The node takes the incoming data stream and converts that data into X.25 format for transmission over the network. The device that performs the conversion is called a packet assembler/disassembler (PAD).

The PAD accumulates incoming data in a storage area until it has enough for a packet and appends control information.

Because the packets that make up a message will travel different routes over the network, they might arrive out of order at the receiving node. X.25 is designed to provide sequential numbering so the PAD at the receiving node can assemble packets in the correct order.

A primary advantage of public VANs is that pricing is distance independent. For example, costs at off-peak times of $6 per connect hour can be compared with charges that run as high as $20 or more for WATS service and as much as $30 for regular telephone line service, depending on distance.

APPLICATIONS OF PUBLIC DATA NETWORKS

For any corporation that has to move data to various locations, the public data network is an option. These networks are more cost-effective than leased lines if the distance between devices to be connected is long and traffic volume is light. However, data transmission at rates higher than 9,600 bits per second is rarely used.

VANs offer a number of enhancements in addition to their basic transmission capabilities. Detailed usage information is provided in printed or machine-readable form for bill back, statistical usage analysis, and projection of future communication needs, for example. Most VANs also do protocol conversion that allows asynchronous microcomputers to access applications that normally require synchronous terminals. One of the VANs, Tymnet, has introduced a new protocol called X.PC that supports error checking over the local loop, thus eliminating the errors that creep in when users are linked to the packet switched network over ordinary phone lines. X.PC also provides simultaneous access to multiple host computer sessions over this single physical connection.

Many corporations use the VANs to access their own private computers, which are connected to the network most commonly through dedicated X.25 interfaces, supported by more than 60 different equipment vendors. VANs can automatically route a data call to alternate hosts if the primary host is down or lacks free ports. And any device on the network can connect to any other device, provided it is authorized to do so, making hosts that support public services as easy to access as a corporation's own hosts.

The application services provided by these public hosts are numerous. Examples include order entry, inventory control, credit verification, on-line data bases, computer services, manufacturing distribution systems, accounting and statistical analysis, data base management, computer-aided instruction, message switching, text editing, court scheduling, flight and reservations planning, and library management and many other home and business information services.

SUMMARY OF PUBLIC DATA NETWORK OFFERINGS

The number of packet-switched networks has grown significantly over the past few years. A few of the major ones and their key features include:

- ADP Autonet links major U.S. cities and interconnects with other networks to reach 45 countries.
- Tymnet, Inc. serves more than 500 metropolitan areas in the United States and numerous foreign countries.
- GTE Telenet is available in more than 300 U.S. cities, Canada, Mexico and more than 50 other international locations.
- Uninet, Inc., is available in 275 cities in the United States with links to foreign data networks.
- RCA Cylix provides dedicated services between major cities in the continental United States, Alaska and Canada.
- CompuServe Network Services is available in major metropolitan areas.
- Graphnet Freedom Network provides data and facsimile services at data speeds from 50 bits per second to 56 kilobits per second for directly connected terminals from major metropolitan areas.

- IBM Information Network is accessible from 16 U.S. cities.
- Infonet provides international data transport and purports to be the most extensive data network.

QUESTIONS FOR REVIEW:

1. What are public data networks? Value added networks?
2. What are some of the elements of packet switching?
3. Describe some early packet networks.
4. Describe the X.25 standard.
5. Describe some of the uses and benefits of VANs.

FOR DISCUSSION:

1. What are some home services offered by public data networks?
2. Why doesn't the PSN offer public data networks?

REFERENCES

ANONYMOUS. *Packet Switching—Concepts and Networks*. Datapro Research Corporation, October 1984.

ANONYMOUS. *Planning Network Development*. International Data Corporation, 1984.

BARTEE, THOMAS C. *Data Communications, Networks, and Systems*. Ma: Howard W. Sams & Co., Inc., 1985.

MARTIN, JAMES. *Future Developments in Telecommunications*. New York: Prentice-Hall, 1977.

MEADOW, CHARLES and TEDESCO, ALBERT. *Telecommunications for Management*. New York: McGraw-Hill, 1985.

Bypassing the Public Switched Networks

OBJECTIVES

- Understand the concept of "bypass."
- Understand the varieties of bypass.
- Match the suitability of various bypass schemes to transmission potential.
- Understand major bypass services.
- See how some companies are using bypass.

A GOOD STORY OF HOW WE GOT THERE & THE SITUATION ANALYSIS

The phone lines that connect office buildings to the public switched network were set up to handle voice, not data. Modems must be used to convert data to analog form for transmission on phone lines, and they typically carry data reliably no faster than 9.6 kilobits per second. Higher quality analog leased lines have long been available from the telephone company, but even these support modem speeds of no higher than 19.2 kilobits, and error rates remain relatively high compared with digital transmission. Moreover, such lines can be expensive, and their use for a single data connection may not be cost-effective.

In some cases, the public data network is a better alternative than the public switched network for data transmission. The packet switching networks offer reduced error rates and access to a large number of sites. But even with direct connection to a packet switched network, transmission speeds are usually limited to 9,600 bits per second. *COMMUNICATIONS DEVICES*

For companies with high volumes of high-speed data transmission, these deficiencies make the public switched network and public data network unattractive. Even if these networks can provide the needed data communication services, a backlog *CONFLICTS* of other users' orders might prevent them from installing the necessary facilities in a timely manner. Also, there is the issue of cost: The public switched and public data networks are rarely the most cost-effective alternatives. For these reasons, an increasing number of companies are bypassing the public switched and data networks.

REASONS FOR BYPASS

Bypass is not a new concept. It has been available for many years in the form of private line services provided by local phone companies. But as we will see, technological advances have made it possible to bypass the public networks using a number of increasingly cost-effective transmission media: These include satellite, CATV systems, private microwave, and fiber optic cable.

The competitive environment created by divestiture has also contributed to the growing trend toward the use of bypass technology by corporations. Indeed, the term *bypass technologies* could as easily be *competitive technologies*—i.e., cost-effective alternatives to using the telephone system.

Bypass has a slightly pejorative meaning, however, derived from a historical circumstance. Before divestiture, long-distance rates were artificially high and local residential rates artificially low. The idea was to subsidize local calling costs to make residential service feasible for everyone.

Divestiture's segmentation of the public switched network into the distinct local and long-distance operations was designed to provide a level playing field for all competitors; phone services were to be priced according to actual costs. Critics charged that this actual-cost basis for service charges would put local phone service out of the reach of the poor. Thus a fee was charged of the interexchange carriers for access to the local loop. Those carriers recouped the fee by adding it to long-distance calls that traveled the last mile through the local loop.

Ironically, a side effect of this charge for local loop access was to threaten local rates, because it provided an incentive for businesses to bypass the local loop. If enough businesses bypassed to avoid access fees, local telephone companies would be forced to raise rates for residential service. Thus, the fee designed to subsidize residential rates seemed likely to cause them to go up. (See Figure 9–1.)

Meanwhile, the FCC was fearful that bypass would undermine the financial viability of the local operating companies and thus cause a deterioration of local phone service. Thus, the

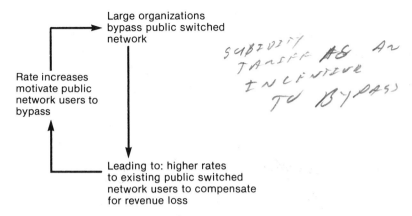

[handwritten annotation:] SUBSIDY TRANSFER AS AN INCENTIVE TO BYPASS

FIGURE 9–1: A bypass model—the reinforcing cycle based on rate increases.

FCC proposed to shift access charges to the local telephone subscribers to remove the incentive for bypass. Such a shift would lead to residential rate increases, however, and once again protests streamed in from consumer groups and state and congressional opponents. The FCC relented and delayed the institution of monthly access charges for single-line residential and business users.

As this is written, the future of access fees is still uncertain. However, it seems likely that strong political opposition will prevent the elimination of access fees that are added to long-distance calls that use the local loop. Thus, access fees, along with the limitations of local analog links, insure continuing incentive to establish digital links that bypass parts of the public switched network.

A survey of International Communication Association members (organizations with annual telecommunications budgets of $1 million or greater) showed that 45 percent of these large companies were using various bypass technologies for one or more of the following reasons:

[handwritten annotation:] TEST

- To save costs.
- To stabilize prices.
- To enter new markets, such as electronic banking.
- To use the communications network as a strategic weapon.

[handwritten annotation:] - BACKUP FACILITIES

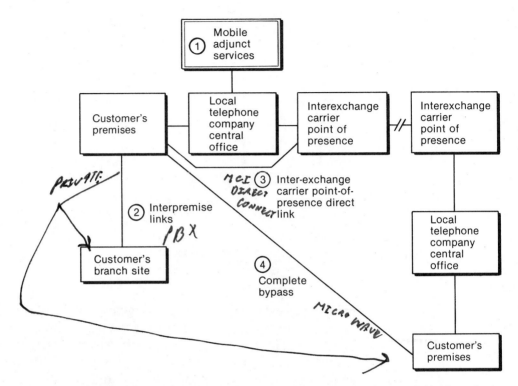

FIGURE 9–2: The four distinct types of bypass are shown: 1) Mobile adjunct services. 2) Interpremise links. 3) Interexchange carrier (IXC) point-of-presence (POP) direct link. 4) Complete bypass.

Although there are a number of disincentives—among them the need to make large capital outlays and the expense of labor-intensive maintenance—corporations with high-volume communication needs are considering bypass technology as a key method for cutting costs.

VARIETIES OF BYPASS TECHNOLOGY

To this point, we have simplified matters by lumping all of bypass together. There are actually four distinct types of bypass, as shown in Figure 9–2. These are:

- Mobile adjunct services, which extend the reach of the telephone system to mobile users.

- Interpremise links (and the so-called leaky PBX).
- Bypass of the local loop by establishing a direct link between the customer premises and a nearby IXC POP.
- Complete bypass, from customer premise to customer premise.

The Mobile Adjuncts

The public switched network has been extended in recent years by new, mobile services. These are lumped together with bypass technologies more because they are "competitive" with the public telephone network than because they circumvent the telephone network. Although cellular radio and radio paging were designed primarily to provide a mobile tie to the local loop for voice communication, mobile data communication is also becoming common. Indeed, the latest mobile technology, mobile satellite, is completely data oriented.

Interpremise Links

The PBX is considered a form of bypass technology when it provides switching services between business premises without need for the telephone network. As noted in Chapter Eight, PBXs with distributed architectures are capable of connecting widely separated premises with a unified phone system. Each of these premises contains PBX modules that are individual pieces of that unified PBX system. The link between modules of such a PBX system may be tie lines, T1 lines or proprietary fiber optic links, depending on the amount of traffic and the distance between modules.

The term *leaky* PBX refers to the fact that once a call has traveled over a private link to another module of a unified PBX system, it can "leak" out into the local loop. In effect, long-distance calls can be made without involving an interexchange carrier and are charged as if they were local calls.

Bypass of the Local Loop

Interexchange carriers and RBOCs are taking a hard look at the second type of bypass, which involves establishing direct links between large customers and long-distance networks. This bypass avoids access fees and may provide service better than that available through the local loop, resulting in better telecommunications at lower cost to corporations.

Complete Bypass

Corporations with very large networks may take the initiative and bypass not only the local loop but the interexchange carriers as well. Specialized telecommunication providers are also establishing such links.

BYPASS MEDIA

There are a number of media available with which to implement these various types of bypass, including fiber optic cable, satellite links, microwave links, and CATV coaxial cable systems. However, selection of media is less dependent on the variety of bypass being implemented than on a medium's appropriateness for carrying a particular volume of transmissions over a particular range of distances, as illustrated in Figure 9–3.

This categorization can become a bit confusing because one of the most common measures of high-volume transmission over any medium by any means also defines a particular transmission method over twisted-pair lines. Thus we begin with an explanation of the so-called T1 line and the measurement it defines, the T1 rate.

The T Carriers

One of the main measures of the capacity of a particular bypass medium is in terms of multiples of the basic transmission capability of a T1 line. T1 lines, first used internally by AT&T in 1962, are composed of two twisted-wire pairs. Instead of carrying the usual analog voice conversations, however, they carry 24 digitized conversations at a 1.544 mbps rate.

As we mentioned, however, T1-like service can be provided over most media, including terrestrial microwave, fiber optic cable, or satellite links.

T1's provision for 24 separate digital channels means voice, data, and video can be carried through the same physical link.

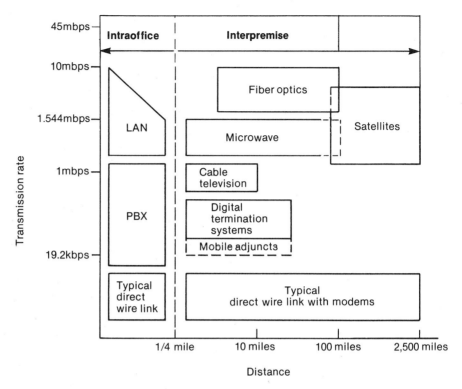

FIGURE 9–3: Bypass alternatives mapped to cost-effective distances and transmission rates. Note that there are considerable differences in transmission rates among these bypass media.

Unfortunately, the original T1 specification would not allow dividing or "submultiplexing" any one of the 24 channels—any data connection had to use a full 64 kilobits per second even if it ran at 1.2 kilobits—but that situation has been corrected by AT&T. Indeed, AT&T has offered a number of variations on the basic T1 channel, first as part of its dataphone digital service (DDS) in 1977, later as part of its high capacity terrestrial digital service (HCTDS) and Accunet T1.5.

AT&T has also defined a T-carrier hierarchy to accommodate transmission rates higher than 1.544 megabits per second. T2 is a scheme for multiplexing four T1 lines together; T3 lines carry the equivalent of 28 T1 lines; T4 equals 6 T3s or 168 T1s, as shown in Figure 9–4.

The earliest use of leased T1 lines was to connect two cus-

Type of transmission facility	Data rate	Name of digital signal	Number of multiplexed T1 lines	Number of voice channels transmitted
T 1	1.544 mbps	DS—1	1	24
T 2	6.3 mbps	DS—2	4	96
T 3	44.7 mbps	DS—3	28	672
T 4	274.2 mbps	DS—4	168	4032

FIGURE 9–4: The T carrier hierarchy.

tomer premises. By the mid-1980s, however, 50 percent of AT&T's T1 circuits were used to bypass the local loop, connecting customer premises to a local office. In general, reaching a central office that supports AT&T's interexchange T1 service is cheaper and easier in the more densely populated states, but it is generally available nationwide. Many of the local telephone companies also supply T1 services in the local loop.

The popularity of T1 lines for bypass has been increasing steadily. In 1985, the number of AT&T customer T1 circuits tripled, for example; one RBOC, Pacific Bell, saw its number of T1 customers increase sixfold.

T1 lines are expected to get stiff competition from the proposed integrated services digital network (discussed in the next chapter). Today, however, the strong market presence of T1 indicates it will coexist with the roughly equivalent ISDN primary access service at least through the 1990s.

As we mentioned, T1-like or any other service can be provided over microwave, fiber optic cable, and satellite links. We will discuss these media after we discuss analog transmission using CATV.

Cable TV

CATV technology is appropriate for the transmission of high-speed data (up to T1 rates) over relatively short distances (5 to 10 miles). The acronym CATV comes from a phrase that is misleading today (community antenna television), although it was accurate when the first system was installed. That was in 1949, when an enterprising TV repairman ran coaxial cable from an antenna on a mountaintop into a village in an Appalachian val-

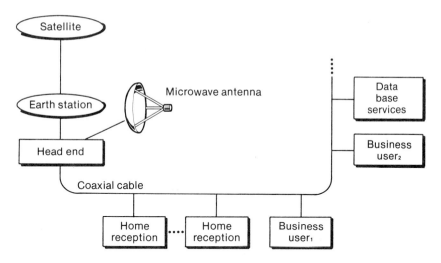

FIGURE 9–5: An illustration of a cable TV network with business users. Satellites offer businesses the possible transmission and reception of data, along with television program feeds. Microwave antennas are used for line-of-sight transmission and reception.

ROUTE THE SIGNAL THROUGH THE EXCESS CAPACITY OF CATV

ley with poor reception. Today, most cable TV systems involve no community antenna. Instead, programming gets distributed to the originating point of the system via satellite feeds. Figure 9–5 illustrates the main components of CATV.

Although CATV once was limited to rural areas with poor receptions, it is now in use in most urban areas as well to provide superior reception and additional programming. A single CATV coaxial cable can carry as many as 60 channels, and despite an expansion of programming material available from subscription networks, all-news networks, sports networks, public access programming, and so forth, most systems will still have a great deal of excess capacity on the cable.

The primary advantage of putting data on a cable television system is that the system is already in place in more than 40 percent of premises in the United States and is generating revenue from subscribers. Routing feeders from large corporations into this system is all that is necessary to take advantage of such systems' significant amount of excess capacity.

CATV technology is ideal for data; systems can carry as much as 1.5 megabits per second of data over distances as great as 10 to 20 miles without degradation. Coaxial cable used in such systems is extremely good for carrying integrated voice, video, and data and becomes relatively inexpensive if the total volume of traffic is high enough. Telecommunication specialists expect CATV operators to skim the cream of the market and provide subscribers with bundles of 56 kilobits to 1.544 megabits per second links.

CATV cable systems broadcast radio frequency signals using radio frequency modems over coaxial cable much as broadband local area networks do. The source of the main broadcast in most systems is typically at one end, called a "head end." The system fans out from the head end in a system of trunks and feeders. Amplifiers are required about every 2,000 feet and whenever the trunk cable is bridged by a feeder.

Many CATV systems use only a single cable; the bandwidth available on that cable is divided to provide bidirectional communication. Three frequency splits are possible, as described below and shown in Figure 9–6.

Subsplit, which provides capacity for 56 standard 6 mHz channels on a forward path and four on the return path. For data, this translates into 208 T1-rate forward channels and 20 T1-rate return channels. That capacity can also be allocated between TV and data as desired in 6 mHz chunks. Subsplit has been the most popular scheme with the CATV industry; it allows two-way communications—making possible interactive applications such as teletext—yet TV channels can occupy their normal frequency assignments.

· Midsplit provides more bandwidth on the return path. This is the most commonly used format for data-only coaxial networks because the increased bandwidth for the return allows for more full-duplex data communication links.

· High-split provides even more bandwidth on the return path for two-way communications. Because the TV stations 7 through 13 are not supported in high-split configurations, its use in a CATV system requires installation of converters.

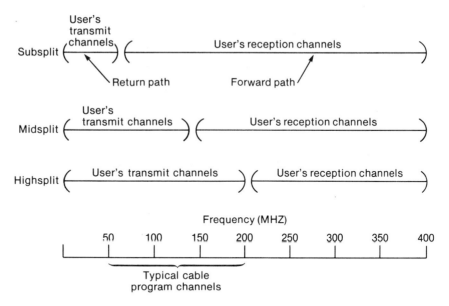

FIGURE 9–6: Single-cable broadband LANs (CATV-based) use one of three frequency schemes: subsplit, midsplit, or highsplit.

CATV can provide two of the four types of bypass. In the example of the large New York bank we will consider soon, the Manhattan Cable system links several premises. MCI Telecommunications, on the other hand, is considering the use of CATV systems to bypass the local loop.

However, CATV has no advantage over the use of ordinary phone lines for low-speed, interactive terminal traffic, which typically runs at 9,600 bits per second. The expense of the radio frequency modems needed to transmit data on a CATV system limits its advantage to high-speed links. If there is a problem with using CATV technology, it is that many of the approximately 6,000 CATV system operators in the United States may choose not to provide data services. There is simply not enough demand for high-speed links in their service areas.

Private Microwave Links

Private microwave links are cost-effective for transmissions of 10 miles and more and can be used to establish direct digital

Courtesy of AT&T

FIGURE 9–7: A typical picture of a microwave tower.

links to an IXC POP. Although limited by the earth's curvature or terrain because of the need for line-of-sight transmission paths, the use of repeaters can make microwave systems viable for links of hundreds of miles. Microwave is often used to skip from mountaintop to mountaintop, over lakes, and across rough terrain. It is equally useful in establishing communication links between buildings within a city or region.

The biggest advantage of microwave is the low fixed costs involved. A microwave system typically costs $100,000 to $200,000 per location. That includes the transmitter, receiver, multiplexing equipment for up to 1,344 voice circuits, antenna, local power, and installation. A microwave tower is shown in Figure 9–7.

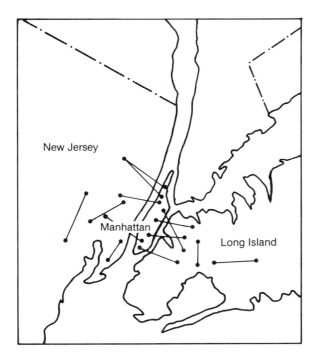

FIGURE 9–8: Congestion of microwave beams in the metropolitan New York area. As a result, many C-band (4–6 gHz) earth stations for use with satellites are miles away.

Typically, microwave equipment is an alternative to phone company T1 circuits. The expense can be justified against a single T1 link given a two-year payback and even more quickly if more T1 links are needed. In the mid-1980s, the ratio of T1 terrestrial lines (earthbound wires) to microwave links was 7:3 but falling rapidly.

Microwave is not without drawbacks, however. The need for a line-of-sight transmission path can eliminate it as an alternative in congested metropolitan areas. Even when a transmission path is available, permission to use it is needed.

Microwave is also not completely reliable. Large buildings and hills may cause interference, as can frequency congestion in downtown areas. Figure 9–8 shows the congestion in metropolitan New York. There is also the problem of rain and snow, which interferes with high-frequency microwave transmissions. The seriousness of this problem with inclement weather depends on location and length of the link. An 18 gHz microwave system that transmits over a distance of 15 miles in Phoenix will be usable 99.99 percent of the time. If you want that level of service in Houston, where it rains quite frequently, links will be limited to no more than five or six miles.

The primary difference between microwave transmission and ordinary radio is that smaller and cheaper antennas can be used. Moreover, microwaves behave much as light waves do. They can be focused with parabolic dishes and reflected around obstructions with passive reflectors. This means microwave stations can operate on the same frequency in close proximity to each other with little interference.

Unfortunately, the similarity to light extends to undesirable characteristics, such as the just-mentioned interference caused by bad weather. There is significant attenuation of signal strength caused by the absorption of frequencies higher than 10 gHz by heavy rain. (Absorption is greatest in areas of rainfall with large drop sizes, such as the Gulf Coast and the southeastern United States.) Multipath reflections, caused by atmospheric conditions such as temperature inversions or heavy cloud layers, can also cause fading of microwave signals.

Microwave systems are either analog or digital. Digital microwave has an advantage: Regeneration of the signal, rather than amplification, allows digital microwave to provide the same low error rates that T carrier provides. Unlike analog microwave, which becomes progressively noisier, digital microwave remains relatively quiet until the number of errors in transmission exceeds the scheme's ability of error-correcting circuitry to handle them, which causes the link to suddenly "crash."

The data-handling capacity of digital microwave radio is approximately 12 times greater than analog equipment. A single voice channel can be used for up to 56 kilobits per second of data, for example. Thus, on a 384-channel radio link it is possible to carry 21.5 megabits of data. And unlike analog microwave, digital microwave can carry voice and data in any combination without worry of interference.

Digital Termination Systems

One of the main problems with microwave transmission—frequency congestion in metropolitan areas—can be overcome for short-distance links with a technology known as digital ter-

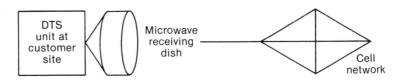

FIGURE 9–9: A simplified depiction of a DTS network.

SERVICES TO LOCAL AREAS

mination systems (DTS). By dividing a metropolitan area into cells and using low-power transmission, the same microwave frequencies can be reused in alternate cells without interference. Thus DTS is suitable for intracity transmission. This alternative to the local loop is illustrated in Figure 9–9.

Interest in DTS is widespread. Possible uses include:

③

• As a "last mile" local link bypass for specialized interexchange carriers trying to avoid local access charges and the rising cost of leasing lines from local telephone companies.

② *TO PRIVATE NETWORK* ④

• As a vehicle for high-speed data transmission to packet switching networks such as Tymnet and Telenet.

APPLICATIONS

Generally, DTS is cost-effective for data transmission in the 56 to 488 kilobits per second range, placing its effective capacity between that of ordinary phone lines and CATV cable. It is most suitable for high-speed document distribution, video conferencing, remote terminal-to-host transmission, and high-speed trunks linking local area networks.

PERFORMANCE CRITERIA

DTS offers links with error rates that are several orders of magnitude lower than those of analog phone lines. Just as in other microwave-based transmission, weather can interfere, but reliable links (defined as links with less than two minutes of system outage in any given month) can be approximately 2 miles in the heavy rain regions of the southern United States to more than 10 miles in the arid areas of the country.

BACK UP

The typical DTS unit installed at a user site is not much larger than an office typewriter. The microwave receiving dish attached to it may be installed behind a window. Because of its transportability, DTS equipment can be used for temporary installations and emergency services.

DTS is one of several media that can be useful for the last few miles of satellite-based links to avoid the satellite system bottleneck that can occur when the higher throughput of a satellite channel has to be fed through local loops operating at 9,600 bits per second.

Fiber Optic Links

Both the local telephone companies and the companies trying to bypass the local loop want to put the enormous capacity of fiber optic cable to use. It is an ideal medium for carrying high volumes of high-speed data between a customer premise and an IXC POP, although only the largest customers generate enough data traffic to make it cost-effective. The point at which it becomes effective, therefore, is highly sensitive to the level of access charges that must be borne by the interexchange carriers.

NEW LINES

The greatest attraction of fiber optic technology is the bandwidth of light. The frequency of visible light is in the thousands of gigahertz.

HIGH CAPACITY

Current techniques for encoding information using light waves get nowhere near that theoretical limit. Capacities of 375 T1 carriers and more have been achieved, however, and all on a cable much thinner than coaxial or twisted-pair cable. A sample of fiber optic cable is shown in Figure 9–10.

Fiber optic technology has a number of advantages over using copper wire or coaxial cable for telecommunication. These include:

BENEFITS

- Potential bandwidth greater than any other type of system, including coax.
- A single cable can act as the medium for all current data, voice, and video needs and provides room for expansion without laying additional cable.
- Harsh or noisy environments do not affect the signal. Indeed, optical cable can be run nearly anywhere: It even withstands temperatures up to 1,000° centigrade and is not susceptible to lightning strikes. The only "must" is to protect it against water seepage, because freezing can physically interrupt the transmission path.
- Reliable data transmission. Lower error rates than other media.
- Cheaper than copper with the price of copper rising.
- Uses less electricity and fewer repeaters.

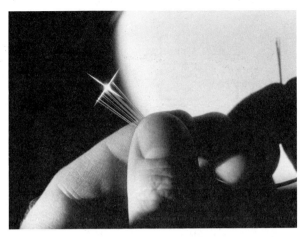

Courtesy of AT&T Bell Laboratories

FIGURE 9–10: Twenty-four hair-thin fibers like the one shown are now used to carry voice, data, and video traffic under streets of Chicago and other cities.

- Surreptitiously installed taps can be detected, making fiber optic relatively safe for carrying confidential data.

TREND

The primary application of fiber optic technology during the mid-1980s was for long-haul telephone communications, but eventually fiber optic cable is expected to become the dominant terrestrial communications medium in the United States and throughout the world. Certainly this lightwave transmission technology will play a major role in bypassing the local loop. Indeed, the RBOCs are looking to fiber to provide video, data, and telephone services for the integrated services digital network that may replace today's analog public switched network.

A fiber optic link consists of a transmitter, a fiber optic cable, and a receiver or detector, and other components. The complete end-to-end use of fiber optic cable is depicted in Figure 9–11. The transmitter accepts analog or digital input and projects it along the cable in the form of light pulses; the detector accepts the light input and converts it back to analog or digital form.

How

The transmitter has to use a light source that emits a bright, highly directional light and is able to be turned on and off

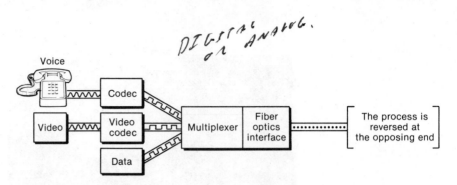

FIGURE 9–11: A diagram showing how voice, data, and video travel on optical fibers.

quickly. LEDs like the ones used in pocket calculators are used for less demanding applications; the highly directional, powerful light of lasers that can turn themselves on and off millions of times a second are better for higher bandwidth links.

At either end, a multiplexing technique allows the data streams from many end-user devices to be merged onto a single cable. Time division multiplexing (explained in Chapters Four and Six) or wave division multiplexing create multiple channels to carry the various signals. Wave division multiplexing simply uses different wavelengths, or colors, or light to carry different signals. Diodes sensitive to only a single color of light decode the separate signals at the receiving end of the link.

Fiber Optic Cable. At the core of fiber optic cable is a piece of glass or plastic, stretched thin as a human hair, that serves as a waveguide for light. That core is wrapped in a second layer of glass or plastic called the cladding, which keeps the light traveling down the cable by the reflection or refraction. Finally, around those is a jacket that protects against moisture, crushing, burrowing animals, and other environmental factors; different jackets are designed for specific environments. Cable designed for suspension in harsh aerial environments, for example, incorporates a steel-reinforced cable to strengthen against wind and ice formations. For any kind of harsh environment, the jacket may be surrounded by plastic or other hard casing for additional protection.

There are three types of optical fiber cable: multimode step-index, multimode graded index, and single mode, as depicted in Figure 9–12. They each carry light in a different manner, and

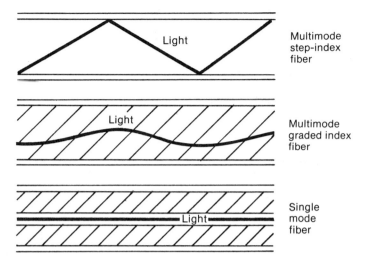

FIGURE 9–12: The three main varieties of optical fiber.

there are major differences in their bandwidths, ease of installation, and ease of manufacture, as follows:

- Multimode step index, the oldest, is found in short-distance, low bandwidth systems (10 to 100 mHz/km). Its core is surrounded by glass cladding with a lower refractive index. Thus, at the boundary there is a sharp step in the refractive index that causes light waves to bend sharply, totally reflecting them back toward the center of the core. With large diameters approaching a millimeter, the rays have a lot of room for bouncing back and forth. Each wave can thus take many different paths of varying lengths as it makes its way down the cable. As a result, the light pulses slowly spread out, or disperse, as they travel along, which reduces the potential bandwidth (governed by the number of pulses per second that may be sent down the cable). Pulse spreading, as it is called, worsens as the fiber core increases in diameter.

   The advantage of multimode step index is that it is easy to splice and install. There is no need to worry about alignment of the core.
- Multimode graded index cable guides light through refraction, instead of reflection. The refractive index of the

material making up the core gradually decreases from the center outward to and including the cladding. The boundary between core and cladding is thus not clearly defined. Instead of a step in the refractive index, there is a slope. Light heading out from the center is gradually bent back toward the center of the core as it hits material with a lower refractive index. Although light waves still travel many different paths through the cable, on average they travel nearly the same distance, minimizing pulse spreading. Another advantage is that graded index is cheaper to manufacture than multimode step index cable.

With its higher bandwidth (200 to 1,000 mHz/km, and order of magnitude greater than the older variety cable) and lower cost, multimode graded index cable became the cable of choice for long-distance links. It was used by AT&T in the more than 40,000 miles of fiber optic telecommunication links installed by 1984. By 1990, 40 percent of AT&T's network will be fiber optic, although much of it is likely to be the latest kind of cable, called single mode.

• Single mode cable was the last to be developed. It has extraordinary bandwidth (50 gHz/km) but is difficult to splice and to transfer light into because it is so small. The principle is to limit the core diameter to a few micrometers, thus limiting the light waves to a single pathway, eliminating pulse spreading.

Its current expense to manufacture and install limits its use to high-bandwidth applications with a need for long distances between repeaters: undersea transmission, for example. Its bandwidth makes it a logical candidate, however, for long-haul integrated services digital networks that include voice and data, teleconferencing, and broadcast over a single fiber optic link.

Installation of fiber optic cable is similar to other cable installation except for the problems raised by splices. When connecting fiber optic cables, the fiber cores must be precisely aligned with a minimum amount of space separating the ends of the two cables (otherwise too much light is lost). The introduction of easier-to-use splicing technology in the next few years eventually should make single mode cable the best choice for most applications.

Courtesy of AT&T Bell Laboratories

FIGURE 9–13: An artist's conception of a satellite in orbit around the earth.

Satellite Links

T V NETWORKS ↓ CATV

BYPASS

Satellites have been used primarily to carry TV programming. Today, the wide dispersal of programming from the various television networks and other sources via satellite is what makes it possible for so many CATV networks to carry a large number of channels.

For data, satellite transmission is cost-effective only over long distances. It is therefore a vehicle primarily for customer premise to customer premise bypass.

A communication satellite is, in essence, a microwave relay in the sky. (See Figure 9–13.) Satellites appear to hang motionless in the sky because they are in geosynchronous orbits. That is, they are in orbital paths approximately 22,300 miles above the equator where their orbiting speed exactly matches the speed of the earth's rotation. Because they are so high, a satellite's broadcast range can easily cover as much as one fourth of the earth's surface.

Satellites began to be taken seriously when a Bell Labs study in the 1960s showed that a few powerful satellites could handle more traffic than the entire AT&T long-distance network and would cost a fraction of terrestrial facilities.

The microwave equipment employed for satellite transmission needs to be much more powerful than that used for terrestrial microwave links, which as we have seen are limited in length by the truncation of line-of-sight paths by the earth's curvature and terrain.

The equipment that receives a signal, amplifies it, changes its frequency, and retransmits it is called a transponder. Most satellites have more than one. (Each of the RCA SATCOM's 24 transponders can handle 60 megabits per second, for example, or a total of 1.44 gigabits per second). Transponders receive microwave signals in a given frequency band and retransmit them at a different frequency to prevent the powerful retransmission from interfering with weaker, incoming signals.

The bandwidth of satellite communications is very large. (Only fiber optic has the potential to exceed it.) There is room for at least 38 satellites in geocentric orbit over North America, with typical data capacities of from 432 mHz to more than 1 gHz per satellite. Such capacity is best used by a constant heavy transmission, such as the T-channel voice circuits and television broadcast traffic that dominated early satellite use. Today, a great deal of satellite traffic is composed of digital signals for voice, data, and video. The data portion is most often bulk message delivery and batch file transfer, although new, packet-oriented protocols are making possible interactive communications over satellite links without wasting bandwidth.

There are three bands available for satellite transmission, each with special characteristics that make it useful for particular applications:

- C-band, with uplinks in the 6 gHz range and downlinks in the 4 gHz range, is the most commonly used. C-band transmissions spread quickly, making them useful for broadcasts that must cover a wide area. However, that spreading makes the signals relatively weak, requiring the use of large, expensive earth stations. The atmosphere is nearly transparent in the 4 to 6 gHz range; thus C-band transmissions can pass through fog and rain without interference. This makes the band useful for terrestrial microwave links, however, and there is a great

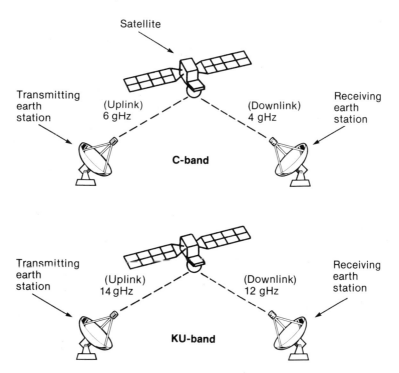

FIGURE 9–14: Most satellites use C-band or Ku-band, usually, for transmission.

deal of C-band congestion in major metropolitan areas. Thus C-band earth stations must be located many miles from cities and have expensive terrestrial cable or microwave links to user sites.

- Ku-band transmissions use uplinks in the 14 gHz range and downlinks in the 12 gHz range. They lend themselves to strong, narrow broadcast beams, making them ideal for point-to-point use. Unlike C-band transmission, Ku band is immune to interference from terrestrial microwave; it can be downlinked to earth stations in the center of cities. (C-band and Ku-band links are shown in Figure 9–14.) Moreover, those earth stations can be relatively small and inexpensive because the tightly beamed signals are strong. Thus, Ku band has brought satellite communications to the roofs of subscribers, making satellite links more attractive for use in private networks.

Unfortunately, Ku-band signals are extremely sensitive to interference from the heavy rainfall associated with thunderstorms. Two Ku-band earth stations can be installed several miles apart to circumvent this problem (they will rarely be affected by storms at the same time).

- Ka band, with uplinks in the 30 gHz range and downlinks in the 20 gHz range, is the latest technology. The Ka signal can be beamed even more tightly than Ku band, making even smaller, less expensive earth stations possible.

The increasing demand for satellite communication has created a need to share the available satellite channels. This is a common requirement for communications trunking, but satellite links complicate the necessary coordination because users of a single transponder may be scattered over a wide area.

An early attempt at solving the problem, the Aloha protocol, assigned the bandwidth of a single satellite channel at random with provisions for retransmission in case of collisions caused by two earth stations trying to use a channel at once. A refinement of this technique interleaves transmission from many different earth stations by preassigning time slots for transmission. Very high-speed burst modems are used to achieve reasonably fast data rates despite the brief duration of each time-slot transmission.

Other unique characteristics of satellite transmission include:

- A 270 millisecond (approximately one-quarter second) propagation delay as the signal travels the 45,000-plus miles to and from a satellite. Some transmission techniques require acknowledgment by the receiver that a "packet" has been received correctly before the next packet is sent, resulting in unacceptable throughput over satellite links because most of the time is spent waiting for acknowledgment.
- Transmission cost is independent of distance. That means a regional computer center can be set up anywhere within range of the satellite without affecting transmission costs.
- Even Ka-band transmissions spread and reach many earth stations; coding and encryption is necessary to insure security and to limit reception of the signal to a single earth station.

Satellite Costs. A typical earth station with access to one satellite channel will cost $200,000 to $300,000, although newer technology, smaller scale systems can be purchased for less than $100,000. Very Small Aperture Terminals (VSAT), the latest technology, which uses a four-foot earth station, costs less than $5,000, but it is only a substitute for using a modem to send data over phone lines because it can be used to send and receive only low-speed data.

As an alternative to a leased T1 terrestrial line, the payback period for satellites over a distance of 500 miles is approximately two years. That payback period is shortened if there is a need to broadcast data to several points: It is quite simple to broadcast from one location to many using satellite technology. The greater the number of downlinks from a single uplink, the more cost-effective a satellite channel becomes.

Some corporations are making satellite transmission cost-effective by reselling use of their satellite earth stations and leased satellite channels to smaller companies.

Cost aside, satellites have a major advantage over other bypass technologies. In many cases, an earth station can be installed on the customer's premises much more quickly than other forms of bypass can be put into operation.

Teleports

Although the option of installing any of the bypass technologies just discussed is usually open only to large corporations, the opportunity for saving on telecommunication costs through bypass is available even to small businesses via "smart buildings" or "shared tenancy PBXs" (discussed in Chapter Six) and a new development called teleports.

Teleports are business parks that offer a lower-cost alternative to the services of the local telephone company and, to a limited degree, the interexchange carriers. In effect, the teleport is an interexchange carrier. The Washington, D.C., teleport, for example, owns a 1,000-mile mirowave distribution system with ties to IXC POPs in 20 locations. It also is tied to satellite service with eight geographically distributed earth stations. Buildings within the business park may include a leaky PBX that is shared among tenants. The San Francisco Bay Area teleport is shown in Figure 9–15.

Courtesy of Bay Area Teleport

FIGURE 9–15: San Francisco Bay Area Teleport's control center and central microwave terminal site are located together in a 138-foot-high structure at Harbor Bay Business Park.

In short, the real estate developer bundles integrated voice and data services that utilize all three types of bypass into the lease package. Users enjoy the convenience of one bill for all communication services.

SPECIALIZED BYPASS SERVICES

Four services are available that bypass the public networks. The first provides continuous data service that would be too expensive using the telephone network; the other three provide mobile adjuncts to the public networks. These services can be compared, as shown in Figure 9–16.

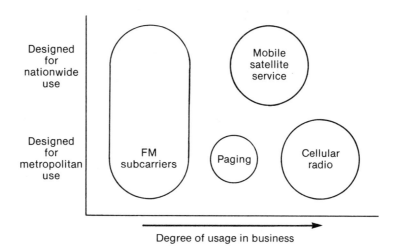

FIGURE 9–16: A comparison of bypass services that are growing in popularity.

Cellular Mobile Radio

Cellular radio allows users to conduct business by telephone from wherever they happen to be; it is a way to make productive use of time spent stuck in traffic or when commuting to a distant location.

Ordinary radio telephones have been available for many years, but their use was not widespread because of the limited number of frequencies available. In New York, for example, only several thousand users could be accommodated, and waits for service were often as long as 20 minutes.

The newer, cellular mobile radio service makes it possible to reuse the few available frequencies and thus accommodate a far greater number of subscribers. Cellular radio works by scattering a number of low-power transmitter/receiver base stations throughout a metropolitan area. Transmissions to and from car or briefcase radio phones to the various base stations are passed to the local loop. Each base station has enough power to send and receive reliably in only a single cell in a honeycomb pattern of cells. Adjacent cells use different frequencies to avoid interference, but a frequency can be reused in a nonadjacent cell. A sophisticated computer system assigns a frequency to

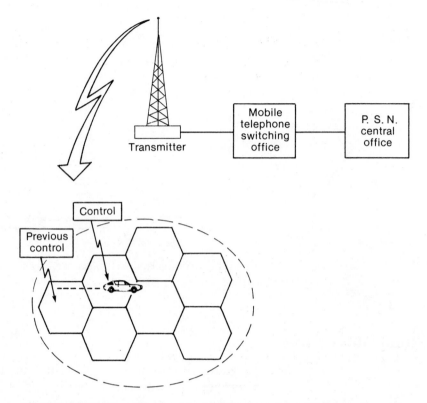

FIGURE 9–17: A cellular mobile telephone system divides an area into hexagonal cells. Each cell has a different set of frequencies than its neighbors. Calls are transferred to different control centers upon crossing cell boundaries.

each subscriber requesting service within a particular cell; as that subscriber drives across the boundaries between cells, the computer "hands off" the call from one cell to another by assigning the call to a new frequency in the new cell, as shown in Figure 9–17.

The result is a tremendous increase in capacity over earlier citywide systems. New York can now handle 100,000 to 200,000 subscribers with no wait for service.

Cellular mobile radio is relatively expensive, but nevertheless has proved surprisingly popular. The need to be constantly in touch even when commuting is a far greater motivation than cellular operators in Chicago expected, for example. Ameritech

Mobile Phone was forced to double its projection of the number of subscribers for the first year.

Most cellular radio systems were constructed in regular patterns, with smaller cells where service demand was expected to be highest. To some extent, traffic patterns were overlooked. A few systems may suffer from that oversight as the exceptional traffic experienced at rush hour at major interchanges overloads the local cell capacity, causing lines to be blocked. System operators are responding by splitting such cells, thus restoring the proper level of service.

The technology that provides voice service can be used for data service as well. The primary technical problem comes with truly mobile operation. A voice link may not be disrupted when the system's computer passes a subscriber from a channel in one cell to a channel in the next cell. Data links, however, are much more sensitive. The hand-off causes an intolerable error rate and resulting distortion of transmission.

The three different technologies that may provide cellular radio data service are the following:

- Modems can be used with cellular radios, establishing a data link similar to that available through voice lines with a personal computer and modem. This option would not improve on local loop service except for the provision of mobility. A typical application might be telemetry of vital signs from an ambulance to an emergency room.
- Cellular radio sideband transmission, technically similar to FM SCA, may provide subcarrier services for data as a low-cost adjunct to existing cellular radio operations.
- The arrival of ISDN's end-to-end digital network eventually may prompt migration from current analog cellular radio systems to a digital system better suited to data transmission.

FM Subcarriers (FM SCA)

FM radio stations use only the center of the bandwidth assigned to them by the FCC. It is possible to broadcast on two subchannels of 9,600 bits per second each that exist on either side of the primary signal without undue degradation of that signal. For many years, however, the FCC limited the use of these subchannels to the transmission of private music services. The Muzak heard in department stores, for example, is transmitted using FM subcarrier technology.

In 1983 the FCC opened the use of FM subcarriers for the transmission of data. Equipment installed at the FM station's transmitter allows one-way point-to-multipoint broadcasting of data at up to 9,600 bits per second within an area roughly equivalent to the broadcast range of the FM station.

Current rental fees charged by radio stations for use of FM SCA are excessive, however. Unless an application requires continuous updating of information—providing "ticker tape" financial market quotations to investors, for example—FM SCA is generally too expensive to consider.

Most FM SCA broadcasts are nationwide in scope. In a typical application, data is carried through a satellite link to an earth station in each major metropolitan area. From there, the data are fed to special broadcast equipment at an FM station for transmission over the station's subcarrier.

At the user site, a special receiver that looks like an ordinary modem with an antenna translates the FM subcarrier signal into a standard format, such as RS-232, and passes the data to a local computer system or printer.

Mobile Satellite Service

Mobile satellite service extends the kind of service provided by cellular radio in a specific metropolitan area to the entire continental United States. Instead of a honeycomb pattern of cellular base stations, MSS achieves broad coverage with only a single repeater that happens to be 22,000 miles high. Figure 9–18 illustrates the concepts within MSS.

MSS is expected to be data oriented from the beginning. Mobile voice communication is possible but would be very expensive. Only a few thousand voice users could be served by a satellite link, as compared with several hundred thousand data users. Voice transmission would also require a 3-foot diameter earth station on the top of vehicles as compared with a small antenna for data services.

MSS will be used in conjunction with a global positioning

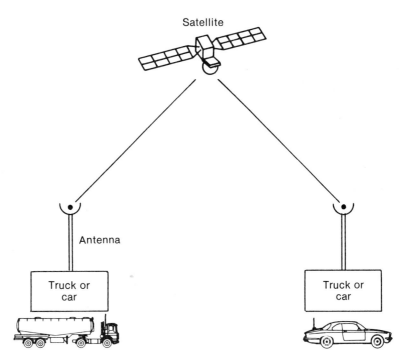

FIGURE 9–18: Mobile satellite service allows direct lines between mobile vehicles via satellite up-links and down-links.

system (GPS) scheduled for deployment before 1990 by the Department of Defense. MSS receivers with links to the GPS will be locatable to within 100 meters of their position. This facility will make MSS popular, for example, with firms that need to track their interstate trucking fleets.

Radio Paging

Paging is a means of notifying an individual who is away from his or her normal base location that there is a need to call in. Paging companies provide service to large metropolitan areas. See Figure 9–19 for a schematic depiction of a paging service.

The most primitive form of paging is the simple "beeper." Although the information content of such a beeper signal is small, it is useful. Doctors can be reached on the golf course in case

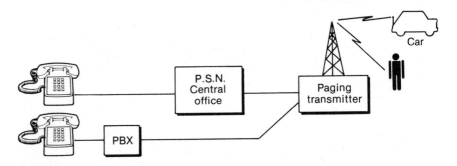

FIGURE 9–19: Radio paging systems can help locate persons away from telephone contact.

of emergencies. Salesmen or any field representative can be informed of changes that will affect their schedules, saving money by avoiding lost time or unnecessary travel. (Pages are prone to poor reception as the subscriber moves about, however. The presence of a building can block signals; at frequencies in the 800 to 900 mHz range, for example, reception in a modern office building can be wiped out by closing metallic blinds.)

The introduction of voice capabilities made paging a true messaging medium, however. Although bandwidth limits keep the voice messages short, the paged person could at least be told to call a particular number.

The next generation of paging devices were digital, with the ability to display short messages on an LCD screen.

In the early 1980s, radio paging's potential was restricted because it was a strictly local service, limited to a single metropolitan area. A 1982 FCC decision opened the possibility for nationwide paging, although at this writing no such system is in operation.

EXAMPLES OF BYPASS

There are a number of compelling reasons for a large corporation—and sometimes even a small company—to consider using the various bypass technologies. A look at how the technologies are being used by five corporations illustrates some of these reasons.

Hewlett-Packard's International Bypass Network

Hewlett-Packard (HP) has such a dispersed sales and manufacturing operation—and places such a heavy emphasis on data communication—that it had little choice but to bypass the U.S. telephone company for data and intracompany voice communications. The phone company simply cannot do the job economically; in most cases, HP has instituted complete, premise-to-premise bypass.

The oldest of HP's several discrete networks is its own Telnet system. Designed to carry voice and data among 70 HP sites, it uses private lines leased from local phone companies for intercity traffic and lines leased from a variety of interexchange carriers for traffic that crosses LATA boundaries. Besides saving 20 percent to 30 percent on telecommunication costs, Telnet eliminates the need to dial area codes—anyone on the network can be reached by dialing seven or fewer digits.

In the 1970s and early 1980s, HP used minicomputers to store and forward batches of inventory and sales data as well as electronic mail to minicomputers in its main office. Batches were forwarded to the next node in the network only when traffic on Telnet lines was low. The trade-off for the economy of utilizing only excess capacity of the Telnet network was that data took anywhere from 20 minutes to two days to reach its destination. A new, more efficient system called ROUTS was evolving to take its place in the 1980s.

The heart of HP's worldwide network, in and around the San Francisco Bay Area where HP is headquartered, consists of microwave links installed by HP in 1984. It didn't take long for HP to begin to push the capacity of those links, however. Negotiations are now under way for the local RBOC to build a fiber optic network to replace the microwave links.

HP utilizes private links to GTE Telenet's packet switching network for interactive data applications. Eventually, however, HP plans to switch to its own private X.25 network as the backbone for all data transmissions, both interactive and "batch." To give an idea of the total volume of HP's data traffic, its private data network, when completed, will rival the volume and size of each of the two largest public data networks, Telenet and Tymnet.

Eventually, Hewlett-Packard plans to move most of its telecommunications, data, video, and intracorporate voice traffic to a private, completely digital network. When completed, HP's network will circle the globe with circuits of T1 bandwidth or greater. Overflow from that network (during peaks of video transmission, for example) will be handled by public ISDN facilities that should become generally available during the 1990s.

HP's telecommunications system will be discussed in greater detail in Chapter Seventeen.

Hercules Goes Satellite

Hercules, a leading specialty chemical company, has 11 sites in the United States and overseas. In 1980, the company leaped into bypass by leasing a private satellite network from Satellite Business Systems (SBS). The network interleaves digital voice, data, and video signals into a single stream and beams it down to seven geographically distributed earth stations. One of the earth stations is in England. The earth stations all have a built-in switching capability that allows connections to the company's outlying sites using Dataphone Digital Services facilities leased from AT&T in the United States and similar service from other carriers elsewhere. The network is a form of complete premise-to-premise bypass.

Hercules management estimates that the introduction of services made possible by the satellite-based digital network saves the company millions of dollars a year. Video teleconferencing alone saves more than $1.5 million annually in time and travel expenses; voice mail saves $3 million a year in employee time.

Most of the data going to the company's main computing site in Wilmington, Delaware goes over the satellite backbone. The volume of data transferred between that main site and Hercules' regional data center in Magna, Utah, on the other hand, was high enough to justify leasing a number of dedicated T1 lines.

Hercules' telematic corporate network will be discussed in greater detail in Chapter Sixteen.

Bank Bypass in Manhattan

A major New York-based bank has a private, 40-node packet-switching network leased from Tymnet. Sites with low volumes of data traffic access Tymnet through local dial-up lines, while heavy users are connected directly.

In Manhattan, where terminal-to-mainframe traffic is especially heavy, the bank uses Manhattan Cable TV's data service. Because the cable system is ubiquitous throughout the bank's Manhattan buildings, personnel can relocate within the bank's offices without additional cabling. Another advantage is that the CATV system, unlike the private cabling it replaces, provides redundant data paths, reducing terminal down time.

The bank has installed its own interoffice local area network in its four lower Manhattan buildings. Empire City Subway ducts provide a conduit for dual broadband cable that provides high-speed connection of minicomputers, teleconferencing, and microcomputer communication among buildings.

The bank has also installed a private microwave system of T1 circuits to its large data processing centers on Long Island. No line-of-site route was available, however, because of the tremendous congestion of downtown New York. Thus the bank is forced to beam data to a repeater located past the data centers, which then beams the data back.

Finally, there was a need to connect the bank's midtown Manhattan, lower Manhattan, and Long Island sites into a single network. A five-mile fiber optic link between the bank's uptown and downtown offices was laid with no repeaters necessary to complete the triangle. The bank estimates that this link in the network alone saves it $500,000 annually in phone and data-transmission costs.

Insurance Bypass

One of the largest insurance organizations in the world, with assets of more than $30 billion, has a communications budget for voice and data of more than $40 million per year. A large portion of that goes to the local phone company: The firm has more than 20,000 Centrex lines into its two headquarters locations and uses WATS and tie line service as well.

The company's data transmissions bypass the local loop: They are carried by AT&T's Dataphone Digital Service wherever it is obtainable in the United States. Although the DDS 9,600 bits per second point-to-multipoint transmission and 56 kilobits per second for point-to-point and point-to-multipoint service has served the company well, DDS does not provide the diagnostic controls the company desires. Moreover, the company faced unacceptably long waits before AT&T could install the increased DDS capacity the company needed. Thus it was necessary for the firm to build its own network.

The company's new premise-to-premise private data network consists of a combination of analog and digital private lines, a private Telenet packet-switched network, and three earth stations for satellite service.

The satellite link is new. Until recently, Telenet carried all low-speed terminal traffic from the firm's outlying locations, with traffic between key concentration points in the company's various regions carried by leased terrestrial T1 lines. Unhappiness with T1's high cost over longer distances, the year-long wait for installation, and the difficulty in achieving redundancy for critical data links, however, prompted the insurance giant to investigate satellite transmission.

A decision was made to transfer most of the T1 data to a private satellite network. Six 56 kilobits per second channels are used for bulk data transfer among all the data centers except one; three more channels carry the batch and interactive terminal traffic from that site.

The company plans to replace several more of its leased T1 links, this time with microwave links that are 0.6 and 13 miles long. Payback of this investment is expected to take three years. The insurance giant also is looking at a microwave-based digital termination system (DTS) to interconnect 5 to 15 sites centered around its headquarters that exchange moderate data traffic.

Northwest Bypass

The same forces that lead a billion-dollar electronics firm to install a number of Ethernet LANs, microcomputer networks, and high-speed links between mainframe computers has pushed

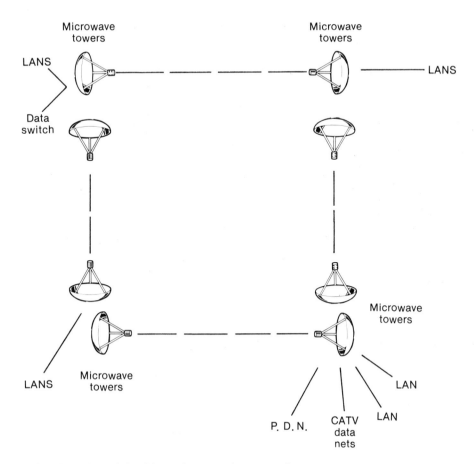

FIGURE 9–20: A backbone interpremise network.

this company into bypassing the local telephone company. In the fast-paced, information-intensive high technology business, it is not possible to be competitive using old technology.

The company uses interpremise PBX links to carry integrated voice and data traffic among several Portland, Oregon locations. Higher volume data is handled via a 12 gHz terrestrial digital microwave system that the firm owns and operates. Two leased T1 lines between its two largest sites save the firm approximately 10 percent over WATS charges. The company also uses a CATV system that links several of the company's sites and supports telecommuters, a data transfer link to financial institutions, and an order entry system with several suppliers and vendors. Figure 9–20 illustrates this network.

The company is considering an additional form of complete bypass via packet switching networks, more CATV use, and possibly satellite systems. The packet switching network will provide protocol conversion and access to other networks.

There were several factors behind the use of bypass technology. Ironically, this high-tech firm did not anticipate the need to bypass; its system was not designed to save money. Rather, rapid corporate growth, a management style based on decentralization, a decision to integrate voice and data, and an increasing demand for communications from its user communities, coupled with unavailability of sufficient support from the local telephone company, left the firm little choice.

QUESTIONS FOR REVIEW:

1. Describe the concept of "bypass." What are some of its benefits?
2. Recount the story of access fees.
3. What are some of the disincentives to bypass?
4. Describe the four categories of bypass.
5. Sketch the categorization of bypass media to transmission volumes and distances.
6. What is the role of the T carrier in bypass?
7. What are some of the components needed for bypass through CATV?
8. What are the advantages and disadvantages of microwave links?
9. What is DTS? How is it used?
10. What are the advantages and disadvantages in fiber optics transmission?
11. How do fiber optic links work?
12. Contrast the three types of fiber optic cable.
13. Describe the advantages and disadvantages of satellite transmission. Contrast it specifically for C and Ku Bands.
14. What is a teleport?
15. How do FM subcarriers work?

16. How do cellular mobile radios work?
17. How can cellular radio data service be provided?
18. Describe mobile satellite service.
19. Describe radio paging.
20. Describe one of the examples c.

FOR DISCUSSION:

1. Relate the reinforcing cycle of bypass to residential service rates.
2. Is bypass a public policy issue? Why?
3. Devise another model to categorize bypass media.
4. Contrast the advantages and disadvantages of fiber optics and satellites for long-distance transmission.
5. How would you choose a bypass technology? Service? Vendor?
6. Give your own example of bypass in an organization.
7. How would IXCs use bypass methods? What is the impact to the local telephone company?

REFERENCES

ANONYMOUS. *Fiber Optics.* Datapro Research Corporation, 1983.

ANONYMOUS. "Paging Industry's Explosive Growth Prompts FCC Action." *Telecommunications,* November 22, 1983.

ANONYMOUS. *An Overview of Transmission Facilities.* Datapro Research Corporation, September 1985.

ANONYMOUS. *An Overview of Satellite Communications.* Datapro Research Corporation, 1984.

DAVIS, DWIGHT B. "Making Sense of the Telecommunications Circus." *High Technology,* September 1985.

FELDT, TERRY. "Satellites—The Push Is On." *Electronics Week,* January 21, 1985.

International Data Corporation. *Special Report: Bypass Alternatives.* November 1984.

Link Resources Corporation. *New Communications Markets.* 1984.

MEIER, ALBIN. "Technology Is Adding New Dimensions to Paging." *Business Communications Review,* July–August 1984.

NOREEN, GLENN. "Mobile Satellite Service: 22,000-Mile-High Repeater?" *Telecarrier,* April 1985.

SHUFORD, RICHARD S. "An Introduction to Fiber Optics." *Byte,* December 1984.

STIX, GARY. "Many Bands=Light Work." *Computer Decisions,* September 10, 1985.

SWANSON, RAYMOND. "Primer: Satellite Communications for Managers." *Data Communications,* July 1984.

VIOLINO, BOB. "Special Report: Mobile Communications." *Communications Week,* June 24, 1985.

WATT, PEGGY. "Communications Managers View Bypass as Opportunity to Save Money and Gain Greater Control." *Communications Week,* August 19, 1985.

Integrated Services Digital Networks

OBJECTIVES

- Understand how local telephone companies and IXCs are fighting bypass.
- Understand the ISDN concept.
- Understand the potential benefits of ISDN.
- Understand how the ISDN market is being developed.

The term "Integrated Services Digital Network" (or simply ISDN) refers to a consistent body of evolving international telecommunications standards recommendations being established by the CCITT which are providing the only coherent vision for the future evolution of the world's public communications networks.

The technical work of formulating comprehensive ISDN guidelines is several years away from completion. But once the CCITT's work is concluded, the standards will guide the manufacturers, telephone companies, corporations, and state-run telecommunications monopolies of any country in constructing all elements of a modern digital network. The network elements standardized by ISDN will include:

- Local and long-distance digital transmission channels.
- Central office digital switching facilities.
- ISDN "network terminators" at the home or small business site or ISDN-compatible PBXs at the large corporate user's site.
- A defined set of digital voice, data, and image communications services to run over the network.

ISDN frees telecommunications system builders from the worry of attempting to interconnect a myriad of incompatible network pieces. The ISDN standard attempts to guarantee—regardless of the equipment or service supplier—that all elements of a nation's or corporation's network will be compatible, and that they will link easily with the ISDN of any other organization or country.

The ISDN standard is, therefore, an integral part of the grand vision of the approaching Information Age: universal end-to-end digital connectivity over a single nationwide or even world-wide network; support for simultaneous voice, data, and image transmission over a single-access link to that network; and transparent network access for all users regardless of the transmission protocols involved or the type of terminal device used.

Such a result would be unthinkable without the existence of international standards. Indeed, it is already being foreshadowed by ISDN trials and the early phases of ISDN implementation by numerous countries. Nations as diverse as France, Italy, Japan, and New Zealand have taken significant steps toward designing and deploying their own ISDNs. These developments provide us with a glimpse of how the standardized networks of the future will operate.

The initial impetus for ISDN came in the early 1970s from western European countries, whose analog telecommunications networks at the time lagged considerably behind those of the United States and Canada. The Europeans represented in microcosm a major world dilemma: As individual countries began making the large investments needed to upgrade their networks, they were in danger of locking in a new generation of incompatible national communication systems. Thus, the European countries initiated the establishment of an international standard to coordinate the efforts of all nations upgrading their telephone networks. That standard, now called ISDN, has ever since provided the path and the design goal for any country migrating its network into the information age.

INSTITUTING THE ISDN STANDARD

The formulation of the ISDN proposals began in the late 1970s by the CCITT. By the time of the Eighth Plenary of the CCITT in October 1984 in Spain, a comprehensive set of ISDN recommendations had been presented and accepted unanimously by the CCITT member nations. New recommendations are issued periodically by the working committees of the CCITT, the most recent regarding ISDN occurring in late 1985. Despite this progress, it should be understood that much of the work of defining the recommendations still remains to be done.

The long-term goal of the CCITT planners is the construction of a compatible worldwide network in which essentially all communications services will be provided under one common set of standards. Clearly, this result, if fully achievable at all, is decades away. In the meantime, non- or pre-ISDN services will coexist along with a growing array of ISDN services.

Thus, as the industry awaits the outcome of early ISDN trials and the full completion of standards recommendations, ISDN may appear for a time to be only one of a wide range of available communication services. Nevertheless, there should be no doubt that ISDN is coming. It represents the inevitable and natural direction of network evolution in the digital age. It is already well underway in the ongoing digitalization of the world's public networks.

In the United States, ISDN will be an architecture for an intra-LATA service that will evolve from the local telephone network. It will also provide a digital last mile if the interexchange carriers, VANs and private networks also support the ISDN standard with their interfaces, protocols, services, and performance characteristics.

STRUCTURE OF ISDN

ISDN can be thought of as several pipelines of different capacities through which many kinds of digital services may flow. These services flow through subdivisions of those pipelines called channels. The most important channel types are known as the B channel, which carries 64 kilobits per second of information, and the D channel, which is intended primarily to carry signaling information at rates of 16 kilobits or higher. The "basic access" pipeline provides two B channels and one 16 kilobit D channel. The "primary access" pipeline carries 23 B channels and a single, 64 kilobit D channel. Figure 10–1 depicts the basic and primary services.

The basic and primary access pipelines are designed to provide nearly all ISDN services over the next two decades. A third interface known as the hybrid interface structure, expected to be important for the residential market, will not be discussed here. Basic access provides a vehicle suitable for integrated voice and data; local telephone companies can use it to provide voice/

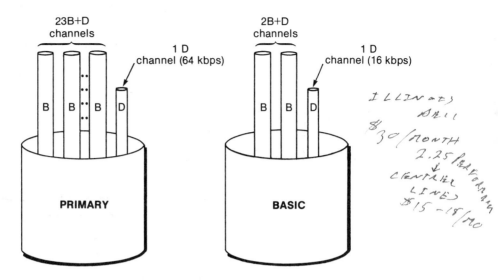

FIGURE 10–1: "Pipelines" for primary access and basic access.

data services to their Centrex customers. Primary access is suitable for high-volume voice and data transmission.

It should be noted that the 1.544 megabits per second primary access standard proposed for ISDN is essentially the same as the T1 standard described earlier. The difference is that T1 uses 8 bits from each of its 64 kilobits per second channels for signaling information (each channel actually carries data at only 56 kilobits). ISDN, in contrast, uses a separate channel for signaling, making the capacity of its 23 "clear" channels a full 64 kilobits per second. What is new about ISDN's primary access is that it brings high bandwidth digital service to the local loop.

ISDN Switches

The first step on the path to ISDN is the installation of digital central office switches; ISDN is at first a set of digital communication services available on specific digital switching stations.

Today, nearly one quarter of all U.S. Centrex facilities already have some digital capabilities, though none—with the exception of a few test sites around the country—conform to

ISDN standards. In addition, about 10 percent of the local subscriber loops originating at these switches are digital lines. As we have noted before, these lines are commonly leased at premium rates to large corporate customers for specialized high-speed data links to their on-premise PBX equipment.

A major benefit of ISDN is that as these switches migrate to the new standard, high-speed end-to-end digital connectivity will become affordable to small business and even to the home subscriber. Subscribers will no longer have to invest in special digital leased lines and expensive PBX equipment; ISDN on central office switches will provide them with the ability to use *existing phone lines* for all services, including circuit- or packet-switched voice and data services, plus high-resolution graphics and video.

The ISDN Signaling Channel

Unlike existing telecommunications networks, ISDN separates "message" information from the signaling (routing and control) information. (This is known as Common Channel Interoffice Signaling, specifically CCIS/CCITT Signaling System Number 7.) Thus, basic access ISDN splits an ordinary phone line into two 64-kbps B channels, each able to handle voice and data traffic, and a third 16 kbps D channel, primarily devoted to carrier signaling but also capable of transmitting voice or low-speed packet data. By moving the signaling data "out of band" to the separate D channel, ISDN frees the full B channel for carrying message information. ("Inband" signaling leaves only 56 kbps of a 64-kbps line available for message information.) This scheme for turning existing phone lines into triple-lane thoroughfares is commonly known as "2B + D."

ISDN and On–Premise Equipment

Since ISDN provides end-to-end digital connectivity, modems can be eliminated from the network. But additional hardware and software is still needed at the end user's site in order to take advantage of ISDN. Users of microcomputers or voice/data terminals will need a terminal adapter (a plug-in board that handles conversion to ISDN protocols) and a network terminator, which would be plugged into an ISDN standard wall jack. The network terminator would function much the same way as a concentrator/multiplexer, accommodating microcomputers, phones, video monitors, and other terminal equipment. Existing communications software would function normally on an ISDN line, but such programs will need modification in order to gain access to ISDN's many specialized capabilities.

BENEFITS OF ISDN

An integrated services digital network will surely not be fully implemented in the United States before the 21st century. But even in the 1980s, we can begin to envision some of the effects of ISDN on users and their organizations and on providers of telecommunications services around the world.

For users, the fulfillment of ISDN's potential will provide them with transparent access to the resources needed for nearly any communications application. From their desktop voice/data/video workstation or other devices, they will have the power to choose easily among a practically unlimited menu of software-based services. These will include:

1. The ability to send electronic mail and voice mail across once-incompatible networks.
2. Links to data bases of virtually any size and location.
3. The bandwidth necessary to send or access still video or high-resolution graphics or to conduct full-motion video teleconferencing at an affordable cost.

And, notably, these voice, data, and image applications will be available to users through their multimedia workstations over a single-line interface to the network.

Staying abreast of ISDN developments should be a central concern for telecommunications planners in corporations and other user organizations. Numerous features of ISDN can improve their organizations' operational costs and the communication productivity of their information workers. These benefits should be integral to corporate strategies for staying competitive in world markets. They include the following:

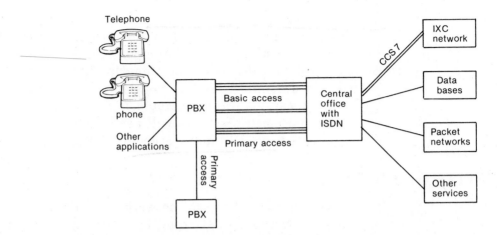

FIGURE 10–2: A structure for ISDN.

1. *Economies of scale.* ISDN provides a single pipeline for connecting workstations or PBX environments directly to the local central office. (See Figure 10–2.)

PBXs today require a jumble of connections: to tie lines, T-1 terrestrial lines, or fiber optic cable when linking to other PBX modules; to separate WATS and FX long distance lines; to various packet-switched and circuit-switched voice and data networks; and to numerous trunks for local loop access. All these lines use different signaling schemes; they must be handled separately.

ISDN's primary access will allow PBXs to transmit the information carried by all these lines over a *single, standard link*.

2. *Lower transmission costs.* Since ISDN can be implemented via lower-cost fiber optics, microwave, and satellite links, local and long distance usage rates should be lower over the long run. In addition, ISDN allows dynamic allocation of bandwidth; customers will be billed only for services used, as opposed to paying standard rates for prearranged capacities and services.

3. *Network flexibility.* ISDN will allow network managers to use the D channel to dynamically reconfigure their networks in near real time. Software on ISDN switches will allow reconfiguring of the number, type, and transmission speeds of circuits to meet the changing needs of an organization. (This ca-

pability is sometimes generically referred to as the "software-defined network.")

4. *Universal connectivity*. ISDN provides universal or near-universal connection with other networks. Protocol conversion occurs within the network, eliminating the need and the expense of customer premise equipment. A universal port will be provided at the customer's premise, with which users could interchange many vendors' terminals and avoid constant incompatibility problems.

TIIE RBOCs AND ISDN

The regional Bell operating companies are realizing that in this new post-divestiture environment, network digitalization, with the eventual implementation of ISDN, is the best long-run solution to their biggest problem: preventing the bypass of the public networks by their large corporate customers. At the same time, ISDN is also decidedly best for the regionals themselves; it provides them with the most practical path of network evolution, promising greater economies of scale. And finally, if introduced properly, ISDN will bring greater transmission efficiencies and will stimulate a large demand for a potpourri of service options for residential and business customers. No wonder ISDN is a major factor in recent attempts by the RBOCs to persuade regulators to roll back many of the restrictions to their activities which resulted from the divestiture decree.

Divestiture and the RBOC's Problem

As we have seen in earlier chapters, these restrictions include orders which bar the regionals from selling long-distance services, making their own equipment, or offering "enhanced" services. They were instead restricted to offering ubiquitous phone service at reasonable rates within local access transport areas (LATAs) while passing calls that cross LATA boundaries to the "point of presence" (POP) of an interexchange carrier such as MCI and AT&T.

In addition, to keep local phone rates down, the divestiture decree compels local phone companies to charge the long-distance carriers prices for access to the local network far higher than actual costs. (This access fee is used to subsidize local service.)

Unfortunately, the divestiture accord did not take into account that rapid changes in technology would erode the Bell's monopoly of local service and thus subvert the subsidy-pricing system. But as we saw in Chapter Nine, the new technologies—satellite, microwave, and fiber optics—are having just this effect. Major network users have available a wide variety of alternatives to the use of the local network and its attendant charges: Bypass vendors are offering to build these users their own private intracompany networks or give them the ability to reach their long distance carrier without using the local exchange network. For their part, the long distance companies, wishing to avoid inflated payments to the local companies, are increasing their own presence at their customers' premises as well as offering to build complete bypass networks for their customers.

This situation has the local telephone companies very concerned. Nearly half of their revenues are derived from business customers. Moreover, the top 10 percent of these customers provide 80 percent of business revenues—and these are the very customers most likely to bypass. One recent study, for example, estimates that large companies can save up to 50 percent on telecommunications costs through bypass of the local exchange, making the payback period for investment in a private bypass network only a few years.

As the large customers bypass the local network, the remaining customers—mostly small businesses and residence users without the means to use bypass technology—are left to bear a greater proportion of the fixed costs of operating the network, thus subverting the original intention of the divestiture agreement.

The RBOCs Fight Back with ISDN

The regionals are fighting to regain ground lost to the bypass vendors in several ways. Many are arguing before regulators that prices of telephone service must be restructured: on one hand, prices for inter-LATA calls must fall if phone companies are to be able to compete for large customers in their territories; at the same time, they argue, local rates for small businesses and residential customers must be raised.

The regionals are having some success in arguing for rate restructuring, but their key strategy for fighting back is to beat the bypass vendors at their own game. Thus, throughout the United States, local phone companies are building fiber optic and microwave systems that, in effect, bypass themselves. More importantly, however, they are also modernizing their plant and enhancing their network capabilities with the ultimate goal of being the leading supplier of integrated-voice and nonvoice digital communications.

The real thrust of the regionals' efforts is to become full-service telematics providers competing openly in the communications marketplace; they want to offer one-stop shopping to corporations, much as IBM and AT&T do. This would mean not only the digitalization of their networks, but gaining permission from regulators to sell customer premise equipment, offer enhanced services, and become value-added resellers of the long distance services of the interexchange carriers. Of course, this is tantamount to scrapping the divestiture accord as it affects the RBOCs.

As the regionals fight this larger regulatory battle in Washington, they are using ISDN—to the extent allowed under regulatory guidelines—to position themselves as the telematics providers of the future. *ISDN is the mainstay of their long-term network strategy.*

The general plan is that ISDN will gradually evolve out of an ongoing upgrade of the existing phone network. In the meantime, all seven regionals are planning extensive ISDN marketing efforts, including the introduction of intermediate (or "pre-ISDN" services), such as:

1. Circuit Switched Digital Capability (CSDC), which provides 56 kbps service to a few large local customers and is an approximation of ISDN basic access.
2. Local Access Data Transport (LADT), which is a 16 kbps packet switched offering.

The local companies are expected to maintain these intermediate services and their separate standards for several decades as ISDN evolves, simply because ISDN, even at the entry level, provides more bandwidth than most users will require for some time.

Meanwhile, ISDN field trials are getting under way across the United States. The ISDN plans of Pacific Bell, a member of the Pacific Telesis Group, the RBOC covering California and Nevada, are representative of the cutting edge of these efforts.

Pacific Bell's ISDN Plans: A Case Study

"ISDN is the vehicle for delivering on the promise of digital technology," says Lee G. Camp, Vice President of Marketing at Pacific Bell. "The company is planning now to deliver ISDN services for all its customers—residential, small business, and large corporate customers. Our 1986 ISDN trials have the goal of connecting all pieces of a full-scale integrated digital network (IDN) by early 1988."

Like most of the Bells around the U.S., Pacific Bell is just beginning to test the waters for market acceptance of ISDN. Much is at stake in this complex process. On the one hand, Pacific Bell recognizes that ISDN is the key to regaining bypass customers. "ISDN is essentially a competitive weapon against bypass," says Larry Kunke, Pacific Bell's director of ISDN product development. "It's our hope for preventing bypass vendors from eating up the high end of the business market over the next five years." On the other hand, the burden of proof in today's market is on the ISDN provider. The bypass technologies—less complex and already well established—even now have a strong foothold with the large corporate users.

The task of regionals like Pacific Bell is to prove that in time they will be able to provide more cost effectiveness and higher quality than the bypass vendors. But their ability to deliver much on this promise in the next five years will be limited by a number of mitigating factors: essentially, they must implement a plan that embraces the complete overhaul of the public network, guided by a telecommunications standard that is still evolving—all the while struggling with government regulators to restructure their rates and allow them to diversify their offerings. For example, the FCC has taken the position (at the time of this writing) that network terminating equipment (NT-1), a key component of ISDN, is not to be considered a part of an ISDN network. This limits the ability of the regionals to develop integrated technological advancements in the local loop.

Thus, even as the Bells continue losing their high volume customers to bypass, the process of introducing competitive ISDN services will need to be slow and deliberate.

Because ISDN represents a significant departure from traditional industry marketing efforts, Pacific Bell has restructured its internal marketing organization. An integrated planning organization consisting of six company vice presidents from differing disciplines was formed to develop and monitor the overall plan to deploy digital services in a cost-effective, customer-responsive fashion. The members of the planning organization will watch closely how the complex technological, social, economic, and political factors influence the timing and market acceptance of both pre-ISDN and future ISDN services.

According to one Pacific Bell vice president, market acceptance for ISDN (assuming a minimum of regulatory interference) will revolve around customers controlling their own networks, cost-efficient pricing, an integrated features package, and the RBOCs' ability to provide ISDN accessibility for all users.

Pacific Bell's strategy for achieving this result combines careful market introductions of both "pre-ISDN" and "true" ISDN services. Chief among the pre-ISDN offerings is Project Victoria, a unique ISDN-like technology for converting a standard twisted-pair telephone line into a multiplexed digital line consisting of seven simultaneous channels. Plans for full-scale ISDN implementation will begin with the initiation of a major four-phase ISDN field trial in three cities in late 1986.

Thus, technology for both ends of the potential ISDN market is being tested by Pacific Bell in 1986: Project Victoria will offer economical access to an ISDN network for residences and small businesses, and the three-city ISDN trial late in 1986 will be "an equally important effort to integrate all of the other network components crucial to an ISDN," according to Camp, thus making ISDN services widely available to both small and large business customers.

Project Victoria represents a highly original course in the testing of ISDN-like services. The system is now being tested among 200 residential and business users in Danville, California (a small town 35 miles east of San Francisco) who have been supplied with Apple IIe computers.

As noted, Pacific Bell's upcoming ISDN trial has the goal of connecting all the pieces of a full-scale integrated digital network (IDN) by early 1988. The trial has four phases:

1. In the initial test phase, Pacific Bell will send end-to-end digital signals between three circuit switches—each using digital circuitry provided by a different manufacturer. "Showing that ISDN works within a dissimilar analog/digital central office equipment environment is essential if ISDN is really going to make it big in the United States," says Larry Kunke, director of ISDN product development.

The test will upgrade an analog switch with digital adjunct equipment supplied by a specialized manufacturer. This station will in turn be connected to two digital switches from different manufacturers. Digital signaling at 56 kbps between the three switches will then be implemented.

2. In early 1987, Pacific Bell will connect a half dozen users to its test ISDN network from more than 10 locations in the San Francisco Bay Area using ISDN terminal adapters. The adapters will enable users of Centrex in different cities to send and receive end-to-end digital signals throughout a LATA via any exchange office regardless of the type of switch involved.

3. The third phase involves connecting the ISDN network to Pacific Bell's LATA-wide packet switching network.

4. In the fourth phase, Pacific Bell will add the ISDN signaling system (Common Channel Signaling 7) to the trial network, thus allowing inter-LATA ISDN transmission.

It remains to be seen whether plans such as these, which are echoed by regionals across the country, will be fulfilled in time to regain large business customers—customers who are increasingly becoming locked into various bypass options or who are even building their own private networks.

> Divestiture has profoundly complicated the introduction of ISDN facilities into the local loop, and the technology and standards of ISDN are still uncertain. Given these conditions, formidable challenges surely lie ahead for the RBOCs in the next decade.

THE LONG-DISTANCE LINK

If the local telephone companies succeed and ISDN becomes a reality, the local loop of the telephone network will be digital. What about the interexchange carriers? AT&T Communications is ahead of the other long-distance carriers in its ability to provide the interexchange equivalent to ISDN's primary access, called common channel signaling 7 (CCS7). AT&T also hopes to sell the local telephone companies much of the digital switching equipment they will need to convert to ISDN capability, although other large switch providers such as Northern Telecom, Ericcson, and Siemens will be stiff competition.

Some experts question whether ISDN will solve the problem of bypass for the local telephone companies. If the local telephone networks go digital, and the interexchange carriers are digital, wouldn't the long-distance carriers simply provide end-to-end digital service much as they are providing bypass today? AT&T and the other long-distance carriers such as MCI rapidly are modernizing facilities for CCS7 to make that a possibility. The intent of AT&T is to regain the end-to-end network control it lost with divestiture, only this time it will have to compete with IBM, which has entered this business with its recent investment in MCI.

Clearly, given the probable face-off against both IBM and AT&T, and with the public utility commissions protecting against sharp increases in residential phone service rates, the local telephone companies have their work cut out for them.

TO BYPASS OR NOT TO BYPASS?

Let's return to one of the major predictions of the information age: Eventually, there will be a single, multimedia workstation on users' desks that provides for all communication needs via its attachment to a unified digital network. That network will provide a transmission path for voice, data, video, text, facsimile, graphics, and any other form information may take in order to cope with the burgeoning communication needs of corporations in the future. Clearly, the public switched and public data networks cannot provide such service today, nor is ISDN yet a reality; if a true telematic solution is sought in the short run—say, over the next 5 to 10 years—bypass is a necessity.

In many cases, it is not a case of striving for the best possible solution. Companies experiencing rapid business expansion may have no more choice than did the major electronics supplier from the Pacific Northwest: The telephone company simply cannot meet its needs, and bypass will be a necessity.

QUESTIONS FOR REVIEW:

1. How are local telephone companies fighting bypass?
2. What does ISDN stand for? What is its structure?
3. What do "basic" access and "primary" access mean?
4. What are some benefits of ISDN?
5. What are some uncertainties in ISDN?
6. How is ISDN being marketed? Focus on field trials.
7. Describe the role of ISDN in the long-distance link.

FOR DISCUSSION:

1. What are some of the impacts of ISDN on residential charges?
2. What are some possible mechanisms to establish *one* standard ISDN in the United States?
3. How could IXCs bypass ISDN?

REFERENCES

ANONYMOUS. *Special Report: Bypass Alternatives.* International Data Corporation, November 1984.

"The Baby Bells—Special Report." *Business Week,* December 2, 1985.

Communications Systems & Services. *Interfacing with ISDN.* The Yankee Group, October 1983.

CAMP, LEE. "Pacific Bell Brings ISDN to California." *Telephony,* September 23, 1985.

Data Communications in the Local Loop. Link Resources Corporation, 1984.

DAVIS, DWIGHT B. "Making Sense of the Telecommunications Circus." *High Technology,* September 1985.

"Divestiture: Two Years Later—Special Report." *IEEE Communications Magazine,* December 1985.

RUDOV, MARC H. "Wanted: Concerned Users to Join ISDN (R)evolution." *Data Communications,* June 1985.

SAPRONOV, WALT. "Technical and Regulatory Issues are Challenging ISDN's Progress." *Data Communications,* November 1985.

PART FIVE

Applications in Telematic Networks

Now that we have surveyed the transmission technologies, we can turn to a consideration of the newer communication services available to users over these information pathways.

There are two fundamental kinds of telematic applications: those that facilitate communication between people, and those that facilitate communication between people and data bases.

Micro-to-mainframe links (Chapter Eleven) and business videotex (Chapter Twelve) are on-line data base communication applications. Micro-to-mainframe technology provides private links to sensitive files stored on large corporate data bases. Videotex allows on-line data base access, but the data bases in this case are more group-oriented in nature. Videotex data bases are available to virtually anyone in the company with access to a terminal.

Electronic mail and teleconferencing are primarily people-to-people communication systems. Electronic mail allows sending of text, graphics, and voice between two individuals, or as broadcasts from one person to many. Teleconferencing allows electronic meetings among groups and broadcasts to groups, using audio, text, and video as communication media.

In Chapter One we introduced the concept of business intelligence, showing how telematics has the potential to make the mechanics of networks increasingly transparent to users, while giving them the power to easily select or extract needed information. As we explore these four key telematics applications, it will become clearer how they facilitate the transmutation of data into business intelligence.

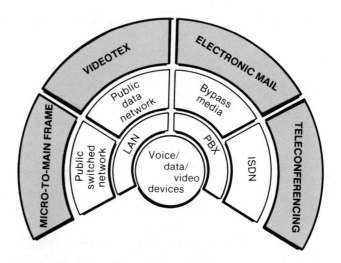

Micro-To-Mainframe Links

OBJECTIVES

- Understand the need for micro-to-mainframe links.
- Describe the players in micro-to-mainframe politics.
- Understand the categories of link options.

AAM

- WHAT IS RIGHT SOLUTION LINKS
- POLICY FOR LANS / LINKS
- DP VIEW OF LINKS POINT/PERIOD [SECURITY]
  DATA INTEGRITY

- UPLOADING

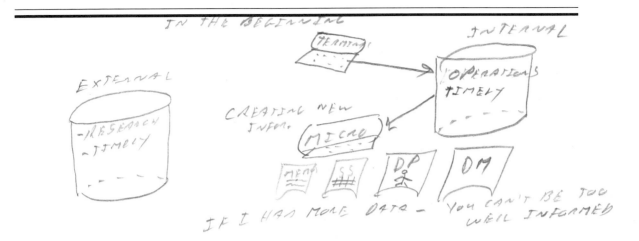

INTRODUCTION

During the 1985 slump in the computer market, there were persistent stories that large corporations that had bought hundreds or even thousands of personal computers were letting many of them sit idle. *Business Week* reported that many companies believed they had acquired "a lot of expensive glass-faced dust collectors."

One authentic story concerns an accountant working for a large international corporation who returned his micro to the data processing department. "You can send it back to me," he told the DP manager, "as soon as there is a way to use it without wasting my time." His main complaint? He could no longer be bothered to manually enter financial data from a mainframe printout every time he wanted to process corporate financial data on his micro.

Lack of easy access to data held on mainframe files is a major barrier to increasing the usefulness of microcomputers. Gaining mainframe access represents one of the most beneficial uses of microcomputers.

Desktop computers have taken much of the drudgery out of users' workday by automating many routine analytical and decision-making chores. But many sophisticated users resent an arrangement in which they have access to powerful integrated software packages but inadequate means for acquiring the data they need to use these tools. Often the most important information is held out of reach, on the company's minis or mainframes (which normally include an extensive library of programs, along with years of accumulated data). Making a user-friendly connection to these large computers—sometimes known simply as "the link"—has become a key element in creating the electronic office of the future. (Gaining access to large public databases is also crucial for many business users; see Chapter Twelve.)

The micro-mainframe connection is the latest step in the evolution toward end-user computing. Two motives have spurred this migration.

1. The need to reduce ever-mounting data processing backlogs of data processing (DP) departments.
2. End-users' desire for more computational power distributed to where they are—where it is most needed and can be most effectively utilized.

At first, DP departments acquired terminals for end-users and taught them the rudiments of mainframe database access. The next initiative was taken by the end-users themselves. To avoid the DP center's backlog, many began buying personal computers out of discretionary budgets and doing their own processing work. A short time later, terminal emulation products appeared that allowed end-users to use their microcomputers to mimic the ability of mainframe's native terminals to view and even download mainframe data. This step threatened the ability of DP managers to control database security and integrity. The current challenge is to preserve the benefits of end-user access while bringing the micro-to-mainframe link under proper control by the company's data processing experts.

We can envision a future in which micro-to-mainframe software automatically handles the two-way transfer of data, offers (transparently to the user) access to whatever level of processing power or to any database required, while guaranteeing appropriate control of information flow by management. Ultimately, the very distinction between "small" and "large" computers may disappear; the link will allow micro users to easily transmute mainframe data into business intelligence.

Courtesy of IBM Corporation

FIGURE 11–1: An IBM 3270 PC is an example of the many link products available. It combines the capabilities of an IBM personal computer with the ability to emulate a dumb terminal. *— NO STORAGE OR PROCESSING ABILITIES*

PLAYERS IN MICRO-MAINFRAME POLITICS

MOVING OUT FROM THE LAN TO ACCESS CORPORATE DATA SERVICES

POLICY STD LINK
- ACCESS
- AUTHORITY TO CHANGE
- SECURITY
- INTEGRITY

We have seen how LANs help create improved systems for sharing information and hardware among work groups. Micro-to-mainframe links raise the stakes higher in the corporate information game. Link technology epitomizes those forces (see Chapter One) that are driving the convergence of those once-separate domains of technology: telecommunications, data processing, and office automation. It connects the automated office for the first time directly to the data processing center, using a wide range of telecommunication media. It shouldn't be surprising that an industry that bridges such a range of technologies, having got its start in 1983, is still in its infancy. Link solutions that make both office workers and DP professionals happy are still rare.

Much of the difficulty is in choosing the right solutions from among the variety of link options. Potential buyers are snowed under by a diversity of products offered from more than 400 vendors. Offerings that range between $500 and $150,000 all come under the rubric of "the link." These products have differing capabilities, ranging from simple terminal emulation to bi-directional transfer of data. (See Figure 11–1.) In addition, there are a number of inherent technical difficulties in each type of link, with each vendor tackling it in a unique way.

End-users of link products are concerned most about increasing their efficiency and effectiveness and less about the technical issues of the link. On the other hand, data processing and telecommunications professionals must concern themselves with the difficult hardware and software issues. In addition, data processing managers are extremely wary of end-users once they are empowered by link technology to violate the integrity of the corporate data bases. Bridging these differences requires the guidance of what can be called the corporate approach as opposed to the DP or end-user view.

The corporate approach encourages link users and data processing managers to coordinate their differing interests. Only corporate management can reconcile DP's imperative to protect data integrity and security with the desire of end-users for user-friendly, timely access to whatever data they need to do their work effectively. Much of the difficulty of choosing micro-to-mainframe links amounts to the problem of finding the right solutions within this highly charged environment.

Users

Microcomputer software, such as spreadsheets, graphics programs, and data base management programs, allows managers to perform a variety of operations at fairly sophisticated levels. These programs are increasingly easy to learn, with a single command structure serving a variety of applications. Micro software is easier to use than most interactive mainframe software packages, and most managers believe they can do far more with a micro on their desktop than with a terminal.

As mentioned earlier, the microcomputer entered organizations through the back door. Most agree that it has achieved the status of a necessary tool for today's professionals. It is increasingly a foolish policy to prevent the more efficient use of micros by blocking their access to mainframe data.

Perhaps the major advantage of microcomputers, from the user's point of view, is the ability to perform financial analysis on an ad hoc basis. The electronic spreadsheet is the tool that made the micro popular in business and is still its primary ap-

POINT IN TIME

SENSORY IN TIME

plication. The user's problem, of course, is that much of the data used in spreadsheet analysis is resident on the host data base. Users must either rekey the data or find a way to download it from the mainframe. As spreadsheets have grown in size and complexity, manual data entry has become increasingly irritating. This problem has provided the major impetus behind the movement toward micro-mainframe communications.

Data Processing

The micro-mainframe link will perhaps be the major DP issue of the late 1980s and is surely one of the hottest topics in the software community today.

Initially, micros gave information workers impatient with DP's backlogging of their requests the ability to bypass DP and do their own processing work. In many companies, the invasion of micros threatened to usurp the DP professionals' dominance over an organization's data and computing resources. However, the link to the mainframe may reverse that trend. The desire of end-users to access corporate data electronically can give DP a way to regain credibility with end-users. The time is coming when local processing of mainframe data will be essential, and information *must* be made available. End-users will not tolerate inflexibility or ignorance on the part of the data processing department. Because of their traditional role of maintaining control over the corporate data base, it is in the best interest of DP managers to implement a coherent policy that incorporates link users' needs.

How can DP RESPONSE + MAINTAIN control ?

PROCEDURES

The issues DP will face will not be entirely new. Links that allow micros to extract and download mainframe data or to upload locally processed data simply raise many traditional DP concerns in a new form. Chief among these are data integrity, data security, mainframe processing time, and user training and regulation.

Data Integrity. As long as data is processed within the closed environment of the host-terminal connection, traditional data control measures are in place. But once vital information is transferred to user-owned diskettes, a DP manager has lost control of data integrity. Diskettes can be lost, stolen, or dam-

STORY OF TWO SPREADSHEETS WITH SIMILIAR CALCULATEONS AND WITH DIFFERENT ANSWERS.

SINCE I HAVE NO SENSE MY DATA OF URGENCY TO UPDATE DATA BASE

REFORMAT TO INPUT TRANSACTIONS

ASSIGN A CLASSIFICATION TO INFO. RELATE TO ACCESS LEVEL

DUMP TERMINALS PRODUCE MORE INTERRUPTIONS

aged. A greater problem is multiple copies. If one copy is available for off-line processing on the micro, while another resides on the mainframe, which data is the most current? How can these two versions be merged? These issues must be resolved by DP departments working closely with users.

But upoading data to the mainframe is a far greater threat to data integrity. Some companies simply prohibit uploading. Such fears may be unnecessary if data is uploaded to a buffer or intermediate storage area. Information can later be transferred to the mainframe from this shadow data base after review and validation by DP staff. But this procedure can be cumbersome and expensive.

Data Security. DP must install appropriate security measures to regulate who is entitled access to which kind of data. At a simple level, data could be identified by importance. "Critical" data might include purchase orders, costs, billings, or accounts receivable/payable. "Noncritical" data would include newsletters, everyday departmental documents, or memos. Users could be separated into "read only" and those who have the right to change data.

Multiple levels of security could be implemented by regulating the amount of functionality available to users. These levels of authorization could include no access, data viewing only, download only, upload only, download and upload, or combinations of these.

Mainframe Processing Time. The good news for DP is that the micro-to-mainframe link can run more efficiently than dumb terminal links. Before the personal computer influx, information workers tapped mainframe power with the aid of terminals built for mainframe access. Compared with micros, most of these terminals had little or no memory, storage capacity, or internal processing power. As a result of this and other factors, once on-line, these dumb terminals occupied the mainframe's power. As more and more of these dumb terminals came online, the host's response time to user requests began to plummet.

Micros acting as smart terminals take much of this pressure off the mainframe. Their internal processing power and separate storage capability allow them to tap into the mainframe just long enough to gather needed data and log off for off-line processing. This frees the mainframe to do what it does best: large-scale, high-speed number crunching, data storage, and file transfers.

On the users' side, link technology allows replacement of dumb terminals with terminal emulating micros. This allows these users to retain the stand-alone computing power of micros: the ability to analyze data quickly and efficiently under their own control.

User Training and Regulation. Data processing managers in many companies will find that users demand assistance in micro-to-mainframe hardware and software evaluation and selection, as well as support in installation and training. Training is an especially important consideration because users must be made aware of how their actions can affect the corporate data base. The need to train users may provide an opportunity for DP to expand its control over the proper uses of mainframe data.

Corporate Telecommunications Policy

Corporate communication planners should recognize that the link's contribution to telematics is more of a goal than a proven capability. Unfortunately, the potential payback is perceived by many to be so great that some organizations will commit themselves without proper planning or technical resources needed to correctly implement the link. Indeed, the potential advantages of the link for a corporation are many:

- Cost savings through nonduplication of terminals, through access to cheaper mass storage on the mainframe, and so on.
- More rapid data distribution under control of DP.
- Reduction of DP workload.
- Improvements in data access for information workers coping with information overload.

The best approach to implementing the link properly is to begin by encouraging dialogue between users, data processing, and

① INFO. S.T.P
PROVIDERS
KNOW THE +
POTENTIAL
POSSIBLE
SOLUTIONS
THEY SHOULD
INITIATE
CHANGE
② DECLARE VALUE
BY CUSTOMERS
BY

telecommunication staffs. (See Chapter Nineteen for more on these three parties.) The first initiative in the dialogue should come from the end-users. After all, the reason for harboring valuable corporate data on the mainframe is to serve the needs of end-users. Thus corporate management should see to it that the link issue first is presented—clearly and in written form—from the standpoint of end-users. To facilitate the clear expression of user needs, it may be helpful to have an overview of just which link options are available to end-users. This can help users present their needs to DP professionals, telecommunications professionals, or others with responsibility for purchasing link technology, offering hope that users' needs will be translated into appropriate hardware and software choices.

THE MAINFRAME ENVIRONMENT

But before describing available link options, it is important to understand the technical challenge of establishing a micro-to-mainframe link. If a micro is to fit into the mainframe's native communications environment, the micro must be made to "appear" to the mainframe as one of the mainframe's own standard devices. However, the mainframe's operating environment is in sharp contrast to that of the micro.

The Mainframe Hierarchy

TECHNICAL
CONFIGURATIONS

Mainframe computers traditionally sit at the top of a hierarchy composed of intermediate communication controllers, terminals, and peripheral devices. Mainframes can be connected to these devices through physical outlets called interface ports. Generally, terminals and peripherals (such as printers) are not connected to the mainframe directly through the ports. Each port is far too valuable a resource for dedicated service to one end-user only.

FEP

Instead, the communications controller, or front-end processor, acts as the direct interface device. The front-end processor (FEP) services the communication requests made by terminals, passing to the mainframe only that portion of a terminal's request needing the mainframe's attention. Data returning from

Courtesy of IBM Corporation

FIGURE 11-2: A typical IBM mainframe environment.

the host is routed to the appropriate terminal or other peripheral device by the FEP.

The IBM mainframe hierarchy commonly includes another intermediate-level interface device, known as the cluster controller. Typically, the cluster controller is connected to the FEP directly or remotely through the telephone network; sometimes, it is directly connected to the host itself. When present, the cluster controller services the terminals' requests and provides printers, plotters, and other peripherals with needed data from the host.

The combination of a mainframe with front-end processors and, optionally, cluster controllers allows the mainframe to service thousands of devices without a corresponding number of physical ports. Figure 11-2 illustrates the various devices in a mainframe environment.

Transmission Media

Mainframes are normally connected to their peripheral devices by coaxial cable, a slight variant of the type used for home cable TV. (Off-site peripherals can be connected to the mainframe via modem-based telephone lines.) In the non-IBM mainframe environment, requirements for cable are less stringent. Most hosts use high-grade twisted-pair wire to interconnect the mainframe and its associated devices.

Sometimes, of course, minicomputers contain data needed by a micro. In this case, it is a mini's environment that must be mimicked by the micro. This is less difficult than connecting to the mainframe environment because many of the intermediate communication handlers, such as FEPs, are not present. It should be noted, though, that in the IBM minicomputer environment, the micro must connect to the mini through a twin-ax cable, a variant of coax cable having two conductor wires.

LINK OPTIONS FOR END-USERS

Now that the mainframe environment has been introduced, we can proceed to a presentation of the variety of link options available to end-users. Figure 11–3 contains a summary chart of the six major link categories. These are classified according to the level of technical sophistication of the link application.

Terminal Emulation

As stated before, the micro normally replaces the terminal hardware (often known as the dumb terminal) in the mainframe's environment. However, terminals are normally connected to the mainframe hierarchy via coaxial cable, while micros have communication interfaces (known as RS-232C ports) that are oriented for communications via twisted-pair wire. Also, mainframes use synchronous protocols to communicate, while micros characteristically use asynchronous protocols. (The difference between these protocols was presented in Chapter Three, Module 4.) To emulate a terminal in a mainframe environment, the micro must be able to resolve these two incompatibilities.

Emulation Hardware and Software. Specialized terminal emulation hardware and software are needed to bridge this technical gap between the micro and mainframe.

On the hardware level, a common approach is to intercept the micro's asynchronous transmissions with a protocol converter external to the micro. This device converts between

FIGURE 11–3: Matching link technology to application.

	Types	Capabilities
Dumb terminal emulation	1. 327X emulator 2. ASCII emulator	View mainframe data only
Simple downloading	1. Screen capture 2. File downloading	Store to disk or print out screens Store or print out screens or complete files
Selective data access	*APPLICATION LINKS* *4GL'S*	Select specific data from file or multiple files Simple query language or precanned queries
Simple uploading	1. Batch entry 2. Auto data entry	Emulate RJE applications Micro storage to mainframe storage
Integrated links	1. Virtual diskette 2. Data insertion	Multiuser access Host integration option Archival storage Extracted data is read directly into micro software
Cooperative processing		Application mirroring Advanced data security/integrity

asynchronous and synchronous protocols and usually is attached to a PBX. The protocol converter is then linked to the mainframe, often via coaxial cable. (See Figure 11–4.)

Another approach involves directly inserting hardware into the micro. Rather than converting protocols, these add-on boards perform the same task as the circuitry of the terminals. Figure 11–5 depicts a product of this variety.

Once one of these hardware options is chosen, software can be added to the micro to mimic the dumb terminal according to the mainframe's requirements. Thus, traditional dumb terminal operations such as querying the mainframe and performing simple transactions can be performed by the micro.

Emulation and the User. There are two main advantages in dumb terminal emulation. First, many terminal users today are converting to personal computers. They will continue to work with mainframe data in a terminal mode, but they need or want to add the local processing power of a personal computer. Dumb terminal emulation allows these information

Courtesy: ROLM, an IBM Company.

FIGURE 11–4: A protocol converter located on the table adjacent to a PBX.

Courtesy of CXI, Inc.

FIGURE 11–5: An add-on board placed inside a personal computer allows terminal emulation.

workers to avoid having two separate devices on their desktops. The other advantage springs from the traditional need to provide relief for mainframe backlog problems, which are caused by the ever-mounting quantity of requests in most companies for traditional data processing services. By adding inexpensive terminal emulation programs to selected micros, the data processing center may gain by offloading simple processing tasks.

However, the numerous dumb terminal emulation packages on the market have significant disadvantages. Their basic design causes them to emulate a device, usually an IBM 3270 family terminal, that possesses no local processing or storage power. Users make a simple physical connection that allows only the viewing of data. They are unable to upload data to the host, download to the micro, or convert files between mainframe and microcomputer formats. In some of these packages, the micro's native capabilities are also not available during emulation. Finally, users accessing host files may need to understand complex mainframe data access commands.

[handwritten margin note: LIMITED UTILIZATION + ACCESS OF COMPANY DATA BASES]

Simple Downloading

The next level of mainframe interface allows the downloading of screens or files in bulk for capture by the micro. The data can be saved on a disk or printed. Of course, in order to be used in a micro application, the mainframe data must be manually rekeyed; much more sophisticated software would be needed for reformatting the desired mainframe data for storage or use in the micro.

Two types of simple data downloading are covered here, along with a discussion of other features that may be present in such packages. These types are *screen capture* and *file downloading*.

Screen Capture. One step beyond straight terminal emulation are those simple packages that allow users to capture screens to an existing micro file. One vendor's offering in this category adds this capability to simple terminal emulation. It allows the user to transfer the contents of the emulation screen to disk or to string screen images together on disk. However, neither of these features allows the user to make very efficient use of the data because extraneous information is captured along with the needed data.

[handwritten margin note: CAN BE AN EXTENSION TO EMULATION. SCREEN DATA IMAGE NOT FILE FOR A STD PROCESSING]

Software packages in this class, plus all higher-level link packages, allow the user to toggle between the emulation mode and a micro application, with a feature known as "resident mode." Imagine that a user is emulating a 3270 device but suddenly needs data from a micro application program. An emulator in resident mode maintains the mainframe link while the user toggles to the micro application to retrieve the data. Upon returning to the host session, the screen looks the same as when the user left emulation mode. The IBM 3270 PC and products

[handwritten margin note: MULTIPLE SESSIONS OF RESIDENT TO 3270]

Courtesy of CXI, Inc.

FIGURE 11–6: CXI's 3270 PC connection allows window displays of up to five mainframe computers.

patterned after it (see Figure 11–6) extend this capability by allowing windowing of both the host and micro sessions. Users are able to "jump" from window to window by pressing keys.

Downloading Files. In some cases it may be better to be able to download mainframe files in bulk to the micro. As with simple screen capture, these programs do not have the sophistication to allow selection of data from within mainframe files. The files are simply made available as is for storage locally on the micro.

File downloading can be problematic. Mainframe files are organized differently than those for the microcomputer and are often much larger than the microcomputer is able to handle. When downloaded in bulk, these files may overwhelm a micro's storage or memory capacity. In addition, products at this level may require users to learn tedious mainframe access commands in order to retrieve host files.

One vendor's offering in this category allows IBM PCs to emulate several popular DEC terminals for simple file downloading from DEC's VAX minicomputers. This inexpensive link product downloads files in bulk to PC storage or memory. Users may need to have a DP manager verify that the size of the downloaded file does not exceed their PC's memory or storage capacity before attempting a transfer. This product is used, for example, by internal auditors working at worldwide branch sites for Monsanto Corporation to convert portable PCs into DEC terminals. The auditors are able to download updated financial data files over phone lines from a VAX computer in Monsanto's St. Louis, Missouri, headquarters.

Selective Data Access

More advanced forms of the link allow end-user selection of data from mainframe files without resorting to esoteric search commands. Specifically designed mainframe enquiry software installed on the micro and the mainframe allows users to make very particular requests for mainframe data without the response flooding the storage capacity of the micro. The benefit is that only the data needed from the mainframe file (or from several files) are downloaded.

In addition, in most of these packages, microcomputer data may be uploaded to the host. Selective data access packages normally do not address the issue of what is done once data is uploaded. Mainframe software must be added or customized to make this data useful to the host. Some vendors already in the business of providing mainframe software are offering such "two package solutions." These are also known as "application interface links" because they allow micros to access files in vendor-specific mainframe application programs. One vendor's offering, for example, running on an IBM PC, allows the users to extract financial data and later upload new data through a link with the vendor's applications running on IBM mainframes.

A few data extraction packages allow the user to query the mainframe system in languages approaching ordinary English. Queries may include requests for specific data from mainframe spreadsheets, for reports or for other text, and they may even support trial-and-error searches through the corporate data.

One approach to this kind of selective access makes predefined or canned queries available to end-users. The DP department customizes a report and assigns it a simple name. Perhaps it's a marketing department's year-to-date budget from the corporate accounting system. By typing "marketing department budget," for example, a marketing manager would receive a display of everything spent to date and what is budgeted for the remainder of the year.

Executives of Hardee's Hamburgers, one of the five largest franchise operators in the United States, use such a technique to obtain daily sales and expense figures for the more than 200 restaurants the company operates across the Southeastern United States.

[handwritten note: SPECIFIC DATA FROM APPLICATION LINKED TO ALL CONCERNED]

- Hardee's uses a link product that connects the corporate mainframe to IBM Personal Computer XT's on the executives' desktops. The link improves information flow for corporate executives at the home office and Hardee's six district managers. Before the link, the district managers would make business decisions based on mailed weekly sales reports plus mailed monthly reports on payroll, food and materials cost, and gross and net sales. The link software allows those managers to log onto the mainframe over telephone lines to access figures that are updated on a daily basis. In addition, corporate executives in the home office use the link to access more timely figures for making decisions on prices or expenses.

[handwritten note: EDI — STOCK TRANS. TO MEMBER — SETTLEMENT TKNS TO PSE]

- The Pacific Stock Exchange (PSE) uses a selective data access package for downloading selected stock exchange transaction data to its member brokerage houses or banks. Members use PCs utilizing the link program to log onto the host over public or leased telephone lines. At appropriate batch cycles, relevant information reflecting traded stocks can be transmitted to the PSE member and printed out.

  The link package's uploading capability is also useful to PSE. To settle a stock transaction, the fact that trading information was received and verified must be authenticated. In the past, couriers traveled up and down the West Coast carrying authentication messages between PSE members and the two stock exchanges (located in San Francisco and Los Angeles). Now PSE members can upload this information directly to the host using their PCs.

Uploading from the Micro

Uploading from the micro involves the direct or indirect transfer of microcomputer data to mainframe data bases.

Micro-to-mainframe links for uploading data or files to the host are more technically complex than those that offer downloading only. They require significant changes to both the micro and the mainframe environment.

There are two specialized forms of uploading at this level of link communications.

Batch Entry. The most elementary form of uploading to the mainframe involves batch entry. This simple micro-mainframe application derives from the classical DP environment where remote job entry (RJE) workstations, tied to RJE controllers at any branch office, were used to ship large batches of data to and from mainframes. Now less expensive and less bulky micros can emulate devices that perform this task. (RJE devices are dumb terminals with large storage capability, which allows them to store multiple transactions so these can be sent together to the mainframe at prearranged times.)

In the IBM environment, this device is usually a cluster controller. In such a micro-to-mainframe link, the microcomputer must be altered so it emulates a cluster controller; the micro would thus appear to the mainframe as a complete RJE station. The micro will also act as a controller for attached devices such as printers and other micros using dumb terminal emulation. Significant cost saving would result as there is no need for the purchase of an actual cluster controller.

Data Systems Corporation, a service bureau for banks and savings and loan institutions, uses an RJE batch entry package to allow PCs to emulate 3770 RJE workstations or to emulate an 8100 series IBM minicomputer running an RJE application. In addition, the PC is able to emulate an RJE terminal, accomplishing error checking and recovery.

Auto Data Entry. Further up the scale in uploading functions is auto data entry for insertion of ASCII files directly into existing host text-editing applications. Here a single micro program is added to a micro running dumb terminal emulation hardware and software. The auto data entry program reads data from a micro file and passes it on the terminal emulation program as if it were entered from the micro's keyboard. Users must be sophisticated enough to perform any required data conversions before uploading to the host.

Micro-Mainframe Integration

By combining uploading and downloading capabilities found separately in less expensive packages, "integrated" link packages further narrow the gap between micros and mainframes. They also are known as "universal" links because they are able to tie in with more than one vendor's mainframe application program and can interact with numerous mainframe file structures. These packages can thus be defined as those that allow greater flexibility both in uploading and downloading data, along with increased ease of use. Two types of integration packages, virtual diskette and data insertion, are considered here.

MULTIPLE VENDORS

Virtual Diskette

What if transferring data to the mainframe required only the most elementary knowledge of the mainframe environment? Virtual diskette packages make uploading data to the mainframe appear as if the user is simply transferring files between two floppy disk drives on a micro. The only difference is that instead of dealing with disk drive A or B physically located in the PC, the user is talking to C, D and E, which are virtual disk "images" on the mainframe. Virtual diskettes provide a safe environment on the mainframe for data uploading and offer more flexibility for data downloading.

Most virtual diskette products are able to offer the following capabilities:

FILE EXTENSION

1. **Less user education.** Virtual diskette packages typically allow simulation on the mainframe of micro operating systems such as MS–DOS, PC–DOS, and UNIX.

SHARING

2. **Multiuser access to the same data.** The original user would have read-and-write access, whereas all subsequent users would have read-only access.

REFORMAT + TRANSFER

3. **Mainframe integration.** By adding hardware and software for code conversion from ASCII to EBCDIC, or to any other mainframe code, the data on virtual diskettes can be integrated into any host application. Meanwhile, the data remains in mainframe storage in microcomputer format.

STORAGE EXTENSION

4. Archival storage. Storage of micro data on the host can replace investment in more expensive hard disk storage facilities.

- Traveler's Insurance Company uses the virtual diskette technique for linking its insurance agents in the field with the corporate data base. Agents use their micros to download new insurance rates or other news from what appears to them to be an additional microcomputer disk drive. The virtual diskette link also allows them to leave messages that other agents or management can access from mainframe storage without going through format conversions.

Data Insertion

Some "integrated" link packages allow automatic conversion of the data selected from a variety of mainframe data base files into a form understood by micro spreadsheets, data bases, or word processing programs. The data are read directly to the micro's application software. This capability fulfills one of the most important desires of end-users: to be able to convert mainframe data into a format immediately compatible with their existing micro software, such as Lotus 1-2-3®, Symphony®, or dBase II®. Once they have extracted and inserted the needed mainframe data, they can return directly to their micro program.

DOWNLOAD TO A COMPATIBLE FORMAT

One data insertion link package allows users to extract only the fields or records needed from one mainframe file or several files simultaneously. The data is automatically reformatted and downloaded into the microcomputer-based Lotus or dBase (as well as Framework and Symphony) software. The package includes basic security procedures for limiting access to mainframe data, especially if files are being accessed in combination.

Cooperative Processing

The general goal of the link is the closest possible integration of data on the mainframe with that held on the micro while allowing management to monitor and control the use of information. Cooperative processing links allow users to establish an intelligent connection between mainframe and micro applications along with enhanced data transfer, data security, and data integrity procedures. These packages usually require a costly mainframe resident software component. "Intelligent link" products can cost between $20,000 and $150,000.

Cooperative processing better leverages the unique capabilities of the mainframe and the micro. Mainframe computers are best at manipulating large amounts of data. The micro excels at displaying information the way an individual wants. Within limits imposed to insure security and integrity, cooperative processing allows a closely coupled working relationship between the personal computer and the mainframe, permitting data to be passed back and forth and displayed according to the user's needs. Thus, each machine does what it is best at doing, allowing greater productivity for both computers.

One package from a link provider specializing in human resource management systems provides mainframe communications in the context of micro applications. The micro applications encompass data held on the mainframe; in other words, portions of the mainframe data base are distributed to the micro and maintained synchronously. A fourth-generation command language allows data base access through the link, and users can write command language statements that allow them to build applications over the link. They can adjust the link to a particular application, and they can further "personalize" the application by customizing screens and interactions to suit different users. All this functionality is provided through mainframe and micro application software.

- One user of this cooperative processing product is customizing a software package to create an interactive employee benefits questionnaire. A new employee sits at a personal computer and responds to prompts for personal or family information. The printout of this information becomes the formal document for signature by the employee. Later an operator can upload the employee data and use this information to complete the enrollment process using an application in place on the mainframe.

This incomplete list of link options for end-users can help users specify what they need from data processing managers responsible for implementing micro-mainframe connections. A wide range of capabilities are available. Users who understand their options are more likely to persuade understandably reluctant DP personnel to accommodate their needs for more timely access to corporate data and to mainframe processing power.

QUESTIONS FOR REVIEW:

1. What motivations have spurred micro-to-mainframe links?
2. Who are the players in micro-to-mainframe politics?
3. Describe the role users have on developing the link.
4. Describe the role of DP in the link. What are the DP departments' concerns?
5. Why is a corporate telecommunications policy needed?
6. Describe the components in the mainframe environment.
7. Sketch the categories of link options.
8. Describe terminal emulation and its advantages.
9. Describe simple downloading of screens or files.
10. Describe selective data access.
11. Describe the two forms of uploading—batch entry and auto data entry.
12. Contrast virtual diskette and data insertion.
13. Describe cooperative processing.

FOR DISCUSSION:

1. What would happen if the mainframe vendors eased the link requirements for micros?
2. Why did the micro-to-mainframe market stay small for a period of years?
3. Where do you see the micro-to-mainframe product direction going in the next five years?

REFERENCES

BASIL, RICHARD. "Linking Micros to Mainframes." *Micro Communications*, February 1984.

BELITSOS, BYRON. "Specialized Solutions." *Micro Communications,* October 1985.

BLACK, UYLES D. *Data Communications, Networks, and Distributed Processing.* Reston, Virginia: Reston Publishing Co., 1984.

"The Computer Slump." *Business Week,* June 2, 1985, pp. 74–78.

DURR, MICHAEL. "Ins and Outs of Data Integrity." *Micro Communications,* January 1985.

GALLANT, J. "Navigating the Micro-to-Mainframe Seas." *Computerworld,* October 3, 1984, pp. 15–18.

GOODING, C. "Links Start to Meet Promises." *Management Review,* March 1985, pp. 18–21.

EMMETT, ARIELLE. "Micro-to-Mainframe Links." *Popular Computing,* August 1985.

LISKER, PETER. "The Missing Link." *PC Week,* March 19, 1985.

MAGID, LAWRENCE J. and BOESCHER, JOHN. *The Electronic Link: Using the IBM PC to Communicate.* New York: John Wiley, 1985.

"Micro-Mainframe Choices Expand." *Mini-Micro Systems,* May 1985.

MOREL, CHARLES. "Micro-to-Mainframe Link Allows Five Sessions." *Mini-Micro Systems,* May 1985.

PHILLIPS, STUART G. "Micro-to-Mainframe Communications: What Managers Should Know." *Telecommunications,* November 1984.

SIMPSON, RICHARD. "Stepping into File Transfers." *Micro Communications,* June 1985.

THISTLETHWAITE, GLENN, JR. "Micro-Mainframe Links Help DP Professionals Regain Lost Credibility." *Data Management,* April 1985, pp. 14–17.

CHAPTER TWELVE

— RESALE OF DIRECTORY INFO.

Videotex in Business

OBJECTIVES

● Define business videotex and see current applications.

● Describe why business videotex is growing in use.

● Understand system design, architecture, and standards.

● Contrast videotex against print media, micro-to-mainframe links, electronic mail, and public data bases.

[Handwritten annotations: EIS, ELECTRONIC PUBLISHING, EDI, IDENTITY CRISES; WHAT IS IT: EM, EBB, INFO UTILITIES, CONNECTED, PC's, TV's, PHONES, WHO'S CONNECTED, FIRST TIME, NOVICE, SOPHISTICATED; INFORMATION COMMONS?, COMMUNICATION ORIENTED]

INTRODUCTION

In the near future, the operations of many information-intensive businesses will be dramatically affected by the use of private videotex systems. Most telecommunications industry analysts expect the application of videotex in U.S. business, after overcoming a difficult early growth period, will soon mature into a significant corporate (and consumer*) force, similar to its recent growth in Europe.

[Handwritten annotation: PUBLIC ACCESS / RESPONSE TO INFORMATION SUBJECTS]

Business videotex refers to a data base communications and display application running on an existing company computer network that has been designed so workers with no knowledge of computers can quickly and easily select needed information from company data bases; users are given menu-driven ("multiple choice") access to stored text—often enhanced by graphic displays—via a desktop personal computer or dedicated videotex terminal.

[Handwritten annotation: EXAMPLES FOR PUBLISHING]

Videotex is a form of electronic publishing, a way to make widely used company information electronically available. An office videotex system could give access, for example, to a complete listing of the company's current sales literature, an up-to-date copy of personnel policies and procedures, or a quick look at the corporate annual report.

Many business videotex networks also allow users to con-

---

*The most popular consumer videotex services are electronic banking and "tele-shopping" via a personal computer in the home.

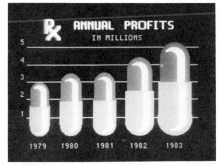

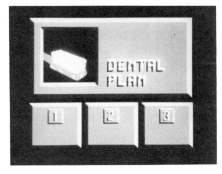

Courtesy of Aesthetics, Inc.

FIGURE 12–1: Typical graphics—
enhanced pages used in corporate
videotex systems.

duct electronic transactions. For example, in-house users can
order such items as office supplies or sales literature, and customers can electronically order products from point-of-purchase
terminals or from their own desktop terminals after viewing
product information.

The ability to transmit color graphics in videotex displays is not as essential for business videotex applications as it is for consumer videotex or teletext[1]; many in-house applications of videotex rely on relatively simple ASCII-based text displays. But color graphics displays may be necessary when businesses use videotex as a sales and marketing communications vehicle. Moreover, as the graphic enhancement of electronic text becomes less expensive and as transmission capacity becomes more plentiful, more in-house videotex systems will feature color graphic displays like those pictured in Figure 12–1.

Finally, we include public on-line data base services used by business (such as Dow Jones News/Retrieval or DIALOG) in our definition of videotex, even though these employ ordinary ASCII-formatted displays and are not menu-driven. These systems still fulfill the fundamental videotex criterion of easy electronic access to public information.

Though it is less conventional to include these (and even ASCII-based communication and display systems) in the videotex category, our purpose is to make a simple distinction between data bases created mainly for distribution of information that already exists (videotex) and those more traditional data base systems that must be manipulated to create new information through sophisticated data inquiry languages. As seen in Chapter Eleven, micro-to-mainframe systems require users to enter sensitive, private files and define what information they need and how that information will be presented; by contrast, videotex is a simple way of organizing public information in advance of any user's request. The information could be an airline schedule, stock market information, product specifications, or corporate policy that needs to be quoted in a memo—data that already is written down but is difficult to find. Videotex provides a way to organize and display this information so it can be accessed quickly and easily.

THE FUTURE OF VIDEOTEX

Videotex is a corporate information management system well suited for the age of business telematics. Videotex software, which is easily installed on a company's existing data processing equipment, can link the user's desktop to digitized text and graphic information resident on company data bases or other remote data bases over existing telephone lines or data communications networks. These systems go beyond traditional data communications: They allow access to authoritative data bases for a far greater number of users, while offering them the ability to transact much of their business electronically rather than on paper—and all this with little or no training in using the system.

Electronic Connections

Companies that install videotex systems will be able to enfranchise more employees—as well as customers, vendors, distributors, and suppliers—into their corporate networks. Videotex is a window through which they can see information; it provides an effective way of making up-to-the-minute information available to everyone in the company or everyone who interacts with the company. Indeed, videotex will be the vehicle through which large numbers of information workers will first put their hands on and use computer-related devices in the workplace. But it should be remembered that the improved user interface offered by videotex is gained by sacrificing the flexibility and greater functionality offered by more specialized systems, such as advanced micro-to-mainframe links.

Influencial Factors

Two factors will aid in the spread of videotex: (1.) The demand for better means of distribution of already existing information that is needed by information workers; and (2.) the increasing penetration of personal computers in the business environment. In the future, personal computers will help increase communication productivity in business through playing a dual role. They will function as communication systems linked both to traditional corporate data bases and to the simpler menu-driven videotex systems.

Ultimately, videotex will become a pervasive business tool in three ways:

EBB

1. As an *in-house communication medium* that improves information access for all employees, regardless of geographical location, position in the company, or computer literacy, and that allows employees to conduct simple transactions such as ordering company sales literature by filling in the blanks on an electronic order form.
2. As a *business-to-business* or *marketing communication system* that can enhance a company's competitive posi-

APPLICATION DATA ENTRY

tion through improved responsiveness to external demands for product or service information. This includes giving customers the ability to conduct sales transactions electronically through videotex terminals installed on the customer's premises or at the point of purchase (see Buick example below).

3. As a means of gaining *access to hundreds of on-line business, science, and engineering data bases* offered via public on-line data base services (according to our expanded definition).

INFO. UTILITIES

CURRENT USES OF VIDEOTEX

The following examples illustrate the first two ways cited above in which videotex will become an important communications tool in today's corporate environment: Digital Equipment Corporation's (DEC) in-house videotex system, currently the world's largest, and Buick Motor Division's point-of-purchase videotex system for information retrieval at the Buick dealer's site. (An example of the use of public on-line data bases in a corporate environment is given at the end of Chapter Fifteen.)

- DEC is a pioneer developer and user of in-house corporate videotex, with more than 7,000 employees participating worldwide and more than 100 installations of its videotex system in the marketplace.

  DEC departments that had been responsible for providing traditional hard copy communications within the company began by using videotex as a secondary communications medium. Once electronic publishing was proven the more effective tool, most of them moved to primary reliance on videotex. Now any department that needs to disseminate information internally simply has its departmental "videotex system operator" create the videotex pages and load them into "infobases" stored on VAX computers. Employees use DEC personal computers and terminals to gain access to the system.

  Most of DEC's infobases lack graphics, but terminals located in common areas of the company, such as lobbies, cafeterias, or conference rooms, use the North American Presentation Level Protocol Syntex (NAPLPS) videotex protocol to build graphics displays for a more attractive presentation of the company newsmagazine, electronic maps, stock market updates, new product announcements, or stockholders' meetings.

- Applications targeted for desktop access to the system normally use the simpler ASCII (text-only) protocol. A selection of these include the following:

Electronic Happenings at DEC

1. Electronic newsletters.
    Manufacturing and engineering.
    Update on competitors.
    Site newsletters.
2. Manuals and indexes.
    Administrative and sales forms index.
    Software and hardware manuals.
    Personnel policies.
    Index of promotional literature.
3. Company bulletin boards.
    Job openings.
    Upcoming events.
4. Schedules.
    Seminars and training.
    Transportation and lodging.

Many of these applications allow transaction processing, such as electronic ordering of office supplies, or on-line registration for training classes. According to William Carlyle, manager of Publishing Services and Videotex, such interactive services "receive the most visibility and interest. Without them, a corporate videotex system will not succeed."[2]

Buick Motor Division first piloted videotex in 1983. Today Buick is using videotex to aid in providing product information to both dealers and end-users. (The system is also used internally among Buick employees.)

- Buick's videotex system provides detailed information on an increasingly complex product to 3,000 dealers and millions of potential customers. The simple menu-driven terminals located on the Buick showroom floor offer access to information on financing terms, models available, status of an ordered vehicle, prices, customer-selected options, and more. The information is updated frequently from a central point at company headquarters in Flint, Michigan. Potential customers can quickly and easily comparison shop over videotex terminals instead of waiting until a salesperson is available; Buick salespeople also use the system to access detailed dealer-specific product information.[3]

Business videotex applications like these are just coming of age in the United States, but have been in broad use in Europe for more than a decade. Soon after the first television-based videotex system (or teletext) went into operation in England in the mid-1970s, the concept spread quickly to other European countries, branching out into both consumer and business applications. In mid-1985, more than 1,000 business videotex systems were operating in Europe, and more than 40 percent of large companies in Britain had internal videotex services. By contrast, only about 150 U.S. companies were operating videotex systems. However, business videotex installations in the United States may jump to more than 3,100 by 1990, according to Link Resources, an industry consulting firm.[4]

As the videotex industry enters the 1990s, most Fortune 1000 corporations will have their own private videotex systems and will also make extensive use of public data base services. A large minority of smaller companies will also find videotex in its various forms to be cost-effective.

But there are numerous hindrances to the full development of the American business videotex market. Videotex systems are expensive, and it is difficult to quantify their cost-effectiveness. Another major barrier springs from misunderstanding its potential. Although videotex is a much-publicized communications concept, it is often perceived as being limited to one marketplace: electronic delivery of information to home television sets via television signals. It is well known that most of these home-services experiments have failed financially in the United States. Only recently has the videotex industry recovered from its association with this unhappy market, which has obscured understanding of the usefulness of the medium in other far less ambitious applications.

At the same time, a specialized form of videotex targeted to home and business users of microcomputers—the popular on-line data base services such as The Source and CompuServe—quietly gained wide acceptance in the U.S. business community.

Today, business videotex in its several forms is the fastest growing segment of the videotex industry. The public on-line data base services are offering an increasing variety of data bases useful to business. But perhaps the most significant development for business is the private business videotex systems developed to serve a particular corporation's information needs.

VIDEOTEX SYSTEM DESIGN AND ARCHITECTURE

Videotex systems consist of four essential components: the host computer, the transmission media, the composing/data entry devices, and the users' display devices. The typical system architecture is illustrated in Figure 12–2.

1. The *host computer* can be as small as a microcomputer or as large as a mainframe. Its size depends upon the amount of storage, the number of users needing simultaneous access, and the speed of access desired by users.

In many business videotex systems, the videotex system host is adapted to the existing in-house system and data base. One common approach in a large company is to front-end the company's existing hardware system with a dedicated host minicomputer such as VAX 11/780 or IBM Series/1. This front-end processor then can be used to reformat data bases stored on the existing system into whatever videotex protocol is being used or simply to store ASCII-format "pages" created and entered from videotex composing devices (see below).

Some videotex systems used for point-of-purchase product marketing are equipped with videodisk players for still-frame or full-motion video transmission. Some industry analysts predict that in-house training departments may also find video a useful component in business videotex applications.

It should be noted that in some cases, no new hardware is required to establish a videotex system. A company may opt to add videotex application software to its existing computer system (if the use of a simple protocol such as ASCII is acceptable).

2. *The transmission system* used for business videotex signals is the same as that used for other forms of voice and data communication.

3. *Composing/data entry devices* are needed for manually composing and entering "pages" of information into videotex systems. This labor-intensive process of page creation may re-

LOADING
SUBJECT
DATA

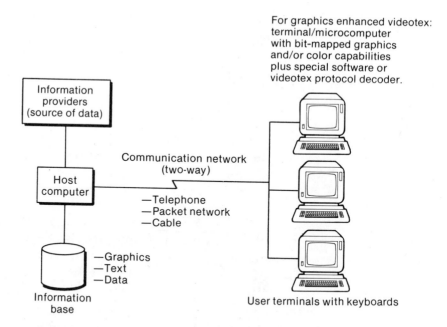

For graphics enhanced videotex:
terminal/microcomputer
with bit-mapped graphics
and/or color capabilities
plus special software or
videotex protocol decoder.

Information
providers
(source of data)

Communication network
(two-way)

Host
computer

—Telephone
—Packet network
—Cable

—Graphics
—Text
—Data

Information
base

User terminals with keyboards

FIGURE 12–2: Videotex system architecture.

quire several minutes or as much as an hour, depending on the complexity of the data and graphics involved. (However, creating videotex pages for use on typical business videotex systems is often less expensive and time consuming than it is to set type and paste up a page of material for the printer; and it probably costs less to create and maintain a videotex "infobase" than it does to create and maintain a traditional data base.)

Videotex programmers normally use microcomputers as the data and graphics entry device; devices such as digitizing tablets can be used when page creation involves sophisticated graphics.

4. *The display system* for the end-user of a videotex system is normally a microcomputer. Applications that make use of color and sophisticated graphics require addition of either special software or hardware decoders to a display station (a terminal or personal computer) that has bit-mapped and/or color capabilities.

In addition, a number of manufacturers offer dedicated videotex terminals that are more functional and less costly than microcomputers.

Videotex Standards

Several videotex protocols are in use in the United States. The most predominant standards are ASCII and the specialized videotex standard NAPLPS; each offers different text and graphic display capabilities.

1. ASCII (American Standard Code for Information Interface) is the traditional U.S. standard for computer communications. ASCII can be used to encode videotex software when the videotex system is to be a close adaptation of a company's existing data processing system. ASCII handles text and has minimal color and graphics capabilities.

2. NAPLPS (North American Presentation Level Protocol Syntax)—whose encoding system is a subset of ASCII—has become the de facto American standard for videotex systems with graphics capabilities. A special terminal decoder must be added to the display stations accessing NAPLPS videotex systems. Most U.S. videotex hardware manufacturers are now including NAPLPS decoders in their hardware.

(NAPLPS is actually an AT&T enhancement of the Canadian videotex protocol, Telidon. NAPLPS is particularly efficient for generating graphics forms and colors and for formatting information on the typical 80-column-by-25-line-frame of a computer screen.)

Two other noteworthy videotex protocols are the British Prestel and the French Antiope systems. Though NAPLPS has superior program flexibility and display resolutions, Prestel in particular is considered less expensive, simpler to use, and may be a better choice where graphic quality is not as important.[5]

USING VIDEOTEX

Videotex is a technique for packaging user access to data bases and electronic transactions. It provides a "front end" or envelope around the traditional computer-user interface, so a broad spectrum of users without specialized training with computers can enter the system. Thus, from the standpoint of the novice user, a videotex system is designed so (1.) The procedures to be followed by the user are intuitively obvious (no training or manuals are needed); (2.) The available operations at the ter-

[handwritten: Human Factors for Selection Process]

minal are limited and consistent so the user can't get lost or "crash" the system. These operations include the following:

- Selecting an item from a menu by number or letter.
- Selecting a page by number or name.
- Moving to the next page in sequence.
- Backing up one page or to start.
- Backing up to a previous menu for a new item selection.
- Access to HELP.

The use of videotex can be better understood by comparing it to other communication systems. Videotex has important advantages (and a few notable disadvantages) when compared with other text-oriented communication systems such as the print media, micro-to-mainframe links, electronic mail, and public information services.

Videotex Versus Print Media

The advantages of videotex over printed information include speed and selectivity. But there are important trade-offs to keep in mind.

The *speed* of distribution of new information is the most striking advantage of videotex. In conventional publishing, the time needed to research, write, and edit a page of information is usually far less than the time consumed in the print production process. Electronic distribution of information allows an organization to shortcut most of the physical steps involved in the print production cycle, which includes typesetting, printing, and physical distribution. Videotex, on the other hand, is *electronic publishing:* New information is made available almost immediately after the page creation process; once the text and relatively simple graphics display are entered into the videotex system by a skilled operator, the information is available electronically to users at terminals. From this point, the timing of the actual information transfer is really up to the recipient of the information, not the publisher or distributor. In sum, the information is made available far more promptly, while the cost of publishing can be significantly less.

The *selectivity* of videotex, like its speed, arises out of the telematic convergence of telecommunications and computer technology. The economics of producing printed publications dictate that they are printed and assembled in one physical unit. In a videotex system, users employ simple key words and menus to search a computer data base for the line, page or pages of information they need, without accumulating, filing, and storing stacks of useless paper.

Electronic clipping services (available from the public on-line data base services) offer even greater selectivity and increased speed of retrieval. A user can request that the host computer be programmed to make continuous, automatic keyword searches of its data base and copy items of interest into the user's private files.

- One midwestern electroplating company employs an online clipping service to obtain news stories about its clients and suppliers. This company's officers logged on to the service one morning to find that the Rhode Island plant of a key industry supplier had burned to the ground the night before. This gave them an advantage of days and even weeks over their competitors in locating alternate suppliers.[6]

The main disadvantage of videotex when compared with the print medium lies in the physical limitations of a display terminal for conveying information. A screen can display only one page at a time, and terminals are not easily portable like booklets or sheets of paper. Terminal screens are also tiresome to gaze at for long periods of time.

Videotex Versus Micro-to-Mainframe Links

Videotex and micro-to-mainframe links can be compared by considering the following factors: type of information made available, system flexibility, and ease of use.

Information. Micro-to-mainframe links help a narrow range of professionals access specialized, sensitive corporate information. This information is stored as traditional mainframe files—and zealously safeguarded by DP departments. Such information can include the key data bases used by accounting, engineering, finance, and marketing departments. Access to it is restricted to specialized users who have been entrusted with secret access codes or passwords.

Videotex leaves most of these specialized files intact in the traditional mainframe environment. The point of videotex is to make less sensitive, more general-interest information electronically available through menu-driven selections. Much of this information was formerly available only in hard copy form; a private videotex system can make it easily and cheaply available to a wide range of users, including secretaries, clerks, and other office workers; nontechnical managers and executives; and customers and suppliers. Many of these users may never have had a compelling reason to use a computer in the workplace before the advent of videotex.

Issues of data integrity and data security are very important in micro-mainframe links. On videotex systems, however, such issues have no import; information is meant to be located, retrieved, and stored; it is assumed that information available on a videotex system is "safe" for users—no matter how inexperienced—to freely access.

(On the other hand, videotex can be used to keep confidential information out of general circulation through the use of passwords or access codes. Electronically published documents are easier to safeguard than paper documents.)

Flexibility. Sophisticated micro-mainframe links allow far more flexibility than videotex systems. Users can download data from mainframes, manipulate the data, and even upload new data to the mainframe. "Integrated links," for example, allow users to search mainframe files, extract a unique set of financial figures, and download this data into spreadsheets on their desktop micros; this data can later be uploaded to the same mainframe file. Cooperative processing links offer users even more flexible operations.

Greater information selectivity than that available from videotex is provided by any micro-to-mainframe link that goes beyond the simple downloading of screens of information ("screen capture"). With the use of a data-inquiry language, the user can produce new information. For example, a manager may want a listing of first-quarter results over the past five years. The mainframe can be commanded to go through existing files to produce an ad hoc report.

Users of videotex, on the other hand, are interested in retrieval of publicly available information and in performing simple transactions such as the electronic ordering of products. The limited set of operations available at a videotex terminal were discussed above.

LESS PROCESSING
+
MORE INQUIRY
+
DATA ENTRY
TRANS.

Ease of Use. The use of advanced micro-to-mainframe links requires a high degree of computer literacy, including programming experience and an understanding of mainframe file access and data manipulation procedures. Users often must understand how mainframe files are organized and need to know exactly what they are looking for in these files.

Videotex is a service-oriented information system. The user is led through the system by simple menus. In addition, the use of color graphics and even full-color, full-motion video obviously makes videotex more attractive to the typical user. Graphic displays are rarely found in micro-to-mainframe systems.

It should be noted that some applications on micro-to-mainframe links have been designed for user-friendly access through fourth-generation query languages; here is an area of overlap with videotex. However, the major distinction remains: Even in these cases, the files are restricted to certain authorized users, and access is through English-language queries and not through simple "multiple choice" menus.

Videotex Versus Electronic Mail

Although some private electronic mail systems have evolved into "ad hoc" videotex systems, and though many corporate videotex systems include some sort of electronic mail service, the two terms cannot be used interchangeably.

Electronic mail is basically point-to-point communication, usually with the capability to store communications off-line. Generally, it refers to the ability of any one person on a network to compose and send text to one person or to a small distribution list on the network; videotex, on the other hand, is a

NOT MUCH DIFFERENT OR

data base-oriented *broadcast* communication medium. Electronic mail involves composing and sending electronic messages; videotex involves electronic publication and distribution of manuals, booklets, newsletters, price lists, and so forth for independent access by a multitude of videotex users. In addition, the special color graphics display capabilities of a videotex terminal differ from the simple text displays available on electronic mail systems.

FORM {

Private Videotex Versus Public On-Line Data Base Services

Information services such as The Source, CompuServe, and Dow Jones News/Retrieval are huge, centrally located mainframe data bases, (See Figure 12-3) with nationwide general audiences and with greatly varying information sources. Business videotex, on the other hand, refers to a private corporate data base, with input only from corporate information resources. The difference is the degree of public access: Public on-line data bases are "highly public" services accessible by anyone with a subscription and a computer; corporate systems are meant for wide access within one company or by the company's customers, vendors, and suppliers.

BUSINESS APPLICATIONS OF VIDEOTEX

Simply installing a private videotex system does not guarantee greater communication productivity in a company. Some companies have dropped videotex systems after trying them, often because the systems turned out to be more complicated to operate than promised. One data communications director shut down a videotex system after one year and a $100,000 investment, because the "interaction of workers with the terminal was the critical success factor, and it failed miserably."[7]

Another company, Pacific Bell, has had to skillfully shift the offerings available on its system as it has adjusted to unexpected usage patterns.

- In November 1983, Pacific Bell installed a corporate videotex system to be used by approximately 400 middle and upper managers.

FIGURE 12–3: Disk drives used for storage of on-line data bases on the DIALOG information retrieval system.

All employees participating in the "executive information system" were given desktop personal computers.

The system includes the following services:

- Corporate (Pacific Bell) news.
- Marketing and sales information.
- Financial information.
- Conference, exhibition, and seminar schedules.
- Electronic mail.

The information included in the system is entered by about 25 "information providers" within the company, who also distribute their information in more traditional ways via newsletters, telephone recordings, and bulletin boards. According to Jeff Richards, videotex product manager in Pacific Bell's New Business Opportunities division, one of the original intentions of the videotex system was to eliminate the need to disseminate some executive information via paper-based media. But the competition from existing media was stronger than expected. The pilot revealed that users were not completely willing to change their usual habits in favor of retrieving information from a screen display. The result is that Pacific Bell has decided not to allow the duplication of the same information in several media; the current thrust is to allow hard copy, voice recordings, and videotex to complement one another as information sources.

Despite such implementation difficulties, videotex applications in business are proliferating. Figure 12–4 indicates the variety of possible applications. These come under two major classifications: in-house videotex and business-to-business videotex.

In-House Corporate Videotex

Among the more important applications of in-house corporate videotex are the following; marketing and sales, administration, engineering and manufacturing, and companywide communications.

1. MARKETING AND SALES: Because sales information in most organizations is constantly in flux, marketing and sales departments probably have the greatest need for in-house videotex systems. This is especially true if they need to communicate with remote sales offices or distributors. A videotex system can give sales personnel electronic access to constantly updated information about price changes, inventory levels, customer order status, and credit terms, or to electronically published product catalogs, account profiles, and sales literature.

2. ADMINISTRATION: Publishing administrative procedures often requires expensive printing costs, cumbersome physical distribution, and storage of large quantities of paper in pervasive file cabinets and bookcases. Many of these documents—policy and procedure manuals, health and medical insurance forms, office supply catalogs, corporate directives, employee manuals, and such—can be more efficiently produced, stored, and distributed in a videotex system. Rather than hunting through file cabinets or making phone calls, employees can bring the desired forms or documents to the videotex terminal screen by calling up a simple series of menus.

FIGURE 12–4 Videotex applications.

Corporate Videotex Applications

FORD AEROSPACE

Administration	Marketing and Sales	Engineering and Manufacturing
Policies and procedures	Sales literature index	Product specifications
Manuals	Product catalogs	Project management
Personal benefits	Account profiles	Service manuals
Vendor agreements	Price books	Plant safety procedures
Budgets and financial reports	Customer order status	User manuals
Office supply catalogs		Reference tables
Signature authorization and approval lists		Order status
		Project management
		Product cross reference

Communications	Education and Training	General
Job postings	Course schedules	Timetables (railroad, bus, air)
Lobby directories	Newsletter	Emergency data
Newsletter	Course cancellations	First aid
Bulletin boards	Registration systems	
Cafeteria menus	Training manuals	
AP news		
Weather reports		
Promotions		
Phone directories		
Plant/office directory		

Business-to-Business Videotex Applications

Administrative	Sales and Marketing	Manufacturing and Distribution
Credit policies	Electronic newsletters	Order status
Billing problems	Price books	Order inquiry
Electronic bulletin board	Online ordering	Manufacturing capabilities
Customer visits	Discount schedules	Parts lists
Trade show schedule	Product promotions	Parts cross-reference
Offices by region	Product specifications	Transportation schedules
Sales reps by region	Product applications	
Problem reporting	Competitive applications	
	Selling tips for wholesalers	
	Directories	
	Market surveys	

Once administrative information is on-line, it can be up-dated quickly and cheaply. The most obvious examples are employee directories or personnel files. Instead of periodically compiling and printing a new company telephone directory to account for department reorganizations, promotions, hirings, and layoffs, a videotex-based telephone directory can be kept current at an absolute minimum of trouble and expense.

3. ENGINEERING AND MARKETING: Research and development, engineering, and manufacturing departments traditionally produce numerous paper documents that need to be carefully prepared, distributed, and "signed off" on before they are just as carefully filed. Technical specifications, parts lists, reference tables, order status reports, milestone dates, and progress reports are just a few examples of such documents. Better and more accurate communication and filing of such delicate and timely information can be achieved using videotex.

4. COMPANYWIDE COMMUNICATIONS: Videotex is very suitable for general, corporatewide applications. For example, job postings, internal newsletters, lobby directories, Associated Press news, weather reports, and cafeteria menus all can be distributed using an in-house videotex system.

Business-To-Business Videotex

Business-to-business videotex is probably the fastest growing segment of the business videotex industry. As illustrated in the Buick case study cited earlier in this chapter, one of the most dramatic applications of videotex is providing product information to customers, vendors, suppliers, or dealers through terminals at their own site.

Business-to-business videotex often gives a company an advantage over competitors that have not yet discovered it. It allows for the advantages of "narrowcasting" versus print media or television broadcasting: Advertising messages can be targeted over the videotex network to the subscribing clientele, who can "tune in" when they need to get access to sales and product information.

Some systems are fully interactive: Customers are given the option to send feedback messages to product managers, participate in on-line conferences or electronic bulletin boards focusing on specific product issues, or even complete and send in market research surveys.

But perhaps the most important advantage offered by many business-to-business systems is product information coupled with on-line ordering capability. This is illustrated in American Hospital Supply Corporation's (AHSC) use of a videotex system for the distribution of product information and accompanied by what AHSC calls "automated order entry."

EDI

- American Hospital Supply Corporation of Chicago manufactures and distributes medical and hospital products, grossing more than $3 billion annually. Its videotex system, called ASAP, offers AHSC customers electronic access to information on thousands of products and the ability to order AHSC products from their videotex terminals. Each year, more than $1.5 billion in product orders — nearly half of AHSC's gross total—are taken electronically; the company's customers use the videotex system to perform marketing and sales functions that used to cost AHSC an estimated $6 million a year in salaries and commissions for a large sales force.

  Customers using the ASAP can save 40 percent to 60 percent in order processing; can receive printed confirmation of an order within minutes of placing it; and can leave special messages for sales representatives. Customers can even arrange for "automatic ordering," in which their remote computer can communicate with the ASAP host computer on a regular basis, automatically checking inventories and ordering new supplies when needed.[8]

Other Types of Business-to-Business Videotex. There are two other categories of business-to-business videotex: industry-specific and advertising-supported.

Industry-Specific Videotex. A variety of information providers have developed industry-specific videotex systems. Such systems attempt to provide a complete information service to a narrowly defined segment of a particular industry.

- AT&T offers an industry-specific videotex service for real estate agents and brokers. The Real Estate Information Service (REIS) provides brokers and customers with extensive property-listing information, as well as community news, school zones, maps, real estate news, and other information pertinent to a potential buyer of real estate. The system has sophisticated color graphics capabilities, and full motion video became available on the service at the end of 1985.

Courtesy of Regis McKenna, Inc.

FIGURE 12–5: David Schneer, on-line data base researcher for Regis McKenna, searches through a full-text file in NEXIS.

Advertising-Supported Videotex. Some business-to-business videotex services employ on-line "advertising" in order to reduce the user's costs. The Phycom videotex service, for example, allows doctors and other medical professionals to retrieve up-to-date information on more than 1,700 pharmaceutical products; sponsors of the system have a ready-made narrowcasting medium for reaching busy health care practitioners.

PUBLIC ON-LINE DATA BASE SERVICES

Currently, the most successful videotex services (in terms of number of subscribers) appear to be those that offer access to public data bases displayed in the ASCII format to both businesses and consumers. The giants of this industry segment are The Source, CompuServe, Dow Jones News/Retrieval, DIALOG, and NEXIS.

Both The Source and CompuServe have added a multitude of business videotex services to their general public offerings.

Dow Jones News/Retrieval has always maintained a strong core of business and financial data bases that can be browsed, searched by key words, and downloaded; these include the full

```
·PRINTS    User:030605   13oct85                              PAGE:    4
P028: PR 16/5/ALL (items 1 3)                       Item    1 of   3
```

DIALOG (VERSION 2)
DIALOG File 16: PROMT - 72-85/Oct, Week 3 (Copr. Predicasts Inc. 1985)

1120593
  IBM DEVELOPING MAJOR VIDEOTEX SYSTEM.
VideoPrint   September 10, 1984   p. 1,2

    IBM will introduce a large scale videotex system for the corporate market in 6
mo. The system will be standard-independent but will initially emphasize ASCII to
take advantage of the large number of installed ASCII terminals and PCs. It will
run on existing IBM installations concurrently with other applications. IBM does
not have to develop its own system because a suitable French system exists, but it
apparently wants full internal control over design and development.

    *1USA *United States *4811528 *Bsns Videotex Svcs ex Database *36 *services data;
      *International Business Machines; Duns No: *00-136-8083; Ticker: *IBM; CUSIP:
      *459200

1002819
  FEATURES/Video/A-V: Should You Invest in Private Videotex.
#Business Marketing (formerly Industrial Marketing)   March 1984   p. 66-77

    Most future growth for videotex will be in business-to-business marketing
applications, according to N Wiener of Strategic Futures (New York), graphics
consultants. As computers continue to penetrate business management at a quickening
pace, private videotex systems offer communication efficiencies unmatched by other
technologies. Moreover, achieving those efficiencies is more within the grasp of
business than for consumers. Three types of private videotex systems a company can
install include an internal system within a company's own operation; an external
system which ties customers and suppliers to an expanded version of the internal
system; and a semi-public external system which opens selected company databases to
a wider audience. Article examines the potential and pitfalls of private videotex
as a business-to-business marketing tool and presents flow charts of its
applications. A related article examines the more limited option of becoming a
corporate 'information provider' to established videotex systems.

    *1USA *United States *4811528 *Bsns Videotex Svcs ex Database *33 *products
                            (cont. next page)   **DIALOG**
  ──────   INFORMATION SERVICES, INC.
  003024

FIGURE 12–6: Samples of bibliographic extracts available through DIALOG.

text of *The Wall Street Journal* back to January 1984, plus selected stories from *Barron's* and *The Wall Street Journal* back to 1979. The Dow Jones News offers daily on-line financial and business news reports supplied by *The Wall Street Journal* reporters; their stories go on-line only 90 seconds after being received by the *Journal*.

NEXIS and DIALOG, the leading specialized bibliographic services, offer access to a multitude of data bases relevant to business users. Both services offer full-text on-line versions of most daily and weekly publications, as well as abstracts of many

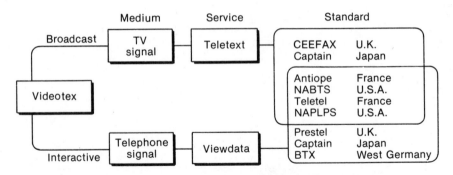

FIGURE 12–7: A comparison of teletext and viewdata (or videotex).

other publications. NEXIS carries the largest number of full text publications; more than 120 newspapers and magazines, including the *New York Times* back to 1980, are available electronically. DIALOG has an especially complete bibliographic indexing feature that allows users to search for specific topics in more than 400 periodicals covering virtually all fields, some of which are indexed back to 1959.

QUESTIONS FOR REVIEW:

1. Describe business videotex.
2. What are some factors making business videotex popular?
3. Illustrate a current example of videotex use.
4. Describe the four essential components of videotex systems.
5. Describe the two predominant videotex standards.
6. Contrast videotex and print media.
7. Contrast videotex and micro-to-mainframe links.
8. Contrast videotex and electronic mail.
9. Contrast videotex and public on-line data base services.
10. Describe one of the applications of in-house corporate videotex.
11. What is business-to-business videotex? Give some examples.

FOR DISCUSSION:

1. Why doesn't videotex, with its user-friendliness and simplicity, replace other forms of data viewing?
2. What can prevent business videotex from growing in use?

NOTES FOR CHAPTER TWELVE

1. Videotex in the broadest sense actually includes two separate applications: teletext, a one-way text service delivered through standard television signals, and viewdata, an interactive service delivered via a telephone network or cable system through a series of menus. Figure 12–7 illustrates the traditional differences between teletext and viewdata. However, in this book, the term *business videotex,* or simply *videotex,* will be used to refer specifically to business applications; the term *viewdata* is European in origin and unlikely to gain popular usage in the United States.

Videotex varies substantially from teletext because of its use of interactive menus. From the minute users access a business videotex system, they are taken progressively from one menu level to another; this continues until the desired information is located. Teletext, by contrast, involves the broadcast of pages of information that are displayed under control of the teletext provider.

Menu-driven systems do have their drawbacks. For more experienced users, menus can become very time consuming and tedious; the user must follow the same path—perhaps involving multiple selections off multiple menus—taken many times before. Fortunately, many videotex systems now allow shortcuts to those who know their way around the data base structure; use of artificial intelligence interfaces are also cutting down on the tedium of menus without detracting from their easy-to-use characteristics.

2. William Carlyle, "DEC's Internal Use of Videotex," *Videotex '84,* (New York: Online Conferences, Inc., 1984), p. 181.

3. The Business Council of the Videotex Industry Association, "Business Videotex Comes of Age," Draft of White Paper, May 3, 1985.

4. "Hardware Vendor Influence Seen Boon to Videotex Systems," *Computerworld,* January 21, 1985, p. 55.

5. The Business Videotex Council of the Videotex Industry Association, "An Executive's Guide to Understanding and Implementing Business Videotex," July 11, 1985.

6. G. Berton Latamore, "The Business Connection," *Popular Computing,* March 1985, p. 76.

7. Anne R. Field, "Making a New Match for Videotex," *Business Week,* July 22, 1985.

8. Bruce Page and Harry Newton, "Let Your Customers Work For You," *Teleconnect,* July 1985.

REFERENCES

"The Changing Priorities of Videotex." *Broadcasting,* July 1, 1985.

CONNELLY, MIKE. "Ailing Videotex Ventures Haven't Slowed Plans to Market the Information Services." *The Wall Street Journal,* March 28, 1985.

A Guide to Corporate Videotex. Digital Equipment Corporation, 1984.

HEYWOOD, PETER and KEZEMIS, PAUL. "If Not Booming, Videotex in Europe Has At least Taken a Leap." *Data Communications,* February, 1985.

MEADOW, CHARLES T. and TEDESCO, A.S. *Telecommunications for Management.* New York: McGraw Hill, 1985.

METZGER, STEPHEN. "Videotex in Business: The Second Market." *Engineering Manager,* May 1985.

SEELINGER, WILLIAM W. "Videotex in the United States." *Telephony,* April 23, 1985.

SIGEL, EFREM. *The Future of Videotex.* Englewood Cliffs, N.J.: Prentice-Hall, 1983.

Electronic Mail

OBJECTIVES

- Understand the concepts and roles of electronic mail.
- See current uses and limitations of electronic mail.
- Categorize types of electronic mail systems.
- Contrast the various types of electronic mail systems.

INTRODUCTION

Electronic mail is the generic term for a wide array of telematic messaging systems. (In its broadest sense, the term includes computer-based messaging services (CBMS), telex, TWX (teletypewriter exchange), and teletex communications, facsimile messaging, voice messaging systems, and others) The modern forms of electronic mail are telematic technologies because they combine computer control (i.e., computers store and forward messages and microprocessor-based terminals originate and receive messages) with digital transmission capability. The modern concept of electronic mail also implies asynchronous, desk-to-desk messaging of text, voice, and graphic information from one person to another or from one person to a group. (Desktop facsimile devices and telex terminals are just now entering the market.)

Electronic mail will play a major role in tomorrow's corporate networks. CBMS, facsimile, telex, and voice messaging services will act as the central nervous system for the communication of information in many future office systems. In addition, electronic messaging *among businesses*—the creation of international networks for electronic business communication—will benefit greatly from the establishment of international electronic mail standards and eventually from ISDN.

Worldwide interconnection of electronic messaging sytems can be envisioned by the end of this century. Point-to-point connections between users of any electronic mail vendor's equipment anywhere in the world will be possible, much like today's telephone system. The varieties of terminal equipment—telephones, microcomputers, facsimile machines, and so on—will converge to allow voice, text, and graphic communication through a single end-user device. As a result, a typical business message could combine voice, text, or graphics components, allowing users to blend the special communication qualities of each for maximum communication effectiveness. This integrated electronic mail system will act simply as an electronic envelope for all of these forms of messaging, forwarding the information to and from various pieces of compatible equipment, performing the necessary translations of forms of data.

CURRENT USES OF ELECTRONIC MAIL

Today most corporate networks still employ the older electronic messaging technologies—telegraph, telex, TWX, and facsimile. But many are moving forward to messaging systems based on new telematic technologies, building their systems around one or a few forms of electronic mail and, incidently, using systems that at this time are often incompatible with those used by outside organizations. The following case studies illustrate applications of CBMS, facsimile, and voice mail currently in use.

- Tandem Computers' 5,000 employees are heavy users of TRANSFER/MAIL, the company's proprietary messaging system. More than 90% of workers at Tandem have terminals linked to the messaging network. Tandem does not use voice messaging; phone messages are taken by message center clerks, who enter them directly into the electronic mail system. According to one account by a Tandem manager, "Life at Tandem revolves around the electronic mail system."

  Richard works for Tandem's headquarters marketing organizations as the manager of a technical support group of 40 or 50 people. The first thing he does when he arrives at the office in the morning is to log on to his terminal and scan his electronic mail. The system's scan function allows Richard to view a list of all messages in his electronic "in box." The list gives the sender's name, the message type (original, forwarded from another receiving party, reply to an earlier message, and so forth) and a subject line. Having scanned his mail, Richard can then select the most important messages to read first. The first batch of messages he chooses for immediate reply includes the following items:

- An invitation to a strategy meeting with the Software Development Group.
- Minutes of a meeting he attended last week.
- A request from the vice president of marketing asking him to provide people to help with a design review for a large customer's application.
- A request from an analyst in Australia for performance information on a new hardware product.

The mail system allows Richard to respond immediately to the meeting invitation and to electronically file the minutes of last week's meeting. He then composes a short addendum to the design review request (providing more specific instructions) and forwards the whole package to a subordinate, who will follow through for him. Richard doesn't have the performance information needed in Australia, but he knows of someone at the Performance Research Center in Germany who might. He forwards the message there electronically and replies to the analyst in Australia indicating what he has done.[1]

Meanwhile, in another part of the building, Jim Treybig, founder and chief executive officer of Tandem, has arrived at his office. He switches on his terminal and finds more than 20 messages sent to him from virtually every department and rank within his company. One message is from an employee in Austin, Texas, who complains that workers who had worked for his supervisor at another

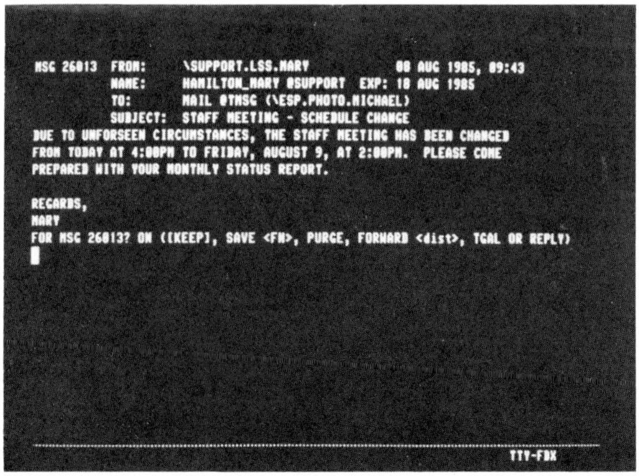

Courtesy of Tandem Computers

FIGURE 13–1: A message on a recipient's screen in Tandem's electronic mail network.

company were being favored for promotions. Mr. Treybig checks out the complaint and, finding the allegation to be false, electronically dispatches a reply message to the employee to quell his concerns.[2]

- Pacific Bell (one of the seven regional Bell operating companies) has installed a videotex system with electronic mail capabilities for use by its managers. The system supplements the company-wide voice messaging system. The company has found that many executives greatly prefer the convenience of using the voice mail system instead of typing memos for electronic delivery.

- The National Cooperative Bank, centered in Washington, D.C., relies heavily on facsimile machines for communications to headquarters from numerous regional locations. Loan documents and other contractual or financial papers are routinely sent by facsimile; there is also limited use of ITT Dialcom's nationwide electronic mail network for sending administrative reports and memos.

These cases illustrate emerging electronic corporate cultures based on choices of particular forms of corporatewide messaging. These different mixtures reflect specific advantages of input and delivery offered by each system. Comparative advantages of each will be considered later in this chapter.

TYPES OF ELECTRONIC MAIL SYSTEMS

There are four distinct types of electronic mail: computer-based messaging services, telex and teletex, facsimile, and voice messaging systems (VMS).

Messaging systems that can be regarded as forms of "electronic text mail" or "document transfer" will be considered in this chapter. These include the older technologies of telegraphy, teletypewriters, telex, TWX, and analog facsimile, and the new computer-based systems such as teletex, CBMS, and digital facsimile.

Voice messaging is covered in detail in Chapter Six because such systems often appear in association with a PBX installation. However, because the benefits of voice mail are closely related to those of text messaging technologies, VMS is often considered a member of the larger electronic mail family.

COMPUTER-BASED MESSAGING SYSTEMS

CBMS is the technical name for a large class of electronic mail products capable of transferring text between desktop micros, terminals, and word processors. CBMS systems are often referred to with the generic term *electronic mail*. But it is important for this discussion to distinguish CBMS systems from the varieties of electronic mail systems discussed above and especially from facsimile and telex, because as these two technologies begin to incorporate computer capabilities, they are becoming less distinct from CBMS.

All types of CBMS require four fundamental components:

1. *Terminals*. Messages are keyed in, edited, and displayed on personal computers or dedicated terminals.
2. *Software*. Sophisticated software systems, which can be quite costly, are the heart of telematic messaging systems.
3. *The host computer*. A computer with large memory or at least hard disk storage capacity is needed to store incoming messages, forward messages from one terminal to another, and process commands. The end-user's electronic mailbox, or "in box," is physically located on the host computer.
4. *The transmission system*. Public and private telecommunications media link the system host with sending and receiving terminals.

The Electronic Mailbox

The differentiating feature of CBMS technology at this time is the central importance of the *electronic mailbox*, which permits users exclusive access to electronically stored messages via their desktop (or portable) computing device. The electronic mailbox capability is so essential to the current technology of CBMS that these systems are sometimes called "computer-mailbox services." The following example shows the central importance of the electronic mailbox function for a midwestern hardware distributor.

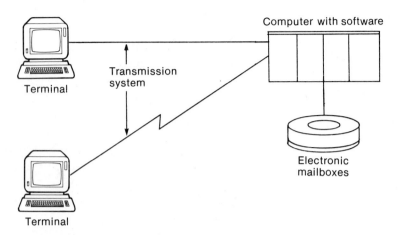

FIGURE 13–2: Basic components of a CBMS.

● Mike is a field salesman for a wholesale hardware distributor. Sitting in his hotel room in a small town in Indiana, he dials a number in a nearby large city. Connecting his portable computer, he gains access to his electronic mailbox. After reading a message from the sales manager on last month's overall sales figures, he types a command requesting a sales form. The form prompts him to enter the information from his five sales calls that day. The sales information is automatically posted to a mailbox to be read the next morning at the company headquarters in Cincinnati. Finally, Mike sends a private message to the sales manager, mentioning new leads.

There are three notable aspects of the mailbox concept:

1. _Ownership_. Usually a mailbox is assigned to a single user who has sole access to it (though sometimes a group of users can be joint owners). Some systems limit the owner's access to one particular terminal only, while others enable users access to their mailboxes from any terminal on the system.
2. _Mailbox address_. All mailboxes in CBMS systems have electronic "addresses" to which messages are sent. Because a mailbox is associated with its owner, the owner's name or some abbreviation of it is often used as the address, which must be typed in by the sender of the message.

3. _Storage_. An electronic mailbox stores messages waiting to be received by its owner. The system notifies the owner of each new message and allows storage of messages in the mailbox even after they have been received.

Other typical features of CBMS systems include facilities for message preparation, sending, receiving, and message retrieval.

Message Preparation

Message preparation features commonly available on electronic mail systems include:

1. _Word processing_. Text editing capabilities and even full word processing capabilities can be provided in a mail system.
2. _Annotation_. The best method of response to some messages is to simply attach written comments to the original message and then forward the annotated message on to the next recipient.
3. _Forms capability_. Some advanced systems provide the electronic equivalent of fill-in-the-blank forms such as expense reports, purchase orders, and so on. (In the previous example, Mike, the hardware salesman, filled out an electronic sales form from his hotel room using a personal computer.)
4. _File merging capability_. Many electronic mail systems are capable of appending files to mail messages, enabling them to accomplish crude but quick file transfer.

Message Sending

The following are integral aspects of the sending facility of typical electronic mail systems:

1. _User directory_. Electronic mail systems always maintain a directory of their users. The directory contains a variety of information such as the user's full name, office location, and job title.

2. *Timed delivery*. This capability allows a sender to specify the time a particular message is to be delivered to the receiver.
3. *Automatic distribution lists*. The computer can allow for creation of specialized electronic distribution lists for the sending of one-to-many "broadcasts"; the same list can be stored and recalled on demand for sending new messages. The public relations manager of one large company says he periodically sends press releases to about 90 editors using the automatic distribution feature of his CBMS systems; setting up and sending the broadcast takes him about five minutes.

    The most sophisticated CBMSs require the sender only to identify the names of the recipients on the distribution list; no knowledge is required of the terminal location of the recipient.
4. *Message confirmation*. CBMSs provide for confirmation to the sender (via a notice on the computer screen) that the message has been sent and received by the recipient.

Message Receiving

CBMS systems should provide ease-of-use features for recipients as well as senders of messages. Common message receiving features include:

1. *Message notification*. All CBMS systems have techniques—such as a brief flash on the receiving party's display screen—that notify the user of the presence of new messages.
2. *Mailbox scanning*. This feature provides a user, upon logging on, a single line of information about each new message, detailing who the sender is, message priority, time and day sent, and so on.
3. *Message selection*. Virtually all systems allow users to specify an order in which to scan their mail. This feature allows users to select individual messages one at a time or to group certain messages together such that each message in the group is presented automatically as the previous one is read.

4. *Message forwarding.* In many circumstances a message recipient may want to send a copy to another individual. Many systems have the ability to easily forward original or annotated messages.
5. *Mailbox management.* Electronic mail systems usually allow a variety of mailbox management functions. Users can delete messages or transfer them from the mailbox to some filing system. Some systems provide an automatic filing facility whereby once a message is read, it is automatically removed from the mailbox and stored in a separate file.
6. *Message filtering.* Many electronic mail systems provide a message filtering facility to stop the flow of irrelevant information. The recipient simply specifies the name of some sender, a particular message title, or some other distinguishing characteristic and all messages meeting this condition are diverted to a separate file or automatically deleted.

Message Retrieval

The system for retrieval of old messages from a user's electronic mailbox often includes the following features:

1. *Retrieval facilities.* Messages can be retrieved by title, sender, recipient, date sent, date received, and date filed.
2. *Archiving.* Users should be able to transfer messages from the on-line filing system to off-line storage.

Advantages of CBMS

Electronic mail systems compete with the telephone, overnight mail delivery services, and combination services, such as Zapmail™ from Federal Express, which uses both electronic transmission and a human courier to deliver documents within hours. CBMS systems offer numerous advantages over these conventional message delivery systems. Once they begin communicating regularly with electronic mail, users generally become very attached to their electronic mailboxes and use them often.

Many of the following advantages of CBMS apply to the other

forms of electronic messaging, which will be examined later in the chapter.

BENEFITS

1. *Reduction of telephone tag.* Telephone tag is one of the greatest scourges of office work. Only about one out of four phone calls reach the intended party the first time; according to another estimate, it can take an average of three to six calls before two busy people finally connect. By contrast, virtually 100 percent of electronic messages reach their destination. (Or if two parties do need to connect by phone, electronic messaging can be used to set up a mutually agreed upon appointment for a telephone conversation.)

2. *Reduction of telephone interruptions.* The other side of the coin from telephone tag is the problem of telephone interruptions. CBMS systems allow asynchronous communication; that is, the message is stored on the recipient's electronic mailbox and can be forwarded at the recipient's own convenience, thereby eliminating untimely and irritating phone interruptions.

In addition, a large proportion of phone calls require only one-way communication of information; such messages are better off received and stored electronically, allowing both parties to avoid unnecessary real-time telephone interaction and conviviality.

3. *More timely communication.* Electronic messages can be dispatched to a recipient's electronic mailbox as quickly as a few seconds, whereas land mail takes several days. (The use of mail couriers or express mail is more timely but obviously more expensive.) In addition, much of the time-consuming work of typing hard copy documents and stuffing and mailing envelopes is avoided with the use of electronic mail.

4. *Lower mailing costs.* Conventional mail systems are usually more expensive because of the cost of secretarial labor, paper supplies, and physical delivery.

5. *On-line storage.* Documents received or sent as electronic mail can also be stored on-line. It is easier and less costly to store such documents electronically than to maintain files for hard copies.

6. *Easier one-to-many distribution of information.* The automatic distribution capability in most CBMS systems allows

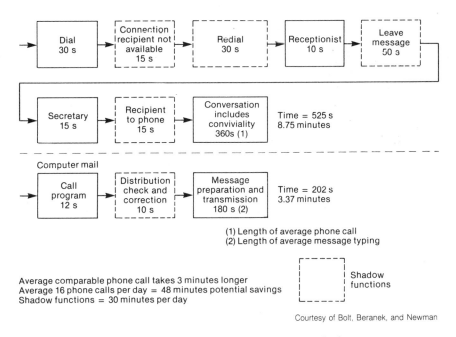

(1) Length of average phone call
(2) Length of average message typing

Average comparable phone call takes 3 minutes longer
Average 16 phone calls per day = 48 minutes potential savings
Shadow functions = 30 minutes per day

Shadow functions

Courtesy of Bolt, Beranek, and Newman

FIGURE 13-3: Potential time-saving of CBMS versus telephone.

information workers to simultaneously dispatch electronically stored messages to multiple recipients.

7. *Accessibility 24 hours a day.* Messages can be sent and received at any time during the day or night, thus eliminating time zone differences.

LIMITATIONS OF ELECTRONIC MAIL

The most fundamental limitation of CBMS and other forms of electronic mail is that users must possess a microcomputer or other terminal capable of messaging; clearly, these relatively expensive devices are not as ubiquitous in offices as telephones are, and thus many companies currently have a very small base of potential electronic mail terminals. (Of course, the telephone itself can be turned into an electronic voice messaging terminal.) Beyond this elementary point are two prominent difficulties that any company faces as it installs an electronic mail network—incompatible systems and system misuse.

The Need for Standardization

[handwritten annotation: WHO'S ON THE SYSTEM & ABILITY TO CROSS SYSTEMS]

The most obvious disadvantage of electronic mail in all of its forms is that senders and receivers must use the same electronic mail system. This limitation is especially problematic for messaging outside a given corporate network. The receiving party—more often than not—uses some other incompatible system, and, to make matters worse, a growing number of vendors are offering incompatible systems.

The problem of incompatible electronic mail systems is very similar to the situation that prevailed early in this century when there were numerous independent telephone companies vying for a piece of the new voice communications market. In many cities it was necessary to have three or four different telephones on one's desktop in order to talk to business associates in various parts of town. (This problem was solved when AT&T bought out most of the independents. See Chapter Four.) Worldwide standards are already in effect for telex and facsimile messaging systems, as discussed later in this chapter. However, because of the current lack of a prevailing CBMS standard, users who message outside the company network often must go to the expense of subscribing to a number of systems and deal with the added inconvenience of keeping track of multiple electronic mailbox addresses. This is especially problematic for small supply or service businesses that need messaging links to numerous clients or vendors.

[handwritten annotation: STOP]

The key to overcoming this limitation is for system vendors to implement the X.400 series of international standards developed by the CCITT. X.400 is a set of specifications that describes the format for messages and the logical steps for exchanging them. The standard's existence does not mean vendors will implement it; but most industry analysts agree that the market will not reach its potential unless there is interconnection of public and private messaging systems worldwide, effectively eliminating the problem of incompatibility. Major electronic mail vendors, such as IBM, AT&T, Xerox, GTE Telenet, and ITT, participated in efforts to define X.400, and many have announced plans to implement the standard. But many issues still need to be resolved, such as how customers will be billed for messages that cross services, and who would be liable if such messages are lost.

A parallel effort has been launched in the electronic mail industry to standardize message system directories, thereby allowing the creation of a universal on-line user directory. Some envision that "The Directory," as it is called in industry circles, would list users on all CBMS, facsimile, telex, videotex, and telephone systems in one massive, distributed data base. Without access to such a directory, users wouldn't be able to send messages to others outside their own company network (particularly if the recipient uses a different vendors' system) any more than they can telephone someone without getting access to the telephone number through an operator or a phone book.

Electronic Junk Mail

One of the most important aspects of building a successful electronic mail network is properly training users. Without proper support, a company's electronic mail system may become a "ghost network" with few office workers and even fewer executives using the assigned mailboxes. Users may become discouraged by how few messages they receive or by the lack of response to their messages and thus may underutilize the system.

But poor management of an electronic mail system can have an even worse result than underuse—misuse of the network to send junk mail.

Automatic distribution lists are an integral part of any good electronic mail system. A departmental manager, for example, can quickly get a message out to a large group of subordinates by simply entering a memo into her terminal and electronically dispatching it to the relevant distribution list. The automatic distribution feature allows a myriad of such practical uses, but also affords a great deal of room for abuse. According to Paul Strassman:

> It is very easy to generate a 10-fold to 30-fold increase in the amount of information received by an individual when he becomes involved with the electronic medium and gets onto all sorts of public distribution lists. Central authorization of access to distribution lists may remedy some of the excesses, but it will create restraints on information flow—thus eliminating most of the advantages of easy interconnection between people.[3]

One example cited in *Computer Decisions* illustrates how far abuse of automatic message distribution can go.

> Managers at a major bank recently received a strange inquiry in the morning's electronic mail. A group of bank staffers who regularly played backgammon during lunch had lost a leather dice cup in the office. By way of an electronic memo, they asked if anyone had seen the missing cup. The whole thing seemed harmless enough. However, the staffers sent their memo to every one of 2,500 mailboxes in the bank's worldwide electronic mail system.[4]

This incident represents an exaggerated case of the kind of abuses that can pose a problem for companies implementing electronic mail systems. How can employees be encouraged to become familiar with a new messaging system without prompting a flood of wasteful, frivolous uses?

Some organizations respond by cracking down on electronic junk mail. Because junk mail is annoying and tends to trivialize the system's productive capabilities, it can become a barrier to user acceptance, according to this point of view.

The alternative approach would be to accept nonsense uses and even abuses of the system as an inevitable part of the user familiarization process. Many analysts believe that allowing such casual use helps make electronic mail appear less threatening and may encourage appropriate use of the system for business purposes. Then, once users have become accustomed to the system, management might begin to regulate system usage by publishing guidelines. Perhaps the best remedy for excesses and abuses is "to price network usage at commercial rates, as a direct cost to the user. Applying overall budget limits is a much more effective way of restraining unreasonable usage than exercising direct control."[5] Hewlett-Packard has begun to phase in such a mechanism to help regulate use of its large in-house system. (See Chapter Seventeen.)

TYPES OF CBMS SYSTEMS

Many analysts expect that by the 1990s, the majority of information workers in many companies will be CBMS users. Because of the ongoing invasion of microcomputers in these companies, messaging terminals will be nearly as ubiquitous as telephones. (Some current examples of this phenomenon: Tandem Computers, cited earlier, with more than 90 percent usage rate among employees; the example of Software Publishing Corporation below; and the case of Hewlett-Packard's HP Mail system, presented in Chapter Seventeen, with more than 45,000 electronic mail in-house users.)

A diverse array of highly competitive electronic mail providers has arisen to meet the growing demand for CBMS. These vendors can be divided into two classes of providers: those offering in-house systems and service bureaus offering universal electronic mail systems on a subscription basis.

In-House Systems

Most in-house CBMS installations consist of software customized for use on existing in-house computer networks. In addition, a number of major computer hardware vendors provide complete turnkey electronic mail systems, including terminals, large computers, and storage devices required for mailboxes, plus the needed software and communication links. (Some industry analysts define the term *CBMS* as designating an in-house electronic mail system, strictly speaking.)

CBMS capability can also be added to an existing departmental local area network. In many LAN packages, CBMS is a feature provided by the original LAN vendor. The communicating word processor network used by the writing and production department of Regis McKenna, Inc., is an example of turnkey word processing and electronic messaging system provided by one LAN vendor (Exxon).

A low-cost (and rather cumbersome) alternative is to simply use communications software and modems to link two micros over the switched public networks; in this case, because of the lack of electronic mailboxes, both sender and recipient must be simultaneously present at their terminals to make the connection.

Service Bureaus

CBMS service bureaus allow users to buy mailbox space and other messaging services from a time-sharing computer vendor.

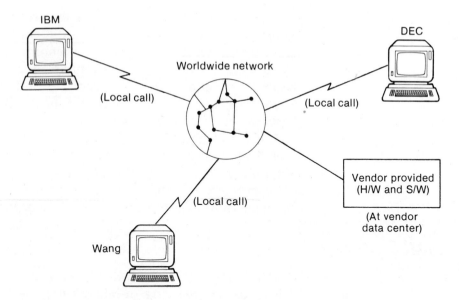

FIGURE 13–4: Dedicated service bureaus can link users of any variety of microcomputer.

A company choosing this option provides its own terminals and modems for accessing the vendor's system through public voice or data networks. Users generally pay according to the number and length of messages transmitted and stored.

It is not usually economical to use a service bureau if most of a company's messaging goes on in-house (despite the example of the Software Publishing Corporation cited below). The best strategy is to use one of the public service vendors to supply outside messaging services and use a separate vendor's product for in-house messaging; public vendors such as MCI and Western Union now offer gateways to in-house systems, and many vendors of in-house systems are working to supply gateways in the other direction.

Nationwide information services such as The Source and CompuServe offer CBMS in addition to their on-line data base services. This choice of a CBMS system may provide a cost-effective approach for intermittent messaging among geographically dispersed sites for those companies that also require access to on-line data bases.

However, a dedicated CBMS service bureau is probably re-

FIGURE 13–5: Tymnet's worldwide packet switching network is monitored and controlled in this network control room at company headquarters.

quired when a defined group of people needs to communicate regularly. Figure 13–5 shows the control room of such a network.

Leading vendors of dedicated CBMS networks include Tymshare's On Tyme II, GTE's Telemail, General Electric Information Service's Quick-Comm, Easy Link from Western Union, and MCI Mail from MCI.

The following example illustrates the use of a service bureau by Software Publishing Corporation, a producer of business productivity software.

- Each of Software Publishing Corporation's 165 employees has a personal computer and a telephone. Instead of installing a local area network, the company opted to use its own communications software package in conjunction with MCI Mail; the employees' electronic mailboxes reside on MCI's computer, which is linked to the company's personal computers through telephone lines. Employees communicate with each other (and with outsiders who also use MCI Mail) via MCI's host computer.

  Using a service bureau allows the company to have a reliable CBMS capability without owning its own CBMS hardware. Incidently, Software Publishing Corporation has no secretaries among its 165 employees.

A low-cost approach to hiring a service bureau, which is used by some small businesses, is to build a "virtual" CBMS system by using a special-purpose electronic bulletin board offered by a local bulletin board service (BBS). BBSs lack computer store and forward capability (electronic mailboxes), but it is possible to use electronic bulletin boards as a crude version of electronic text mail by having employees post messages on the board in the hope that the intended recipient will eventually read it.

TELEX AND TELETEX

Telex

A historian of technology could trace a distinct line of evolution for electronic mail, beginning with telegraphy in the 1840s, evolving to the teletypewriter, and finally to telex and TWX machines with computer store and forward capability in the 1960s. Today approximately 1 million users worldwide use telex to send electronic messages at relatively low speed over the public telex network. In the United States, telex is still the most prevalent electronic mail technology, with more than 500,000 subscribers sending messages over dedicated transmission lines leased from Western Union. Now, a new technology called telc-

Courtesy of Western Union

FIGURE 13–6: Modern telex terminals resemble an ordinary computer terminal with CRT display and printer.

tex—offering greater transmission speed and other value added features—is the potential successor of telex, at least in Europe. Teletex can be seen as a telex technology transformed by telematics.

The disadvantages of telex are well known. Compared with other forms of electronic mail, the telex transmission rate of 50 bits per second (approximately 66 words per minute) is slow. Also, because a 5-bit code is used for encoding symbols, a rather limited character set is available. (The telex character set consists of upper case letters only, numbers, spacing, plus 13 special characters.) The cost of a telex transmission is at a fixed rate (no off-peak rates), which makes it quite unsuitable for long messages. Moreover, the failure rate on international connections is distressingly high for telex. And telex machines are not located on or near the user's desktop but in a separate area of an office.

But telex does have important advantages. It is internationally accepted and well established, with fairly strict regulations and standards agreed upon by all users. Telex also covers more area geographically than any other messaging system and has a world directory containing the telex numbers of all users.

Teletex

Teletex, by contrast, is a high-speed, desk-to-desk message service that allows users to type and edit letters and transmit them error-free over telephone lines or packet switched data networks. The 2,400 bits per second transmission speed of teletex allows significant savings in transmission cost when compared with the 50 bits per second capability of telex service. And teletex does not require the use of a specialized terminal; word processors, electronic typewriters, and even personal computers can be converted to teletex terminals.

Another important difference between telex and teletex results from the use of an eight-bit character code for teletex transmission instead of telex's five-bit code. This permits transmission of upper and lower case characters plus a larger set of special characters, allowing a standard letter format to be adopted.

FIGURE 13–7 Telex and Teletex compared.[7]

	Telex	Teletex
Medium	dedicated low-grade network	network independent (protocols to link into PSN, packet or circuit switch, as appropriate)
Terminal	special telex machine	microcomputer, word processor, electronic typewriter
Rate of transmission	50 bits per second	1,200–2,400 bits per second (varies with network used)
Character code and set	5-bit code, 50 characters only	8-bit code, more than 200 characters

Where teletex-to-teletex communications can be used, it will be much cheaper then telex because of the much faster transmission rate. Teletex is also a more flexible medium. Teletex terminals will be located directly at the point of need—for instance on the secretary's desk—rather than in a communications room or reception area, and teletex terminals can also be linked to the external telecommunications network via the PBX.

Teletex is far more prevalent in Europe than in the United States. The following example illustrates the advantages of teletex for a German company.

- A West German company recently replaced its telex-based network used for transmitting order information with a teletex system. Now its branch office can send orders directly to a variety of desks at the head office, eliminating delays formerly caused by having to carry hard copy to and from the centralized telex room. Order clerks can key details of each order directly into their teletex terminal while the customer is on the telephone. Teletex transmission charges are a fraction (about one-eighth) of equivalent telex charges.[6]

Teletex provides a much-needed international, manufacturer-independent, standard for communications between word processors, electronic typewriters, and microcomputers. Some view teletex as being among the most important developments in telecommunications since the standardization of international telephone services. The major growth in electronic mail that is now starting to occur will certainly be spurred by the teletex standard.

H 3 FACSIMILE

Facsimile (or "fax") is a messaging technology that allows transmission and output of a replica, or facsimile, of an original document containing both alphanumeric and graphic information. Facsimile provides an efficient method for sending photos, graphs, drawings, charts, business forms, business letters, and ordinary text to a party with a compatible machine.

During facsimile transmission, the characters in the original document are translated into analog or digital impulses by means of a scanning device, conveyed over public telephone lines or private lines, and then reconverted into hard copy by a compatible facsimile machine at the receiving end. Because the receiving machine can generate the facsimile output in unattended mode, computer store and forward capability is not a necessary feature of a facsimile system.

Until the mid-1960s, facsimile technology did not provide the cost, convenience, speed, or flexibility required to meet the needs of most business offices. The event that turned the tide in favor of business facsimile was not a technological or marketing breakthrough but the Carterfone decision in 1968, which required that telephone companies give independent manufacturers of communication devices access to the public telephone network. This landmark deregulatory decision encouraged a new wave of technological innovation and a new emphasis on business applications in the facsimile industry. The subsequent introduction of the Xerox Telecopier line triggered the real impetus for the growth of business facsimile in the United States. Today, facsimile is the next most prevalent electronic mail technology after telex, with nearly 500,000 machines in use.

Facsimile and Telematics

The facsimile industry is currently benefiting from a telematic convergence with computer technology. In the newer models, everything works digitally, including the camera and the copy printer. The most advanced machines are built for digital transmission of up to 30 pages per minute using private data lines or packet switched networks. The output copy is almost indistinguishable from the original. Another recent innovation would allow integration of facsimile machines with other office automation equipment, such as word processors, telexes, and personal computers, by using an ASCII interface over RS-232 lines. Beyond this is the distinct possibility that desktop facsimile terminals will function as a peripheral to the personal computer. According to this scenario, the fax machine will act as an "electronic communicating copier" that will handle all printing, whether it be to copy, to retrieve hard copy from an electronic file, or to send facsimile documents.

The Japanese are responsible for much of the current innovation in facsimile technology. The complexity of the Japanese alphabet, with more than 2,500 distinct characters, has motivated a fundamental search for an efficient means of transmitting graphic information. Japanese technology is currently dominant in the U.S. fax market.

According to the market research firm Dataquest, annual shipments of facsimile equipment will double between 1984 and 1989. Improvements in quality and transmission speed will aid this growth, but the establishment of worldwide fax communication standards have helped immensely.

Facsimile Standards

Unlike the computer and word processing industries, key U.S. companies first involved in the introduction of office facsimile (Magnavox and Xerox) adopted a strategy of standardization and compatibility early on. These pioneers were instrumental in the development of the so-called Group I facsimile standard.

As the telephone-coupled facsimile technology of this early period became internationally accepted, the focus for fax standardization shifted to the CCITT. The result was the establishment of the international Group III standard.

Sales of facsimile machines began to accelerate after the CCITT introduced the Group III standard in 1980. Group III allowed for speeds that exceed one page per minute, which significantly lowered transmission cost. This was the threshold that allowed facsimile transmission (which for Group III occurs over phone lines) to compete with other forms of electronic mail. Group III also allowed for crisper, higher resolution output copies.

Once the Group III standard was adopted, prices plummeted. In 1980, when the standards were set, Group III digital terminals cost $12,500. Since then, prices have gone down steadily because of reduced component costs, competition, and the existence of standards. A typical Group III machine is currently priced at less than $3,000.

According to the CCITT protocols, Group I can transmit a page in four to six minutes; Group II, in two to three minutes; and Group III, in less than a minute. The Group IV standard, which will come into common use in the late 1980s, can transmit a page in less than five seconds. It's capable of 400 pixels per inch resolution, twice as good as that offered by Group III.

The development of these facsimile standards by the CCITT has enabled facsimile companies to manufacture equipment that can communicate with any other company's machine. It is now customary for Group III terminals to also be compatible with Group II and sometimes Group I. Most existing facsimile terminals, and virtually all new facsimile terminals, are compatible. Thus, even though word processing terminals and microcomputers greatly outnumber facsimile terminals, and though CBMS systems have been extensively promoted, the early establishment of fax standards has allowed the volume of electronic mail carried by facsimile to exceed the volume of CBMS traffic, according to some estimates.

COMPARISON OF ELECTRONIC MAIL SYSTEMS

The following section summarizes the specific advantages and disadvantages (for use in business) of the electronic mail systems introduced in this chapter.

Computer-Based Message Services

CBMS offers asynchronous desk-to-desk text messaging among users with compatible terminals. It is especially suited for messaging activities within information-intensive companies among employees using desktop personal computers or word processors. The electronic mailbox feature of CBMS offers the distinct advantages of message store and forward, automatic distribution, and numerous other value added-features.

The establishment of the X.400 standard for CBMS will put it on par with telex, teletex, and facsimile for universality of service and international standardization.

Telex, TWX, and Teletex

Telex and TWX continue to be the main carriers of electronic messages across national boundaries. The main advantage of telex and TWX is the ubiquity of terminals in businesses throughout the world, coupled with well-established international standardization. Teletex also offers international standardization, but is not wellestablished in the United States.

The major disadvantages of telex and TWX are slow transmission capability, high error rates, limited character rates, and centralization of terminals in special rooms. But these disadvantages are largely overcome by the emerging teletex standard that allows error-free, 2,400 bits per second transmission, a much expanded error rate, and desktop access.

Facsimile

Facsimile offers international standardization and ubiquity of service approaching that of telex, with the added advantage that the output is a replica of the original document.

The ease of reading the received document is an important part of the total value associated with facsimile and is one of the "human factors" often overlooked in comparing the various forms of electronic mail. At the current state of display technology, a sheet of hard copy is significantly easier to read than a screen, particularly where the information is detailed or complex.

If the text of a message is long, keying it into a CBMS terminal can be time consuming and wasteful. Very often, the message that needs to be transmitted is a document that already exists (such as a memo, received letter, marked-up draft, newspaper clipping, page from a manual, engineering-change order, and so on). In this case, feeding it into a facsimile terminal may be the best alternative when speed of delivery is desired.

If the nature of the message is such that it is best expressed in graphic form (such as engineering drawings, graphs, charts, photos), facsimile has the clear advantage. But if the message is short and its content can be adequately carried by a few sentences of text, then computer-based message systems are suitable, provided the sender and recipient have compatible terminals.

The distinct disadvantage of facsimile when compared with CBMS, of course, is that facsimile technology does not currently allow desk-to-desk messaging. CBMS expands the already powerful role of personal computers and other desktop devices in the workplace. With CBMS, information workers can use these devices not only to create, analyze, and retrieve information, but also to communicate with other terminals or data bases.

#4 PBX and Voice Mail

Voice messaging eliminates typing and provides desktop access to store and forward messaging service through the ubiquitous telephone terminal. The convenience and ease of use of voice messaging may explain why many executives prefer this medium to CBMS. It preserves the nuances of the human voice, which is crucial in much managerial communication. Also, like CBMS, voice mail eliminates the scourge of telephone tag with a minimum of effort.

Voice mail is largely a substitute for the inefficiencies of real-time telephone service and is not suitable for formal or complex correspondence.

WHAT HAPPENES TO ZAP MAIL

QUESTIONS FOR REVIEW:

1. What is "electronic mail?"
2. What are the roles of electronic mail in corporate networks?
3. Describe a current use of electronic mail in a corporation.

4. Briefly describe the four types of electronic mail systems.
5. What are the main components of CBMS?
6. What are some of the limitations of electronic mail?
7. Describe telex, its advantages and disadvantages.
8. Contrast telex, TWX, and teletext.
9. Describe facsimile.
10. Describe the evolution of standards in facsimile.

FOR DISCUSSION:

1. What would be some reasons for not endorsing the use of electronic mail? What are some consequences of using this system regarding privacy?
2. Will the use of electronic mail ever overtake the volume of phone conversations? If so, what would the impact be on human communication patterns?

NOTES FOR CHAPTER THIRTEEN

1. Example supplied by Tandem Corporation.

2. "More Corporate Chiefs Now Seek Direct Contact With Their Workers and Customers," *The Wall Street Journal,* February 27, 1985.

3. Paul Strassman, *Information Payoff* (New York: The Free Press, 1985), p. 52.

4. John Seaman, "Is Electronic Junk Mail Good For Users?" *Data Communications: A Manager's View,* ed. John Seaman (Hasbrouck Heights, New Jersey: Hayden Book Company, 1985), p. 3.

5. Strassmann, Information Payoff, p. 52.

6. I. A. Galbraith, "Teletex and Electronic Mail: The Shape of Things to Come," *Telephony,* June 1984, p. 42.

7. R. A. Hirscheim, *Office Automation: Concepts, Technologies, and Issues* (Wokingham, England: Addison-Wesley Publishing, 1985), p. 123.

REFERENCES

GILBERT, NAT. "The Role of Facsimile in Telematics." *Telecommunications,* October 1983.

HEFTER, DONNA. "Huge Growth For Fax This Year." *Communications Week,* August 26, 1985.

HILDEBRAND, J. D. and STRUKHOFF, ROGER. "LAN E-Mail." *Micro Communications,* April 1985.

LOUIS, ARTHUR M. "The Great Electronic Mail Shootout." *Fortune,* August 20, 1984.

MEADOW, CHARLES T. and TEDESCO, ALBERT S. *Telecommunications for Management.* New York: McGraw-Hill Books, 1985.

ROSENBERG, ARTHUR M. "Successful Telemessaging Systems Will Be Built for Speed—and Comfort." *Communications Age,* December 1984.

SIRACUSA, GAIL. "Facsimile: On the Verge of a Breakthrough." *Office Administration and Automation,* August 1985.

Teleconferencing

OBJECTIVES

● Define teleconferencing.
● Understand the five forms of teleconferencing.
● Overcome some of the popular misconceptions about teleconferencing.
● Contrast some of the major uses of teleconferencing in business.

[handwritten notes:]
- MORE PEOPLE
- FAST DECESIONS
- STRUCTURED MEETINGS
- REDUCE MINUTES ARE KEPT + HOURS WASTED

Teleconferencing is best understood as a medium that enables people to meet electronically when they would otherwise find it inconvenient, too costly, or impossible to do so through physical travel. Of course, many business meetings will always need to be face to face. But teleconferencing allows in-person meetings to be much more a matter of choice than they are now. At the same time, teleconferencing should be regarded as much more than a rational but mediocre substitute for business travel. As we will see in this chapter, electronic meetings can work just as well as, and in some cases even better than, in-person meetings.

Two-way video is not the best representative of the potential of teleconferencing in business. There are a number of other techniques for arranging electronic meetings that are usually more cost-effective and in many cases more preferable than full-motion video.

Basically, teleconferencing occurs in five forms, which businesses use singly or in combination: audio, audiographics, freeze-frame or slow-scan video, full-motion video, and computer teleconferencing. All forms of teleconferencing—but especially the full-motion video and computer variants—are becoming more cost-effective and easier to use because of the digitalization of telecommunications media and equipment.

Audio teleconferencing is the foundation of all the other conferencing forms except computer conferencing. An audio teleconference transmits the voices of multiple participants through conventional telephone equipment; speakerphones are used at each site to transmit and amplify the voices of participants.

Audiographic teleconferencing is essentially audio teleconferencing augmented by the simultaneous exchange of printed documents through facsimile transmissions or written messages through an electronic writing pad (telewriting) or AT&T's Electronic Blackboard.

Freeze-frame video conferencing supplements audio teleconferencing with a series of "television snapshots," which are transmitted to remote monitors over regular telephone lines. The still images are refreshed at 35-second intervals or less.

NETWORKS **Video teleconferencing** is full-motion, live video transmission. It can be a one-way broadcast from a single site to multiple remote sites or a two-way, fully interactive broadcast simulating a face-to-face meeting. Videoconferencing can also combine a one-way video broadcast with a two-way audio connection.

Computer teleconferencing is an advanced software system used to structure and coordinate electronic text communications among widely dispersed microcomputer users. Computer conferencing allows ongoing, asynchronous, electronic meetings among multiple participants.

TELECONFERENCING: A GROWING TREND

Market research suggests that teleconferencing is entering a period of substantial growth in the business environment, following upon a long period of gradual but rather slow growth.

One of the most optimistic forecasts of the growth of business teleconferencing is based upon a study conducted by the Center for Interactive Programs at the University of Wisconsin, an internationally recognized resource center on teleconferencing. The teleconferencing market—including equipment, services, and transmission—reached $279 million in 1984; the Center predicts the market will grow to $3.7 billion by the end of 1990.[1] The Center's findings are summarized in Figure 14–1.

Most other teleconferencing market forecasts are less optimistic (see Figure 14–2), but all agree that this market will no longer experience the sluggish growth that has always been its earmark.

FIGURE 14–1   Projected growth rates of three major teleconferencing market sectors.

Market Sector	Projected Growth ($)	Projected Rate (%)
Audiographics	from $217 million (1986) to $1.58 billion (1990)	7.2%
Video conferencing	from $254.1 million (1986) to $1.6 billion (1990)	6.3%
Audio conferencing	from $186.7 million (1986) to $469.2 million (1990)	2.5%

For the time being, the market for teleconferencing is still underdeveloped, and the industry itself appears more technology-driven than user-responsive. But signs of approaching maturity are clearly discernable: The range and quality of teleconferencing products is increasing; equipment and usage costs are slowly decreasing; and users are growing more aware of how teleconferencing can enhance communication productivity. One-third of the excellent companies described in *In Search of*

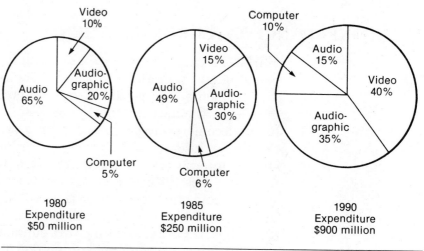

SOURCE: Gnostic Concepts, Inc.

FIGURE 14–2: Gnostic Concepts, Inc. predicted in 1982 that teleconferencing expenditures would rise to 900 million by 1990.

Excellence, for example, use teleconferencing on a regular basis. And, as we will see in Part Six, two companies with advanced telematic networks, Hercules and Hewlett-Packard, have very large investments in teleconferencing. Use of teleconferencing is especially heavy at Hewlett-Packard, where all five forms of the medium are in regular use throughout the company.

MISCONCEPTIONS ABOUT TELECONFERENCING

There are many reasons for organizations to be skeptical of teleconferencing. Conferencing technology, especially if it involves video transmission, can be expensive and unreliable. In some instances, the use of teleconferencing, just like any other form of electronic communication, can lead to a decreased sense of interpersonal contact among users—less sense of the "high touch" quality of human interaction, as John Naisbitt pointed out in *Megatrends.* Also, the availability of teleconferencing facilities could lead to an increase in the amount of nonproductive time spent in unnecessary meetings, simply because teleconferences are easier to arrange. Or it could lead to an increase in management control of workers at remote sites, through a form of "Big Brother" surveillance.

Convening geographically dispersed groups of people electronically is a complex social and technical phenomenon. It is too soon to predict the eventual impacts of teleconferencing in the workplace. But recent studies appear to refute some widely held misconceptions about teleconferencing systems. In order to gain a full understanding of the drawbacks and benefits of teleconferencing, such stereotypical ideas must first be re-examined.

Misconception #1: The Purpose of Teleconferencing is to Cut Travel Costs

Using travel substitution to justify teleconferencing is a simpleminded approach, and one that is largely illusory. One leading authority on teleconferencing, Robert Johansen of the Institute for the Future, summarizes the problem in the following way:

MAJOR REASONS FOR TRAVEL IS NOT COMMUNICATIONS AS MUCH AS FACE TO FACE CONVERSATIONS ON PREMISE SOCIALIZING AND WALK AROUNDS.

Travel substitution is still the most common justification for teleconferencing, even though it is mostly a mirage. Unfortunately, new entrants in the field are almost always drawn to this idea. However, 10 years of experience yield few convincing examples of direct travel substitution. Indeed, in some cases, travel increased along with the introduction of teleconferencing.

These factors do not mean that teleconferencing cannot facilitate a net reduction in travel or eliminate certain types of undesirable travel. However, there is more to it than unlocking the door to the teleconferencing room and adding up the travel savings. Teleconferencing, if it works, will change the way business communication occurs. Travel patterns may change, but probably not predictably, and, almost certainly, teleconferencing will not substitute directly for travel.[2]

Johansen does recognize that net travel reductions are possible through the careful implementation of teleconferencing. For example, he points out that a company could impose a corporate policy that would require travelers to provide a reason why each trip they take cannot be replaced by a teleconference; or incentives could be provided that make electronic meetings more attractive than travel.

Thus, setting corporate guidelines may lead to decreased travel costs, but a more appropriate corporate approach should view teleconferencing in terms of qualitative productivity criteria, such as increased managerial productivity. The following organizations provide examples of this orientation.

- Langley Research Center of the National Aeronautics and Space Administration judged its teleconferencing systems to be successful according to nontravel criteria. Langley considered the payback of its teleconferencing system to be the involvement of more people in decisions and the delivery of fresher, more accurate information.

MORE PEOPLE

- Lesle Kayser, supervisor of ARCOvision, Atlantic Richfield Co.'s extensive video teleconferencing system, has said, "In our original justification, we based savings on a 15 percent reduction of travel costs between the cities in the system. Actually, the obvious advantages to the conference system are not so much [decreases in] travel as increases in productivity and innovation, as well as the keener competitive edge we get by being able to meet with a full group and arrive at faster decisions."

Although it's an unmeasurable benefit, faster decision making is indeed a key benefit of teleconferencing. Executives often tend to delay making decisions until they are able to travel to face-to-face meetings. Teleconferencing, by contrast, allows managers to make real-time decisions on an as-needed basis. As one IBM executive put it, "We saved $1 million in travel, but more importantly, we cut our product development cycle by one-third."

Another key benefit of teleconferencing is indirectly related to travel substitution: The medium can allow lower-level managers who would ordinarily not travel to participate in meetings with higher-level managers and executives. One of many applications of video teleconferencing at Hercules Incorporated (see Chapter Sixteen) vividly illustrates the expanded management participation afforded by the medium. Hercules' Management Committee meetings used to include only the company's six most senior executives; now more than 100 managers at 14 sites are able to participate in the monthly meetings.

Misconception #2: Teleconferencing Can Never Be as Good as Meeting Face to face

Many users find teleconferencing valuable in renewing or maintaining contact first established at a face-to-face meeting. But evidence does not support the assumption that teleconferencing can never be as good as "live" meetings. In fact, for certain tasks, teleconferencing has been shown to facilitate communication as well or even better than face-to-face meetings.

For example, one study found that audio and audiographic teleconferencing can substitute effectively for 45 percent of face-to-face meetings. A study conducted by AT&T concluded that audiographics teleconferencing could substitute for 80 percent of such meetings.

Kathleen Kelleher and Thomas Cross summarized almost two decades of research on teleconferencing with the following conclusions about electronic meetings:

- Meetings are shorter, as people tend to concentrate specifically on the task at hand.
- Meetings are more task-oriented.
- Meetings are better structured.
- Meetings are more orderly, even though less hierarchically organized and less status oriented.

- There is generally more equality of participation.
- More opinion exchange occurs and persuasion is more successful.
- In computer conferences, there is more time for reflection and thought before the necessity for response and decision.[3]

In a comprehensive study conducted by Satellite Business Systems in association with Booz-Allen & Hamilton and the National Opinion Research Center at the University of Chicago, three-fourths of the large-corporation video conferencing users surveyed reported they experienced an increase in their personal productivity and one-half reported an increase in meeting effectiveness. Figure 14–3 summarizes their perceptions of the effects of video conferencing.

A British study found that teleconferencing enhanced group decision making in several ways, and that in conflictual situations it actually facilitated negotiation, leading the researchers to the following conclusions:

1. In negotiations and bargaining, the group with the soundest case was more likely to win in a teleconference than in a face-to-face meeting.
2. Opinions changed during the meeting and fewer coalitions formed because teleconferencing participants tended to be less dogmatic and more compromising.
3. Those holding a minority opinion were more easily persuaded to line up with the majority.

This study leads to another possible conclusion—that the participants were more manageable because the teleconferencing medium itself intimidated them. According to the study, however, participants reported a heightened level of feedback from other members and perceived the videoteleconference to be less threatening than a face-to-face meeting.[4]

Another study, carried out by the University of Wisconsin-Extension Educational Telephone Network (ETN), compared the effectiveness of training presented in a face-to-face group with a group that was trained electronically via ETN. Results showed no significant difference between the mean scores of the face-to-face group and the ETN group, though the scores of both were

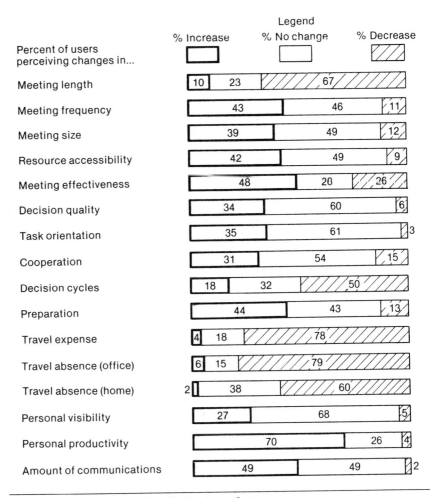

Legend

Percent of users perceiving changes in...	% Increase	% No change	% Decrease
Meeting length	10 23	67	
Meeting frequency	43	46	11
Meeting size	39	49	12
Resource accessibility	42	49	9
Meeting effectiveness	48	20	26
Decision quality	34	60	6
Task orientation	35	61	3
Cooperation	31	54	15
Decision cycles	18 32	50	
Preparation	44	43	13
Travel expense	4 18	78	
Travel absence (office)	6 15	79	
Travel absence (home)	2 38	60	
Personal visibility	27	68	5
Personal productivity	70	26	4
Amount of communications	49	49	2

SOURCE Green/Hansell, Satellite Business Systems

FIGURE 14–3: Some effects of videoconferencing.

significantly higher than the control group, which had no training.

Misconception #3: Full-Motion Video Teleconferencing Is Always Preferrable

Potential teleconferencing users often think that a system is first-rate only if it provides full-motion video. However, some studies indicate that audio conferences, especially when enhanced by graphics, can be just as effective as face-to-face meetings or full-motion video conferences.

For example, a major study conducted by the Institute for the Future revealed that users or potential users of multimedia communication systems show no strong preferences for full-motion video. When asked to select input functions for an optimal system, respondents chose audio and keyboard inputs over video at a rate of nearly 2:1. When asked to select the output functions of an optimal system, respondents again preferred motion video the least. By far their preference was for text, still video, and audio. These preferences held both for optimal systems and for budget-constrained systems.

TYPES OF TELECONFERENCING TECHNOLOGIES

Audio Teleconferencing

How many use it?

Conferencing via telephone is the simplest, most widely used and least expensive form of teleconferencing. Audio teleconferencing in its most basic form joins groups of people at each end of a regular telephone circuit. Participants speak through a common microphone and listen via a speaker amplifier. A more sophisticated installation may include elaborate meeting rooms with built-in, high-quality microphones and loudspeakers, such as in the special audio teleconferencing facility used by executives at Bank of America, cited later in this chapter.

An "audio bridge" is needed for audio teleconferences that connect more than two conferencing sites. One site acts as the bridging location, or else telephone company operator assistance can be used to establish the needed connections among participants. Audio bridges can link any location in the world served by telephone; some bridges incorporate new technology that improves signal quality and reduces echo, ensuring high-quality transmission among the sites.

Audio Plus Graphics Teleconferencing

An audio teleconference can be supplemented by the simultaneous interchange of images via facsimile machines, telewriting, and the AT&T Electronic Blackboard.

Facsimile is an invaluable tool for exchanging detailed text and graphics before and during a teleconference.

Courtesy of The Telephone Museum, San Francisco

FIGURE 14–4: An early teleconference among corporate executives of AT&T. Audio teleconferencing has been in use since the 1920s.

Telewriting refers to fully interactive graphics systems that consist of an electronic writing pad and pen, graphic processor, and color television monitor. Conference participants can write or draw figures and schematics and transmit what is written to remote TV monitors.

AT&T's Electronic Blackboard, Gemini, consists of a large writing surface used for writing or drawing upon with an ordinary piece of chalk. Whatever is written or erased on the "blackboard" is transmitted to a television monitor at the remote sites. The Electronic Blackboard operates in black and white only and requires a separate circuit.

Freeze-Frame Video

Video transmission of one frame at a time adds a dimension of interaction not possible with facsimile and provides greater de-

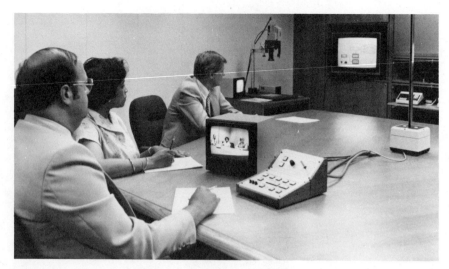

Courtesy of Hercules Incorporated

FIGURE 14–5: An audio/graphics/video teleconference.

tail than is possible by the transmission of line drawings. This technique is known both as freeze-frame or slow-scan television. Video cameras are used to take "snapshots" at approximately 35-second intervals or shorter. The video information is transmitted via regular telephone lines or data lines to receiving video monitors.

With recent advances in microcomputer graphics hardware and software, the ubiquitous micro will increasingly be used to conduct freeze-frame teleconferences, though the transmission speeds of such products are not yet up to par with current video-based freeze-frame systems.

One of the first such products is AT&T's Truevision™ line of microcomputer-based image capture graphics boards, introduced in late 1985. These boards allow users of AT&T's PC 6300, the IBM Personal Computer, and IBM PC compatibles to capture and store on a hard disk electronic images from any standard video source, and to retrieve, manipulate, transmit, and display this information as full-color, television-quality, still-frame images.

In addition, teleconferencing software available from AT&T allows users to send the digitized electronic photographs at 9600

PRODUCT OPTIONS

bps over ordinary telephone lines so that any action on the monitor at one teleconferencing location appears simultaneously at a receiving location. Functions of the teleconferencing system include control of an electronic "slide show" of pretransmitted and stored images; pointing to items on local and remote screens simultaneously using the computer cursor; and annotating the local and remote screens simultaneously with text, graphics, or numbers.

The limitation of the system at present is that "reduced color" images take about one minute to arrive, while full color images arrive on the screen after about two minutes. AT&T engineers have designed a special technique to mitigate this problem which allows the receiving personal computer to begin to reconstruct the image after only 25 percent of the picture data has been transmitted.

The advantages of freeze-frame (both video-based and microcomputer-based) over full-motion video teleconferencing include equipment portability, ease of use, relatively inexpensive initial cost of the equipment, and comparatively low cost of transmission because it requires much less bandwidth and channel capacity than full-motion video teleconferencing.

Full-Motion Video Teleconferencing

The transmission of full-motion, live television images offers the closest approximation of face-to-face meetings. Of course, full-motion video television technology requires wide-band transmission capability, and therefore is the most costly form of teleconferencing.

Early video conferencing systems used transmission channels that were prohibitively expensive for the majority of potential customers. Audio and video signals for full-motion video conferencing were transmitted in analog form at very high data rates—6 megahertz. Sending signals at such a high transmission rate used the full capacity of a communications satellite's transponder, and transmission costs ran as high as $1,200 per hour.

This situation was improved somewhat in 1981, with the development of the video coder/decoder (codec). A codec converts analog video into digital signals that occupy less transmission capacity. Recent improvements in signal compression have cut the necessary bandwidth even further. A number of these narrow-bandwidth signals can be relayed simultaneously by a single satellite transponder, bringing transmission costs into an affordable range for many companies.

Transmission costs were not the only economic drawbacks associated with video conferencing. Many video conferencing customers found that obtaining the proper combination of equipment and transmission capabilities was a costly, frustrating process. In most cases, users have been forced to piece together systems with components provided by a number of separate vendors. This was a process that could take more than a year to complete at a typical cost of $600,000 to $1 million per video conferencing site. And the majority of video conferencing systems available have been difficult to install and use.

But video teleconferencing technology is moving forward along with the rest of the telematics industry. The digitalization of television technology and ongoing improvements in video signal compression continue to make video conferencing less expensive and more accessible to business. Also, an important new factor is that competition among carriers is leading to lower video transmission prices.

Video teleconferencing can be carried out in a fully interactive mode, which includes two-way video and two-way audio, or a broadcast mode, which includes one-way video with two-way audio.

Two-Way Video/Two-Way Audio

The goal of two-way video conferencing is to convey a sense of being in the same room, even sometimes at the same conference table. A major advantage of full-motion video is that it can transmit body language, a vital element of communication.

The teleconference participants face the TV monitor where the distantly located participants can be seen; a camera located on the same wall as the TV monitor they are watching picks up and transmits the images of the local participants. The effect is that all participants are looking directly at one another. Camera switching is activated by a speaker's voice, and the camera automatically focuses on each new speaker. Other cameras pick up and transmit overview shots of all the participants.

Courtesy of Vitalink, Inc.

FIGURE 14–6: Two-way full-motion video and two-way audio.

A recent and exciting innovation in two-way video is the introduction of voice/data/video workstations. For example, Datapoint's MINX System adds both voice and full-motion video teleconferencing capability to the IBM Personal Computer, Personal Computer XT or AT, or its own Datapoint VISTA-PC Professional Computer.

One-Way Video/Two-Way Audio

This type of teleconferencing typically involves full-motion video broadcasts, usually via satellite, from the main site to the remote sites and return audio connections via regular telephone lines that allow voice interaction between all the receiver sites and the broadcast site. Interaction between sites through the two-way audio connection is usually for a scheduled question-and-answer period following the one-way broadcast.

COMPUTER CONFERENCING

The preceding discussion has involved conferencing forms based on audio transmission, augmented by graphics or video. Computer conferencing, by contrast, is based entirely on the exchange of electronic text through a computer with an elaborate store-and-forward message-handling system.

Each participant in a computer conference has a microcomputer connected by phone lines to a central computer that organizes and stores all of the communications. The communications are typed by the participant, transmitted to the central computer, and accessible to any participant for as long as the conference lasts. The conference administrators can delete messages, set up conferences on new topics, and include or exclude users.

Even if new participants join the conference late, they can review all preceding communications and add new comments of their own. Conference members can interact with each other directly and immediately, or they can tune in and out at their own convenience and still not miss the chance to contribute. Communications are read on a video screen as they scroll by, and/or they may be received in hard copy on a printer.

Computer conferencing differs significantly from real-time audio or video conferencing because participants can take or add messages at their convenience. It also differs from electronic mail because conferencing software facilitates group "dialogue" via key word search and retrieval of text from among the complete text of conference proceedings.

The search and retrieval capability of computer conferencing software is a key feature of these systems. Conferencing software (which runs on the central computer) usually allows the following retrieval methods:

- By time: retrieval after a date, before a date, between dates.
- By name: retrieval of messages written by or addressed to a specific person.
- By subject: retrieval of messages by key word search of a subject line, or full-text search.

Thus, computer conferencing has some distinct advantages as a way of linking people together, such as:

- A permanent written record of all discussions and convenient, quick access to prior comments.
- Asynchronous communication, meaning that people can use the system at a time convenient for them and do not have to use it at the same time.

- Increased group resources (more people are available who otherwise could not participate).
- Different communication linkages—cross-groups and more lateral links within and outside organizations.
- Increased quality of participation because of time for reflection and some research before the response.
- Greater sense of community with people even though they are geographically widely dispersed or even in different fields and institutions.
- Tailoring of the communications process to meet a group's particular characteristics, project goals, and types of participants.

This chapter concludes with a case study of Hewlett-Packard's use of computer teleconferencing, which illustrates many of these benefits in action.

USES OF TELECONFERENCING IN BUSINESS

Some of the most useful applications of teleconferencing in the business environment have been for the following kinds of meetings:

- Executive meetings.
- International meetings.
- Company broadcasts and crisis management.
- Product introduction/customer outreach.
- Teaching/training.
- Integration of decentralized work groups.
- Orchestration of separate task forces.

Executive Meetings

Only a handful of executive teleconferencing systems are in routine use. Interestingly enough, most successful executive systems to date have been audio rather than elaborate full-motion video systems.[5]

Bank of America installed an ultra high-quality audio system in 1968 to reduce executive travel between San Francisco and Los Angeles. The teleconferencing room in San Francisco headquarters looks like a typical bank executive conference room. Except for a small microphone, the technical features of the system are invisible to the users. The users flip one switch and are immediately connected to their colleagues.

CONOCO is one of the other success stories in executive conferencing. The company has regularly conducted its executive meetings via an audio conferencing system since CONOCO became decentralized in 1960. As was true with Bank of America, CONOCO's teleconferencing room in Houston has the ambience of a board room, not an equipment room.

Crisis Management

American Airlines' broadcast audio conferencing system, which is in daily use throughout the company, is also used as a crisis management tool. The system enables American to link all airports, and even the cockpit of the plane, to the Federal Aviation Administration and the Federal Bureau of Investigation, and thus receive valuable information required to make critical decisions.

Ad hoc or single-event video conferences have also been successful means for crisis control. After the 1984 Tylenol deaths in Chicago, Johnson & Johnson, using a single-event video conference transmitted throughout the country with video feed available directly to network television stations, announced a way of repackaging the drug so the bottle was much more tamper-resistant. Johnson & Johnson was able to gain airtime on network television that evening, and within weeks regained its market share.[6]

Ad Hoc Broadcasts

Many companies rent time on a vendor's teleconferencing system on an as-needed basis. For example, in 1982, when money market interest rates were sliding, Merrill Lynch & Company produced a special hour-long broadcast titled "Strategies for High-Yield Investments." The ad hoc video teleconference was broadcast live to 30,000 viewing customers at 30 specially wired hotels around the country. The show's impact on viewers was stunning to company executives: 35 percent of the viewers bought one of the products suggested in the broadcast. Shortly thereafter, the company installed a permanent video network encompassing all 500 of its sales offices.[7]

Teaching/Training

Teleconferencing in some cases may be a better medium for instruction than traditional face-to-face classroom meetings. Travelers Insurance Company recently conducted a series of training sessions both in person and by audio teleconference. Surprisingly, results showed that the audio conference sessions were more effective. Only 80 percent of the participants passed the face-to-face course, while 90 percent passed the audio conference course.

Hoffmann-LaRoche Pharmaceutical Company uses audio conferencing to conduct weekly and monthly sales meetings as well as to hold seminars for physicians. The seminars feature an expert in a particular field of medicine. Through the audio conference seminars physicians can converse with the expert in the convenience of the hospital conference room.

Integrating Decentralized Work Groups

The most successful applications of teleconferencing so far, according to Robert Johansen of the Institute for the Future, have been in integrating decentralized work groups. Large, geographically dispersed companies such as IBM, Aetna Life & Casualty Company, Hughes Aircraft, Honeywell, and Boeing have all successfully used this approach. To develop the 757 aircraft, Boeing's flexible, even subtle use of its teleconferencing system illumines the potential of this application.

- The extreme complexity of designing and manufacturing aircraft requires that work groups operate closely together. To facilitate the design and development of its 757 aircraft, Boeing installed 12 video conferencing rooms in locations at its airfield and at engineering and manufacturing facilities scattered around the Seattle metropolitan area.

    Under the pressure of meeting deadlines, engineers used teleconferencing regularly and learned to use the medium to communicate with great subtlety. For example, engineers requested that cameras zoom in on the faces of pilots answering questions about the aircraft's performance. By observing the pilot's facial expressions as he spoke, engineers believed they could learn much about the way an aircraft handles. During one large engineering meeting, one project manager requested close-ups on a speaker's face as well as on his own while they answered difficult questions.

Frequently, teleconferences were halted temporarily so engineers might be brought into the meeting electronically to react to potential design changes. Boeing reported that in at least three cases the suggestions of engineers called into the conference in this way saved the company more than $1 million each. According to a company spokesperson, Boeing's video conferencing network helped the company to complete the development of the 757 *ahead* of schedule.[8]

Coordination

Teleconferencing is also beneficial for groups that are decentralized and simply need to stay in touch to share knowledge and experience.

Computer conferencing is particularly well suited for coordination. Operators of nuclear power plants all over the world keep in touch with each other daily by checking into an industrywide computer conferencing system. In an emergency, participants can come together quickly over the system and exchange ideas on handling the situation.

We conclude this chapter with the following case study of computer conferencing at Hewlett-Packard. The study illustrates the wide applicability of the medium for group coordination in a multinational corporation.

Computer Conferencing at Hewlett-Packard

Hewlett-Packard's extensive computer conferencing network is based on CONFER—a conferencing software program purchased from Advertel Communications, Inc. CONFER runs on a portion of an Amdahl mainframe computer located in HP's headquarters computer center in Palo Alto, California. Among the software's features are key word full-text search of a conference's proceedings, posting of temporary bulletins, and electronic messaging. Plans are to install an updated version of

CONFER on a dedicated IBM mainframe, which will be able to handle up to 8,000 participants. Transactions on the conferencing systems are transmitted over HP's worldwide interactive X.25 data communications network.

HP was fertile soil for the proliferation of a computer conferencing community. The company consists of more than 50 divisions; each one conducts itself much like an independent business, with full product development capability. Most divisions have their own accounting, personnel, quality assurance, and manufacturing units, even to the point of making their own chips. The small size of HP's divisions allows an intense focus on product development, but makes the sharing of technical and managerial knowledge across divisions somewhat difficult. Computer conferencing provides an electronic vehicle for solving such communication problems.

SUBJECT SHARING FOR INTEREST GROUPS

- One heavily "attended" conference links about 50 of HP's industrial designers across numerous division. Many of these industrial designers—all of whom are visual thinkers concerned with ergonomics and product design—began the conferencing experiment convinced that the medium would not be very conducive to their needs. But the group is currently very active, accumulating connect times of more than 200 hours per month.

- Another important electronic meeting on CONFER links printed circuit board engineers in more than 10 divisions. All of the engineers work with "surface mount technology." The engineer who first convened the group was concerned that each division was independently making the same discoveries about this controversial technology. Their electronic conference, with a connect time of 10 to 20 hours per month, allows a convenient forum for the exchange of engineering ideas, preventing the possibility that engineers in numerous locations throughout the company are not all "reinventing the wheel."

These two examples illustrate the two main benefits of CONFER, according to Anthony Fanning, manager of the computer conferencing program at HP. "Computer conferencing helps spread the best practices of each division companywide and allows us to avoid duplication of efforts across divisions. These benefits apply to communication within a division or even within offices too.''

Fanning is a member of the research and development information resources unit of the corporate engineering division in Palo Alto, whose charter is to support the information needs of HP's diverse research community. First started as a service to that community, the conferencing network has expanded to include a diverse range of nontechnical interest groups as well as a great number of specialized technical conferences.

Electronic Meeting Styles. HP's conferencing networks support two distinct styles of meeting that have long been entrenched in the company's corporate culture: informal or ad hoc discussion meetings, and formal working meetings for technical or managerial decision making. CONFER organizers report that the electronic analogue of each type of meeting can easily be set up on the company's computer conferencing system. Moreover, these electronic meetings are able to significantly enhance the communication productivity of participants, when compared with person-to-person meetings of the same type.

HP is well known for its high degree of informal communication; a great deal of information is exchanged in "coffee pot" meetings with broad participation or through encounters resulting from MBWA ("management by walking around"). These informal interactions provide the working basis of ideas and proposals that are then decided upon (or even just ratified) in formal face-to-face meetings.

Anthony Fanning coaches the six electronic "coffee pot" meetings that he says have become an electronic analogue for HP's culture of informal sharing. These conferences are not particularly goal oriented; they give participants a forum for self-expression on topics of general interest, similar to the conferences flourishing on public networks around the United States. For example, about 250 participants from more than 50 divisions in a half dozen countries log in at least once daily to the MICROS conference, which Fanning moderates. Users simply chat about their experiences with microcomputers, HP or otherwise. Another electronic meeting place open to all participants is Fanning's ERGO conference, which sponsors on-line discussions of the "ergonomics" of working conditions at HP. In ERGO, a small but vocal group of participants informally examines topics ranging from video display terminal radiation to complaints about back pain.

The MOTMOR conference is a bit more controversial; it was set up to allow participants at any level of HP to contribute to ongoing discussions of motivation and morale issues. According to Fanning, the conference gives valuable feedback to management about how employees feel about working conditions and improves the morale of users who see that their complaints have a forum for expression. Many solutions to complaints appear from other on-line participants; a few personnel and human relations managers are beginning to participate. However, some employee complaints appearing in the conference have reportedly gone too far for some observers; indeed, discussion has sometimes turned to complaints about bosses. Some management critics of Fanning's "electronic coffee pot" conferences say it is inappropriate for the company to support forums that can encourage electronic dissent. Fanning replies that electronic "coffee pot meetings" work just like the company's traditional informal communications network, providing the working basis for management decision making in formal meetings. "A central part of the HP Way has always included the idea of a working community based on intense, informal communication among people at all levels and across functions," says Fanning. "The informal computer conferences on CONFER now allow people to 'bump' into one another electronically, with similar intensity and the same effect. MBWA has become logistically more difficult as the company has grown and spread out; CONFER returns the values of MBWA and the HP way through an electronic medium."

There are other, more practical reasons for the open conferences, as well. "I think it's essential to offer these more amusing conferences, just from the standpoint of giving people the motivation to log on to the private working computer conferences of which they are members," says Fanning. "The open conferences generate the underlying energy needed to keep the whole conference system operating, just as face-to-face meetings in hallways and around coffee machines have always provided the emotional infrastructure needed for more formal group activities at HP."

The vast majority of meetings on CONFER, of course, are private working teleconferences. According to Bert Raphael, a founder of HP's computer conferencing system, these conferences have quickly found a ready-made audience at HP. A common complaint around the company, similar to complaints heard at other large corporations, has been that flying into headquarters for periodic face-to-face meetings is time consuming and marginally productive. Multipoint audio or video conferences have been found to be inadequate substitutes for travel; both still require synchronous meetings. In addition, facilities and connect time for two-way video conferencing are prohibitively expensive for convening people across numerous divisions (but note how Hercules Incorporated, has been able to arrange successful multipoint conferences through the use of leased satellite services in Chapter Fifteen); though audioteleconferencing is far less expensive, Raphael points out that multipoint audio meetings are difficult to arrange and very awkward to conduct.

But text teleconference meetings are flourishing on the system, especially for technical groups. The list of conferences among the 50 or so technical meetings on CONFER includes ones for corporate engineers, mechanical engineers, computer-aided manufacturing engineers, productivity managers in HP laboratories, users of drafting design workstations, microprocessor engineers, quality control managers, and evaluators of third-party software. One remarkable conference links engineers in 17 different divisions who are involved with a certain IEEE standard. Another joins MIS managers in charge of service computers at most of HP's worldwide sites; members of this group were particularly isolated from their peers until the computerized conferencing became available.

QUESTIONS FOR REVIEW:

1. What is teleconferencing?
2. Briefly describe the five forms of teleconferencing.
3. Briefly describe the three misconceptions about teleconferencing.
4. Contrast freeze-frame video and full-motion video teleconferencing.
5. What is the role of the video codec?
6. Describe computer conferencing.

7. What are five useful applications of teleconferencing in business? Briefly describe these applications.

FOR DISCUSSION:

1. Do you foresee a picture-phone being useful at home? Why or why not?
2. If teleconferencing in all forms becomes commonplace in business, how would a manager's workload change?
3. Speculate on alternate technologies to teleconferencing.

NOTES FOR CHAPTER FOURTEEN

1. Lorne Parker, "Working Toward a Perfect Fit," *Telecommunication Products + Technology,* September 1985, p. 74.

2. Robert Johansen, *Teleconferencing and Beyond* (New York: McGraw-Hill, 1984), p. 5.

3. Kathleen Kelleher and Thomas Cross, *Teleconferencing* (Englewood Cliffs, N.J.: Prentice-Hall, 1985), p. 52; for a summary of findings of approximately the first decade of laboratory and field research on the social and psychological effects of teleconferencing see Robert Johansen, Jaques Vallee, and Kathleen Spangler, *Electronic Meetings: Technical Alternatives and Social Choices* (Reading, Massachusetts: Addison-Wesley Publishing Company, 1979), pp. 141–91.

4. J. A. Birrell and Ian Young, "Teleconferencing and Long-Term Meetings: Improving Group Decision-Making," The Economist Intelligence Unit, London, England, no date, p. 447, in Kelleher and Cross, *Teleconferencing,* pp. 51–53.

5. Robert Johansen, *Teleconferencing and Beyond,* pp. 62–63.

6. *Businessweek,* "Videoconferencing: No Longer Just a Sideshow," November 12, 1984, p. 117.

7. Raymond Grenier and Susan Pereyra, "Teleconferencing: The Medium is NOT the Message," *Telephony,* August 20, 1984, p. 38.

8. Robert Johansen, *Teleconferencing and Beyond,* pp. 52–58.

REFERENCES

KERR, ELAINE B. and ROXANNA STARR HILTZ, *Computer-Mediated Communication Systems.* (New York: Academic Press, 1982).

SINGH, INDU B., ed. *Telecommunications in the Year 2000.* (Norwood, New Jersey: Ablex, 1983).

WILLIAMS, JEFF. "Micro Meetings." *Micro Communications,* November 1984.

PART SIX

Case Studies in Telematics

The case studies presented in Part Six are based largely on original field research. The intent is to illustrate in detail how three very different companies have matched telematic technologies to their unique business communication needs. In each case, the real-world challenge of building a corporate network is presented according to the divergent viewpoints of corporate management, end-users of communication networks, and telecommunications or data processing managers. Part Seven examines in more detail the newly emerging roles of these three groups in the era of business telematics.

The case of Regis McKenna, Inc., in Chapter Fifteen, shows the predicament of a small, information-intensive organization that must make crucial choices for integrating stand-alone personal computers and its corporate minicomputer in a headquarters data network. The company is also making important decisions about upgrading voice, facsimile, and video communications.

Hercules Incorporated, (Chapter Sixteen) is a pioneer in business telematics. It was one of the first American corporations to build its own integrated voice, data, and video digital network serving multiple sites. Hercules is also a model of the strategic management of corporate telecommunications, where leadership in harnessing the productivity potential of telematics emanates from the company president himself.

The technology, management, and everyday use of Hewlett-Packard's corporate telematic network is presented in detail in Chapter Seventeen. Hewlett-Packard has built one of the most advanced corporate networks in the world, currently linking more than 400 sales, research, and manufacturing sites in 75 countries for voice and digital data and nearly 100 sites for broadcast video. This large, high-technology company, well known in the business world for its innovative management techniques, has also developed futuristic techniques for using telematics applications of every kind to enhance employee performance and company profitability.

CHAPTER FIFTEEN

Regis McKenna, Inc.: Initiation into Telematics

OBJECTIVES

- Observe a small firm's initiation into telematics.
- Examine the decision-making process in the selection of telematic technologies.

INTRODUCTION

How does a leading marketing communications firm—one that represents some of the most innovative companies in the telecommunications industry—use advanced communication technology to manage its *own* information requirements? This chapter considers how Regis McKenna, Inc. (RMI), famed for introducing the Apple computer and the Intel microprocessor to the world, is initiating itself into the era of telematics.

Regis McKenna founded the company in 1970 after leaving his position as marketing manager at then-fledgling National Semiconductor. Since then, RMI has helped scores of small and high-technology companies attain success in the volatile start-up electronics industry. Today Regis McKenna presides over a $10 million international public relations firm with eight offices worldwide. RMI continues to offer marketing and communication strategies exclusively for high-technology companies, though McKenna has recently published a book and conducts seminars that apply his seasoned Silicon Valley experience along broader lines.

Among RMI's earliest clients were Intel, which developed the first integrated circuit for Ethernet, one of the earliest LANs, and 3COM, a pioneer LAN equipment manufacturer whose president, Bob Metcalf, was a principal developer of Ethernet. Such involvements preconditioned the agency to the concept of data communications and office networking before these technologies gained general acceptance. Still, the story of RMI's own internal application of new communication technologies is not one of rapid, precocious implementation of cutting-edge technology. Instead, the RMI experience should appeal to nearly any small organization—with access to limited resources—that is considering its own "telematic initiation." RMI's approach has been cautious and evolutionary, marked by trial-and-error attempts to develop unique solutions to equally unique communications problems.

INCREASING INFORMATION PRESSURES

Since 1980, RMI has grown from representing fewer than 10 clients to more than 70. Its information requirements have increased exponentially with this expanding client base. To be successful, the agency has had to keep pace with the exploding complexity of the high-technology marketplace, providing extremely timely information access for its executives and professionals.

The agency's method of guiding emerging high-tech companies requires access to two major sources of information: data about the market environment surrounding new products and "internal audits" of the client's own resources and capabilities.

In addition, as RMI has grown with the maturing high-technology industry, the company has had to develop many more specialized categories of information work. Long-standing clients have diversified their offerings, requiring the addition of more account executives along with several more layers of account management. (For example, the number of account executives on the Apple account increased from 4 to 10 between 1980 and 1985.) As a result, efficiently handling the increasing volume of intraoffice communications is now a major challenge facing the agency. Successfully meeting this challenge is also imperative for the following reasons:

1. Virtually all of RMI's 160 employees work with information in some form.
2. More than 80 percent of information work in its offices is estimated to be of a nonroutine nature.
3. The company has expanded in the past several years from

Regis McKenna, founder of Regis McKenna, Inc.

its headquarters in Palo Alto to small branch offices in Portland, Phoenix, Costa Mesa, Boston, Paris, Munich, and London.

Emergence of a Corporate Information Policy

Regis McKenna's general attitude toward the use of information technology parallels the marketing communications advice he proffers to clients: "Decisions about communication technology should be based on an analysis of the qualitative impact of the transmitted information on its recipient. It's best if a firm begins by classifying its communications in terms of the end purpose—the intended impact of the communication on the recipients. With this in mind, the company can go on to the quantitative or economic issues, exploring and choosing among the range of available communication technologies."

It happens that his company is currently in the midst of

Robert Brownstein, a vice president of RMI, is de facto manager of office automation and telecommunications.

making its own major decisions concerning voice, data, and text communications. The company's aging PBX is often choked when the high volume of phone calls reaches peak capacity. In addition, at the time this is written most of the company's 80 desktop micros still operate in stand-alone mode, and an HP 3000 minicomputer was also recently purchased.

This hardware situation, plus the pressure of RMI's increasing information requirements, is pushing senior management toward the formulation of a coherent approach to information management.

MANAGEMENT VISION OR NECESSITY

Robert Brownstein, a vice president of RMI and former senior manager in the writing and production department, has become de facto manager of office automation and telecommunications. Brownstein handles acquisition and installation of new information technology at the agency, in addition to a number of other roles. "We are not quite ready to add a full-time vice president of information resources," says Brownstein. "However, we recently hired a manager of human resources and will likely add an office automation department in a year or two."

EVOLUTION

WITHOUT A CIO THIS TAKES MORE TIME

"At the same time," he comments, "senior management is intimately involved in helping to make acquisition and implementation decisions concerning new technology. We're moving into a growth phase where a specific corporate information policy will be a necessity."

EARLY EXPERIENCES WITH INFORMATION TECHNOLOGY

Beginning in the early 1970s and extending to 1979, all documents produced at RMI were generated on electric typewriters. The agency's first word processor—"a clunky and expensive machine," according to Brownstein—was installed in late 1979. The first drafts of all texts generated by the writing department were to be entered on the new machine to permit easy revisions of future drafts.

Apple computers first entered the agency a year later. "One has to remember that personal computers were not yet considered word processing tools," Brownstein says. "The IBM PC wasn't even on the drawing board until two years later."

ENTRANCE OF COMMUNICATING WORD PROCESSORS

By 1982, RMI entered a period of more rapid growth as a result of the upsurge in the microcomputer industry. The agency's writing and production department—the key group for developing client proposals, product positioning statements, and product literature—was adding many more personnel. This led to a decision to acquire word processing workstations for the enlarged writing staff.

Numerous products were reviewed, and the large field of offerings was narrowed to five, each of which were tested by the department. This field was narrowed to two for continued testing. After two months of deliberation and a great deal of end-user input, Brownstein opted to purchase Exxon word processors for the agency's eight writers. "We chose Exxon because it was one of the very first turnkey local network products for a text processing environment," Brownstein recalls. The eight word processors were tied together in a 1 megabit per second communicating word processor network, giving the company its first data communications capability. Today, the Exxon network has grown to its full capability, with 16 workstations.

The network has simplified the writing, editing and production of RMI's documents, with local area network features such as file sharing, electronic mail, and peripheral sharing.

Document filing and the transfer of documents among writ-

A shared printer on the Exxon local area network.

ers and editors, whose offices are spread around the agency, is done largely electronically. Writers of first drafts dispatch their copy for storage in an "electronic file cabinet" (a 30 megabit hard disk file server), from which the copy can later be forwarded at an editor's convenience; the writer sends a separate electronic message over the network to notify the editor regarding document completion. Alternately, the writer may send the text itself directly to the editor's screen.

In addition, the system's security features enhance the editor's control of the writing process; a writer's place in the editorial hierarchy determines whether he has "read/write," "read only," or no access to shared files.

The writers rarely used electronically stored text as background for developing new texts. Writers find it easier to retrieve hard copy documents from file cabinets because key word searches of shared electronic files are not possible on the Exxon system.

The Exxon file server allows sharing of three letter-quality printers—one a high-speed daisy wheel printer—within the department.

Writers and editors are enthusiastic about the network. "From the beginning, the issue for our writers has been quality, rather than simply greater productivity. The communicating word processing environment has enhanced the quality of everyone's work and improved job satisfaction," says Brownstein.

TOWARD OFFICE INTEGRATION

The decreasing costs of computer and telecommunications equipment, plus increasing information requirements at RMI, led to a turning point in the company's evolution.

By 1983–1984, amid the personal computer revolution it helped launch, the agency decided to equip a large portion of its information professionals and their support staff with personal workstations.

In addition, the company's old Diablo business computer (installed several years earlier to handle financial and accounting functions) was in need of replacement.

Getting timely access to information about the company's financial status had become especially critical for executives. "Our business managers should have desktop access to a centralized corporate financial data base on the HP 3000," says Paul Dali, president of Regis McKenna. "This has become a key requirement of executives needing to make, say, a large capital equipment decision or a decision to hire more personnel. Unfortunately, with our current system, overall corporate financial data is only compiled monthly. This makes it quite awkward to gather information needed to make major ad hoc spending decisions in midmonth. Executives should instead be able to enter a financial data base on demand and query it about the daily status of the whole agency or any single department."

Thus, senior management was able to perceive two major communication needs within the company: the need to improve messaging and document interchange among writers and other professionals and to improve the flow of financial data to business and accounting managers. As a result, the agency's executive committee began to consider developing a corporatewide electronic network.

After a thorough review of the company's needs, Brownstein recommended conversion to a high-end, multiuser microcomputer network featuring a large disk, several fast printers, and off-the-shelf software. But senior management had more ambitious plans. The final recommendations of the executive staff

RMI's minicomputer facility.

provide the first evidence for the evolution of an ad hoc corporate information policy at RMI. A system 10 times more powerful than the multiuser network—in terms of on-line storage capacity and cost—was to be implemented. The agency's leadership was clearly looking ahead to their mounting information requirements of the coming decade.

The initial solution called for installation of a Hewlett-Packard 3000 minicomputer with RS-232C links to HP 150 personal computers. Seventeen HP 150s were brought in for testing by agency business managers and support people. Plans were made to supply the rest of the agency with 150s (and HP 110 portables) after successful completion of the test.

However, like many small organizattions implementing new office technology, an unplanned turn of events complicated the process. This was now mid-1984 and RMI's client, Apple Computer, had just introduced the MacIntosh 512 for the business environment. Regis McKenna, having launched one of the most ambitious high technology product introductions ever for the MacIntosh, was able to also negotiate a discounted bulk purchase of "Macs" for his company. The result was that the agency found itself equipped both with a set of HP 150s and approximately 50 Macs—all in stand-alone mode. This situation raised the issue of creating an electronic office network to a new stage.

RMI'S NETWORKING "SOLUTION SET"

RMI is currently faced with three major options for creating a corporate network around its HP 3000 minicomputer, 50 Macs, and 15 HP 150s. Brownstein and RMI's executive committee is carefully considering the following three approaches:

Centralized, Time-Shared

One obvious solution is to build a star-shaped companywide computer network around the HP 3000 minicomputer. Both the Macs and HP 150s are capable of emulating HP terminals linked to an HP 3000 for timesharing. In this configuration, the Exxon word processing network would need to be replaced with micros because of its incompatibility with the HP environment. The installation of this system would include inserting terminal emulation boards in each micro and running RS-232 wires from each desktop device to the minicomputer.

Distributed, Inter-Networked

Another possibility is clustering the micros into departmental LANs networked through file servers provided by 3COM, one of RMI's clients. (A LAN for micros would replace the Exxon

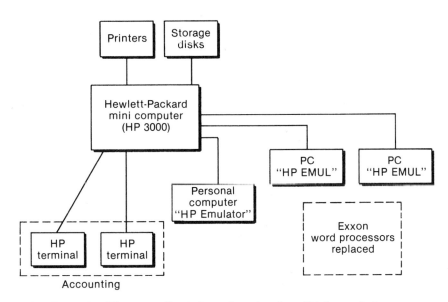

FIGURE 15–1: The centralized, time-shared option. Printer and storage are shared and electronic mail between users is possible.

system under this scheme.) This approach would not constitute a companywide network, at least initially. "Ninety percent of the messaging and file sharing activities occurring in a department remain within that department," according to Brownstein. "So LAN clusters could in effect handle 90 percent of the micro communication needs of our people. Bridges or gateways to neighboring LANs and ultimately to the HP 3000 minicomputer could be added later. In addition, the company could avoid installing a big web of RS-232 lines."

Unfortunately, the agency would have to wait to execute this solution. 3COM still needs to complete writing the software that permits messaging and file sharing between Macs and HP 150s.

Mixed Environment

A final possibility is to upgrade the text processing environment for the agency's writers by replacing the Exxon system with an IBM-compatible office automation system from Wang or Harris-Lanier. LAN clusters of IBM PCs and Macs and HP

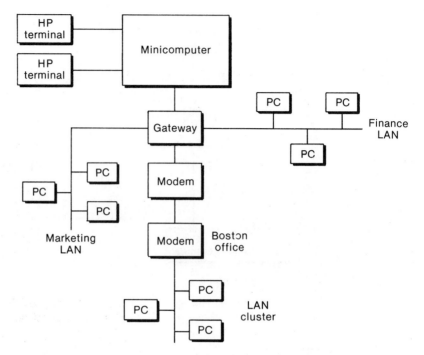

FIGURE 15–2: The distributed, internetworked system option. Clusters of LANs in marketing, finance, and the Boston office are shown.

150s (which can talk to IBM networks) would be set up in other departments much like alternative 2.

NEW OPTIONS IN VOICE COMMUNICATIONS

In 1979 RMI installed an analog PBX, with common features such as call transfer and conference calling. Telephone speaker sets for audio teleconferencing are in limited use at the agency.

RMI is considering replacing this old device either with a digital PBX, with voice and data communications capabilities, as well as options offered through the phone company's Centrex. According to Brownstein, "The old system we have now is totally inadequate. We are a strategic communications and marketing company; a huge volume of phone calls are constantly coming in and going out. Consequently, our phone lines get tied up a lot, which of course is intolerable."

Brownstein wants to see a voice messaging feature on the

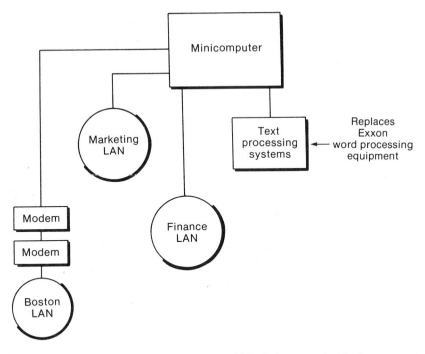

Figure 15–3: A mixed environment would include upgraded text processing plus LANs for each department.

switching system RMI acquires. "There's a place for voice mail in this company. Unlike electronic mail, voice messaging supplies the emotional content of the message and preserves the spontaneity and texture of the sender's vocal delivery. These subliminal qualities are a key factor in many forms of one-way managerial communications."

VIDEO TELECONFERENCING

Brownstein has adopted a wait-and-see attitude concerning use of video teleconferencing for his own organization. The fact that RMI represents a major vendor of the equipment, and has even arranged product introduction video conferences for several large clients, is not relevant for Brownstein. "At this point, the cost of renting teleconferencing facilities is simply too high to justify its use in most small organizations. We expect its cost to fall significantly in a few years, however. And as the agency's business becomes increasingly international, face-to-face teleconferencing should appear more cost-effective."

LONG-DISTANCE MESSAGING

RMI's Palo Alto headquarters office constantly sends documents and artwork to remote branch offices, clients, and its own vendors. The agency has worked out a simple formula concerning the use of facsimile versus overnight mail (or telex).

Overnight mail is, of course, the only medium suitable for sending original graphics and artwork. The use of facsimile is considered the best choice when documents or a short, written message needs immediate delivery domestically. But because faxing to Europe is quite expensive, the agency encourages the use of telex whenever possible for time-sensitive international messaging.

When a sender requires no better than overnight delivery, page count determines the choice of fax versus overnight mail. RMI's Group III fax machines operate at $30 per hour and send 25 pages per hour. After a page count exceeds about 25 pages, overnight mail becomes more economical.

Brownstein is quick to point out—in line with Regis McKenna's own stated philosophy of business communication—that the main criterion for choices of long-distance communication techniques are qualitative. "Not enough people make a clear distinction between the means of a communication and its end purpose. Looking at the end purpose involves considering the impact on the person at the other end—how the timeliness of a communication and its form of delivery affects their ability to respond to or use the information. Telex, fax, long-distance telephone calls, and overnight mail each have unique and intangible qualitative impacts. In the long run, these impacts have a definite economic effect."

USE OF PUBLIC ON-LINE DATA BASES

Access to timely information about products and markets is especially important for a marketing communications agency that handles high-technology clients. RMI's market research de-

David Schneer, RMI's information retrieval
specialist, inspects the printout of the full text of an
article downloaded from the NEXIS on-line data
base service.

partment uses two main research techniques for capturing such
information: primary research using telephone interviews and
focus groups and secondary research for printed information
stored electronically on on-line public data bases.*

RMI's information brokers can access close to 1,500 data bases
through nearly a dozen on-line public information services.
NEXIS is the most heavily used data base, followed by DIALOG

---

*Secondary research also includes occasional use of libraries to find information that
is not stored on-line or to find information in those rare categories in which it is less expensive to conduct a library search.

and Dow Jones News/Retrieval. David Schneer, RMI's manager of secondary research services, says use of his department's services saves the company and its clients thousands of dollars a day. "Computerized searches of electronic data bases are far more efficient than library research," says Schneer. "And much of the information we access on-line cannot, practically speaking, be found in any other way. For example, we were asked by one of our account executives to find all the pertinent information about IBM's plans for marketing the IBM PC in China. We were able to find this odd bit of data in only 20 minutes. This kind of accuracy is possible only because the tremendous processing power of these public information utilities allows key word searches of millions of on-line records."

Applications of RMI's data base service for in-house users and clients fall into four major categories of "intelligence": markets, competitors, the media, and industry infrastructures. Typical searches performed in these categories have included the following:

Market Intelligence.

- Determine the major players in the data base software market.
- Find out how many 2,400 baud modems were shipped in 1984.

Competitive Intelligence.

- Gather financial information about a client's competitors.
- Locate reviews of a client's products.

Media Intelligence.

- Find out which magazines write most about voice synthesis.
- Find out which writers/editors write most about the software market.

Industry Infrastructure Intelligence.

- Find out, on behalf of a telecommunications client, who are the leading experts, luminaries, and most-quoted analysts in the voice/data networking industry.

RMI's data base service is used by most clients and by nearly everyone in the company, from junior account executives to Regis McKenna himself. For example, account executives routinely ask for comprehensive searches of secondary source material when preparing public relations plans for new clients. The company's president, Paul Dali, relies on an on-line electronic news clipping service to provide him with a daily dossier of news stories on the agency's major clients. Even Regis McKenna himself is said to be a frequent user of the agency's information retrieval service.

QUESTIONS FOR REVIEW:

1. Give a brief history of RMI.
2. Recount some early experiences in RMI with information technology.
3. What are the three major options for creating a corporate network for RMI?

FOR DISCUSSION:

1. Which of the three options should RMI choose? Why?
2. Which of the three options would you choose if this situation occurred in a company you owned? Why?

CHAPTER SIXTEEN

Hercules Incorporated—Telematics Pioneer

OUTLINE

INTRODUCTION
COST EFFECTIVENESS
ORGANIZATIONAL EFFECTIVENESS
COMPANY BACKGROUND
INFORMATION MANAGEMENT STRATEGY
IMPLEMENTING AN INFORMATION POLICY
THE AOS STRATEGY
A TECHNICAL OVERVIEW OF THE HERCULES CORPORATE NETWORK
    Problem Areas
TELECOMMUNICATIONS APPLICATIONS
    Voice Communications
    Voice Messaging
    Video Teleconferencing
    On-Line Information Retrieval
    Electronic Mail
    High-Speed Data Communications
THE IMPORTANCE OF USERS

OBJECTIVES

- Understand why Hercules chose to use a telematics network as a competitive weapon.
- Understand the role of a CEO in shaping information management strategy.
- Understand how Hercules' strategy was implemented.
- See a technical overview of the corporate network.

INTRODUCTION

In 1979, Alexander F. Giacco, who had recently become new president and chief executive officer of Hercules Incorporated, set out to transform the work environment of his company. Giacco knew his company's survival depended on cutting costs in the face of increasing competitive pressures in the chemical industry. Well aware of the huge initial investment required, he committed Hercules to one of the most comprehensive information productivity programs ever undertaken in a large corporation. The clear result of Giacco's extraordinary foresight, half a dozen years later, is that Hercules leads the world chemical industry in cost control and in office and managerial productivity.

Another result is that Hercules now has in place the kind of corporate network most large companies will be scrambling to build in the late 1980s.

Giacco and his 26,000 employees are end-users of one of the few private integrated services digital networks in the world. Hercules' corporate network represents second-stage telematics: Its leased satellite network transmits digital voice, data, and video signals at high speed among geographically dispersed earth stations situated on Hercules' premises; video conferencing, electronic mail, and voice messaging are integrated into the same end-to-end digital network that handles long-distance voice and data communications.

In addition, backed by a carefully implemented corporate information policy supported by senior management, Hercules' information and telecommunications system managers have been able to harvest significant gains in cost efficiency and organizational effectiveness from the newly installed technologies.

COST EFFECTIVENESS

By late 1984, Ross O. Watson, vice president of information resources, estimated the following cost savings from the new information tools:

1. Word processing used for the production of text and for electronic mail had allowed a 40 percent reduction in secretarial work hours, saving about $3 million per year.
2. Voice mail had saved more than $3 million annually in employees' time.
3. Video teleconferencing had saved more than $1.5 million yearly in time and travel expenses.
4. New information technologies installed since 1977, in sum, had enabled Hercules to trim 1,800 jobs, or 6.6 percent of its work force.[1] Clerical staff, for example, was reduced from 1,200 to 800.

ORGANIZATIONAL EFFECTIVENESS

If organizational effectiveness is indicated by reductions in layers of management, Hercules can be said to have made significant progress. In a period during which Hercules increased sales from $1.7 billion to $2.7 billion, the new technologies have allowed the stripping away of six layers of management, including the elimination of assistant department managers, assistant plant managers, and one level of vice presidents.[2] As a result, the total number of top management positions has been reduced by half since 1977, and managerial staff at the company's largest factory, for example, was reduced by 15 percent. "We believe that layers of middle management inherently generate work and costs, contribute few significant decisions, and garble communications," says Giacco. "That's why we've set up major data processing, word processing, and telecommunica-

Ross O. Watson, vice president of information resources at Hercules Incorporated.

tions resources over the past three years: to streamline and reduce hierarchical layers."[3]

COMPANY BACKGROUND

Hercules Incorporated, headquartered in Wilmington, Delaware, is a multinational specialty chemical firm with annual sales approaching $3 billion. Its broad product line of more than 1,000 natural and synthetic materials includes cellulose and natural gum thickeners, flavors and fragrances, rosins and resins, polypropylene fibers and films, explosives, graphite fibers, and propellants for rocket fuels.

To be near its customers and sources of raw materials, Hercules has locations dispersed across the United States and in many foreign countries. The company has 80 domestic and international sites, with only about 10 percent of its employees working in the Wilmington area.

INFORMATION MANAGEMENT STRATEGY

Giacco's innovative approach to management began to emerge when he became head of Hercules' planning group in 1974, amid the world oil crisis. "It was obvious that we could no longer afford our previous management system. My job was to develop a new management organization plan," Giacco remembers. "One of the first things we did was to accelerate data automation. We slowly began to see some changes, yet by the end of 1977, progress had been minimal. We saw that we had to take drastic measures to stay competitive. Accordingly, when I became CEO early in 1978, we started a complete top-to-bottom management restructuring."

As part of that restructuring, Giacco led the company in a greatly increased use of computers and telecommunication systems to support the new management system. "At Hercules, our use of new computer technology, information systems, and telecommunications is very much a reflection of our new management style," Giacco claims.

"In fact, we believe that new computer technology, with its faster and more accessible information, is leading to a revolution in industrial management. Computer technology is allowing us as managers—I should say forcing us—to move to new and different organization types so that we can better meet competitive needs. And the people who can best harness these new technologies in the future will be the most successful."

Hercules' large investments in new information technology plus its management restructuring over the past decade reflect Giacco's fundamental belief that "Success follows information. . . . Information is more and more getting to be the central capital and key to economic strength—particularly in the competitive battleground of the world marketplace."

[handwritten margin note: BASED ON TECHNOLOGY]

Alexander F. Giacco, president and CEO of
Hercules Incorporated.

IMPLEMENTING AN INFORMATION POLICY

Giacco and Hercules' senior management launched the information productivity campaign with the founding of the Advanced Office System (AOS) program in 1979. The AOS staff group was given a charter to look at evolving technology, to recommend how it might help control costs, and to implement the program in such a way as to support the company's extensive management restructuring.

Ongoing encouragement and guidance from Giacco and other high-level executives gave a tremendous impetus to the fledgling AOS program. Their support permitted a full-time staff to research, plan and publicize the project from its inception; insured adequate financing; and moved the program along much faster than it otherwise might have. According to Ross Watson, vice president of information resources, "Alexander Giacco has really been the top supporter of AOS. That has given us the flexibility to plan for what is best in the long term—a critical factor when you're dealing with expensive and fast-changing technologies. In addition, in some companies, information technology is approved strictly on a cost-displacement basis. Giacco has led senior management to perceive new technology on the basis of value added as well as cost displacement."

THE AOS STRATEGY

Soon after its founding, the AOS group returned to senior management with a three-pronged strategy for introducing new information technology:

1. **To improve the productivity of professionals as well as clerical employees.** Hercules was typical of U.S. industry over recent years in that manufacturing productivity had steadily increased while office productivity remained constant.
2. **To link more closely the company's widely scattered manufacturing and sales locations, many of which are in remote areas.** The goals were to decrease travel requirements and to improve communications between sites even when travel was not a factor.
3. **To take advantage of the move to a new corporate headquarters facility.** The Hercules Plaza building was constructed to provide more space and improve the corporate image, but the move also offered an opportunity to equip Hercules' headquarters with the latest office technology.

To implement this strategy, AOS recommended immediate expenditures on office automation equipment and development of a new telecommunication system to tie these applications together.

Finally, the new telecommunications and office system was

The Hercules headquarters in Wilmington, Delaware, is an "intelligent building."

to be made the responsibility of a newly established Advanced Office Systems Department. This department and the Computer Systems Department both report to Watson, who in turn reports to Giacco. Pairing these two groups at the highest level in the organization shows the importance placed on information resources by Hercules' executive management.

A TECHNICAL OVERVIEW OF THE HERCULES CORPORATE NETWORK

The new telecommunications system recommended by AOS was to be built around the private, high-capacity, ISDN service supplied by Satellite Business Systems (SBS). According to Watson, "We picked the SBS Communication Network Service because we wanted a system that would integrate our voice, data, and image communication requirements into one transmission path. We also liked the SBS technical features—digital wideband transmission, switching capability, and on-premise earth stations that we could control."

The network, also known as Hercules Integrated Telecommunications System (HITS), became operational in 1982. Few organizations use satellite services so extensively in their private networks. But making satellite links the backbone of its corporate network is a logical choice for a company as widely dispersed as Hercules.

Figure 16–1 shows the major components of the SBS portion of the network: one of four satellites now in orbit, the earth stations (called network access centers), and the SBS control center. Seven earth stations are located throughout the United States on Hercules sites. Hercules terminal equipment (consisting of computers, video conferencing equipment, and PBXs) is connected to the SBS network by twisted-pair wire or coaxial cable when the link runs locally. Outlying locations are linked to the network through dataphone digital services lines operating at 9.6 to 56 kilobits per second. (The geographical location of earth stations is shown in Figure 16–2.) The network's performance is monitored by SBS's network control center in McLean, Virginia. SBS field engineers are also stationed at each Hercules site.

At the heart of each earth station is the satellite communications controller. The controller contains the hardware and software that format the signals received from information systems and other equipment into a single integrated digital stream. A "burst modem" collects the digital bit stream from the sat-

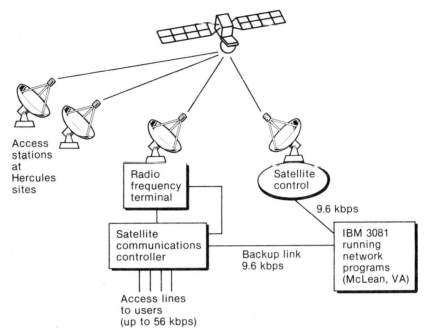

Access
stations
at
Hercules
sites

FIGURE 16–1: Major components of Hercules' backbone satellite network.

ellite communications controller, places the information on an analog carrier wave, and transmits the data to the radio frequency terminal in bursts of 48 megabits per second. The radio frequency terminal amplifies, transmits, and receives signals. Data is transmitted to the satellite at a frequency of 14 gHz and receives from the satellite at 12 gHz. Figure 16–3 shows these components of the network access center.

Least-cost call routing for all off-network calls is also provided by the SBS satellite communications controller (SCC) at each earth station, rather than through a switch on premises at a Hercules site. Thus, least-cost routing is provided for all network users, not just those with a sophisticated PBX.

Soon after the HITS network was installed, Hercules began substituting satellite links for its terrestrial data communication circuits. All remote earth stations now have data links to the Wilmington computer center. Applications include both interactive and batch data transmission at speeds from 9.6 to 56

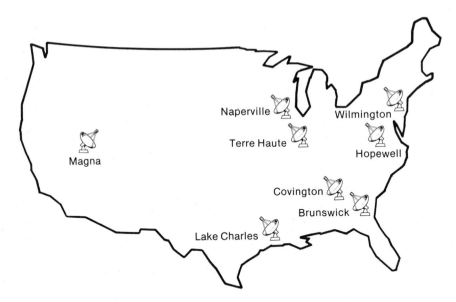

FIGURE 16–2: Hercules integrated telecommunication system locations.

kilobits per second between the host computer in Wilmington and the regional locations.

Terminals on Hercules' data network number more than 4,000, including some 1,700 Wang word processor stations worldwide and more than 1,000 IBM or IBM-compatible PCs.

The headquarters' Wangs are linked for office communications by a broadband cable local area network known as Fast-lan. Wang's gateway to the wide area network, called Mailway, includes a connection to an IBM mainframe with the help of a protocol converter.

Many of the IBM PCs are linked to the mainframe via terminal emulation boards and IBM's PROF software.

One implementation of the micro-to-mainframe link over Hercules' corporate network allows mainframe data extraction for insertion into LOTUS spreadsheets running on IBM 3270 PCs. The PCs (with IRMA terminal emulation boards) are used by professionals in the corporate accounting department.

Problem Areas

Jay Kocher has a number of technical concerns at this period in the growth of HITS. Chief among these are the following:

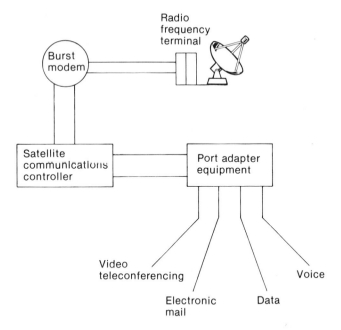

FIGURE 16–3: The earth stations accept voice, data, document or electronic mail, and video teleconferencing transmissions.

1. Electronic mail: improving the system's ability to transfer revisable text between different electronic mail systems; adding gateways so electronic mail can be sent to more European countries.
2. Security: the issue of opening up the corporate data bases for improved ease of access versus the need to maintain system security.
3. Software: finding improved filing and text retrieval software.

TELECOMMUNICATIONS APPLICATIONS

Many "bypass" corporate networks are initially cost justified solely as a replacement for conventional long-distance telephone service. While Hercules has realized significant cost savings from bypassing AT&T, the major savings from the network have accrued from the addition to the basic voice and data network of voice and text messaging, video conferencing, and high-speed data transfer.

FIGURE 16–4: Users of Fastlan at company headquarters.

The Growth of a Corporate Network

The following are some landmark dates in the development of Hercules' corporate network:

1973   OPEC oil embargo throws the petrochemical industry into crisis.

1978   Alexander G. Giacco assumes leadership of Hercules; initiates complete management restructuring.

1979   Major corporate reorganization continues; Advanced Office Systems (AOS) planning group appointed.

1980   Company embarks on program to implement advanced information technology; signs agreement with Satellite Business Systems (SBS), satellite network services vendor.

      Hundreds of Wang word processors installed at corporate headquarters, linked for electronic messaging.

      Voice messaging pilot tested with 50 corporate managers.

1981 Cost-cutting and productivity measures result in $60 million savings in operating expenses, reduction in 1,600 staff.

1982 Company invests additional $8.5 million in office technology, amid economic recession in the American economy.

Hercules' satellite network becomes operational.

Video teleconferencing operational over the network.

1983 Number of network calls per month doubles because of increased voice circuit capacity.

Begin voice mail and electronic mail over the satellite network.

1984 Tenth private workstation installed (three of these removed in 1985 in cost-cutting measure that reduced the number of sales locations.

1985 Hercules becomes first International Business Services (IBS) customer with an earth station installed on premises for communication to an international site (Holland).

Hercules and SBS sign contract for two-year extension of service.

1986 ·Completion of leased fiber optic network connecting Hercules buildings in Wilmington.

Second IBS circuit added to connect European headquarters in London to HITS.

T1 data link completed between Wilmington and Salt Lake City, Utah.

Voice Communications

Since the network became operational, voice usage over the satellite system has increased at a rapid pace. Bill Phile, manager of Network Services, explains why: "Before the network, people trying to make long-distance calls at most locations had to queue up for one or two WATS or tie lines that were manually controlled by a PBX attendant. That sometimes meant long periods of waiting and priority bumping. Now it's cost effective to have enough capacity on the earth stations for near-peak usage periods."

The wideband and broadcasting features offered by SBS's satellite network are well suited for Hercules' data and video transmission needs, but it should be remembered that voice signals transmitted over satellite links arrive at their destination with a half second propagation delay because of the long distances the signals must travel to and from the satellite. However, Jay Kocker, director of technology and development for AOS, says user complaints about the voice delay are minimal.

Voice Messaging

Hercules' voice messaging system was tested in 1980 with 50 corporate-level managers and was so enthusiastically received that 1,600 more users were quickly added. The system has now grown to more than 3,000 users who send about 50,000 messages a month. About half of this usage is routed via the satellite network among geographically dispersed sites. (Before the satellite network became available, it was not cost-effective to provide voice mail to regional locations; now the incremental cost to do so is virtually zero.)

Watson calls the voice messaging service "one of our most successful and popular services on the network. If we tried to take VMS away now, there would be a real employee outcry!"

Video Teleconferencing

Satellite communications is ideal for video teleconferencing because of its broadcast capability and its relatively low cost and wide bandwidth compared with terrestrial lines.

According to President Giacco, "We're generating a good rate of return on our video teleconferencing investment through reduced travel costs, but even more important, we're getting more timely horizontal and vertical communications—with much less wear and tear on our executives."[4]

Hercules has 24 operational video conferencing rooms, including 5 in its headquarters building, 18 at other U.S. locations and 1 overseas in London. The system can connect up to 17 rooms together simultaneously if the need arises.

Each video conferencing room on the network can be connected for one-way broadcast or two-way interactive conferences. The rooms house five color video cameras and two color monitors. Three cameras are focused on the conference table, a fourth is positioned on a document stand, and another rests on a movable tripod for coverage of flip charts, a blackboard, or objects out of range of the other cameras. The conference moderator operates a control panel to switch between cameras and transmit images.

The video conferencing system transmits in a color still-frame mode. Eighteen of the conferencing rooms communicate at 56 kilobits per second, allowing for 12-second throughput of images. The remaining locations multiplex four standard telephone circuits for 19.2 kilobits per second transmission, which provides a new image every 35 to 40 seconds.

Full-motion video conferencing has been piloted over T1 lines at selected locations, as an adjunct to the less-expensive freeze-frame system. However, according to Jay Kocher, senior management has put off approval of proposals for the permanent installation of a full-motion capability on the grounds that the extra quality is not yet cost-justifiable because of the current high cost of codecs. It is interesting to note that the most common request in video conferencing questionnaires (regularly submitted to users) is for full-motion video.

Hercules' use of video has accelerated rapidly since its inception in 1982, both in terms of connect time and breadth of application. Aside from the usual applications for internal problem solving, Hercules managers use video teleconferencing sites to communicate with suppliers, customers, and clients.

However, one of the most dramatic examples of the company's effective utilization of the medium is the multipoint video conference for corporate management explained below. It illustrates one of the key benefits of video teleconferencing discussed in Chapter Fourteen: greater participation by middle-level management in upper-level management deliberations.

- The Hercules Management Committee, whose members are Alexander Giacco, Robert Leahy, and four vice pres-

One site of a multipoint video teleconference for corporate management.

idents, used to meet in private sessions at corporate head-quarters. Now Management Committee meetings are held via multipoint video conferencing with up to 100 partic-ipants at 14 Hercules locations. These conferences for the first time have permitted a broad audience of Hercules managers to sit in on top-level discussions and listen to and participate in status reviews of major ongoing proj-ects throughout the company. According to Giacco, "The Management Committee teleconferences give us direct contact with those who have the ultimate responsibility for the success or failure of our investments. We are able to instantly communicate management standards and goals through a number of levels over a wide geographic area."

On-Line Information Retrieval

Hercules managers have desktop access to company data bases through the company's on-line information retrieval system. The system can be compared to corporate videotex, though the soft-ware was developed in-house. Even the most senior managers have terminals in their offices for access to the data bases. For example, Giacco uses his terminal every morning to access real-time information on the status of the company.

The company has a policy of capturing all transaction, production, and administrative data at the point where these data originate. Terminals have been installed at numerous locations in each plant so clerks can input data on operations, maintenance, quality control, and shipping. The Wang word processors located at all Hercules sites are used to capture almost all administrative data generated in the company, such as customer trip reports, complaints, and contracts. These varieties of data are then made available to management through terminals or micro-to-mainframe links. Even salespeople in the field, recently equipped with Radio Shack TRS Model 100 portables, can access or input sales and order information when on-site with customers.

According to Watson, the strong backing of senior management has contributed to the rapid acceptance and expansion of management information systems within the company. "Senior management has led in terms of facilitating user acceptance of desktop computers," says Watson. "Every top manager has a terminal in his office, even Giacco. Senior management's hands-on familiarity with the new technologies sends an important signal to the company: These tools are easy to use, and senior management thinks they can be used to solve business problems."

Electronic Mail

Approximately 900 electronic messages are sent each day over HITS to virtually any Hercules site. Delivery is one day or less anywhere in the United States or several locations in Europe.

High-Speed Data Communications

Hercules' Computer Systems Department operates the corporate computer center in Wilmington, a large data center in Magna, Utah, and many smaller data centers at plant locations and international sites in Canada, Mexico, and Western Europe. The computing facilities installed at the Wilmington center include two large IBM computers and peripheral storage devices, tape drives, high-speed printers, and communications controllers.

The system supports more than 1,000 displays, printers, and remote job entry (RJE) terminals and communications protocols including SDLC (synchronous data link control), BSC (binary synchronous), and asynchronous. Transmission speeds range from 1.2 to 56 kilobits per second over private-line terrestrial circuit and satellite links.

Some of the data communications applications currently operating at Hercules are described below:

- REMOTE DATA PROCESSING: Typical of the data links in operation and planned for other Hercules sites is the Oxford, Georgia, plant. There, a number of batch RJE and interactive data applications are being supported by an IBM 3705 communications controller connected over a 19.2 kilobits per second Systems Network Architecture (SNA) satellite network to the Wilmington computer center.

- HIGH-SPEED DATA TRANSFER: Hercules and SBS have implemented a high-speed bulk data transfer link between Hercules' two main data centers. With a T1 transmission rate of 1.544 megabits per second, the equivalent of a 2,400-foot tape reel can be transmitted in 12 minutes, as opposed to more than 31 hours over land lines at 9.6 kilobits per second.

THE IMPORTANCE OF USERS

A significant factor in the success of Hercules' Advanced Office Systems program—of which the integrated telecommunications system is the heart—has been the careful way in which it was introduced to users. Early surveys of user requirements, design of the system, and procedures for ongoing measurement of user reactions have all been undertaken with users in mind. For example, early in their planning cycle, members of the AOS group met with Hercules managers and their support personnel to discuss the program and explain how it could help them. Managers did not want the traditional working relationship between themselves and their secretaries disturbed, so the AOS group rejected the idea of setting up word processing pools and instead chose to keep secretarial functions near the manager.

The AOS program was introduced in a building-block ap-

Office automation did not disrupt the traditional working relationship between managers and their secretaries.

proach, starting with pilot projects in individual departments and gradually expanding into broader areas of the company. Extensive in-house training was provided at each stage. Depending on location and requirements, the AOS group offered classes, demonstrations, printed materials, audio conferences, and videotapes to explain the program. The reward for this careful implementation of new information technologies is evident in the growing usage and high levels of user satisfaction with Hercules' corporate network.

QUESTIONS FOR REVIEW:

1. Briefly recite Hercules' company background.
2. What are some of the cost savings at Hercules due to information technology?
3. Relate Giacco's information management strategy.
4. How did Hercules implement an information policy?
5. Describe HITS.
6. What are some problem areas in HITS?
7. What are some features offered by HITS?

FOR DISCUSSION:

1. If you were a competitor of Hercules, how would you use information technology to compete now?
2. If you were a customer of Hercules, what are some of the benefits and opportunities HITS provides for you?
3. If you were a supplier to Hercules, what are some of the benefits and opportunities HITS provides for you?
4. How should Hercules improve HITS now? In 5 years?

NOTES FOR CHAPTER SIXTEEN

1. "Beefing Up on Electronics Makes Hercules Leaner," *Business Week,* October 8, 1984, p. 125.

2. Ibid., p. 126.

3. A. F. Giacco, unpublished speech delivered to the Société de Chimie Industriele, September 20, 1984.

4. Ibid.

REFERENCES

GREEN, J. H. *The Handbook of Telecommunications* (Homewood, Illinois: Dow Jones-Irwin, 1986).

PHILE, W. G.; Green; and Cole. "Private Network Integrates Data, Voice and Video Communications." *Data Communications,* May 1984, pp. 125–135.

- LARGE FIRM - TECH. CRITICAL
- MNG. GOAL TO TRANSFORM THE WORK ENVIRONMENT
- COST PLANNING / FULL TIME STAFF ICONL TEAM CIO
- JUSTIFICATION BASED ON COST DISPLACEMENT + VALUE ADDED
- ACTIVE USERS PARTICIPATION

CHAPTER SEVENTEEN

Hewlett-Packard: Business Telematics in Action

Video Teleconferencing at HP
One-Way Video Conferences
Two-Way Video Conferences
Video Conferencing with Graphics
Computer Conferencing

OBJECTIVES

- Understand the impact of sophisticated telematics on Hewlett-Packard's employees.
- Preview some well-conceived plans for HP's network evolution into the 1990s.
- Understand how a corporation manages telematics.
- Understand the possible contents of corporate information policies.

INTRODUCTION

Hewlett-Packard Company is well known for its innovative, employee-centered management practices. Much of the American business community's interest in Hewlett-Packard (HP) has focused on its open corporate culture—its apparent ability to foster informal and intense communication among employees at all levels, resulting in a genuine sense of enthusiasm for corporate goals. HP's corporate objectives are, in turn, very people oriented: The "HP Way" is designed to produce "innovative, capable people throughout the organization" and to generate "enthusiasm at all levels" and proceeds from the belief that, as cofounder Bill Hewlett explains, "Men and women want to do a good job, a creative job, and if they are provided with the proper environment they will do so."[1]

This chapter explores how HP has provided its employees at all levels with an advanced telecommunications environment that is wholly consistent with its commitment to innovation through people.

HP provides, in fact, one of the most remarkable examples of business telematics in action. Between 1979 and 1985, HP increased the amount of raw computing power available to its employees by a factor of 18: The number of desktop computing devices in the company almost equals the number of telephones; one out of every two employees uses a desktop microcomputer or terminal, and among engineers the ratio is 1:1. In addition, HP's television network includes close to 100 video teleconferencing receive sites, and its Group III facsimile network numbers nearly 200 machines.[2] To connect these computing and communication facilities and the employees using them, the electronics giant has implemented a sophisticated worldwide voice, data, text, image, and video network. HP's adept management of this far-flung corporate network has helped make it a continuously innovative company that is often highly responsive to its customers. (More than half of HP's sales in 1985, for example, came from products introduced in just the past three years.)

A number of key telematic applications are used to support the "HP Way" of communications. The most notable among these are the following:

1. A home-grown electronic mail system ("HP Desk") used for messaging, file transfer, and electronic publishing by more than 45,000 users worldwide.
2. A computer communications network allowing interactive and batch data communications links among hundreds of HP 3000 minicomputers and thousands of engineering workstations worldwide.
3. One- and two-way video teleconferencing used many times weekly for training, product introductions, technical communications, press conferences, and managerial and corporate communications.
4. A rapidly growing population of computer conferencing users participating in more than 50 on-line business and technical conferences.
5. A corps of service technicians staffing HP "service centers," accessible by customers through more than 350 toll-free telephone numbers and equipped with master "customer solution" data bases and remote diagnostic tools.
6. An expanding voice-mail capability, soon to be merged with HP Desk to create a combined text-and-voice mail system.

Behind these diverse applications is one of the largest corporate telecommunication systems in the world, currently linking more than 50 divisions dispersed through 400 sites in 75 countries. The voice network that links these sites is increasingly based on private tielines leased from the public telephone company; all data traffic is moving rapidly toward transmission over a private worldwide X.25 packet switching network; and HP currently owns a satellite network capable of one-way analog and two-way digital video transmission and high-speed data transfer.

This increasingly private network is managed by HP's Corporate Telecommunications and Office Systems (CTOS) group, which represents the 1982 merger of once-separate office automation and telecommunications departments. This administrative merger—which the former manager of office automation calls "extremely fortunate"—reflects the technical convergence of office technology, traditional data processing, and telecommunications technology at HP, which is in turn being encouraged by information policies emanating from HP's senior management.

INFORMATION MANAGEMENT FROM THE TOP

Hewlett-Packard provides a useful model for management of an advanced corporate network on a large scale; its approach to telecommunications management derives from an explicit information policy—a policy that is formulated at the top level of the company.

John A. Young, president and CEO of Hewlett-Packard, often enunciates general principles of the company's information policy in public. In a 1985 speech in Singapore, he posed the following question: "How does HP manage information for quality and productivity?" Young, who was at the time chairman of President Reagan's Commission on Industrial Competitiveness, answered with the following words: "I know that lots of companies have an organizational separation between their information resources and the rest of their people. We think this situation takes away the chance to really use information to improve operations. Management of information can't be separated from management in general—information is an integral part of each manager's job. That's why at HP, the strategy for information is set by our management council—the key operational committee in the company."[3]

John A. Young, president and CEO of Hewlett-Packard Company.

Information policies are set by HP's senior management council in cooperation with the executive committee—the 25 most senior executives in the company.[4] While these executives oversee and set policy governing both acquisition and use of telematics and other information technologies, the information systems committee (ISC), consisting of members of the management council, reports to the larger body on the major information technology and management issues facing the company. In turn, technical and staff support for the ISC is provided by the information systems steering committee (ISSC), which is staffed by the directors of each of HP's five functional areas, of which CTOS is one. (See organizational chart in Figure 17–1.)

Young is careful to distinguish these staff support functions from the central direction of how to use information in the company. The following statement perhaps epitomizes the kind of central direction provided by President Young and the rest of senior management. "If you make the information available, if

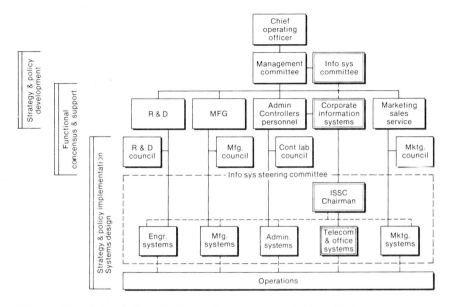

Figure 17–1 Information Systems Management at HP: HP's Telecommunications and Office Systems group, which combines the company's data processing, telecommunications, and office automation departments, implements information policies that are set by the company's senior management committee.

you give employees a chance to get involved—if you open the gate—you will unleash the creativity and commitment of your people."[5] HP's use of telematics to facilitate information flow to employees and customers illustrates this principle.

COMPANY BACKGROUND

Hewlett-Packard designs and manufactures precision electronic equipment for use in business, industry, science, engineering, health care, and education. HP's more than 7,000 products include test and measurement instruments, integrated computer systems, hand-held calculators, medical electronic equipment, and instruments for chemical analysis.

HP is one of the 100 largest industrial corporations in America, with sales of $6.5 billion and earnings of $489 million in its 1985 fiscal year. In addition, it is one of the top 20 U.S. exporters, with slightly less than half its business generated outside the country. Headquartered in Palo Alto, California, the company employs approximately 85,000 people, of whom 57,000 work in the United States. Plants for HP's 50 manufacturing and four nonmanufacturing divisions are located in 23 U.S. cities, most of which are in California, Colorado, the Northeast and the Pacific Northwest. The company also has research and manufacturing facilities in Europe, Japan, Latin America, and Canada and manufacturing operations in Southeast Asia. HP's worldwide sales organization includes sales and support offices in 100 U.S. cities and more than 275 sales and support offices and distributorships in 75 other countries.

AN OVERVIEW OF HP'S CORPORATE NETWORK

HP's Corporate Telecommunications and Office Systems group has set the goal of substantially increasing the company's communications capability by providing a worldwide integrated digital services network for voice, data, and video by 1990. Moreover, the key elements of this network will be privately owned and managed by HP before the decade is over.

Like most high-volume users of telecommunications, HP has made significant efforts to bypass the U.S. telephone companies' public switched networks. In fact, HP is a classic case of a firm whose increasingly dispersed sales and manufacturing operations—plus heavy emphasis on data communication—has forced it to turn to private communications for cost control. As telephone companies have offered economical "bypass" alternatives of their own, HP has turned to these options for the transmission savings they offer.

In 1986, the result of HP's mixing and matching of transmission options is a network consisting of a potpourri of transmission media, which are either shared with the public, leased, or purchased from a variety of sources. The elements of HP's worldwide network include the following transmission technologies operating in a variety of contexts:

1. Public switched voice networks in the U.S. and foreign countries.
2. Leased private lines for data and voice transmission wherever cost-effective.

3. Telenet's nationwide packet switched data network (for batch and interactive data transmission), with gateways to public packet switched data networks in foreign countries, all based on the international X.25 protocol.
4. An emerging privately-owned X.25 packet data network based on private leased lines.
5. T1 lines for high-speed, high-volume voice, data, and video transmission.
6. Limited use of satellite links for long haul data and video transmission.
7. Private microwave for voice and data transmission to numerous sites adjacent to company headquarters.

HP has a number of discrete telecommunication systems built from these constituent elements. These include a worldwide public/private voice and data network with increasing video transmission capabilities, a nationwide television network, a regional microwave network (soon to become a fiber optic network), and a high-speed local area network around company headquarters. These units can be broken up into the following subcategories:

1. The voice network based on public switched facilities.
2. Telnet (the leased private line voice and data network covering the United States and the United Kingdom).
3. The batch data network (COMSYS and ROUTS).
4. The X.25 packet data switching network.
5. The HP television network.
6. HP's Bay Area microwave network.
7. The headquarters LAN.
8. Switching technology.

Each of these is covered in more detail in the following sections. Students of HP's corporate network should bear in mind that these systems will be merged into a worldwide integrated, private telecommunication system by 1990.

The Public Voice Network

A large portion of HP's current voice and data (batch and interactive) traffic is still carried over the public telephone network in the United States and abroad.

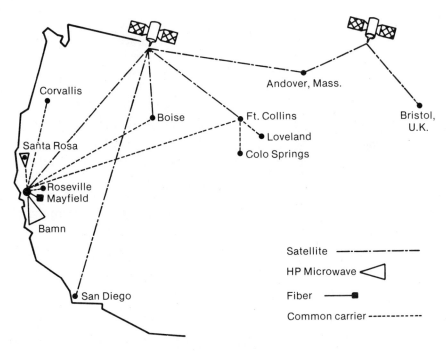

Figure 17–2: T1 carriers in place by late 1985.

Telnet

HP owns an extensive leased private line network known as Telnet, which carries voice and data among 70 HP sites throughout the United States (except in the southern states) and the United Kingdom. In the United States, intercity lines are usually leased from local RBOCs and the long lines from a variety of common carriers; some Telnet lines, such as HP's microwave network in the San Francisco Bay Area, are owned by HP. A few of the more heavily used lines have been converted to T1 digital transmission capability. The switches in the network are typically HP owned. (Figure 17–2 shows T1 lines currently in place.)

HP's Batch Data Network: COMSYS and ROUTS

In a batch transmission, the original sending and receiving computers are never connected in real time. Batches of large

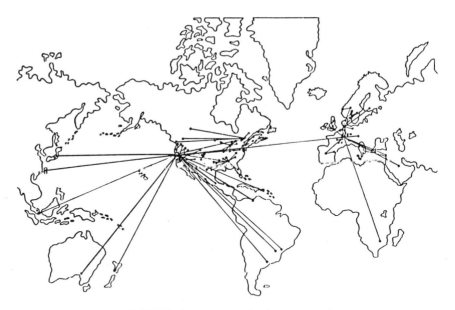

Figure 17–3: HP's ROUTS data communications network.

quantities are transferred for temporary storage at network nodes and then forwarded to the next node when the lines are least crowded or busy. Thus, the arrival of data may take up to two days or as quickly as 20 minutes, depending on availability of line capacity.

HP's first batch data transmission system, COMSYS, was installed in 1970 to replace the use of telephones and teletype machines for sending sales data. COMSYS (short for "communication system") deployed HP terminals and minicomputers for store-and-forward batch data transfer over telephone lines. Each node in the COMSYS network required real-time attendance by on-site operators.

COMSYS (and the ROUTS system that succeeded it) is a hierarchical transmission system with a star topology. (See Figure 17–3.) Remote sites sent daily inventory, sales, and order information to minicomputers at regional sales offices; this information was forwarded each night to factories via an IBM mainframe in Palo Alto. (Later the system allowed direct links to Palo Alto for each sales office.)

Over the past five years, HP has replaced COMSYS with a

new batch-oriented data transmission system called ROUTS (regionally oriented unattended transmission system). New network software (developed at HP) for ROUTS allowed "unattended transmission" of data at higher speeds and allowed transmission as often as needed. As HP began installing new ROUTS nodes, it also began acquiring leased lines for the heavily used data links. (These include the T1 lines shown in Figure 17–2.)

HP's X.25 Packet Data Switching Network

An increasing proportion of HP's data traffic consists of interactive data transactions, as opposed to the simple batch transmission of sales and order data.

Interactive transmission involves a real-time connection over a real circuit (or virtual circuit) where one device is always talking to another, exchanging data, or acknowledging receipt of data. Typical interactive applications include "urgent" electronic mail, inquiries from micros or terminals to internal or external data bases, or computer-to-computer communications where large computers send requests and exchange files.

To handle its increasing volume of interactive traffic in the U.S., HP has turned since 1983 to the use of GTE Telenet's X.25 packet switching data network. Telenet's network is based on the international X.25 protocol standard, which offers superior transmission error correction and detection capabilities. Because of its use of the X.25 standard, data running on Telenet can enter X.25 public data networks in foreign countries through gateways provided by International Record Carriers.

Important examples of interactive applications running over HP's packet data network include interaction with customer support data bases, "urgent" electronic mail, and electronic dispatching of financial reports. These are considered in more detail below.

    a. Customer support data bases. Technicians and other customer support personnel at HP's "Response Centers" can access data bases for product information, hardware and software troubleshooting procedures, customer records, and to aid coordination of field support technicians. Later in this chapter we will present how support engineers perform on-line software diagnosis and troubleshooting remotely from Response Centers.

b. "Urgent" electronic mail. COMSYS allowed transmission of general messages (short memos, reminder, letters, and so on) along with sales and order information. This ad hoc messaging has evolved so the volume of electronic mail currently running over HP's extensive "HP Desk" messaging system (covered in detail later in this chapter) accounts for 20 percent of all HP transmissions. "Urgent" HP Desk messages—about 15 percent of the total electronic mail volume—is routed over the X.25 network for nearly immediate delivery.

c. Financial reporting. All HP divisions and regional sales offices use the interactive network to send monthly financial reports to Corporate Accounting. A complete summary of HP's worldwide financial data can be compiled and presented to the company's executive committee just a few days after the end of each month. Recently this system has been upgraded to allow the *daily* compilation of worldwide order information.

An increasing amount of HP's interactive traffic is being carried over private lines leased from various common carriers. HP's current thrust is to build a private X.25 network that will eventually become the backbone for all data transmissions, both interactive and batch. HP purchased its own packet switching and network monitoring equipment in late 1985, and at least 20 private nodes will be installed over the next two years. In addition, the company is pressing forward with a program to substitute the remaining public telephone lines used for data transmission with leased lines, including T1 or leased satellite links where cost-effective. With its tremendous volume of interactive batch data traffic, HP will soon be able to boast a private packet switched data network that rivals in volume and size of either of the world's two largest public data networks, Telenet and Tymnet.

According to Hank Taylor, manager of corporate telecommunications and office systems at HP, "The public packet networks are severely restricted in the amount of bandwidth avail-

Hank Taylor, manager of corporate
telecommunications and office systems at HP.

able to high volume users like HP. A private packet network, on the other hand, allows a company like HP to build in bandwidth that meets its requirements. It also offers smarter switches and improved security. The final result will be far greater cost-effectiveness than our current network."

HP's private packet network eventually will interconnect all elements of the company: branch offices to their tactical headquarters; the whole field organization to factories and support divisions; and corporate management to all the elements of the company worldwide. The HP network control center will be able to provide comprehensive information about how the networks are functioning. In addition, gateways from the private network to the public networks will allow access for customers and vendors.

Figure 17–4 shows the large number of sites linked by HP's international packet switching data network: notice the differing topologies of the old star-shaped ROUTS network (Figure 17–3) and the intelligent X.25 network.

HP's Television Network

HP's corporate network includes extensive use of one-way video conferencing plus limited use of two-way video transmission.

The one-way conferences, originating either from Palo Alto

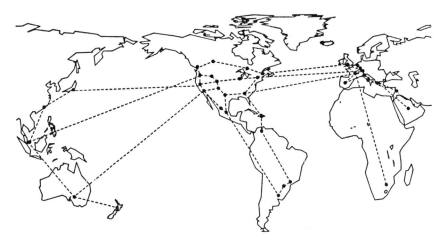

Figure 17–4: HP's packet switching network.

or Roseville, California, use analog 6 Megahertz signals for broadcasting to more than 80 sites worldwide.

HP's two-way conferences allow televised meetings between half a dozen sites. This link employs a video codec to convert the analog video signals into a digital bit stream, which it compresses for satellite transmission over T1 lines.

Figure 17–5 shows the location of HP's one-way and two-way satellite video teleconferencing facilities.

HP's Bay Area Microwave Network

An HP-owned microwave network serves 12 of 19 Bay Area sites with a direct-line radio signal beamed from a station on the 12th floor of a Mountain View, California, building. The network can handle 576 voice and data channels at once and allows some digital video transmission.

HP has recently opened discussions with the local Bell operating company regarding the prospect of "bypassing itself" by being the major supplier of a new regional fiber optic network that will replace HP's privately owned microwave system by 1990. The microwave network will remain as a backup for the fiber optic network.

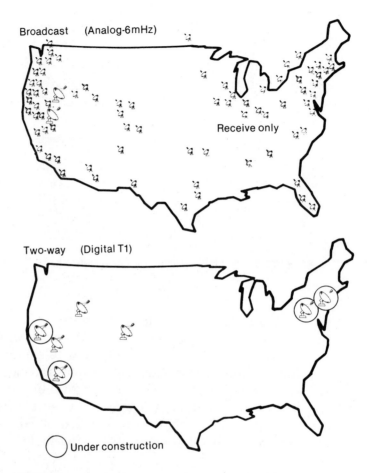

Figure 17–5: HP's broadcast and two-way video conferencing networks.

Headquarters Local Area Network

HP's LAN strategy is similar to that recommended by the authors in the LAN chapter earlier in this book. HP's LAN for connecting its many sites at corporate headquarters is hierarchical: at the highest level of the hierarchy is a buried broadband cable that connects HP Labs and 22 other corporate buildings in Palo Alto, carrying video signals and high-speed data transmission needed by HP engineers and HP Labs research-

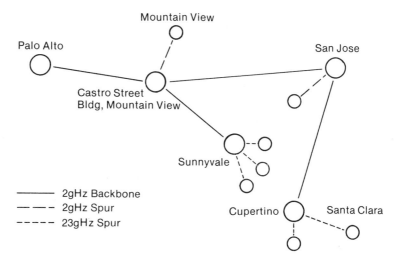

Figure 17–6: The Bay Area microwave network.

ers. This is the backbone of the Palo Alto LAN. The backbone LAN configuration is shown in Figure 17–7.

At the next level of the hierarchy, departments and buildings at the Palo Alto site are interconnected by baseband LANs (802.3 Ethernet-like) which are, in turn, connected by bridges to the broadband LAN. (See Figure 17–8.)

HP's more than 3,000 research and development personnel worldwide, the majority of whom work near the Palo Alto headquarters, use UNIX-based workstations and do their data networking via UNIX's machine-to-machine links; a gateway for these Palo Alto UNIX users to the ROUTS/X.25 network (and thus to the headquarters LAN) is now under construction.

Video communications applications running over the LAN include the following:

1. A "dial-a-tapc" videotape library service offered by HP's Corporate Training Center. This includes plans for the use of interactive videodiscs.
2. Reception of off-campus educational programs offered by universities. This includes satellite links to the National Television University network, which provides seminars

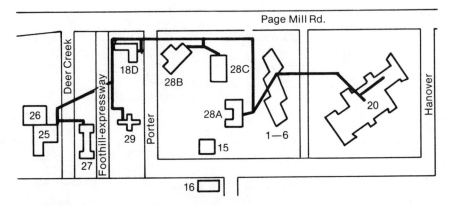

Figure 17–7: Configuration of the Palo Alto backbone LAN.

broadcast from some of the nation's top science and engineering departments.

3. A variety of internal teleconferencing applications: teleconferencing within HP's Palo Alto campus; with HP divisions in Santa Clara 15 miles south (via a gateway to the Bay Area microwave network); teleconferencing with sites nationwide, via a gateway to HP's satellite network.

Switching Technology

Most of HP's voice switching is done by on-site PBXs; data is switched by in-house data switches using the existing telephone wires for data transmission. So far, initial tests of voice/data switches have shown them overly expensive except for use in smaller installations.

THE COST OF HP'S INFORMATION

Between 1966 and 1984, the proportion of HP employees who handle information (managers, professionals, office and clerical workers) grew from 39 percent to 58 percent, which represents a 49 percent increase.

Nevertheless, HP has been able to consistently reduce the per unit costs for transmission of HP's increasing volume of in-

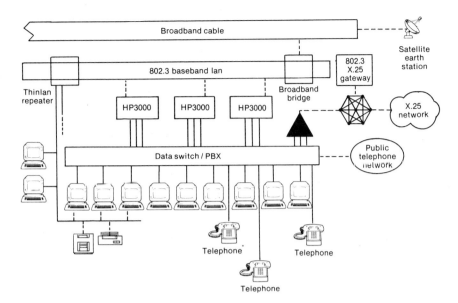

Figure 17–8: Topology of the headquarters LAN.

formation flow. (Transmission cost is the most significant expense involved in operating the HP network.)

Figure 17–9 provides a breakdown of the percentage of transmission costs used for voice, interactive and batch data, video, and facsimile in 1985.

The available statistics for unit costs show that, despite the rapidly increasing volume of network usage, HP has been able to contain costs in the following categories.

1. DATA: Figure 17–10 should give some idea of the greatly increasing volume of data being handled at HP. The chart indicates worldwide totals in terms of characters per month going over ROUTS. Note that between 1979 and 1985, the total volume of all data communication increased from 5 billion characters per month to more than 60 billion. Over the same period, the number of HP employees increased from 52,000 to 85,000. This means per capita generation of characters per month increased nearly 10-fold in six years.

However, the cost (in dollars per megabyte) of ROUTS data transmission has decreased by a factor of three in the past six years.

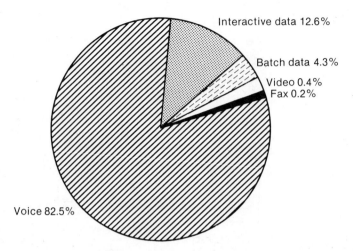

Figure 17–9: Total percentages of transmission costs in 1985.

2. FAX: The cost per page of facsimile transmission, which began at nearly $5 per page in 1982, dipped below $1 per page in 1986, while during the same period companywide facsimile usage has increased fourfold.

3. REGIONAL BYPASS NETWORK: Figure 17–11 shows how bypass technology used to link regional HP sites has greatly increased transmission capability while decreasing costs.

PLANS FOR HP'S CORPORATE NETWORK

Despite the efficiencies currently built into HP's network, much more can be done to improve transmission throughput while decreasing unit costs. This would entail conversion to a private ISDN network or what we have termed here second-stage telematics.

CTOS is planning to make this conversion before the end of the decade. Hank Taylor characterizes the emerging network in the following way: "The goal is to build a wide bandwidth circuit switching digital network, which will 'lie below' X.25, the video signals, and the voice signals; it will provide a consistently managed transmission pathway for common use by voice, data, and video traffic.

"This would be a fully private network in the sense that we

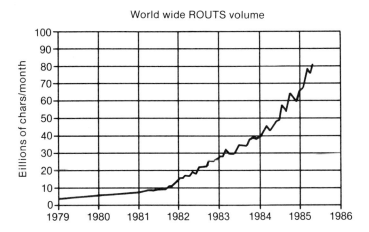

Figure 17–10

would own the facilities and management equipment at all nodes and would lease all lines from common carriers or install our own microwave links."

According to Taylor, HP has historically carried most of its high transmission volumes over voice-grade lines leased from common carriers on a relatively uncoordinated or as-needed basis. "We intend to become much more systematic about how we procure our bandwidth in the future: We are now moving to build a set of circuits around the world at T1 bandwidth or greater, giving us a flexible network that will more economically handle voice, data, and video concurrently and interchangeably.

"These T1 circuits will be dynamically multiplexed so that as the total traffic rises and falls throughout the day, we are able—on the average—to accommodate all these activities within the private network."

A backup plan would come into operation during periods of peak usage of the private network, Taylor points out.

During periods of very heavy use, say, if video happens to come into heavy use at a particular time, the overload capacity would be absorbed by the public networks. If the video dropped off, all the traffic would return to the private lines, and what was formerly video bandwidth would be absorbed for other uses. This interchangeability, with backup capacity provided by public net-

	Capacity	Cost per month
1984 circuits (analog)	335 equivalent voice channels over leased lines [voice and data]	$82K
1985 microwave (digital)	576 equivalent voice channels [voice/data/video]	$10K
1990 fiber (digital)	4032 equivalent voice channels [voice/data/video]	$80K

Figure 17–11: Evolution of the Bay Area regional network.

works, would give HP greater transmission economies and much better leverage over the bandwidth we actually own.

The lines carrying this dynamically multiplexed traffic could be copper, fiber, radio, or whatever—it doesn't matter, really, as long as you have the needed capacity on these links and provided the lines are managed in a consistent way. T1 is a specific approach to managing bandwidth, which is relatively standard. Once we have installed lines using the T1 format throughout the network, we can build the capability to dynamically multiplex all the traffic as I have described.

Relying on the public network for overflow capacity could pose problems for HP's network managers, however. "Once ISDN is in operation around the world, the public networks will be able to provide a trouble-free backup system," says Taylor. "But where it doesn't yet exist, we could have real, though not insurmountable, problems getting access to the appropriate digital line capacity."

TELEMATIC APPLICATIONS ON HP'S CORPORATE NETWORK

"The accessibility of HP networks to everyone in the company is an important part of the HP Way," says Hank Taylor. "For example, everyone can use electronic mail, whether they are clerical, part of the maintenance group, or executives. Basi-

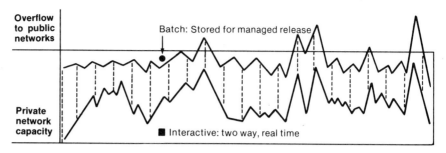

Figure 17-12: Back-up capacity provided by public networks.

cally, everyone has everyone else in their distribution list. Teleconferencing is another good example; these facilities are also accessible to any groups who wish to schedule their use. Even a major broadcast video conference can be scheduled by virtually anyone."

The following pages cover the more significant applications running on HP's corporate network, linking thousands of employees worldwide.

Facsimile

HP has recently upgraded its facsimile capability with the installation of Group III machines. Beginning in 1980, 133 fax locations have now converted to the new digital machines out out of 153 total fax locations. The company is also moving toward fax transmission over the private X.25 network; in addition, a good deal of faxing occurs to non-HP sites over public networks.

HP has experienced significant transmission cost savings because of the conversion to faster machines. The Group III machines reduced transmission time from 6 minutes per page to 40 seconds per page, resulting in 1984 transmission savings of more than $600,000.

"We consider the conversion to the new digital machines to be a giant leap forward," says Taylor. "There's been a big advantage to using the new standard across the board. We used to let our fax machines sit in atrophy. Now they're used appropriately."

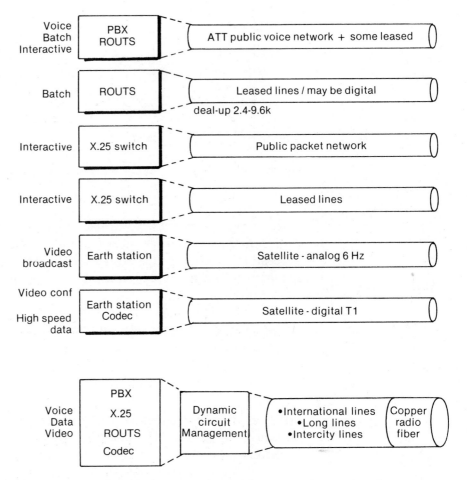

Figure 17–13: Today's fragmented network compared to proposed dynamically multiplexed network.

Voice Mail

HP has a sophisticated, heavily used electronic text messaging system, but voice mail is in its early stages of evolution. By late 1985, five local voice mail systems had been installed on an experimental basis at sites around the United States, including corporate headquarters in Palo Alto. A committee of user groups has reported voice mail to be a very powerful and cost-effective communication tool. Specific findings include the following:

1. Voice mail should be implemented in such a way that it does not antagonize incoming callers. It should offer them helpful features such as multiple options, editing, and group distribution and should operate in such a way that callers come to perceive how the service offers equal benefits to themselves and the receiving party.
2. Voice mail system purchase price per user averaged between $150 and $500 and the monthly cost per user ranged from $6 to $12 per month in 1985.
3. Voice mail can be subject to off-hour transmission to keep bandwidth open for urgent and interactive communications. Voice mail can be transmitted during gaps in transmission load during the day or at night.
4. Voice mail will be a feature on new PBX systems planned and payed for by local sites as needed.
5. Intersite networking for voice messaging became available in 1986.

Plans for voice mail at HP include voice annotation of text and the evolution of speech recognition applications over the network.

Voice annotation will allow an employee to send a complex report via HP Desk and to "append" a voice mail portion that will highlight certain points or "walk" the recipient through the report.

The use of speech recognition for audio transmission of text mail has been used experimentally at HP. "Speech recognition will free employees from dependence on their desktop terminal," says Hank Taylor. "Users who are away from their desks for a long period of time can call in, go through their messages, and choose one that can be automatically read to them over the telephone."

HP Desk Electronic Mail System

HP Desk, with over 45,000 users, is the heart of HP's internal telematic communications system. It's one of the three largest private electronic mail networks in the world and even rivals in size the popular commercial electronic mail networks. In 1985, HP Desk users sent an average of 12 billion characters per month within their own divisions and 6 billion between divisions, or about 40,000 characters per user per month—an awesome volume of electronic communication.

An internal office productivity study among a broad cross-section of the 2,000 employees at corporate headquarters revealed that of the 1,700 registered users of HP Desk, more than 99 percent are at least occasional users of HP Desk and about 75 percent are highly active.

HP Desk actually offers a diverse set of office tools: In addition to electronic mail, it handles word processing, personal electronic filing, and time management. As an electronic mail system, it is able to carry word processing documents, data and graphics, program files, and meeting appointments. Messages can be labeled "urgent," thus arriving almost immediately, or via "bulk data transfer." Users can also monitor the progress of their mail. They are notified when mail has been sent, delivered, read, or a reply received. Other features include automatic distribution and automatic forwarding of messages.

Effects in the Workplace. HP's office productivity survey also indicated significant changes in communication patterns and perception of work resulting from the network. A majority of the managers, professionals, and secretaries surveyed reported increased ease and speed of communication and improved job satisfaction. Secretaries in particular thought that HP Desk had significantly increased their job satisfaction. One professional participant in the survey represented beliefs of many HP Desk users with this comment: "Office automation tools at first seem like a nice luxury, but I have rapidly become dependent on them. HP Desk makes communication with groups of people very easy." (It is interesting to note, however, that in a recent independent survey of HP employees, electronic mail was highly rated, but was still rated behind interoffice paper memos as the most preferred medium of receiving office communications—though it should be kept in mind that HP Desk is not universally available in the company.)[7]

An example cited by company President John Young, in his 1985 Singapore productivity lecture, shows the effect of the electronic mail system on the productivity of a group called PC Central, whose charter was to fully integrate personal computers plus peripherals into the company's HP 3000 minicomputer network:

> The logistics of managing the project proved daunting enough. The project team includes 140 R&D engineers from 10 different HP divisions in the U.S., Japan, and Europe. After waiting one week for an overnight courier to deliver scheduling information to Europe, this team decided to use electronic mail to manage the project. They move software code and all its documentation that way, and they use electronic PERT charts for project management.
>
> If one part of the team's task is going to slip schedule, the computer automatically highlights other parts of the project that will be affected. The entire group is informed immediately, and group resources are reassigned quickly. They've succeeded in introducing some exciting new products, and according to their manager, the project would have been totally impossible without their electronic linkages. . . . The technology allows us a flexibility and responsiveness that we couldn't have had without it. In the PC Central project, information technology wasn't just an individual productivity tool; it was a vital part of the glue that held a project team together.

Network Evolution. The implementation of HP Desk began in 1982. Since then, the network has evolved from a simple messaging system to what Luis Hurtado-Sanchez, manager of HP's Office Utilities Group, calls "a personal networking system." Use of the network has expanded from short business messages to bulk transfer of large documents, data files, and newsletters (electronic publishing); downloading of software; informal interpersonal messaging; and electronic junk mail, which is estimated by Hank Taylor to occupy about 0.5 percent of all HP Desk traffic. Hurtado-Sanchez believes this kind of expansion proves the full acceptance of the system.

The proliferation of HP Desk applications has led to establishment of a two-tier transmission system: Messages can be designated as either "urgent" or "bulk data transfer." *Urgent messages* are usually delivered within 15 minutes if sent within the same site, while the standard delivery time for an urgent off-site message is two hours. *Bulk data transfer,* for example, a large document sent to hundreds or thousands throughout the HP world, would be guaranteed no better than next working day delivery. "Bulk data transfer must go by the cheapeast route possible," says Hurtado-Sanchez. "This is the only way we can optimize the use of the network so that the most urgent messages can always find the needed capacity. It must be remembered that electronically transmitted newsletters or reports are often regarded by many recipients to be mere junk mail. Sending one of these to hundreds of people is so easy that we simply must control the information flow."

Another control mechanism is also being added by network managers: charging users at the corporate site a fee for the use of HP Desk. It is expected that these fees will also serve to discourage temptations to abuse the network. "User fees will make potential authors of junk mail think twice before sending their message," says Hurtado-Sanchez.

Customer Support by Telephone

HP's sales and customer support personnel rely heavily on the telephone for solving customer problems and for disseminating product information. Most of this support activity is provided by sales personnel at local field offices. However, for the more specialized or complex customer problems, HP provides its customers access to more than 350 toll-free "800" lines, which handle nearly 150,000 toll-free calls each month. In addition, expert support analysts in several "response centers" are available to troubleshoot highly technical hardware and software problems with HP's technical and business computers and engineering workstations. The two North American response centers field almost 3,000 calls each week.

HP's "Hotlines." The following randomly chosen list of "800" lines may give some idea of the range of routine customer needs handled by telephone. Note how requests for sales information are handled both by telephone and electronic mail:

- Probably the company's most publicized hotline is 800-FOR-HP-PC. It appears in print and television ads for all HP personal computers and calculators. More than 1,000 calls a day generate sales leads that are sent to field offices overnight via electronic mail for follow-up by salespeople the next morning.

- Potential customers who want to learn more about HP's logic systems can dial a Colorado Springs hotline that will send them a packet of HP 64000 information. The appropriate HP salesperson gets an electronic mail message so a follow-up phone call can be made. The toll-free number started appearing in logic systems product ads in June of 1985.

A high volume of product information requests is also handled by telephone. Here are two examples:

- Owners of HP personal computers can get answers to their software and hardware questions from one of 75 experts in Santa Clara's HP COACH customer center. These former computer programmers, secretaries, personnel reps, and master schedulers field more than 12,000 calls a month.
- Biomedical engineers in hospitals have access to a 24-hour-a-day, 365-day-a-year hotline. If a critical piece of medical equipment fails, an expert can lend assistance over the phone or dispatch a field service engineer.

The HP "Response Centers." HP's specialized response centers for troubleshooting HP computers and workstations were instituted in early 1984. Today, more than 95 percent of incoming software problems and one-fifth of customers' hardware problems are handled over the phone. The two North American centers field almost 3,000 calls each week.

The toll-free call is routed to a coordinator who listens to the problem, enters the information into an on-line tracking system, and dispatches an electronic message to the appropriate team of experienced HP engineers. A support engineer usually calls back in a few minutes.

For handling software problems, HP's Customer Support Division has recently put together a data base containing all the software questions known to HP along with their solutions. Support engineers can consult this data base for quick solutions. For more difficult problems, they can reproduce the customer's difficulty on a duplicate machine at the response center. Once the software error has been detected, the support analyst's terminal can be linked to the customer's computer for remote diagnosis and repair over telephone lines. HP engineers are working on a project that will allow response center computers to routinely dial up and automatically check the functions of customer's machines.

Companywide Electronic Broadcasts

The dissemination of corporate news and information to employees is a challenging task in any large company, and this is especially the case with a company as decentralized and geographically dispersed as HP. Almost out of sheer necessity, HP has turned to electronic broadcasting of text, audio, and audio-visual information from Palo Alto as a major part of its solution to the problem of linking the company's 85,000 employees to corporate headquarters.

"This giant task is made easier by the company's open communications environment, in which managers are already expected to keep their employees informed of everything and anything, and to stay on a first-name basis," observes Brad Whitworth, HP's employee communications manager. "To facilitate this environment, the company provides a great deal of technical support for vertical communication."

The following is an incomplete list of telecommunications vehicles used to keep HP employees in touch with corporate headquarters.

Electronic Broadcasts. "We prefer that HP employees hear company news from HP directly rather than from the media," says Whitworth. "The news media is sometimes tough to beat, but improvements in companywide electronic communications have helped a great deal."

Fast-breaking company news is dispatched to employees via the company's electronic mail system and the facsimile network. When the company needs to disseminate an important item of company news, the corporate employee communications group will first broadcast an "electronic press alert" to onsite communications professionals in the United States and throughout the world. These communicators are then responsible for modifying the message if needed and distributing it electronically or in hard copy to employees at the local site; sometimes they pass it on to the local general manager, who reads it over the public address system.

Figure 17–14: Electronic messaging is in heavy use by about 75 percent of employees at HP's corporate headquarters.

"We've found that the facsimile copies arrive faster, and we can get a quick phone confirmation. Electronic mail can take longer to go through a few nodes, get to the far end, have someone pull it up on the screen, and acknowledge the receipt. In addition, not all sites are connected to HP Desk yet," says Whitworth.

Using the two transmission techniques together, Whitworth can guarantee that virtually every site in the world gets the same information in 20 minutes. "Electronic communications allows us to ensure that everyone gets the full message directly from management and not through the grapevine or from the news media."

HP Video Magazine. Another important form of broadcasting is the dissemination to all sites of videocassettes produced by HP-TV in Palo Alto. Six times a year, HP employees around the world can view a 13-minute videotape showing the company's objectives in action. The feature-oriented television programs have been produced on a regular basis since February 1984.

Companywide Audio Broadcasts. Company President John Young announces the company's financial results—in-

Figure 17–15: HP's studio production control room.

cluding the profit sharing percentages due to employees—in a live, one-way audio broadcast given twice a year; HP's teleconferencing group hooks up the whole company over HP's public address system. The address is repeated for company sites located in significantly different time zones. Thomas Peters, coauthor of *In Search of Excellence,* happened to be sitting in HP's lobby during one of John Young's audio broadcasts. Peters writes, "Young is a soft-spoken individual, but if there is such a thing as quiet cheerleading, that is exactly what Young was doing."[6]

Video Teleconferencing at HP

Hewlett-Packard places heavy emphasis on maintaining close contact with key personnel at more than 400 field locations and on continuing education for employees. Both tasks have become increasingly difficult as the company has grown, but live, one-way, full-motion television—a high impact medium—has helped alleviate the communication burden. In addition, HP is developing the capability for two-way video conferences and "dial up" access to prerecorded training videotapes.

One-Way Video Conferences. The use of one-way broadcasts at HP began in 1981 with a pilot series of satellite video conferences training salespeople at 35 sites. These sessions were so successful in giving the company's sales force the needed technical knowledge that by 1982 the new HP-TV Network began conducting regularly scheduled video conferences at the rate of one per month, using rented facilities.

The next year, HP installed a permanent, private video conference network for use not only in sales training but also for internal problem solving, managerial and corporate communications, administrative meetings, formal employee education, and even customer and press communications.

The first broadcast over the private network—a discussion by four senior managers of management's new concept of "Total Quality Control"—was received by several hundred engineers at 15 sites. The broadcast opened with a prerecorded message from John Young.

Today HP's one-way video conferences usually involve a live broadcast from one location to an audience, often numbering in the hundreds or even thousands. Participants at the receiving sites cannot be seen by the originators, but they are able to ask questions or make comments to the entire audience by means of an audio link. According to Marika Ruumet, manager of the HP-TV Network, "The major benefits of these one-way broadcasts are the uniformity of the message and the immediacy of the audience's contact with key sources of information. All sites receive the same information at the same time, and the audience can hear and see live presentations directly from top people in the company or from those who are closest to the products or ideas being presented; in some cases, we link HP people to customers at remote sites, allowing them to get direct feedback on HP products."

HP's video broadcasts are generally transmitted as analog signals sent via satellite from one of two origination sites—one at Palo Alto headquarters and another at an HP plant near Sacramento. The network now reaches over 100 receive locations across the United States and Canada. HP-TV currently broadcasts several live video conferences each week on the average, and usage is growing rapidly. Ruumet estimates a 20 hour per week average of all private broadcasts over the network.

Professional producers and directors in the HP-TV group work

Figure 17–16: Viewers at a typical receive site in a one-way video teleconference.

closely with Hewlett-Packard divisions that sponsor video conferences to help them present effective programs. Other HP staff members assist users and keep Hewlett-Packard employees informed about the network's capabilities. Newsletters tell corporate training specialists and users about upcoming events and maintain a high level of interest in the network.

The following story illustrates the perceived benefits of a product introduction video conference held in 1984 that included international sites for the first time.

Joe Schoendorf, then director of marketing for technical computers in Cupertino, was the first to use the HP-TV Network for video conferencing overseas. His program was a three-hour live introduction of new products to the Hewlett-Packard field sales force at 35 sites in the United States and one in London.

"We started at 8 A.M. our time, which was 4 P.M. London time. Because it was their first participation in a video conference, the London office invited their people from all over England," Schoendorf recalls.

"That video conference was one of the most motivational experiences the London office ever had. Previously we had flown three or four people to London for new product announcements, and often these were lower-level people because the top executives could not take the time for the trip. For this event, London could see the key players and even ask them questions.

"That first international program was so successful that we decided to expand our next video conference to four additional sites. We used temporary facilities in Paris, Amsterdam, Geneva, and Frankfurt for a program announcing a major new technology.

"After the sales team was trained, we invited members of the European business and technical press for an international video press conference. We made a presentation and let the press ask questions of our senior management in the United States for about an hour. It went so well that we made this a regular feature of our new product introductions."[7]

Two-Way Video Conferences. Two-way video conferences at HP normally involve small groups at two or three sites. Four two-way sites are currently in operation, including one in Bristol, England. Transmission generally uses T1 lines with digital video compression provided by a codec.

According to Ruumet, the uses of two-way conferences are as varied as the kind of meetings that can occur at HP, but two-way electronic meetings "provide an especially ideal substitute for the give and take of face-to-face business and of many technical meetings."

Video Conferencing with Graphics. HP's video conferencing sites also have graphics transmission capability. A rectangular space on each conferencing table can be used to display objects, devices, or graphic information under an overhead camera. The touch screen operator can zoom the camera in close so engineers can focus on details of, say, a circuit design. Both sides see either a still or a full-motion live shot of the object. In addition, all conferencing rooms are equipped with Group III facsimile machines for quick exchanges of meeting agendas and other documents.

Computer Teleconferencing

Hand in hand with HP's emphasis on organizational fluidity is its reliance on a streamlined, decentralized organizational structure. CONFER, the computer conferencing system developed by Advertel Communication Systems, supports both of these key features of HP's corporate culture and especially reinforces HP's emphasis on fostering innovation through intense communication at all levels and across all functions of the company.

In just more than one year of operation, more than 1,000 HP employees joined more than 60 conferences on CONFER, and interest in this unique telecommunications application is spreading quickly at HP despite its limited promotion.

More than half the current participants in CONFER log on to the system at least once a week, and most of these log on to participate in a half dozen open, informal conferences. In addition, 20 or 30 private, working conferences are currently considered to be successful. Membership in these meetings—usually consisting of 10 to 20 members—is by invitation only. These provide an essential forum for serious meetings, which groups would otherwise find difficult or expensive to arrange in any other manner. (The remainder of the story about HP's computer conferencing network appears at the conclusion of Chapter Fourteen.)

QUESTIONS FOR REVIEW:

1. What is the "HP way?"
2. What are some key telematic applications at HP?
3. Provide the basics on HP's private network.
4. How are information policies managed at HP?
5. What are two examples of interactive applications running over HP's packet data network?
6. Discuss HP's LAN strategy.
7. Discuss HP's PBX strategy.
8. Discuss HP's applications strategy. Focus on HP Desk.
9. Describe the future plans for HP's corporate network.

FOR DISCUSSION:

1. What are the risks in going to a private network?
2. What are some of the problems a network manager has in controlling a network as large and diverse as Hewlett-Packard's?
3. What are the benefits of Hewlett-Packard's network to the company and its employees?
4. How would Hewlett-Packard's telecommunications network have to change five years from now to keep pace with the changes it has made in the past five years?

NOTES FOR CHAPTER SEVENTEEN

1. THOMAS J. PETERS and ROBERT H. WATERMAN, JR., *In Search of Excellence,* (New York: Harper and Row, 1982), p. 244.

2. JOHN A. YOUNG, "Information—Powerful Productivity Tool," The 1985 Singapore productivity lecture, June 25, 1985.

3. "Interview with John A. Young," *Information Management Review,* Summer 1985, p. 86.

4. Ibid.

5. JOHN YOUNG, Singapore productivity lecture.

6. PETERS and WATERMAN, *In Search of Excellence,* p. 265.

7. MARIKA RUUMETT and DAVID GREEN, *Communications Age,* March 1985, p. 23.

Strategic Management of Business Telematics

Part Seven concludes this book with an argument for the intelligent management of telematic corporate networks to meet the requirements of the information age.

If managed appropriately, the new digital networks for voice, data, and video communication should facilitate improved access to business intelligence within a company, enhance a company's responsiveness to the needs of customers and others on the outside, and generally provide a significant competitive edge. Properly managing these networks to attain these benefits will require that senior management work with end-users and telecommunication managers to develop specific corporate policies. A correct policy of telecommunication management should be based on senior management's recognition of the unique productivity problems of information workers and its willingness to adjust power relationships in the organization along lines suggested in the next two chapters.

Telematics and Information Productivity

OBJECTIVES

- Understand the need for organizational redesign.
- Understand the changes in information flow in business.
- Understand the new patterns of communications with the outside world.

The telematic technologies and applications surveyed in this book are being introduced just as the information age is mounting its biggest challenge to business. As America crosses over from an industrial to an information economy, business must increasingly face the new problem of information productivity:[1] the need to effectively handle the deluge of information necessary for ordinary business operations.

Unfortunately, information-handling activities in many companies are governed by management techniques more appropriate to the first half of the 20th century. According to the industrial-age management paradigm, the optimal organizational design of a corporation is based on the values of hierarchy, efficiency, and specialization. But management techniques appropriate for these "goods-intensive" industrial organizations, which typically concentrate on the mass production of goods for large markets, are not suitable for handling work flows in *information-intensive* organizations. Industrial-age management can actually obstruct the productivity potential of telematics and allied information technologies.

Two factors inherent in the approaching information age challenge the traditional approach to organization design.

The Information Explosion

The rapid pace of change in the business environment is causing an explosion of information. Companies must handle an increasing volume of information about competitors, customers, suppliers, markets, economic and political changes, government regulations, and scientific and technological advances. The normal response to all this complexity is to hire more office workers and add new layers of management and staff to coordinate their work.

At some point, however, as the volume and complexity of information work continues to grow, the industrial-age mode of office organization causes a loss of productivity. Quicker, more timely flow of information is needed; more and more office workers and managers need access to more information as they attempt to cope with the rapid pace of change. But adding greater complexity to the organization—more specialized tasks and more layers of management—becomes a poor response to environmental complexity. A form of Parkinson's Law comes into effect: Important information needs to circulate across departments, within offices, or between layers of the management hierarchy; however, because of the inappropriately complex design of the organization, the volume of intraorganizational communication events increases out of proportion to the value each communication event is able to add to the product or service. Excessive specialization, hierarchy, and "efficiency" seem counterproductive to effective information handling. Adding information and communication technology to an organization operating under such conditions may worsen the situation.

Demand for Improved Services

Closely related to the factor of the information explosion is the evolution of a postindustrial, service society characterized by a demand for new and superior consumer services in nearly all markets. In a service society, an abundant supply of low-cost agricultural and industrial products is readily available for mass markets. Now, narrow markets proliferate, catering to highly specific tastes and increasingly specialized needs. These markets are inherently information intensive.[2] Customers will choose those companies that are most effective at processing information about their demands and delivering the customized products or services they desire.

But companies with industrial-age management styles that

result in excessive internal communications will be less responsive to these demands; their customers will not be better served if communication technology is used simply to move information around these top-heavy bureaucracies. Instead, such organizations will need to be redesigned so communication resources are shifted outward to serve customer needs.

THE NEED FOR ORGANIZATIONAL EFFECTIVENESS

It should be clear that businesses operating under the weight of the information explosion and the demands of a service society must make organizational adjustments.

First, they will need better means of handling information flow within their companies; bureaucratic paperwork and other redundant intraorganizational communications will have to give way to more streamlined operations and the kind of "organizational fluidity" that Peters and Waterman observed in excellent companies.

And second, information-age companies will need more flexibility for adapting to information flow from the marketplace, resulting in better responsiveness to customers and to other external demands.

To attain these goals, many information-age companies must be redesigned for organizational effectiveness. However, this effectiveness cannot be routinized or automated by adding telematics or other information technologies; it cannot be mechanized by management first.

In the past, engineers designed manufacturing processes for time and motion efficiency, where efficiency was based on extreme specialization of labor controlled by management hierarchies. But information activities being performed by most office workers in the 1980s are nonroutine, ad hoc, and based on group coordination. These activities involve judgment, creativity, knowledge, and experience. The effectiveness of these activities can be measured only by the level of cooperation of employees with company goals and, most importantly, by customer satisfaction with the quality and cost of products delivered.

Then how does organizational effectiveness tie in with communication technology? The new information technologies can improve the performance of office workers and managers, but only if managed in the light of the new imperatives of the information age. *Information and communication technology is not a substitute for the organizational and managerial adjustments that are now required.* We will suggest how companies can begin making the needed adjustments later in this chapter and in Chapter Nineteen. In addition, the case studies presented in the immediately preceding three chapters show how such adjustments are made in practice. But first let's consider the current communication productivity problems of information workers.

COMMUNICATION PRODUCTIVITY IN THE INFORMATION AGE

For our purposes, communication productivity is that portion of the information productivity problem that concerns *how to cost-effectively get the right amount of needed information to the right person in a timely fashion.*

In the following discussion of communication productivity, the broad category "information worker" is divided into two segments, office workers and managers. For both groups, the key concept for evaluating their communication productivity, as we have argued in this book, is whether they are gaining access to business intelligence. The two attributes of networks that facilitate business intelligence are *transparency* and *selectivity.* (See Chapter One for a review.) The transparency afforded by telematics is seen here as more important for office workers; selectivity is presented as the greatest need of managers.

Office Workers. The largest segment of information workers are those who tend various information processing devices, or who are heavily dependent on telephones and mobile communication devices for performing information work. These will be termed the "office worker" segment. (The term "office" becomes increasingly ambiguous, of course, as communication technology erases boundaries between traditional offices and information work performed in factories, in the home, and by sales and service people in the field.)

Most workers in the office worker segment perform "clerical" and technical work and hold a variety of semi-professional job titles. But many higher-level managers and professionals dependent on intellectual technology for doing information-intensive work can also be included in this category. (This group is sometimes termed "information professionals" or "knowledge workers.")

In general, the key concept for understanding the contribution of communication technology to the productivity of office workers is *transparency*. In the information age, office workers' communication productivity is a function of their interface with electronic networks through communication devices that are close at hand. Transparency means an office worker using a voice/data workstation (or mobile communication device) sits at the center of a vast network of easily accessible information resources. Transparent telematic networks increase their desktop power.

Managers. The second segment are those whose work with information involves wider decision-making responsibilities, including middle- to upper-level managers. The key to their communication productivity is *selectivity;* they need to get whatever information they can to reduce the uncertainty and ambiguity of executive decision making. Most are dependent on office workers using information technology to gather and filter relevant information; managers select the needed information from the memos, reports, and summaries submitted by these subordinates. (In the near future, or at least until the introduction of practical speech recognition devices and expert systems, most managers and executives will not heavily interact with the new electronic networks themselves.)

The next two sections consider in more detail the communication productivity problems of these two segments of workers.

Office Productivity

Let us return to the office organization of firms caught in the transitional stage between the new and the old economy. As the business environment has become more turbulent and uncertain, these firms became more bureaucratic and complex. This development is described by Paul Strassman.

The inclination to employ specialists and experts as a way of dealing with new problems led to an explosive growth of staff support groups, which, in turn, necessitated the creation of additional layers of management. Business began adding large numbers of professional, adminstrative, and technical workers in staff positions; they were closely identified with management, since their primary task was the handling of information, rather than direct involvement with the delivery of goods and services to customers.[3]

This description indicates how management principles inherited from the industrial age are misapplied to information work in offices. Let's consider how routine and nonroutine information activities are handled in such an organization.

Routine information activities characteristic of more stable times are handled well by the appropriate staff specialists and their management. The components of this work have been standardized for greatest efficiency, as in a manufacturing process. As long as the work flow is predictable, coordination of its units by a hierarchy of managers is relatively easy.

On the other hand, nonroutine, ad hoc information activities can cause havoc in such organizations. A tremendous volume of reports, studies, memos, meetings, and phone calls are generated. Coordinating the work of so many specialists and layers of management becomes in itself a major management challenge. Indeed, such hierarchical organizations cannot adjust very effectively to changing conditions in the marketplace because they require a great deal of coordination to make any decision.[4]

In short, *the bureaucratic structure itself determines how nonroutine information is handled;* an office worker taking the initiative, say, to directly serve customer needs, will get smothered by all the internal communication events required to get anything accomplished. This is the case even though uncertainty in the business environment (which caused the increase in organizational complexity in the first place) requires the continuous need for innovation and service. Peters and Waterman describe one aspect of the problem well in *In Search of Excellence.*

Most of the institutions that we spend time with are ensnared in massive reports that have been massaged by various staffs and sometimes, quite literally, hundreds of staffers. All the life is pressed out of the ideas; only an iota of personal accountability remains. Big companies seem to foster huge laboratory operations that produce papers and patents by the ton, but rarely new products. These companies are besieged by vast interlocking sets of committees and task forces that drive out creativity and block action. Work is governed by an absence of realism, spawned by staffs of people who haven't made or sold, tried, tasted, or sometimes even seen the product, but instead, have learned about it from reading dry reports produced by other staffers.[5]

Communication technology is certainly not the only factor that can revive effective, fluid communication in such organizations. But it provides a crucial support for the organizational redesign needed to return America's competitive edge. In fact, the new electronic networks cannot add much to business productivity without organizational changes advocated by Peters and by such authors as Rosabeth Moss Kanter in her book, *Change Masters: Innovation for Productivity in American Corporations*.[6] Many of their prescriptions for American business are designed—like information technology itself—to aid adaptation to the new imperatives of the information age.

Paul Strassmann, another writer concerned with office productivity, has spent nearly 20 years studying the flow of information work in offices. His research is helpful in understanding the responsiveness criterion as applied to office work.

> My experience leads me to conclude that for each organization there is a characteristic number of information transactions necessary to get anything accomplished. There is also a benchmark *minimum* number of coordinating steps necessary to take care of a customer's request. That benchmark can be found by examining how the best competitor is performing the function in question.[7]

The *ratio* of actual transactions needed to serve a customer to the minimum required to perform the transaction is a measure of the information productivity of that office, according to Strassman. He has dubbed this productivity comparison the "Parkinson Ratio" for that organization.

For example, he has determined that one customer's non-routine request for a new bank loan should require a minimum of from 50 to 80 internal communications. However, in such cases, "Parkinson's Ratio's of three or four times as much have been observed."[8] Much higher ratios can sometimes be observed in government organizations.

Organizations aware of such problems often add further control mechanisms as safeguards against wasteful internal communications; in addition, office automation and new communication technology may be introduced to add efficiency to the execution of specific tasks. Both techniques are likely to worsen the problem.

Both of these approaches are symptomatic of companies still tied to management assumptions lingering from the industrial era. Isolating individual tasks and attempting to streamline them with tighter procedures and/or with information technology can be counterproductive. Poorly organized information flows are not likely to improve with efficiency analysis. There is no reason to automate or to attempt to improve the efficiency of obsolete patterns of information work.

RE†Iₙk

The potentials offered by properly chosen and well-managed information technology are revolutionary. They require a new approach to the design of office work. According to Eric Trist, professor emeritus at the Wharton School of Business, "Only an internal revolution in the structure and cultural fabric of the office itself can supply the necessary conditions for the realization of beneficial outcomes."[9]

Managerial Productivity

Because of their need to make complex business decisions, managers face greater information productivity problems than typical office workers. The issue for office workers is getting easy access to information sources (or to information recipients) through voice and data networks; for managers and executives the great need is for information selectivity among these sources, particularly when making difficult strategic decisions.

Modern managers face a world almost infinitely more complex and volatile than that faced by, say, their counterparts in the 19th century.

To cope with environmental complexity, their companies have built up support staff, committees, even whole departments to

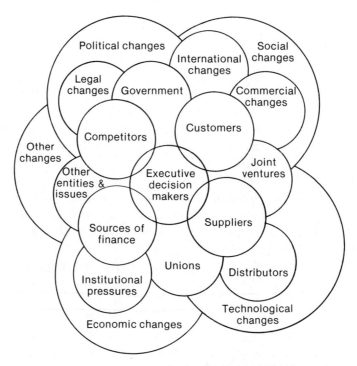

Courtesy: Van Nostrand Reinhold Company Inc.

FIGURE 18-1: The modern excecutive's mental map.

gather, process, and filter internal and external information flows to enhance their decision-making power. Through them, managers or executives need to monitor a myriad of economic, social, technological, and international forces that affect their business, just to stay abreast of their competition. (See Figure 18-1.) They need convenient and timely access to information that decreases the uncertainty and ambiguity of their decision making.

The character in the following futuristic scenario was created to illustrate the contrast between the present information dilemma of most managers and the potential of new communication technologies to improve the information selectivity of managers.

Note that this manager's job functions overlap with those of an office worker as depicted above. This is done intentionally to illustrate the blending of managerial and office duties—the flattening of the management hierarchy—that is a likely occurrence in companies that have adjusted their management styles to the information age.

It's a typical morning in 1992. A marketing manager begins her business day as soon as she pulls out onto the highway for her morning commute. Pressing a button on her car telephone, she activates the voice mail facility at her office. She hears all the messages she received since leaving the office yesterday. She calls in replies to the messages before pulling into the company lot.

Upon entering her office, she switches on her integrated voice/data/image terminal. An updated calendar for her meetings today flashes on her screen. Suddenly she realizes she has forgotten to prepare for a 10AM sales meeting. She needs at least a half hour to prepare. She quickly calls up the calendars of the meeting participants. Finding 10:30 to be free for everyone, she enters the new time and simultaneously transmits an electronic notice (marked "urgent") to each participant's desktop workstation.

Now she checks her text mail by dialing an access code on her intelligent phone. She finds two memos awaiting reply. She composes a reply to the first message and transmits it to the memo sender and a list of other names. The second memo from an overseas sales office requests a contract. She types instructions on her terminal for the facsimile room to select the contract from the contract data base and transmit it over the packet switched network by the end of the day.

To prepare for the 10:30 meeting, she connects to the mainframe computer, requesting sales data from the Southeast region. The data quickly appear on her screen. With the touch of a few buttons, the data are automatically formatted for insertion into her spreadsheet program. The spreadsheet prompts her through the necessary calculations and formats the results for presentation.

Gathering her thoughts on the sales data, she scribbles some ideas and a few questions for her staff. She brings up the computer conference file, reads the other comments her staff people (some of whom are located at remote offices) have entered regarding the upcoming meeting, and types in her most recent thoughts. Just before the meeting, she prints out the complete dialogue between herself and the staff using a laser printer shared with three other managers in her suite. She studies the hard copy document, happy to find answers to her earlier questions.

The meeting is a video teleconference between the southeastern sales office and her department via satellite. As the meeting opens, copies of the updated agenda are sent by a desktop facsimile machine to the remote participants. An electronic blackboard, used for drawing a system diagram, can be simultaneously seen by both parties.

Back in her office around midafternoon, she requests a summary of production data from the factory. Transparently to her, the terminal accesses the corporate mainframe, which in turn gets the latest updates from the factory network. Pressing another button, she accesses the company's videotex infobase; she calls up the file labeled "Visiting Customers—4/19/95," and finds a list of the day's customers plus a status summary of each customer's account.

Now she begins her daily two-hour walk to visit colleagues and employees in the division. Some informal multifunctional meetings are going on. She listens, offers her view, then roams over to the area where presentations are being made to customers. She listens attentively as her customers talk about their needs. One customer is wondering about the next shipment. Our manager dials up the shipping department on her portable phone and reaches a clerk who finds the answer by typing an inquiry in his videotex terminal. (This same infobase would have been accessible from any desktop personal computer at the customer's site.) Another customer informs her that the 24-hour hotline is malfunctioning. Quickly picking up her pager, she uses its data entry section to write a short reminder to herself for follow-up later.

Next she walks into a problem-solving session between a design engineer, manufacturing technician, marketing representative, and a sales representative. The design engineer uses a workstation connected to the engineering local area network to study a customer's specifications. The

---

modification proposed in the session is found to cut manufacturing costs while meeting the customer's needs. The
design change is made on the workstation. Instructions are
entered for transmitting the change electronically to the
mainframe computer's data base during the evening.

Back at her office, the manager finds a number of messages in her voice mail box. One message was sent from
someone in the Southeast region who was assigned to retrieve additional information as a follow-up on the morning's teleconference. As she calls up the voice message, an
electronic document appears on her computer screen. The
recorded voice walks her through the text, explaining the
findings in detail. Realizing it is late, she decides to file
the voice-annotated document for further study the following morning.

This manager's nonroutine, unstructured information work
moves so smoothly because the company has organized the
needed managerial and technical support mechanisms. The remaining pages present our view of how companies can start now
to put these mechanisms in place.

ADOPTING A CORPORATE TELECOMMUNICATIONS POLICY

Programs that properly introduce new communication technology must be initiated and guided at the corporate level. Only
senior management can coordinate the acquisition and use of
technology that electronically links everyone in the organization and connects the organization to the outside world.

Senior management should centralize its control of communications, but other power shifts also need to occur. Senior
management should see to it that end-users are given the power
to reorganize information flow in their own offices, under management guidelines; that's because information workers know
best what their communication productivity problems are. And
finally, the technical management of information technology
(data processing, office automation, and telecommunications)

FIGURE 18–2 Translating technologies into corporate goals.

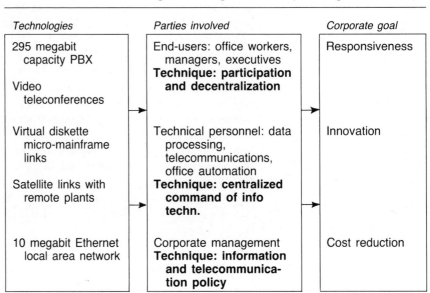

Technologies	Parties involved	Corporate goal
295 megabit capacity PBX Video teleconferences	End-users: office workers, managers, executives **Technique: participation and decentralization**	Responsiveness
Virtual diskette micro-mainframe links Satellite links with remote plants	Technical personnel: data processing, telecommunications, office automation **Technique: centralized command of info techn.**	Innovation
10 megabit Ethernet local area network	Corporate management **Technique: information and telecommunication policy**	Cost reduction

needs to be centralized, as it was in the cases of HP and Hercules, so telecommuncations experts can streamline their communication with top management and end-users.

The Corporate Approach

The adoption of a unique corporate telecommunications policy is the basis of the corporate approach. The heart of such a policy is to select business goals regarding the strategic management of corporate information resources and seek the appropriate communication technologies to support these goals. Figure 18–2 shows that acquisition decisions should be linked with strategic corporate goals. (The choice of strategic goals and specific technologies will, of course, vary widely among companies.) Most importantly, the figure also indicates that senior management—through adoption of an information and telecommunication policy—will need to work with the parties involved to adjust organizational design, so the company will be able to translate features of the technical systems into beneficial applications.

The Context

At the most general level, senior management needs to recognize the ongoing convergence of the three domains of information technology: data processing, office automation, and telecommunications. As we have pointed out before, John Diebold has suggested that a corporate information policy is needed to provide guidelines for managing the acquisition and end use of all these technologies. The guiding principle, according to Diebold, is the realization that "information is just as much a corporate resource as [the company's] work force, its capital, or its plant and equipment."[10] This is why one major shift that needs to occur in organizational design is the merger of data processing, telecommunications, and office automation under one roof.

Figure 18–3 illustrates major components of a corporate information policy (CIP). The model begins with an overflowing "barrel" of information resources. These resources need to be managed on a day-to-day basis under the policy guidelines of corporate management. Mediating the relationship between senior management and the company's information resources are the users of information technology and those who install and manage information technology. Information management policies are adopted for each of the technology domains, but coordinated by the overall CIP.

More specifically, information resources are managed by corporate leaders through the *technical systems* level and through what we will term the *social systems* level.

- The technical level refers to hardware and software used for the capture, storage, and communication of data, voice, text, and visual information anywhere in or outside the organization and the management of these facilities.
- The social level refers to the user rather than the equipment. These are the day-to-day management issues concerning how to correctly manage end-user applications of technology for improvements in communication productivity.

Office automation, telecommunications, and data processing raise separate but interconnected management problems at the social and technical levels. Corporate level management is

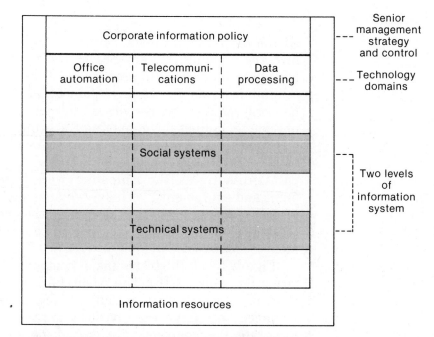

FIGURE 18–3: Major components of a corporate information policy.

needed to integrate solutions to these problems through a corporate information policy.

The scope of this book is limited to a consideration of the application of a CIP to the domain of telecommunications, or what can be called corporate telecommunications policy (CTP). In some sense, CTP is an artificial construct because many companies will implement policies governing each of the three domains as one unified CIP. But from our point of view, "How information flows to and from information processing devices deserves full executive attention."[11] The next chapter explores the elements of the corporate approach to the socio-technical management of telematics.

QUESTIONS FOR REVIEW:

1. Why is there a need for organizational redesign?
2. What are the three major elements to be redesigned?
3. Describe the changes in horizontal information flow.

4. Describe the changes in vertical information flow.
5. Describe the changes in communicating with customers.

FOR DISCUSSION:

1. Create your own scenario for telematics in the next five years.
2. How should you as a potential manager prepare yourself?

NOTES FOR CHAPTER EIGHTEEN

1. The term "information productivity" was coined by Paul Strassmann. The argument of this chapter owes much to Paul Strassmann's treatment of the subject of information work in his definitive *Information Payoff: The Transformation of Work in the Electronic Age* (New York: Free Press, 1985).

2. Perhaps most indicative of the transition to a new information economy is the fact that even manufacturing is increasingly information based.

For the past several years, increases in domestic manufacturing costs have forced businesses to relocate production sites in developing countries, such as Mexico and in the Far East. This increases the need for flow of information between corporate headquarters and far-flung production sites.

The automation of industrial processes is also needed to cut labor costs. As we have seen, the use of robots and microcomputers turns some workers on the factory floor into information workers. For example, assembly-line workers operating fully automatic robots from a control panel are primarily handlers of information.

The information requirements of manufacturing are increasing even more because customers are demanding more customized products, built to varied specifications. Custom product manufacturing requires constant communication between corporate sites, with greater quantities of information than one-product, mass production manufacturing requires. Consequently, increasing manufacturing productivity requires quicker information flow to become more responsive to customer requirements.

Higher consumer expectations for product quality and safety are also creating a new need for information. In many markets, consumer tastes change quickly, requiring companies to keep a finger on the public pulse. Many manufacturers have had to recall products because consumer expectations changed.

3. Strassmann, *Information Payoff,* pp. 25–26.

4. In many information-intensive companies, routine and even nonroutine information work is submitted to this efficiency approach.

Specialization applied to information work (largely in offices) implies that each operation is subdivided into its smallest unit. Each unit is isolated and studied to determine its most efficient means of execution. In addition, the management of each task is strictly divided from its execution. Standardization of operations permits narrowly defined specialists to operate with little special coordination except when rules are to change. The ultimate goal is to

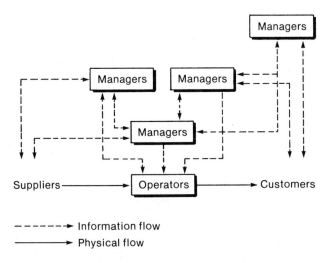

- - - - - ▶ Information flow
────────▶ Physical flow

Information flow among managers in industrial-age setting.

eliminate uncertainty and to ultimately automate the work flow. In the 1960s and 1970s, the programmed automation of office work was a constant topic of discussion in data processing management circles.

Standardization of procedures is required to maintain management control, if not computerization, of a myriad of isolated tasks. Even management practices can become specialized and standardized. Thus management hierarchies come into being. The end result is that management is strictly separate from operations, clerical labor from intellectual work, information gathering and processing from decision making. Simply viewed, information flow within such a hierarchy would look like the following: Information workers gather data about the general environment, the competition, suppliers, and customers. Then the information is passed up the ladder to management for evaluation and decision making. Decisions and policies are passed back down the ladder for implementation. The figure below shows how managers and operators process information from the business environment according to hierarchical organizational design. Note that the management of this process is strictly separate from operations.

The large number of arrows among managers indicates numerous events of intraorganizational communications. This often becomes necessary when managers are many times removed from the actual process of information gathering and when extreme specialization requires a large number of internal communications to handle a *nonroutine* problem.

5. Thomas J. Peters and Robert H. Waterman, Jr., *In Search of Excellence* (New York: Harper & Row, 1982), p. 120.

6. Rosabeth Moss Kanter, *Change Masters, Innovation for Productivity in American Corporations* (New York: Simon & Schuster, 1983).

7. Strassmann, *Information Payoff,* p. 10.

8. Ibid., p. 12.

9. Eric Trist, in an Afterword to Pava, *Managing New Office Technology,* p. 164.

10. John Diebold, *Managing Information* (New York AMACOM, 1985), pp. 40–41.

11. Strassmann, *Information Payoff,* p. 243.

Telematics and Organizational Change

OBJECTIVES

- Understand the role of the telecommunications manager in the future.
- Understand the role of end-users in the future.
- Understand the role of senior managers in the future.
- Reinforce the concept of a corporate information policy.

We have argued that businesses operating under the weight of the information explosion and the demands of a service society should regard the productivity potential of the new communication technologies surveyed in this book as providing an important opportunity—an opportunity to make adaptive organizational adjustments to the information age under the guidance of a corporate information and telecommunication policy. Two basic adjustments need to be made on the social systems level: first, within the company, excessive bureaucratic paperwork and other redundant intraorganizational communications will need to give way to increased communication productivity for office workers and managers; and second, companies should recognize that telematics offers an opportunity for the organization to be redesigned for improved responsiveness to customer demands. At the technical system level, we've seen that the management of office automation, telecommunications, and data processing must be integrated.

Unfortunately, many current discussions on the office of the future "ignore its social aspect completely and instead emphasize technological wizardry, implying a naive faith that technology by itself will boost productivity."[1] Instead, we have emphasized an approach that integrates both social and technical issues as part of a companywide information policy enunciated and carried out by senior management.

The first step in implementing telematic technologies in the workplace, then, is to plan for the socio-technical redesign of the organization.

ORGANIZATIONAL REDESIGN FOR TELEMATICS

One thing is certain today for all information-intensive companies. Telematics has created a new alignment of interests between these three groups: end-users and their immediate management; telecommunication, office automation and data processing managers; and corporate management. The productivity potential of telematics calls upon these groups to collaborate as never before in cutting communication costs while greatly increasing the effectiveness of business communications.

As a first step, it is important that senior management facilitate the integration of end-users into this collaborative process at an early stage. Ideally, they should be invited to participate in organizational design issues before the purchase of new equipment being proposed by telecommunications management; they and their immediate management can contribute the vantage point of specialized departmental or office needs. Then, telecommunications specialists (working together with other technical specialists) can strive to match technical solutions to both corporate goals and the desires of end-users.

Another especially important relationship is the contact between the technical staff and corporate management. These two groups need to learn as much as possible about the issues faced by the other. They will need to learn each other's terminology and concepts and how to carry on a dialogue using each other's languages. To foster this communication, senior management should encourage the merger of those organizations that manage information technologies and in many cases designate one corporate-level information officer. (Note the case studies in Part VI.)

In the next three sections, we will examine more closely the new roles and responsibilities of these three groups involved in organizational redesign. We will first look at the changing role of end-users, then consider the rapport that should be developed between senior management and technical personnel, and finally consider the merger of the departments of data processing, office automation, and telecommunications that will occur in most companies.

END-USERS

If an office is being restructured for the introduction of information and communication technology, senior management should encourage end-user participation, facilitate user training programs, and be prepared for a shift of power in the office.

User Participation. End-users are the only true experts on communication patterns in their office. Their contributions are the essential foundation of office redesign efforts. Their input is especially important if systematic studies of internal and external communications are being carried out before the installation of new equipment. This topic is treated especially well in the book *Managing New Office Technology,* by Calvin Pava of Harvard Business School.[2]

Training of Users. Training of end-users is essential for gaining payoffs from new technology investments. Even substandard equipment will yield satisfactory productivity gains if users are given superior training; if superior equipment is being installed, high-quality training will be an absolute necessity.

According to John Diebold, 85 percent of corporate outlays for data processing education is focused on technical experts. Diebold favors greatly expanding training budgets and diverting a major portion of costs to raising the "information literacy" level throughout the organization.[3] Indeed, as the cost of new technology declines, the people using the technology may well become the dominant cost element.

Increasing Power of End-Users. Introduction of the new technology will change interpersonal relationships, alter the division of labor, and lead to redistribution of power in offices.

As we have seen, communication technology renders traditional management hierarchies obsolete. First of all, because of increasing environmental complexity, there is less time to seek and secure approval for low-level decisions. At the same time, the new technology allows the decentralization of decision making.

> Advanced office technology shifts the distribution of information and enlarges the capacity to process it . . . once there is dispersed capability to process information, developing an overview is possible in multiple locations. Thus, central management loses an exclusive prerogative and hierarchical command loses its raison d'etre."[4]

For example, an early field trial of computerized conferencing showed how computer networks facilitate decentralization of information exchange and decision making.

- Computer conferencing technology was tested in a typical business organization by Bell Northern Research. Before the introduction of conferencing, businessmen at branch offices communicated to other branches by funneling requests through the central office. After introduction of the network, they shifted to direct branch-to-branch communications. Branch managers were able to solve their problems among themselves, rather than involving the central office.[5]

The authors of the book *Information Strategies* also found that decision-making power is rapidly shifting from traditional decision makers to "those responsible for interpreting the organizational environment—staff." Because of the increased complexity of the business environment, executives must increasingly delegate decision-making power downward. In turn, information workers, in order to better accomplish their task of filtering information for top management, demand improved information flow within the company—which is tantamount to a demand for democratic organizational structures. The result is that "staff has emerged as the true controllers of the organization."[6]

Senior management should support expansion of the organizational power of information workers. The new technology may increase office workers' decision-making power and enlarge their job responsibilities, but this should only increase the *information power* of executives. Power shifts should be managed so as to increase communication productivity for everyone.

SENIOR MANAGEMENT

Information systems were once no more than tools used in support of a company's financial and accounting operations; but increasingly they are at the *core* of business organizations. They have become an indispensable ally in manufacturing, operations, marketing, customer service, and human resource management—in short, a strategic tool in the hands of senior management. Telematics is the communications core of most corporate information systems, linking computers, telephones, and other devices for improved information flow within offices and between remote sites.

In information-intensive businesses such as insurance and banking, telematics is the *key* strategic tool. Irwin J. Sitkin, vice president for corporate administration at Aetna Life & Casualty, views the insurance business as "one great big information processing business," where the real problem is communications: how to "get the right information to the right guy at the right time to make the right decision to beat the other guy out in the marketplace."[7]

Making sure that your employee—or your customer—is the one receiving the right information at the right time has become the job of senior management. To accomplish this, executives need not understand exactly how telematic technology works. But they do need to understand its strategic import and develop and implement appropriate policies to exploit this strategic potential. "Just as no general would leave tactical planning to his quartermaster, executives cannot expect their data processing lieutenants to wage this battle," wrote *Business Week* in a cover story on the strategic implications of information technology.[8] Senior management must take charge of the overall strategy. Still, the data processing or telecommunications manager who can speak management's language and explain how a new technology or network can be used as a competitive weapon is an indispensable ally. When it comes to telematics, technical personnel have the additional task of helping management overcome the chaos and confusion in the telematics marketplace precipitated by deregulation and by rapid technological innovation.

Thus, an arrangement has evolved in which corporate leaders can select strategic goals and determine the "information battlegrounds," and then move into a strategic collaboration with technical personnel to acquire and implement the needed technology.

NEW ROLES FOR TELECOMMUNICATIONS, OFFICE AUTOMATION, AND DATA PROCESSING MANAGERS

Thanks to the divestiture of AT&T and the emergence of telematics, a new power and mystique is building around corporate telecommunication management. In the late 1980s and the 1990s, the organizational impact of these changes on telecommunications managers (plus those in allied areas such as data processing and office automation) will be as profound as the impact of computers in the 1960s, when today's DP/MIS structure was assembled. Once arcane technologies such as ISDN, local area networks, digital switches, electronic messaging, and micro-to-mainframe links have suddenly become issues of strategic import to corporate management—in some cases even crucial to competitive survival. As a result, the job responsibilities and general respect for the telecommunication manager's position have increased dramatically.

Telecommunications specialists have come a long way from predivestiture days when AT&T was their major and sometimes only vendor of equipment and services. Now the number of vendors and alternative technologies they must deal with grows at an incredible rate. To stay abreast, today's telecommunications manager must keep track of offerings from scores of vendors, mixing and matching products and services suitable to build the network capabilities that fit a company's unique needs.

Another major challenge comes from the nature of changing technology. As we have seen, digital technology has so permeated vendor products and services that the acquisition and management of telecommunications products must be closely coordinated with that of office automation and data processing. Telecommunication specialists will need new management and business skills to negotiate this uncertain terrain.

At the same time, though they have been elevated in corporate prestige and power, telecommunication managers are not likely to rise to a management position where they will preside over the converging domains of information technology. Just a few years ago, there was much discussion of the future of information processing as a battle for control of resources between DP/MIS managers, office automation managers, and telecommunications managers. This struggle has now been largely resolved. For example, a recent authoritative survey of 130 telecommunication managers revealed that the domains of these two groups are now managed jointly in 40 percent of cases, and that in 90 percent of these companies the manager of the combined activities hails from the DP/MIS side. (In addition, two-thirds of the respondents reported that their organizations will have merged data processing and telecommunications functions within five years.)

Thus, even though telecommunication managers' power and visibility is increasing, it is the DP/MIS manager who is gaining the final authority over the unruly new empire of information technology. Clearly, however, former MIS/DP managers taking on this new position of power will find that their relevant technical knowledge will fall to a small percentage of that needed in the combined data and voice organization. Those who were in the past promoted only on the basis of technical expertise will now survive only through political expertise—the ability to forge a consensus within the organization that combines the technical expertise of telecommunications, office automation, and a number of other specialists. In many organizations, this person will rise or at least report to the highest levels of corporate management, wearing a new title such as chief information officer (CIO). (For example, note the case of Ross Watson, CIO of Hercules Incorporated.)

Within this emerging new organizational structure, the telecommunication specialists will have the responsibility—in fact, what amounts to a once-in-a-lifetime opportunity—to play the advocate of telematics and its still untapped productivity potential. They will also need to educate DP/MIS experts and senior management about the new competitive opportunities resulting from the postdivestiture environment of telematics. The most progressive telecommunications managers will be able to prove to corporate management that their adoption of new equipment, new services, new corporate networks, and new risks is a profit opportunity they cannot ignore. And in the most progressive companies, senior managers will not hesitate to listen to the concerns of telecommunication managers; they will encourage them to have a socio-political as well as a technical role: After all, working with DP/MIS and office automation managers, they are the ones who must become the bridge between telematic technology and corporate goals—they must attempt to build a cost-effective corporate network for the purpose of converting data into intelligence, according to the needs of the end-users of the new communication technologies.

QUESTIONS FOR REVIEW:

1. What changes are occurring in the telecommunications managers' role in the future?
2. How will end-users change in the future?
3. How do senior managers have to change in the future?
4. What is the new role of the corporate information policy?

FOR DISCUSSION:

1. What are some likely impacts on an organization with a profusion of telematic technologies?
2. What will be the impact on your worklife?

NOTES FOR CHAPTER NINETEEN

1. Calvin Pava, *Managing New Office Technology* (New York: Free Press, 1983), p. 1.

2. Ibid, (See Chapters 1, 2, and 7.)

3. John Diebold, *Managing Information* (New York: AMACOM, 1985), p. 43.

4. Pava, *Managing New Office Technology,* p. 132.

5. S. R. Hiltz and M. Turoff, *The Network Nation* (Reading, Mass.: Addison-Wesley, 1978), p. 144.

6. Gerald Goldhaber et al., *Information Strategies,* p. 4.

7. Quoted in "Information Power," *Business Week,* October 14, 1985, p. 118.

8. Ibid.

Abort. To terminate, in a controlled manner, a processing activity in a computer system because it is impossible or undesirable for the activity to proceed.

Access. The manner in which files or data sets are referred to by the computer.

Acoustic Coupler. A type of telecommunication equipment that permits use of a telephone handset as a connection to a telephone network for data transmission by means of sound transducers.

Algorithm. A finite set of well-defined rules for the solution of a problem in a finite number of steps, for example, a full statement of an arithmetic procedure for evaluating sin $(\times)$ to a stated precision.

Alphabet. An ordered set of symbols used in a language, for example, the Morse code alphabet, the 128 ASCII characters.

Alphanumeric. Pertaining to a character set that contains letters, digits, and usually other characters, such as punctuation marks.

Alternate Route. A secondary or backup route that is used if normal routing is not possible.

Alternate Routing. The ability of a switching machine to establish a path to another machine over more than one circuit group.

AM. Amplitude modulation.

American National Standards Institute (ANSI). An organization for the purpose of establishing voluntary industry standards.

Amplifier. A device that, by enabling a received wave to control a local source of power, is capable of delivering an enlarged reproduction of the essential characteristics of the wave. See also repeater.

Amplitude. The size or magnitude of a voltage or current waveform.

Amplitude Modulation (AM). Modulation in which the amplitude of an alternating current is the characteristic varied.

Analog. Pertaining to data in the form of continuously variable physical quantities.

Analog Channel. A data communication channel on which the information transmitted can take any value between the limits defined by the channel. Voice-grade channels are analog channels.

Analog Data. Data represented by physical quantity that is considered to be continuously variable and whose magnitude is made directly proportional to the data or to a suitable function of the data.

Analog-To-Digital Converter (ADC). A functional unit that converts analog signals to digital data.

Analog Transmission. A transmission mode in which information is transmitted by converting it to a continuously variable electrical signal.

ANSI. American National Standards Institute.

Application. The use to which a data processing system is put; for example, a payroll application, an airline reservation application, a network application.

Application Layer. In open systems architecture, the highest layer explicitly defined by end-users that provides all the functions needed to execute their application programs or processes.

Application Program. A program written for or by a user that applies to the user's work.

Area Code. A three-digit number identifying one of the geographic areas of the United States and Canada to permit direct distance dialing on the telephone system.

Arithmetic and Logic Unit. A part of a computer that performs arithmetic operations, logic operations, and related operations.

Artificial Intelligence. The capability of a device to perform functions that are normally associated with human intelligence, such as reasoning, learning, and self-improvement.

ASCII. American National Standard Code for Information Interchange. The standard code, using a coded character set consisting of 7-bit coded characters (8 bits including parity check), used for information interchange among data processing systems, data communication systems and associated equipment. The ASCII set consists of control characters and graphic characters.

Aspect Ratio. The ratio between the width and height of a television screen.

Asynchronous. Without regular time relationship, unexpected or unpredictable.

Asynchronous Transmission. Transmission in which the time of occurrence of the start of each character, or block of characters, is arbitrary; once started, the time of occurrence of each signal representing a bit within the character, or block, has the same relationship to significant instants of a fixed time frame.

Attenuation. A decrease in magnitude of current, voltage, or power of a signal in transmission between points.

Audio Frequencies. Frequencies that can be heard by the human ear (approximately 15 hertz to 20,000 hertz).

Automatic. Pertaining to a process or device that, under specified conditions, functions without human intervention.

Automatic Send/Receive (ASR). A teletypewriter unit with keyboard, printer, paper tape, reader/transmitter, and paper tape punch. This combination of units may be used on-line or off-line and, in some cases, on-line and off-line concurrently.

Auxillary Storage. Data storage other than main storage; for example, storage on magnetic tape or direct access devices.

Availability. The degree to which a system or resource is ready when needed to process data.

Babble. The aggregate crosstalk from a large number of interfering channels.

Backup. Pertaining to a system, device, file, or facility that can be used in the event of a malfunction or loss of data.

Bandwidth. The range of frequencies a communications channel is capable of carrying without excessive transmission impairments.

Baseband. A form of modulation in which signals are pulsed directly on the transmission medium. In local area networks, baseband also implies data transmission digitally.

Batch. A group of records or data processing jobs brought together for processing or transmission.

Batch Processing. The processing of data or the accomplishment of jobs accumulated in advance in such a manner that each accumulation thus formed is processed or accomplished in the same run.

Baud. A unit of signaling speed equal to the number of discrete conditions or signal events per second.

Baudot Code. A code for the transmission of data in which five equal-length bits represent one character. This code is used in some teletypewriter machines where one start element and one stop element are added.

Benchmark. A point of reference from which measurements can be made.

Binary. Pertaining to a selection choice, or condition that has two possible values or states.

Binary Code. A code that makes use of exactly two distinct characters, usually 0 and 1.

Binary Digit. In binary notation, either of the characters 0 or 1. Synonymous with bit.

Bit. The smallest unit of information that can be processed or transported. Contraction of the word BInary DigiT.

Bit Error Rate (BER). The ratio of bits transmitted in error to the total bits transmitted on the line.

Bit Rate. The speed at which bits are transmitted. See also baud.

Bit Stream. A binary signal without regard to grouping by character.

Block. A string of records, a string of words, or a character string formed for technical or logic reasons to be treated as an entity.

BPS. Bits per second.

Bridge. Circuitry used to interconnect local area networks with a common set of higher level protocols.

Broadband. A form of modulation in which signals are modulated prior to transmission. In local area networks, broadband also implies analog signaling typically using frequency division multiplexing.

Broadcast. The simultaneous transmission of data to a number of stations.

Buffer. A routine or storage used to compensate for a difference in rate of flow of data, or time of occurrence of events, when transferring data from one device to another.

Bug. A mistake or malfunction.

Bus. One or more conductors used for transmitting signals or power.

Busy Hour. The composite of various peak load periods selected for the purpose of designing network capacity.

Byte. The representation of a character.

Cache. In a processing unit, a high-speed buffer storage that is continually updated to contain recently accessed contents of main storage. Its purpose is to reduce access time.

Calculator. A device that is especially suitable for performing arithmetic operations, but that requires human intervention to alter its stored program, if any, and to initiate each operation or sequence of operations.

Called Party. On a switched line, the location to which a connection is established.

Calling Party. On a switched line, the location that originates a connection.

Camp-On. A method of holding a call for a line that is in use and of signaling when it becomes free.

Carriage Return. The operation that prepares for the next character to be printed or displayed at the specified first position on the same line.

Carrier. A continuous frequency capable of being modulated or impressed with a second (information carrying) signal.

Carrier Sense Multiple Access with Collision Detection (CSMA/CD). A system used in contention networks where the interface unit listens for the presence of a carrier before attempting to send and detects the presence of a collision by monitoring for a distorted pulse.

Cathode Ray Tube (CRT). A vacuum tube display in which a beam of electrons can be controlled to form alphanumeric characters or symbols on a luminescent screen, for example, by use of a dot matrix.

Cathode Ray Tube Display (CRT Display). A device that presents data in visual form by means of controlled electron beams.

CCITT. The International Telegraph and Telephone Consultative Committee.

Centralized Network. Synonym for star network.

Central Office. In the United States, the place where communication common carriers terminate customer lines and locate the equipment that interconnects those lines.

Central Processing Unit (CPU). The control logic element used to execute instructions in a computer.

Centrex. Central office telephone equipment serving subscribers at one location on a private automatic branch exchange basis. The system allows such services as direct inward dialing, direct distance dialing, and console switchboards.

Channel. In information theory, that part of a communication system that connects the message source with the message link.

Channel-Attached. Pertaining to devices that are attached to a controlling unit by cables, rather than by telecommunication lines.

Channel Bank. Apparatus that converts multiple voice frequency signals to frequency or time division multiplexed signals for transmission.

Channel Capacity. In information theory, the measure of the ability of a given channel subject to specific constraints to transmit messages from a specified message source.

Character. A member of a set of elements upon which agreement has been reached and that is used for a organization, control, or representation of data. Characters may be letters, digits, punctuation marks, or other symbols, often represented in the form of a spatial arrangement of adjacent or connected strokes or in the form of the other physical conditions in data media.

Check Bit. A binary check digit, for example, a parity bit.

Chip. A minute piece of semiconductive material used in the manufacture of electronic components.

Chrominance. The portion of a televised signal that carries color encoding information to the receiver.

Circuit-Switched Connection. A connection that is established and maintained on demand between two or more stations in order to allow the exclusive use of a circuit until the connection is released.

Circuit Switching. A process that, on demand, connects two or more terminals and permits the exclusive use of a circuit between them until the connection is released.

Clock (CLK). Equipment that provides a time base used in a transmission system to control the timing of certain functions such as sampling and to control the duration of signal elements.

Clock Signal. The output of a device that generates periodic signals used for synchronization.

Cluster. A station that consists of a control unit and the terminals attached to it.

Cluster Controller. A device that can control the input/output operations of more than one device connected to it.

Coaxial Cable. A cable consisting of one conductor, usually a small copper tube or wire, within and insulated from another conductor of large diameter, usually copper tubing or copper braid.

Code. A set of unambiguous rules specifying the manner in which data may be represented in a discrete form.

Code Conversion. A process for changing a bit grouping for a character in one code into the corresponding bit grouping for a character in a second code.

Coder/Decoder (Codec). Analog-to-digital conversion circuitry.

Collision. A condition that occurs when two or more terminals on a contention network attempt to acquire access to the network simultaneously.

Common Channel Signaling. A separate data network used to route signals between switching systems.

Common Control Switching. A switching system that uses shared equipment to establish, monitor, and disconnect paths through the network. The equipment is called into the connection to perform a function and then released to serve other users.

Communicating Word Processing Equipment. Word processing equipment capable of transmission and reception of text, data, or both, using telecommunication techniques.

Communication Adapter. An optional hardware feature, available on certain processors, that permits telecommunication lines to be attached to the processors.

Communication Controller. A type of communication control unit whose operations are controlled by one or more programs stored and executed in the unit. It manages the details of line control and the routing of data through a network.

Communication Theory. The mathematical descipline dealing with the probabilistic features of the transmission of data in the presence of noise.

Community Antenna Television (CATV). A network for distributing television signals over coaxial cable throughout a community. Also called cable television.

Compandor (Compressor-Expander). Equipment that compresses the outgoing speech volume range and expands the incoming speech volume range on a long-distance telephone circuit.

Compatible. Pertaining to computers on which the same computer programs can be run without appreciable alteration.

Compile. To translate a computer program expressed in a problem-oriented language into a computer-oriented language.

Compiler. A program that decodes instructions written as pseudo codes and produces a machine language program to be executed at a later time.

Computer. A functional unit that can perform substantial computation, including numerous arithmetic operations or logic operations, without intervention by a human operator during a run.

Computer Architecture. The specification of the relationships between the parts of a computer system.

Computer Assisted Instruction (CAI). A data processing application in which a computing system is used to assist in the instruction of students. The application usually involves a dialog between the student and a computer program which informs the student of mistakes as they are made.

Computer Network. A complex consisting of two or more interconnected computing units.

Computer Program. A sequence of instructions suitable for processing by a computer.

Computer Science. The branch of science and technology that is concerned with methods and techniques relating to data processing performed by automatic means.

Concentration. The process of connecting a group of users to a smaller number of trunks between a remote terminal and the central office.

Concentrator. In data transmission, a functional unit that permits a common transmission medium to serve more data sources than there are channels currently available within the transmission medium.

Concurrent. Pertaining to the occurrence of two or more activities within a given interval of time.

Conditioning. Special treatment given to a transmission facility to make it acceptable for high speed data communications.

Configuration. The arrangement of a computer system or network as defined by the nature, number, and the chief characteristics of its functional units. More specifically, the term configuration may refer to a hardware configuration or a software configuration.

Console. A part of a computer used for communication between the operator or maintenance engineer and the computer.

Contention. A condition arising when two or more data stations attempt to transmit at the same time over a shared channel, or when two data stations attempt to transmit at the same time in two-way alternate communication.

Controller. A device that directs the transmission of data over the data links of a program executed in a processor to which the controller is connected or they may be controlled by a program executed within the device.

Core Image. The form in which a computer program and related data exist at the time they reside in main storage.

Crossbar Switch. A relay-operated device that makes a connection between one line in each of two sets of lines. The two sets are physically arranged along adjacent sides of a matrix of contacts or switch points.

Crosstalk. The unwanted energy transferred from one circuit, called the disturbing circuit, to another circuit, called the disturbed circuit.

CRT Display. Cathode ray tube display.

Cryptography. The transformation of data to conceal its meaning.

Cursor. A movable spot of light on the screen of a display device, usually indicating where the next character is to be entered, replaced, or deleted.

Customer Premise Equipment (CPE). Telephone apparatus mounted on the user's premises and connected to the telephone network.

Cybernetics. The branch of learning that brings together theories and studies on communication and control in living organisms and in machines.

Cycle. An interval of space or time in which one set of events or phenomena is completed.

Cycles Per Second (CPS). Synonym for hertz.

Cyclic Redundancy Check (CRC). A system of error checking performed at both the sending and receiving station after a block check character has been accumulated.

Data. A representation of facts, concepts, or instructions in a formalized manner suitable for communication, interpretation, or processing by human or automatic means.

Data Access Arrangement (DAA). Equipment that permits attachment of privately owned data terminal equipment and telecommunication equipment to the network.

Data Acquisition. The process of identifying, isolating, and gathering source data to be centrally processed.

Data Base. A collection of interrelated or independent data items to serve one or more applications.

Data Circuit-Terminating Equipment (DCE). The equipment installed at the user's premises that provides all the functions required to establish, maintain, and terminate a connection, and the signal conversion and coding between the data terminal equipment (DTE) and the line.

Data Communication. The transmission and reception of data.

Datagram. In packet switching, a self-contained packet that is independent of other packets, that does not require acknowledgement, and that carries information sufficient for routing from the originating data terminal equipment (DTE) to the destination DTE without relying on earlier exchanges between the DTEs and the network.

Data Integrity. The quality of data that exists as long as accidental or malicious destruction, alteration, or loss of data are prevented.

Data Link. The physical means of connecting one location to another for the purpose of transmitting and receiving data.

Data Link Layer. In open systems architecture, the layer that provides the functions and procedures used to establish, maintain, and release data link connections between elements of the network.

Data Over Voice (DOV). A device that multiplexes a full-duplex data channel over a voice channel using analog modulation.

Data Processing. The systematic performance of operations upon data, for example, handling, merging, sorting, computing. Synonymous with information processing.

Data Terminal Equipment (DTE). Any form of computer, peripheral, or terminal that can be used for originating or receiving data over a communication channel.

Debug. To detect, to trace, and to eliminate mistakes in computer programs or in other software.

Demodulation. The process of retrieving intelligence (data) from a modulated carrier wave; the reverse of modulation.

Destination. In a network, any point or location, for example, a node, a station, or a terminal, to which data is to be sent.

Dial-up. The use of a dial or pushbutton telephone to initiate a station-to-station telephone call.

Dial-up Terminal. A terminal on a switched line.

Digital. Pertaining to data in the form of digits.

Digital Signal. A discrete or discontinuous signal; one whose various states are discrete intervals apart.

Digital Switching. A process in which connections are established by operations on digital signals without converting them to analog signals.

Digital-To-Analog Converter (DAC). A functional unit that converts digital data to analog signals.

Digital Transmission. A mode of transmission in which information is coded in binary form.

Digitize. To express or represent in a digital form data that are not discrete data; for example, to obtain a digital representation of the magnitude of a physical quantity from an analog representation of that magnitude.

Direct Distance Dialing. A telephone exchange service that enables the telephone user to call subscribers outside of his local area without operator assistance.

Direct Inward Dialing. A facility that allows an external caller to call an extension without going through an operator.

Direct Outward Dialing. A facility that allows an internal caller at an extension to dial an external number without going through an operator.

Discrete. Pertaining to data in the form of distinct elements such as characters, or to physical quantities having distinctly recognizable values.

Disk. Loosely, a magnetic disk unit.

Diskette. A thin, flexible magnetic disk and a semi-rigid protective jacket, in which a disk is permanently enclosed.

Display. A visual presentation of data.

Distortion. The unwanted change in waveform that occurs between two points in a transmission system.

Distributed Data Processing (DDP). Data processing in which some or all of the processing, storage, and control functions, in addition to input/output functions, are situated in different places and connected by transmission facilities.

Distributing Frame. A structure for terminating permanent wires of a telephone central office, private branch exchange, or private exchange and for permitting the easy change of connections between them by means of crossconnecting wires.

Downstream Channel. The frequency band in a CATV system that distributes signals from the headend to the users.

DP. Data processing.

DTE. Data terminal equipment.

Dual Tone Multi Frequency (DTMF). A signaling method used between the station and central office consisting of a push button dial that emits dual tone encoded signals.

EBCDIC. Extended Binary-Coded Decimal Interchange Code. A coded character set consisting of 8-bit coded characters.

Echo Check. A check to determine the correctness of the transmission of data in which the received data are returned to the source for comparison with the originally transmitted data.

Echo Suppressor. A line device used to prevent energy from being reflected back (echoed) to the transmitter.

Electronic Mail. A service that allows text-form messages to be stored in a central file and retrieved over a data terminal by dialing access and identification codes.

Emulate. To imitate one system with another, primarily by hardware, so that the imitating system accepts the same data, executes the same computer programs, and achieves the same results as the imitated system.

Encode. To convert data by the use of a code or a coded character set in such a manner that reconversion to the original form is possible.

End Office. A class 5 office of a local telephone exchange where a subscriber's loop terminates.

Envelope. A group of binary digits formed by a byte augmented by a number of additional bits which are required for the operation of the data network.

Equal Access. A central office feature that allows all interexchange carriers to have access to the trunk side of the switching network in an end office.

Equalization. Compensation for differences in attenuation (reduction or loss of signal) at different frequencies.

Equivalent Four-Wire System. A transmission system using frequency division to obtain full-duplex operation over only one pair of wires.

Erlang. A unit of network load. One erlang equals 3600 call seconds, or 36 CCS (hundred call seconds). This represents 100 percent occupancy of a circuit or piece of equipment.

Error. A discrepancy between a computed, observed, or measured value or condition and the true, specified, or theoretically correct value or condition.

Error Detecting Code. A code in which each element representation conforms to specific rules of construction so that if certain errors occur, the resulting representation will not conform to the rules, thereby indicating the presence of errors.

Ethernet. A bus local area network developed by Digital Equipment Corporation, Intel, and Xerox. Ethernet formed the basis for the IEEE 802.3 standard.

Exchange. A room or building equipped so that telecommunication lines terminated there may be interconnected as required. The equipment may include manual or automatic switching equipment.

Extension. Each telephone served by a private branch exchange.

External Call. A call involving a public exchange or tie line.

Facsimile System (FAX). A system for the transmission of images. The image is scanned at the transmitter, reconstructed at the receiving station, and duplicated on some form of paper.

Failure. The termination of the capability of a functional unit to perform its required function. A failure is the effect of a fault.

Fault. An accidental condition that causes a functional unit to fail to perform in a required manner.

FAX. Facsimile.

FCC. Federal Communications Commission.

FCS. Frame check sequence.

FDM. Frequency division multiplexing.

FDX. Full duplex.

Federal Communications Commission (FCC). A board of commissioners appointed by the president under the Communications Act of 1934, having the power to regulate all interstate and foreign electrical telecommunication systems originating in the United States.

Feedback. The return of part of the output of a machine, process, or system to the computer as input for another phase, especially for self-correcting or control purposes.

Feeder Cable. The principal cable from a central office.

FIFO (first-in-first-out). A queuing technique in which the next item to be retrieved is the item that has been in the queue for the longest time.

File. A set of related records treated as a unit, for example, in stock control, a file could consist of a set of invoices.

File Protection. Prevention of the destruction of data recorded on a volume by disabling the write head of a unit.

Filter. A device or program that separates data, signals, or material in accordance with specified criteria.

First-Generation Computer. A computer utilizing vacuum tube components.

Five-Level Code. A telegraph code that utilizes five impulses for describing a character. Start and stop elements may be added for asynchronous transmission. A common five-level code is Baudot code.

Flag. Any of various types of indicators used for identification, for example, wordmark.

Flatbed Plotter. In computer graphics, a plotter that draws a display image on a display surface mounted on a flat surface.

Flip-Flop. A circuit or device containing active elements, capable of assuming either one of two stable states at a given time. Synonymous with toggle.

Floating-Point Representation. A representation of a real number in a floating-point representation system; for example, a floating-point representation of the number 0.0001234 is 0.1234-3, where 0.1234 is the fixed-point part and -3 is the exponent.

Floppy Disk. Deprecated term for diskette.

Flowchart. A graphical representation of the definition, analysis, or solution of a problem in which symbols are used to represent such things as operations, data, flow, and equipment.

Flow Control. The procedure for controlling the data transfer rate.

Foreground. In multiprogramming, the environment in which high-priority programs are executed.

Foreign Exchange. A special service that connects station equipment located in one telephone exchange with switching equipment located in another.

Format. The arrangement or layout of data on a data medium.

Four-Wire Circuit. A circuit that uses separate paths for each direction of transmission.

Frame. In data transmission, the sequence of continuous bits bracketed by and including beginning and ending flag sequences.

Framing. The process of selecting the bit groupings representing one or more characters from a continuous stream of bits.

Freeze-Frame Video. A method of transmitting a video signal over a narrow channel by sending one frame at a time without motor.

Frequency. Rate of signal oscillation in hertz.

Frequency Modulation (FM). Modulation in which the frequency of an alternating current is the characteristic varied.

Frequency-Shift Keying (FSK). Frequency modulation of a carrier by a modulating signal which varies between a fixed number of discrete values (a digital signal).

Front-End Processor. A processor that can relieve a host computer of certain processing tasks, such as line control, message handling, code conversion, error control, and application functions.

FTS. Federal Telecommunications System.

Full-Duplex. A data communication circuit over which data can be sent in both directions simultaneously.

Gas Plasma Display. A display that operates on the principle of tubes containing gas that flows above the anodes. Current passes through the tubes so that characters are formed from a variety of anode configurations using the dot matrix principle.

Gateway. Circuitry used to interconnect local area networks by converting the protocols of each to that used by the other.

General-Purpose Computer. A computer that is designed to operate upon a wide variety of problems.

Giga. Ten to the ninth power, 1,000,000,000 in decimal notation.

Grade of Service. A measure of the traffic handling capability of a network from the point of view of sufficiency of equipment and trunking throughout a multiplicity of nodes.

Graphic. A symbol produced by a process such as handwriting, drawing, or printing.

Half-Duplex. In data communication, pertaining to an alternate, one way at a time, independent transmission.

Handset. A telephone mouthpiece and receiver in a single unit that can be held in one hand.

Handshaking. Exchange of predetermined signals when a connection is established between two data set devices.

Hardcopy. A printed copy of machine output in a visually readable form; for example, printed reports, listings, documents, and summaries.

Hardware. Physical equipment used in data processing, as opposed to programs, procedures, rules, and associated documentation.

Hardwired. Pertaining to a physical connection.

HDX. Half duplex.

Head. A device that reads, writes, or erases data on a storage medium, for example, a small electromagnet used to read, write, or erase data on a magnetic drum or magnetic tape.

Head End. The equipment in a CATV system that receives television signals from various sources, modulates the signals, and applies them to downstream channels.

Header. That portion of a message that contains control information for the message such as one or more destination fields, the name of the originating station, an input sequence number, a character string indicating the type of message, and a priority level for the message.

Hertz. A unit of frequency equal to one cycle per second.

Heuristic. Pertaining to exploratory method of solving problems in which solutions are discovered by evaluation of the progress made toward the final result.

Hierarchical Network. A network in which processing and control functions are performed at several levels by computers specially suited for the functions performed; for example, in factory or laboratory automation.

High-Level Language. A programming language that does not reflect the structure of any one given computer or that of any given class of computers.

High Usage Groups. Trunks established between two switching machines to serve as the first choice path between the machines, and thus handle the bulk of the traffic.

Host Interface. The interface between a network and a host computer.

Human-Oriented Language. A programming language that is more like a human language than a machine language.

Hundred Call Seconds (CCS). A measure of network load. Thirty-six CCS represents 100 percent occupancy of a circuit or piece of equipment.

Hybrid Computer. A computer that processes both analog and digital data.

Hz. Hertz.

ICA. International Communication Association.

Identifier (ID). A character or group of characters used to identify or name item of data and possibly to indicate certain properties of that data.

Idle Time. Operable time during which a functional unit is not operated.

Impedance. The combined effect of resistance, inductance, and capacitance on a signal at a particular frequency.

Impulse Noise. High level and short duration noise that is induced into a telecommunication circuit.

Inactive Line. A telecommunication line that is not currently available for transmitting data.

Incoming Message. A message transmitted from a station to the computer.

Incoming Trunk. A trunk coming into a central office.

Independent Company (IC). A non-Bell telephone company.

Information. The meaning that a human being assigns to data by means of the convention applied to that data.

Information Bits. In data communication, those bits that are generated by the data source and that are not used for error control by the data transmission system.

Information Processing. Synonym for data processing.

Information Theory. The branch of learning concerned with the study of measures of information and their properties.

Infrared. Invisible radiation having a wavelength longer than 700nm.

Input Data. Data being received or to be received into a device or into a computer program.

Input/Output (I/O). Pertaining to a device or to a channel that may be involved in an input process, and, at a different time, in an output process.

Instruction. In a programming language, a meaningful expression that specifies one operation and identifies its operands, if any.

Instruction Set. The set of the instructions of a computer, of a programming language, or of the programming languages in a programming system.

Integer. One of the numbers zero, $+1, -1, +2, -2$. . .Synonymous with integral number.

Integrated Circuit. A combination of interconnected circuit elements inseparably associated on or within a continuous substrate.

Integrated Voice/Data. The combination of voice and data signals from a workstation over a communication path to the PBX.

Intelligent Terminal. Deprecated term for programmable terminal.

Intensity. In computer graphics, the amount of light emitted at a display point.

Interactive. Pertaining to an application in which each entry calls forth a response from a system or program, as in an inquiry system or an airline reservation system. An interactive system may also be conversational, implying a continuous dialog between the user and the system.

Interexchange Carrier. A carrier connecting two different LATAs.

Interleave. To arrange parts of one sequence of things or events so that they alternate with parts of one or more other sequences of the same nature and so that each sequence retains its identity.

Intermediate Distributing Frame. In a local central office, a distributing frame, that cross-connects subscriber lines to the subscriber line circuit.

International Standards Organization (ISO). An organization established to promote the development of standards to facilitate the international exchange of goods and services, and to develop mutual cooperation in areas of intellectual, scientific, technological, and economic activity.

International Telecommunication Union (ITU). The specialized telecommunication agency of the United Nations, established to provide standardized communication procedures and practices, including frequency allocation and radio regulations on a worldwide basis.

Interoffice Trunk. A direct trunk between local central offices in the same LATA.

Interrupt. A suspension of a process, such as the execution of a computer program, caused by an event external to the process, and performed in such a way that the process can be resumed.

Inward WATS. A telephone service similar to WATS but applicable to incoming calls.

Jack. A connecting device to which a wire or wires of a circuit may be attached and which is arranged for the insertion of a plug.

Jitter. Short-term variations of the significant instants of a digital signal from their ideal positions in time.

Job Batch. A succession of job definitions that are placed one behind another to form a batch. Each job batch is placed on an input device and processed with a minimum of delay between one job or job step and another.

Jumper. Wire used to interconnect equipment and cable on a distribution frame.

Keyboard. On a typewriter, an arrangement of typing and function keys laid out in a specified manner.

Keyboard Send/Receive (KSR). A combination teletypewriter transmitter and receiver with transmission capability from keyboard only.

Key Telephone System (KTS). A method of allowing several central office lines to be accessed from multiple telephone sets.

Kilo (K). Thousand.

Language. A set of characters, conventions, and rules that is used for conveying information. The three aspects of language are pragmatics, semantics, and syntax.

Large Scale Integration (LSI). The process of integrating large numbers of circuits on a single chip of semiconductor material.

Layer. In open systems architecture, a collection of related functions that comprise one level of a hierarchy of functions and assumes that lower level functions are provided.

Leased Circuit. A service whereby a circuit, or circuits, of the public telephone network are made available to a user or group of users for their exclusive use.

Leased Line. Deprecated term for nonswitched line.

Least Cost Routing. A PBX service feature that chooses the most economical route to a destination based on cost of the terminated services and time of delay.

LIFO (Last-in-first-out). A queuing technique in which the next item to be retrieved is the item most recently placed in the queue.

Light-Emitting Diode (LED). A semiconductor chip which gives off visible or infrared light when activated.

Light Pen. In computer graphics, a light sensitive pick device that is pointed at the display surface.

Line. On a terminal, one or more characters entered before a return to the first printing or display position.

Load. In programming, to enter data into storage or working registers.

Local Access Transport Area (LATA). The geographical boundaries within which Bell operating companies are permitted to offer long-distance traffic.

Local Area Data Transport (LADT). A telephone network-based service to provide a synchronous data channel to the end-user over telephone loops.

Local Central Office. A central office arranged for terminating subscriber lines and provided with trunks of establishing connections to and from other central offices.

Local Loop. A channel connecting the subscriber's equipment to the line-terminating equipment in the central office exchange.

Logical Unit. In SNA, a port through which an end-user accesses the SNA network in order to communicate with another end-user.

Logoff. The procedure by which a user ends a terminal session.

Logon. The procedure by which a user begins a terminal session.

Loopback Test. A test in which signals are looped from a test center through a data set or loopback switch and back to the test center for measurement.

Loop Transmission. A mode of multipoint operation in which a network is configured as a closed loop of individual point-to-point data links interconnected by stations that serve as regenerative repeaters. Data transmitted around the loop is regenerated and retransmitted at each station until it arrives at its destination station. Any station can introduce data into the loop.

Luminance. The portion of a video signal that carries brightness information.

Magnetic Disk. A flat circular plate with a magnetizable surface layer on which data can be stored by magnetic recording.

Magnetic Tape. A tape with a magnetizable surface layer on which data can be stored by magnetic recording.

Main Distributing Frame (MDF). A distributing frame, on one part of which terminate the permanent outside lines entering the central office building and on another part of which terminate cabling such as the subscriber line multiple cabling or trunk multiple cabling, used for associating any outside line with any desired terminal in such a multiple or with any other outside line. It usually carries the central office protective devices and functions as a test point between line and office. In a private exchange, the main distributing frame is for similar purposes.

Mainframe. Deprecated term for main processing unit.

Maintainability. The ease with which maintenance of a functional unit can be performed in accordance with prescribed requirements.

Manual Exchange. An exchange where calls are completed by an operator.

Mass Storage. Storage having a very large storage capacity.

Master Clock. The primary source of timing signals used to control the timing of pulses.

Matrix. In computers, a logic network in the form of an array of input leads and output leads with logic elements connected at some of their intersections.

MDF. Main distributing frame.

Mean-Time-Between-Failures. The average time a device or system operates without failing.

Mega. Ten to the sixth power, 1,000,000 in decimal notation.

Megahertz (MHz). A unit of measure of frequency. 1 megahertz = 1,000,000 hertz.

Memory. Deprecated term for main storage.

Merge. To combine the items of two or more sets that are each in the same given order into one set in that order.

Message. In information theory, an ordered series of characters intended to convey information.

Message Switching. In a data network, the process of routing messages by receiving, storing, and forwarding complete messages.

Metering Pulses. In telephony, periodic pulses sent by a public exchange over a line to determine the cost of outgoing calls.

Microcode. A code, representing the instructions of an instruction set, implemented in a part of storage that is not program-addressable.

Microcomputer. A computer system whose processing unit is a microprocessor. A basic microcomputer includes a microprocessor, storage, and an input/output facility, which may or may not be on one chip.

Microfiche. A sheet of microfilm capable of containing microimages in a grid pattern, usually containing a title that can be read without magnification.

Microfilm. A high resolution film for recording microimages.

Microprocessor. An integrated circuit that accepts coded instructions for execution; the instructions may be entered, integrated, or stored internally.

Microprogram. A sequence of elementary instructions that corresponds to a specific computer operation, that is maintained in special storage, and whose execution is initiated by the introduction of a computer instruction into an instruction register of a computer.

Microsecond. One-millionth of a second.

Microwave. Any electromagnetic wave in the radio frequency spectrum above 890 megahertz.

Millisecond. One-thousandth of a second.

MIPS. Million instructions per second.

Mirror Image. In a document copying machine, an image that has its parts positioned as if the original were viewed in a mirror.

MIS. Management Information System.

Modem. A functional unit that modulates and demodulates signals. One of the functions of a modem is to enable digital data to be transmitted over analog transmission facilities.

Modem Pool. A centralized pool of modems accessed through a PBX to provide data transmission from modem-less terminals to the telephone network.

Modem Turnaround Time. The time required for a half-duplex modem to reverse the direction of transmission.

Modulation Rate. The reciprocal of the measure of the shortest nominal time interval between successive significant instants of the modulated signal.

Module. A program unit that is discrete and identifiable with respect to compiling, combining with other units, and loading.

MTBF. Mean-time-between-failures.

Multifrequency Signal. A signal made up of several superimposed audio frequency tones.

Multiple Access. The capability of multiple terminals connected to the same local area network to access one another.

Multiplex. To interleave or simultaneously transmit two or more messages on a single channel.

Multiplexing. The division of a transmission facility into two or more channels either by splitting the frequency band transmitted by the channel into narrower bands, each of which is used to constitute a distinct channel (frequency-division multiplexing), or by allotting this common channel to several different information channels, one at a time (time-division multiplexing).

Multipoint Link. A link or circuit interconnecting several stations.

Multiprocessing. A mode of operation that provides for parallel processing by two or more processors of multiprocessors.

Nanosecond. One-thousand-millionth of a second.

Network. The assembly of equipment through which connections are made between data stations.

Network Administration. The process of monitoring loads and service results in a network and making adjustments needed to maintain service and costs at the designed level.

Network Architecture. A set of design principles, including the organization of functions and the description of data formats and procedures, used as the basis for design and implementation of a user application network.

Network Layer. In open systems architecture, the layer that provides the functions and procedures used to transfer data received from the transport layer.

Node. The switching machine or computer that provides access to the network and serves as the concentration point for trunks. The term node derives from graph theory, in which a node is a junction point of links, areas, or edges.

Noise. Any unwanted signal in a transmission path.

Non-Return-To-Zero. Non-return-to-reference of binary digits such that the zeros are represented by magnetization to a specified condition, and the ones are represented by magnetization to a specified alternative condition.

Nonswitched Connection. A connection that does not have to be established by dialing. Contrast with switched connection.

Numbering Plan. A uniform numbering system wherein each telephone central office has unique designation similar in form to that of all other offices connected to the nationwide dialing network. In the numbering plan, the first three of ten dialed digits denote area code; the next three, office code; and the remaining four, station number.

Octet. A byte composed of eight binary elements.

Offhook. A signaling state in a line or trunk when it is working or busy.

Off-Line. Pertaining to the operation of a functional unit without the continual control of a computer.

Off-Line Storage. Storage that is not under control of the processing unit.

One-Way Trunk. A trunk between central exchanges where traffic can originate on only end.

Onhook. Deactivated (in regard to a telephone set). A telephone not in use is onhook.

On-Line. Pertaining to the operation of a functional unit that is under the continual control of a computer. The term "on-line" is also used to describe a user's access to a computer via a terminal.

Open Systems Interconnection (OSI). The use of standardized procedures to enable the interconnection of data processing systems in networks.

Open Wire. A conductor separately supported above the surface of the ground.

Operating System. Software that controls the execution of programs; an operating system may provide services such as resource allocation, scheduling, input/output control, and data management.

Operator Console. A functional unit containing devices that are used for communication between a computer operator and an automatic data processing system.

Optical Reader. A device that reads handwritten or machine printed symbols into a computing system.

Optical Scanner. A device that scans optically and usually generates an analog or digital signal.

Original Equipment Manufacture (OEM). A manufacturer of equipment that may be marketed by another manufacturer.

Oscilloscope. An instrument for displaying the changes in a varying current or voltage.

Outside Plant. A collective term describing the cable and all supporting structures used to provide subscriber loops.

Overhead. Any noninformation bits such as headers, error checking bits, start and stop bits, etc. Used for data transmission.

Owned. Supplied by and belonging to a customer as opposed to private and public.

Packet. A sequence of binary digits including data and call control signals that is switched as a composite whole. The data, call control signals, and possibly error control information, are arranged in a specific format.

Packet Assembler/Disassembler (PAD). A device used on a packet switched network to assemble information into packets and to convert received packets into a continuous data stream.

Packet Sequencing. A process of ensuring that packets are delivered to the receiving data terminal equipment (DTE) in the same sequence as they were transmitted by the sending DTE.

Packet Switching. The process of routing and transferring data by means of addressed packets so that a channel is occupied only during the transmission of a packet; upon completion of the transmission, the channel is made available for the transfer of other packets.

PAD. Packet assembly/disassembly.

Parallel. Pertaining to the concurrent or simultaneous operation of two or more devices or to the concurrent performance of two or more activities in a single device.

Parallel-To-Serial Converter. A device that converts a group of digits, all of which are presented simultaneously, into a corresponding sequence of signal elements.

Parallel Transmission. In data communication, the simultaneous transmission of a certain number of signal elements constituting the same data signal.

Parity Bit. A binary digit appended to a group of binary digits to make the sum of all the digits either always odd (odd parity) or always even (even parity). Parity bits are used for error detection.

Partial Dial. A condition that exists when a user hangs up before dialing a complete telephone number.

Password. A unique string of characters that a program, computer operator or user must supply to meet security requirements before gaining access to data.

Path. In a network, a route between any two nodes.

PBX. Private branch exchange.

PDN. Public data network.

Peer. In network architecture, any functional unit that is in the same layer as another entity.

PEL. Picture element.

Performance. Together with facility, one of the two major factors on which the total productivity of a system depends. Performance is largely determined by a combination of three other factors: throughput, response time, and availability.

Peripheral Equipment. In a computer system, with respect to a particular processing unit, any equipment that provides the processing unit with outside communication.

Permanent Virtual Circuit. A virtual circuit that provides the equivalent of dedicated service over a packet switching network.

Phase Modulation. Modulation in which the phase angle of a carrier is the characteristic varied.

Physical Circuit. A circuit created with hardware rather than multiplexing.

Picture Element. In computer graphics, the smallest element of a display space that can be independently assigned color and intensity.

Ping-Pong. A method of obtaining full-duplex data transmission over a two-wire circuit by rapidly alternating the direction of transmission.

Plasma Panel. A part of a display device that consists of a grid of electrodes in a flat, gas-filled panel in which the energizing of selected electrodes causes the gas to be ionized and light to be emitted at that point.

Plot. To draw or diagram. To connect the point-by-point coordinate values.

Plotter. An output unit that presents data in the form of a two-dimensional graphic representation.

Point-To-Point Connection. A connection established between two data stations for data transmission.

Polling. The process whereby stations are invited, one at a time, to transmit.

Port. An access point for data entry or exit.

Portability. The ability to use data sets or files with different operating system.

Post Telephone and Telegraph Administration (PTT). A generic term for the government-operated common carriers in countries other than the

USA and Canada. Examples of the PTT are the Post Office in the United Kingdom, the Bundespost in Germany.

Presentation Layer. In open system architecture, the layer that provides the functions that may be selected by the application layer, such as: data definition; managing the entry; exchange, display, and control of structured data; and definition of operations that may be performed on the data.

Printer. An output device that produces a durable record of data in the form of a sequence of discrete graphic characters belonging to a predetermined character set.

Priority. A rank assigned to a task that determines its precedence in receiving system resources.

Privacy. The right of individuals and organizations to control the collection and use of their data or data about themselves.

Private Branch Exchange (PBX). A switching system dedicated to telephone and data use in a company's communication network.

Process. A systematic sequence of operations to produce a specified result.

Process Control. Automatic control of a process, in which a computer system is used to regulate usually continuous operations or processes.

Processing. The performance of logical operations and calculations on data, including the temporary retention of data in processor storage while it is being operated upon.

Processor. In a computer, a functional unit that interprets and executes instructions.

Programmable Terminal. A user terminal that has computational capability.

Prompting. The issuing of messages to a terminal user, requesting information necessary to continue processing.

Propagation Delay. The time necessary for a signal to travel from one point on a circuit to another.

Protocol. A specification for the format and relative timing of information exchanged between communicating parties.

PSN. Public switched network.

Public Switched Network (PSN). Any switching system that provides a circuit switched to many customers.

Pulse Amplitude Modulation (PAM). A digital modulation method that operates by varying the amplitude of a stream of pulses in accordance with the instantaneous amplitude of the modulating signal.

Pulse Code Modulation (PCM). A process in which a signal is sampled, and the magnitude of each sample with respect to a fixed reference is quantized and converted by coding to a digital signal.

Push-Button Dialing. The use of keys or pushbuttons instead of a rotary dial to generate a sequence of digits to establish a circuit connection. The signal form is usually tones.

Quad. A structural unit employed in cable, consisting of four separately insulated conductors twisted together.

Quantization. The subdivision of the range of values of a variable into a finite number of nonoverlapping, and not necessarily equal subranges or intervals, each of which is represented by an assigned value within the subrange. For example, a person's age is quantized for most purposes with a quantum of one year.

Queue. A line or list formed by items in a system waiting for service; for example, tasks to be performed or messages to be transmitted in a message routing system.

Queuing. The holding of calls in queue when a trunk group is busy and then completing the calls in turn when an idle circuit is available.

Raster. The illuminated area of a television picture tube.

Raster Graphics. Computer graphics in which display images, composed of an array of picture elements arranged in rows and columns, are generated on a display space.

Raster Scan. In computer graphics, a technique of generating or recording a display image by a line-by-line sweep across the entire display space; for example, the generation of a picture on a television screen.

Raw Data. Data that has not been processed or reduced.

Realtime. Pertaining to the processing of data by a computer in connection with another process outside the computer according to time requirements imposed by the outside printing in conversational mode and processes that can be influenced by human intervention while they are in progress.

Record. A collection of related data or words, treated as a unit; for example, in stock control, each invoice could constitute one record.

Recursive. Pertaining to a process in which each step makes use of the results of earlier steps.

Redundancy. The provision of more than one circuit element to assume call processing when the primary element fails.

Redundancy Check. A check that depends on extra characters attached to data for the detection of errors.

Refresh. In computer graphics, the process of repeatedly producing a display image on a display space so that the image remains visible.

Regeneration. The process of recognizing and reconstructing a digital signal so that the amplitude, waveform and timing are constrained within stated limits.

Regenerative Repeater. A device that performs signal regeneration together with ancillary functions. Its function is to retime and retransmit the received signal impulses restored to their original strength.

Regional Center. A control center (class I office) connecting sectional centers of the telephone system together. Every pair of regional centers in the United States has a direct circuit group running from one center to the other.

Relational Data Base. A data base in which relationships between data items are explicitly specified as equally accessible attributes.

Reliability. The ability of a functional unit to perform its intended function under stated conditions, for a stated period of time.

Remote Access. The ability to dial into a switching machine over a local telephone number in order to complete calls over a private network from a distant location.

Remote Access Data Processing. Data processing in which certain portions of input/output functions are situated in different places and connected by transmission facilities.

Remote Job Entry (RJE). Submission of jobs through an input unit that has access to a computer through a data link.

Repeater. A device used to amplify or reshape signals.

Resolution. In computer graphics, a measure of the sharpness of an image, expressed as the number of lines per unit of length or the number of points per unit of area discernable in that image.

Resource. Any facility of the computing system or operating system required by a job or task, and including main storage, input/output devices, the processing unit, data sets, and control or processing programs.

Response Time. The elapsed time between the end of an inquiry or demand on a data processing system and the beginning of the response, for example, the length of time between an indication of the end of an inquiry and the display of the first character of the response at a user terminal.

Restriction. Limitations to a station on the use of PBX features or trunks on the basis of service classification.

Reverse Video. A form of highlighting a character, field, or cursor by reversing the color of the character, field, or cursor with its background; for example, changing a red character on a black background to a black character on a red background.

Ring (Network). A network in which each node is connected to two adjacent nodes.

Ring-Back Tone. An audible signal indicating that the called party is being rung.

RJE. Remote job entry.

Rotary Dial. In a switched system, the conventional dialing method that creates a series of pulses to identify the called station.

Routing. The assignment of the path by which a message will reach its destination.

Run. A single performance of one or more jobs.

Scale. To change the representation of a quantity, expressing it in other units, so that its range is brought within a specified range.

Scanner. A device that examines a spatial pattern one part after another and generates analog or digital signals corresponding to the pattern. Scanners are often used in mark sensing, pattern recognition, or character recognition.

Screen. An illuminated display surface; for example, the display surface of a CRT or plasma panel.

Scroll. To move all or part of the display image vertically to display data that cannot be observed within a single display image.

Sectional Center. A control center connecting primary centers together; a class 1 office.

Sensor. A device that converts measurable elements of a physical process into data meaningful to a computer.

Sequential. Pertaining to the occurrence of events in time sequence, with no simultaneity of overlap of events.

Serial Transmission. The sequential transmission of the bits constituting an entity of data over a data circuit.

Shared. Pertaining to the availability of a resource for more than one use at the same time.

Sheath. The outer jacket surrounding transmission media to protect it from damage.

Shift Character. A control character that determines the alphabetic/numeric shift of character codes in a message.

Sideband. A frequency band above and below the carrier frequency, produced as a result of modulation.

Signal. A variation of a physical quantity, used to convey data.

Signal-To-Noise Ratio (S/N). The relative power of the signal to the noise in a channel.

Simplex Transmission. Transmission in one preassigned direction only.

Simulate. To represent certain features of the behavior of a physical or abstract system by the behavior of another system, for example, to represent a physical phenomenon by means of operations of a computer by those of another computer.

Simultaneous. Pertaining to the occurrence of two or more events at the same instant of time.

Simultaneous Transmission. Transmission of control characters or data in one direction while information is being received in the other direction.

Singing. Sound caused by unstable oscillations on the line.

SNA Network. The part of a user-application network that conforms to the formats and protocols of Systems Network Architecture. It enables reliable transfer of data among end users and provides protocols for controlling the resources of various network configurations. The SNA network consists of network addressable units (NAUs), boundary function components, and the path control network.

Software. Programs, procedures, rules and any associated documentation pertaining to the operation of a computer system.

Source Code Compatibility. Pertaining to a system where changes to the system do not require changes to a user's source code, but may require a recompile or assembly of the source code.

Source Data. The data provided by the user of a data processing system.

Space Division Switching. Interconnecting links in a network by the physical connection of the links.

Special Purpose Language. A programming language designed for use in relatively narrow aspects of broader application areas; for example, COGO for civil engineering, CDL for logical design, GPSS for simulation.

Spooling. The use of auxiliary storage as a buffer storage to reduce processing delays when transferring data between peripheral equipment and the processors of a computer.

Stand-Alone. Pertaining to operation that is independent of another device, program or system.

Stand-Alone Data Processing System. A data processing system that is not served by telecommunication facilities.

Stand-Alone Modem. A modem that is separate from the unit with which it operates. Synonymous with external modem.

Standby. A duplicate set of equipment to be used if the primary unit becomes unusable because of malfunction.

Star Network. A network configuration in which there is only one path between a central or controlling node and each endpoint node.

Start Bit. In a start-stop system, a signal preceding a character or block that prepares the receiving device for the reception of the code elements. A start signal is limited to one signal element generally having the duration of a unit interval.

Start-Stop Character. A character including one start signal at the beginning and one or two stop signals at the end.

Start-Stop Transmission. Asynchronous transmission such that a group of signals representing a character is preceded by a start element and is followed by a stop element.

Station. One of the input or output points of a system that uses telecommunication facilities; for example, the telephone set in the telephone system or the point where the business machine interfaces with the channel on a leased private line.

Statistical Multiplexing. A form of data multiplexing in which the time on a communications channel is assigned to terminals only when they have data to transport.

Station Message Detail Recording (SMDR). The use of equipment in a PBX to record called station, time of day, and duration on trunk calls.

Step-By-Step Switch. A switch that moves in synchronism with a pulse device, such as a rotary telephone dial. Each digit dialed causes the movement of successive selector switches to carry the connection forward until the desired line is reached. Synonymous with stepper switch.

Stop Bit. In a start-stop system, a signal following a character or block that prepares the receiving device for the reception of a subsequent character or block. A stop signal is usually limited to one signal element having any duration equal to or greater than a specified minimum value.

Storage. The retention of data in a storage device.

Storage Device. A functional unit into which data can be entered, in which they can be retained, and from which they can be retrieved.

Store and Forward. A manner of operating a data network in which packets or messages are stored before transmission toward the ultimate destination.

Stored Program Computer. A computer controlled by internally stored instructions that can synthesize and store instructions, and that can subsequently execute these instructions.

Stored Program Control (SPC). A common control central office that uses a central processor under direction of a computer program for call processing.

String. A linear sequence of entities such as characters or physical elements.

Structured Programming. A technique for organizing and coding programs that reduces complexity, improves clarity, and makes them easier to debug and modify. Typically, a structured program is a hierarchy of modules that each have a single entry point and a single exit point; control is passed downward through the structure without unconditional branches to higher levels of the structure.

Substrate. In microcircuit, the supporting material upon which or within which an integrated circuit is fabricated, or to which an integrated circuit is attached.

Supervisory Signals. Signals used to indicate the various operating states of circuit combinations.

Swap. In systems with time sharing, to write the main storage image of a job to auxiliary storage and to read the image of another job into main storage.

Switch Hook. A switch on a telephone set, associated with the structure supporting the receiver or handset. It is operated by the removal or replacement of the receiver or handset on the support.

Switch Room. That part of a telephone central office building that houses switching mechanisms and associated apparatus.

Switched Connection. A mode of operating a data link in which a circuit or channel is established to switching facilities, as for example, in a public switched network.

Switched Line. A telecommunication line in which the connection is established by dialing.

Switched Network. Any network in which connections are established by closing switches, for example, by dialing.

Switching Center. A location that terminates multiple circuits, and is capable of interconnecting circuits or transferring traffic between circuits.

Sync Bits. Synonym for framing bits.

Synchronization. The process of adjusting the corresponding significant instants of two signals to obtain the desired phase relationship between these instants.

Synchronous. A method of transmitting data over a network where the sending and receiving terminals are kept in synchronism with each other by a clock signal imbedded in the data.

Synchronous Data Link Control (SDLC). A discipline for managing synchronous, code-transparent, serial-by-bit information transfer over a link connection. Transmission exchanges may be duplex or half-duplex over switched or nonswitched links. The configuration of the link connection may be point-to-point, multipoint, or loop.

System. In data processing, a collection of people, machines, and methods organized to accomplish a set of specific functions.

Systems Analysis. The analysis of an activity to determine precisely what must be accomplished and how to accomplish it.

Systems Network Architecture (SNA). The description of the logical structure, formats, protocols, and operational sequences for transmitting information units through and controlling the configuration and operation of networks.

Tandem Switch. A switching machine that interconnects local or toll trunks to other switching machines.

Tariff. The published rate for a specific unit of equipment, facility or type of service provided by a telecommunication facility. Also, the vehicle by which the regulating agencies approve or disapprove such facilities or services. Thus, the tariff becomes a telecommunication facility.

Task. A basic unit of work to be accomplished by a computer. The task is usually specified to a control program in a multiprogramming or multiprocessing environment.

Telecommunication. Any transmission, emission, or reception of signs, signals, writing, images, and sounds or intelligence of any nature by wire, radio, optical, or other electromagnetic systems.

Telecommunication Facility. Transmission capabilities, or the means for providing such capabilities, made available by a communication common carrier or by a telecommunication administration.

Telegraph. A system employing the interruption or change in polarity of direct current for the transmission of signals.

Telephone Company. Any common carrier providing public telephone system service.

Telephony. Transmission of speech or other sounds.

Teletex. A service enabling users to exchange correspondence automatically between machine memories over telecommunication networks.

Teletypewriter Exchange Service (TWX). Teletypewriter service in which suitably arranged teletypewriter stations are provided with lines to a central office for access to other such stations throughout the United States and Canada. Both Baudot and ASCII-coded machines are used. Business machines may also be used, with certain restrictions.

Telex. An automatic teleprinter exchange service provided by Western Union, similar to teletypewriter exchange service but worldwide. Only Baudot equipment is provided; business machines may also be used.

Terminal. A point in a system or network at which data can either enter or leave.

Text. In word processing, information for human comprehension that is intended for presentation in a two-dimensional form, for example, printed on paper or displayed on a screen. Text consists of symbols, phrases, or sentences in natural or artificial languages, pictures, diagrams, and tables.

Throughput. The effective rate of transmission of information between two points excluding noninformation (overhead) bits.

Tie Line. A privately owned or leased trunk used to interconnect PBXs in a private switching network.

Tie Trunk. A telephone line or channel directly connecting two branch exchanges.

Time Division Multiplexing. A method of combining several communication channels by dividing a channel into time increments and assigning each channel to a time slot. Multiple channels are interleaved when each channel is assigned the entire bandwidth of the whole communication channel for a short period of time.

Time Division Switching. The connection of two circuits in a network by assigning them to the same time slot on a common bus.

Time Sharing. Pertaining to the interleaved use of time on a computer system that enables two or more users to execute computer programs concurrently.

Tip. The end of the plug used to make circuit connections in a manual switchboard.

Toll. In public switched systems, a charge for a connection beyond an exchange boundary, based on time and distance.

Token. A packet that circulates among network nodes.

Token Passing. A method of allocating network access where a terminal can send data only after it has acquired the network's token.

Topology. The architecture of a network or the way circuits are connected to link the devices in a local area network or other networks.

Traffic. In data communication, transmitted and received messages.

Transaction. In systems with time sharing, an exchange between a terminal and another device that accomplishes a particular action or result; for example, the entry of a customer's deposit and the updating of the customer's balance.

Transducer. A device for converting energy from one form to another. Examples are microphones and telephone handsets.

Transistor. A small solid-state, semiconducting device, ordinarily using germanium, that performs nearly all the functions of an electronic tube, especially amplification.

Transmission. The sending of data from one place for reception elsewhere.

Transmission Code. A code for sending information over telecommunication lines.

Transmission Medium. Any material substance that can be, or is, used for the propagation of signals, usually in the form of modulated radio, light, or acoustic waves, from one point to another, such as an optical fiber, cable, bundle, wire, dielectric slab, water, or air.

Transmission Service. A circuit switched, packet switched, or a leased circuit service provided to the public by a communication common carrier or by a telecommunication administration.

Transmit. To send data from one place for reception elsewhere.

Transparent. In data transmission, pertaining to information that is not recognized by the receiving program or device as transmission control characters.

Transport Layer. In open system architecture, the layer that, together with the network, data link, and physical layers provides services for the transport of data between network elements.

Trunk. A telephone channel between two control offices or switching devices that is used in providing a telephone connection between subscribers.

Trunk Line. A telecommunication line that links a private telecommunication system to the public switched network.

TTY. Teletypewriter equipment.

Turnaround Time. The elapsed time between submission of a job and the return of the complete output.

Upstream Channel. A band of frequencies on a CATV cable reserved for transmission from the user's terminal to the headend.

Uptime. Deprecated term for available time.

User. Anyone who requires the services of a computing system.

Validation. The checking of data for correctness or compliance with applicable standards, rules and conventions.

Value Added Network. A data communications network that adds processing services such as storage and error correction on top of the basic transport of data.

Video Codec. Abbreviation for video coder/decoder. A device in television transmission that compresses a video signal into a smaller digital channel.

Video Compression. A method of transmitting analog television over a smaller digital channel.

Video Frame. A complete television picture consisting of two fields of interlaced scanning lines.

Videotex. An interactive information retrieval service that usually employs the telephone network as the transmission medium.

Voice-Band. The 300 Hz to 3400 Hz band used on telephone equipment for the transmission of voice and data.

Voice-Grade Channel. A channel suitable for transmission of speech, digital or analog data, or facsimile, generally with a frequency range of about 300 to 3000 cycles per second.

Voice Store-and-Forward (Voice Mail). A PBX service that allows voice messages to be stored digitally in secondary storage and retrieved remotely by dialing access and identification codes.

WATS. Wide Area Telephone Service. A service that provides a special line on which the subscriber may make unlimited calls to certain zones on a direct-distance-dialing basis for a flat monthly charge.

White Noise. Noise frequencies that are equally distributed across all frequencies within a communications channel.

Word. A character string or a binary element string that it is convenient for some purpose to consider as an entity.

Word Processing Equipment. Equipment used to prepare business correspondence by keying and temporarily storing text for subsequent revision and editing the stored text in groups of characters such as words, lines, paragraphs, or pages, as distinguished from equipment that permits only character-by-character editing. Text may be printed out immediately upon keying or at a later time automatically or semiautomatically from internal storage or from a recording medium such as magnetic cards or tape made by the text originating machine or by a print-only machine.

Zero Suppression. The elimination from a numeral of zeros that have no significance in the numeral. Zeros that have no significance include those to the left of the nonzero digits in the integral part of a numeral and those to the right of the nonzero digits in the fractional part.